Post-Soviet Women Encountering Transition

Post-Soviet Women Encountering Transition

Nation Building, Economic Survival, and Civic Activism

Edited by

Kathleen Kuehnast

and

Carol Nechemias

WOODROW WILSON CENTER PRESS
Washington, D.C.

THE JOHNS HOPKINS UNIVERSITY PRESS
Baltimore and London

EDITORIAL OFFICES

Woodrow Wilson Center Press
One Woodrow Wilson Plaza
1300 Pennsylvania Avenue, N.W.
Washington, D.C. 20004-3027
Telephone: 202-691-4010
www.wilsoncenter.org

Order from

The Johns Hopkins University Press
Hampden Station
P.O. Box 50370
Baltimore, Maryland 21211
Telephone: 1-800-537-5487
www.press.jhu.edu

Printed in the United States of America on acid-free paper ∞

2 4 6 8 9 7 5 3 1

Library of Congress Cataloging-in-Publication Data

Post-Soviet women encountering transition: nation building, economic survival, and civic activism / edited by Kathleen Kuehnast and Carol Nechemias.
p. cm.
ISBN 0-8018-7918-3 (cloth : alk. paper)
1. Women—Former Soviet republics—Social conditions. 2. Women—Former Soviet republics—Economic conditions. I. Kuehnast, Kathleen R. II. Nechemias, Carol, 1947–
HQ1663 .P66 2004
305.42′0947—dc22 2003021823

ABOUT THE CENTER

The Center is the living memorial of the United States of America to the nation's twenty-eighth president, Woodrow Wilson. Congress established the Woodrow Wilson Center in 1968 as an international institute for advanced study, "symbolizing and strengthening the fruitful relationship between the world of learning and the world of public affairs." The Center opened in 1970 under its own board of trustees.

In all its activities the Woodrow Wilson Center is a nonprofit, nonpartisan organization, supported financially by annual appropriations from the Congress, and by the contributions of foundations, corporations, and individuals. Conclusions or opinions expressed in Center publications and programs are those of the authors and speakers and do not necessarily reflect the views of the Center staff, fellows, trustees, advisory groups, or any individuals or organizations that provide financial support to the Center.

Contents

Foreword

The Woodrow Wilson Center's Kennan Institute convened several meetings during 1999 that brought together policymakers and scholars to review and assess the previous decade's assistance programs to the states that had achieved independence following the collapse of the Soviet Union. Those at times contentious sessions sought to evaluate the past successes and failures of a number of U.S. programs in the region—in particular, those funded by the U.S. Agency for International Development—and to set out possible goals for future programs.

Much of what was said at that time was fairly predictable at a moment when the political debate between congressional Republicans and representatives of the Democratic Bill Clinton administration over "who lost Russia?" intensified in anticipation of the 2000 presidential and congressional election campaigns. Scholars and practitioners set out differing views of the past and diverse visions of the future. Unexpectedly, responses among participants from the policy community to one issue in particular startled nearly every scholar participating in these sessions regardless of political affiliation or belief; that issue was gender.

For the policymakers, gender all too frequently seemed to be merely one more box to check off in a project plan, rather than offering a set of concerns that could provide a synthetic and integrative approach to problem solving in the region. A concentration on gender in the form of specifically targeted "women's programs"—for example, support for women's nongovernmental organizations and women's small business incubators—was seen as sufficient and was built into planned programming goals and objectives.

When the policymakers were pushed by the scholars to think about how gender influences programming across the board (from humanitarian assistance to programs on civic education, media, agricultural reform, and environmental issues), and about how attention to gender issues plays into development at a variety of levels (from a program's inception through its implementation and evaluation stages), the policymakers were at a loss. Probing questions quickly revealed that the extensive literature on gender and development that had caught the attention of scholars in the post-Soviet field had only superficially filtered into the consciousness of the Washington community.

The many wide-ranging studies on women and gender in the states of the former Soviet Union published during the past decade and a half have enormously enriched both our understanding of the role of gender in society and our appreciation of the dynamic interaction among gender and cultural, ethnic, social, and political identities. The issues and questions raised by this literature were only just beginning to come clear to those who make policy decisions on development assistance at the time of the Kennan Institute sessions reviewing the performance of U.S. assistance programs.

As this volume indicates, an approach that focuses on women's organizations and women-centered programming is essential to addressing the problems of this region. These programs are critical to the development of civil society and can help to reduce poverty in the region. Many policymakers in the assistance agencies are devoted to bringing gender into development through these types of activities, and they should be commended for their efforts. Still, scholarship suggests that we should take one step further—that a more integrated approach to gender and assistance programs would benefit both the donors and the countries in transition.

Fresh from organizing these 1999 sessions, we approached various funding agencies in 2000 with a proposal to bring together an interdisciplinary group of scholars and practitioners to discuss the implications of gender and the role of women in the transition. These scholars had something interesting to bring to not only the scholarly literature but also to the policy community. The pages to follow are the result of this effort.

This volume represents the collective effort of the 17 scholars and practitioners who were chosen to participate in a working group on the role of women in postcommunist transitions. Group members convened three times between April 2001 and February 2002. The group, which represented various intellectual, disciplinary, and research traditions, had been selected through an international competition that attracted more than 125 applicants. Some of the participants had known one another before meeting in Washington for the first time, but most had not. They nonetheless shared a deep commitment to scholarship and to the study of women in post-socialist transitional societies. They also shared a dedication to engaging with one another in an extended and challenging dialogue.

The Kennan Institute has sponsored nine similar topic-specific working groups and workshops since 1996. Each group was designed to bring together groups of scholars engaged in similar areas of research from varying perspectives. These multidisciplinary, multinational, and multigenerational sessions have explored such topics as civil society, social capital, and development in Eurasia (1996–98); urban civic cultural and democratic transitions (1997–2000); regional Russia (1998–99); rural Russia (1998–2000); Russia's and Ukraine's experience of economic and political transformation (1999–2001); marketization and democratization in Russia (2000–1); the role of women in postcommunist transitions (2001–2); integrating Russia into Europe (2001–3); and multicultural legacies in Belarus, Russia, and Ukraine (2002–3). The general format has been for researchers to present their previous research as a way of posing shared issues for further discussion. That discussion becomes the basis for the plan of a book, with participants returning home to write original papers on the new topics before convening once again for a final manuscript review.

This format challenges each participant to prepare new work that is substantially different from what he or she has published before. It produces a collective voice that rises above the sum of its individual parts. This process thus achieves two important goals. First, it produces a publication of lasting value. Second, it encourages the formation of a thematic and cross-national "invisible college" that takes on a life of its own as the group disperses.

Group leaders are critical to the success of such an effort. The workshop on women in postcommunist transitions benefited immensely from two particularly skillful, tireless, and effective discussion leaders and editors in Kathleen Kuehnast and Carol Nechemias. Kathleen, an anthropologist with primary field experience in Central Asia, and Carol, a political scientist with long-standing research interests in Russia and Eastern Europe, confronted many of the same intellectual challenges that were placed before all the other participants. They had to engage each other as well as group participants well outside their previous research and disciplinary concerns. As readers of this book will discover, the result is an uncommon group exploration of a set of important intellectual issues and practical concerns. This achievement is testimony to Kathleen and Carol's leadership, for which we at the Kennan Institute are most grateful.

Funding for this exciting endeavor was provided by the U.S. Department of State Title VIII Program for Research and Training on Eastern Europe and the Independent States of the Former Soviet Union, the Woodrow Wilson Center's Federal Conference Funds, the George F. Kennan Fund, and the Mary Harriman Foundation. Kennan Institute staff members Lauren Crabtree, Jen Giglio, Jodi Koehn, and Edita Krunkaityte provided invaluable support to the group, with Jodi playing an especially important role during the preparation of the manuscript for publication. We would like to thank the funders of the workshop and our Kennan colleagues for making this series of meetings possible.

This particular workshop is both similar to the other half-dozen Kennan Institute working groups of the past several years and different in three very important respects. As was mentioned above, the subject of the role of women in post-Soviet transitions is one that is more often recognized than understood. As the readers of this volume will learn, women are essential participants in shaping post-Soviet societies, from the household and the marketplace to the state and nation. The meaning of gender in the post-Soviet context is complex, with researchers concerned with issues central to gender studies being forced to confront the relationship between religion and society, state and society, poverty, wealth formation, and civic activism. The intellectual range and achievements of the contributors to this volume are noteworthy in their own right.

Further, this particular group of scholars represents a major new trend in the study of the societies of the former Soviet Union. One third of the workshop participants are anthropologists, and all have conducted significant field research in the region. They represent an approach to scholarship on the region that was unthinkable a generation ago: one based on a deep understanding of local societies derived from extensive research and life experience on the ground. Their research agendas are those of mainstream anthropology, sociology, gender studies, and political science. Consequently, this book casts a spotlight on an approach to scholarship on the region that is rooted in discipline-oriented theory and methodological rigor as well as in deep knowledge of place.

Finally, the contributors to this volume all shared a desire to move beyond their academic research to touch upon issues of how to adapt their findings to the practical realities of development assistance. The resulting chapters revel in the achievements of women in the region and the programs that have supported them in the past decade. Yet they also ask important questions about the approaches of assistance providers, the reactions of recipients, and the implications of the encounter between donors and those assisted for implementing programs. In this respect, the volume can serve to open readers' minds to a radically fresh understanding of the role of gender in development, so that a decade from now, when the Kennan Institute again convenes meetings on the countries of the former Soviet Union, we may hear very different discussions from those in 1999.

No reader who continues beyond this page can fail to understand that there is scant need to doubt the vigor of the study of the former Soviet Union. An exciting group of scholars who first engaged the region following the collapse of the USSR is busily reinventing the field. The result is a new conversation about the region that simultaneously enriches our appreciation of what has taken place there and expand long-standing debates within individual social science disciplines. We therefore close by expressing our thanks to each contributor to this volume for adding so much vitality to the life of the institute and the field.

Blair A. Ruble and Nancy E. Popson

Introduction: Women Navigating Change in Post-Soviet Currents

Kathleen Kuehnast and Carol Nechemias

The Soviet legacy of high educational levels and workforce participation among women left a looming question in 1991: Would the transition to democracy and a market economy open doors or erect new barriers for women in post-Soviet society?[1] A close examination of the "transition" reveals that several developments are having a great impact on women's lives:

This volume's editors owe a tremendous debt of gratitude to Blair Ruble, the director of the Kennan Institute, and to his able deputy director, Nancy Popson, for their support, encouragement, and expert guidance during the course of the workshops that led to this volume. Without their enthusiasm, this project could not have succeeded. Lauren Crabtree, Jennifer Giglio, Jodi Koehn, and Edita Krunkaityte, all staff members of the Kennan Institute, assisted in ensuring that all went smoothly, from arranging transportation to enforcing deadlines. And above all, this project rests on the bonds of scholarship and fellowship that developed over the course of the workshops. Again, on behalf of all the workshop contributors, we would like to thank the Kennan Institute for creating the opportunity to participate in what was truly an exciting and productive intellectual enterprise.

neofamilial ideologies that sharply criticize Soviet-style emancipation and advocate a return to "traditional families"; a gendered division of labor in the market economy, with women flooding the bottom part of the pyramid of small businesses as bazaar merchants; and a gendered division of labor in the political arena, with men dominating formal government structures and political parties and women dominating nongovernmental organizations (NGOs).

The essays in this volume offer an exceptionally rich array of women's experience during the past decade of political, economic, and social transition in the states of the former Soviet Union. The essays reflect a wide range of concerns, including women's political participation, the feminization of civil society, gender-related violence and discrimination, women's role in economic development, women's health and reproductive rights, and the development of gender programs in the new countries of the former Soviet Union. The volume explores this new terrain through four venues: (1) nationalism, transition, and women; (2) women in rural economies; (3) democratization and women's civic activism, and (4) international assistance encounters. In each case, the analysis is provided from the vantage point of women.

The contributors to the volume, all of whom have conducted field research in the post-Soviet states, use case studies to illuminate what life is like for women in these societies. The fact that this research focuses strictly on women of the former Soviet republics differentiates the volume from the important works of Susan Gal and Gail Kligman on gender in Central and Eastern Europe.[2] The two regions—Central and Eastern Europe and the former Soviet Union—have significantly different cultural and historical legacies, with the former more strongly influenced by Europe. This volume details another geographic scenario, where influences from China, the Middle East, and Turkey vie with those from Europe.

Diversity is the hallmark of the volume. In addition to essays about women in Belarus, Russia, and Ukraine, the research examines post-Soviet women in the Islamic societies of Azerbaijan, Kazakhstan, Uzbekistan, and the Tatar Republic of Russia. The essays focus not only on small towns and rural environments but also on women's NGOs, traditional neighborhood social networks, and issues of class and gender.

Post-Soviet Women: Sites of Contention

Amid economic uncertainty, increasing impoverishment, and political instability, women in the former Soviet Union find themselves awash in the crosscurrents of emerging discourses on their position in society, their jobs, and ultimately their control over their own bodies. In the place of former Soviet ideals, more limiting notions of women in society are being propagated. Simultaneously, the public/private split in women's everyday lives has become a chasm, with more and more post-Soviet societies relegating women to the private sphere. Women do still work in the public sphere, but the ideological preference has clearly shifted from the Soviet notion of women in the public workforce to the more traditional notion of women at home with the family.

Women's roles in these new states have become the focus of debate in the post-Soviet transition. Particularly in transitional (and postcolonial) societies, the category of "woman" becomes a pivotal site where tradition and modernization are debated, new governments are legitimized, and age-old traditions are reconstructed in the name of women.[3] Controversial issues, such as women's reproductive rights, women's employment, and even the manner in which women dress, become symbolic discourses about women's position in society and the nature of national or ethnic identity. Such discourses often serve to distance gender debates from the day-to-day reality and hardship of women's lives.

As the anthropologist Lata Mani points out, such debates often are waged to advance the political projects of political contenders, as in the case when both British colonial administrators and local male elites in nineteenth-century India debated the issue of *sati* (widow burning).[4] Rather than seek to improve the status of women, however, Mani argues that the two camps used the gender issue to gain strategic political leverage. Similarly, Lila Abu-Lughod notes a familiar dynamic of postcolonial politics in which the "woman question"—often couched in a new language of cultural authenticity to distance the debate from foreign or postcolonial influences—animates political and ideological contests. Certainly, the former Soviet Union offers many relevant examples of how the category of woman has been used to further political projects. Few other states have so fervently taken up the question of women's roles in society or so quickly altered women's status in education and the workplace.

The Impact on Gender of a Common Soviet Legacy

The Soviet Union was perhaps an unprecedented example of a state in which gender came to represent everything from policies about work to issues of nationalism. During the Soviet period, women reached levels of education equal to and in many cases higher than men; and they provided a substantial percentage of the professional class of physicians, lawyers, engineers, and scientific workers. Workforce participation rates for women were the highest in the world, with 90 percent of working-age women either on the job or attending school. And work meant full-time work—there were few opportunities for part-time jobs.

When the Soviet Union collapsed in 1991, most Soviet women had no experience of being full-time housewives or operating small-scale businesses. Moreover, their educational credentials and workforce experience had not translated into leading positions in Soviet society—only 5.6 percent of Soviet managers were female, and few women rose to the highest levels of the Communist Party hierarchy. Although observers frequently point to the decline in the proportion of women legislators in post-Soviet countries as evidence of their ouster from the political arena, it is continuity rather than change that marks women's political clout. Under communism, Soviet women were largely invisible in key decision-making institutions (as opposed to "show" institutions), a pattern that appears to persist under "democratization."

Gender and Nation Building

The collapse of the Soviet Union significantly altered the ideological landscape for women. As the colossal Soviet state was dismantled into fifteen separate states, each new country began a unique process of disidentification with Soviet ideology. The Soviet legacy of gender ideology was, however, complex and provided opportunities for selective co-optation of particular beliefs. Certain beliefs proved attractive for many post-Soviet countries, particularly the tendency to regard biology as destiny and gender roles as natural and immutable. Such beliefs justified the assumption that women are "naturally" drawn toward placing a central value on motherhood and on feminine qualities such as nurturing.

Many former Soviet republics embraced highly conservative ideals about men, women, and the family at the same time that they turned toward pre-Soviet ethnic and national identities. Motherhood and nurturing often form an important component of the rhetoric of state building. As is illustrated in Gal and Kligman's work, women are identified as fundamental to nation building, namely, as the producers of children, and thus the family and national community.[5] In states such as Uzbekistan, Ukraine, and Belarus, debate over abortion and reproduction emerged as a key aspect of the nation-building process.

Although demographic concerns were part and parcel of the Soviet experience, the neonationalism that swept the former republics after 1991 added impetus to the idea that motherhood formed women's central mission in life. In many cases, women found themselves in the position in which rejecting Soviet ideology meant embracing an ethnonational identity that subordinated women's social role to far more conservative expectations. In part I of this volume, "Gender and Nation Building," each of the four chapters examines the manner in which women and their roles in society have become the focus of debate between new nationalist discourses and more conservative ethnic charters, ultimately influencing everything from policy to everyday survival strategies.

The process of how post-Soviet states are distancing themselves from the Soviet legacy of sexual egalitarianism and embracing a neofamilial ideology of state building is carefully profiled in chapter 1, "Strong Women, Weak State: Family Politics and Nation Building in Post-Soviet Ukraine," by Tatiana Zhurzhenko. She argues that restoring the "traditional family" has become the central strategy for unifying the state, a means to rally citizens around values antithetical to the paternalist communist legacy. The common strand that connects this variation of nationalism in post-Soviet states is its harsh critique of the totalitarian communist past, which it considers responsible for the destruction of the traditional family. Present-day problems are seen to have their roots in the elimination of private property and in state interference in the education of children, ultimately leaving the family without economic or moral autonomy. One of the cornerstones of neofamilial ideology is reducing state interference in family life and returning social and economic autonomy to the family itself. Yet as Zhurzhenko convincingly illustrates, liberation from the control of the state has not necessarily resulted in more autonomy for families, given that the new states have failed to offer a social contract. Families today are left to survive on their own with very little state support. As a result, the cost of the post-Soviet transition has been transferred from the state to the household, placing a particularly heavy burden on women.

We see another variation on neofamilial nationalism in chapter 2, "The Gender of Sovereignty: Constructing Statehood, Nation, and Gender Regimes in Post-Soviet Tatarstan," by Katherine E. Graney. Her study, which is situated in the Republic of Tatarstan, one of Russia's twenty-one national homelands, examines Tatarstan's effort to build a post-Soviet polity through ethnofamilial ideals of nationhood. As in Ukraine and other post-Soviet states, women's roles in contemporary Tatarstan are distinguished from the Soviet ideal of the working woman and instead are assigned the "privileged" ideal of mothers and preservers of national traditions. Yet Tatarstan's leadership is pulled in several different directions. The region's constitution emphasizes traditional socialist paternalism by placing motherhood and—in a nod to contemporary notions of egalitarianism—fatherhood under state protection. Simultaneously, pressure from Moscow and the international community is pushing local elites to adopt a concept of Tatarstan as a multiethnic, civic nation. Within these contradictions, a rich discussion ensues about how women, politicians, and women's groups are navigating the new terrain of neofamilial nationalism.

An equally complex and contradictory nation-building situation in post-Soviet Central Asia is presented in chapter 3, "Engendering Citizenship in Postcommunist Uzbekistan," by David Abramson. In Uzbekistan, the revival of Islam and Soviet-style nationalism are at odds in numerous aspects of everyday life in Uzbekistan, not the least of which is a woman's right to veil. During the past decade, Islam has acquired an attentive following. In part, the revival of Islam has occurred because many in Uzbekistan sense that Uzbek nationalism has little to offer in difficult post-Soviet economic and political conditions. And although Islam does not provide quick answers to the current situation, it does offer an age-old sense of security and so holds great promise for many. Nevertheless, the tension between secular nationalism and Islamic revivalism has resulted not only in different notions of what citizenship means but also in different ideals of citizenship for men and for women.

Abramson contends that these separate "citizenships" undermine the possibility for reconciliation between secularists and Islamic revivalists and further polarize women's place in Uzbek society, especially, but not exclusively, in the domain of education. He examines how veiling has multiple meanings and cannot be placed solely under the Islamic rubric, but must also be considered in the broader context of Uzbek traditional culture. Because Uzbek nationalism also draws on traditional roles for women in society and uses the veil to represent women symbolically, the veil becomes a common denominator of both nationalist and Islamic discourses about women. Although the two ideologies are purportedly different, Abramson reveals the many common notions that exist between the nationalist and Islamic approaches toward identity, and the manner in which women symbolize both discussions.

In chapter 4, "Conceptualizing Gender, Nation, and Class in Post-Soviet Belarus," Elena Gapova turns the nation-building discourse on its head. Instead of focusing directly on how women are problematized, she creatively examines the impact of the elite class on nationalistic rhetoric in post-1991 Belarus. The national discourse that she investigates stems from urban intellectuals, primarily men, and their construction of nationalism not only as they perceive it but also as they benefit from it. She argues that women, whether poor or rich, continue to be viewed from the perspective of their bodies, that is, their reproductive capabilities. In contrast, men and their relative masculinity, she asserts, are not about their bodies but about their accumulation of resources and access, factors that symbolize male strength. She illustrates her case with both literary and ethnographic examples of how women in post-Soviet Belarus have been redefined from a sexual perspective and displaced from public life, with the former Soviet representation of "strong women" replaced by the image of the strong male.

The producers of nationalist discourse, whereby Belarus symbolizes the woman and Russia the man, replay this new imagery in a larger schema. In this way, the Belarus national discourse appeals to the emasculated "native" males "to get off their knees," or what Gapova lays out as the nationalist formula of "male strength equals the nation's strength." All of which, she reiterates, emanates from the elite class, and serves to reify it. She sees the current Belarus nationalism project as emblematic not only of the spiraling decline of equality between men and women in her society but also of a deeper deviation away from equality among classes toward growing social inequality caused by capitalist class formation and emerging class inequality, a divide that cannot easily be bridged, because the elite "authors" of the nation-building efforts are lodged far away from the majority of Belarusian citizens.

Women and Rural Household Economics

A central response to post-Soviet economic trauma has involved the expansion of subsistence agriculture across rural post-Soviet states and the turn, particularly by women, to small-scale entrepreneurial activity at local markets. Janine R. Wedel's important work on Eastern and Central Europe has pointed to how women "merchants" are largely confined to what can be called cottage industries or microentrepreneurial activities. They buy and resell products, and they are largely concentrated in areas such as arts and crafts, textiles, food, and services. Many of these women work in the informal sector in "enterprises" that are not registered with the state, and they therefore either do not pay taxes or do not pay them in full.[6]

In part II of this volume, "Women and Rural Household Economics," the two chapters illustrate these household survival strategies, one that taps entrepreneurial activities as a means of survival and the other that focuses on household-level food production. Both chapter 5, "Feminizing the New Silk Road: Women Traders in Rural Kazakhstan," by Cynthia Werner, and chapter 6, "The Gendered Nature of Viliui Sakha Post-Soviet Adaptation," by Susan A. Crate, focus on women in rural areas. These authors break new ground by turning our attention to women in relatively remote areas that are rarely represented in the scholarly literature, whereas microentrepreneurial activities in urban areas have received much more attention in recent years.[7] Werner's research focuses on the village of Shauildir in southern Kazakhstan, a *raion* (county or district) center with a population of 8,300, almost all of whom are Kazakh-speaking Kazakhs, whereas Crate's study delves into economic survival strategies in the Viliui Sakha village of Elgeeii, located in the Sakha (Yakutia) Republic of northeastern Siberia, Russia.

Werner's study examines the intersection of the effects of post-Soviet economic change on families, the power of the Soviet legacy in shaping Kazakh women's lives, and the sharp expansion of household production and market trade in the post-Soviet era. Except for the local livestock market, she found that women dominated as sellers at the local bazaars and that the number of Kazakh market women increased dramatically during the 1990s. The high visibility of Kazakh—that is, Muslim—women working openly as merchants in public places sets Central Asia apart from the rest of the Muslim world. Werner's work makes clear that "the mobility and freedom that Kazakh women now enjoy should be viewed as an important legacy of Soviet rule."

Another aspect of that heritage involves well-educated women. Virtually all Shauildir women under the age of 50 years were high school or technical school graduates, and their labor force participation rate stood at a stunningly high 89.9 percent for working-age women in the early 1990s. Because school is coeducational, girls were used to mixing with males who were not related to them. Yet, as is highlighted in the chapters on nation building, competing discourses about women could challenge the gains women made in the past. Werner describes how Kazakh women's freedom to choose their own spouse declined in the 1990s with the rise of nonconsensual bride kidnappings. The resurrection of pre-Soviet traditions could thus pose a threat to women's rights and opportunities in the future.

Crate's analysis of the response of Viliui Sakha to economic decline provides many parallels with life in rural Kazakhstan. A major difference, however, involves the greater isolation of these subarctic villages from markets. For most of the Soviet period, the Elgeeii village depended almost entirely on one economic enterprise: a huge state farm that disbanded during the post-Soviet transition, generating massive unemployment, particularly for males. To survive, households adopted what Crate labels a "cows-and-kin" strategy that relies on an expansion of household food production, focusing on cattle herding and a division of labor within and between households. She documents the "gendered" lines of specialization, with women and men contributing to household self-sufficiency through the production of meat, milk, and vegetables, supplemented by hunting, fishing, and foraging for berries.

Although there was a predominant pattern of gender specific activities, Crate shows how economic distress has changed traditional Sakha gender roles, with tasks like caring for household herds, a traditional female responsibility, shared more equally than in the past. Despite the fact that a majority of households produced a surplus that could be sold to supplement household income, only 10 percent of surveyed households sold products, due to a lack of local markets. Entrepreneurial activity thus produces an income for only a small percentage of Elgeeii families.

Crate also describes the impact of rampant alcoholism on the lives of Viliui Sakha and how it fosters an overworked and overburdened lifestyle for women. Yet there is little in the way of state or private resources to tackle the social pathologies generated by alcoholism. It is too early in the "transition" process to assess whether the trends described by Werner and Crate represent budding capitalism or bare-boned subsistence. The latter particularly seems the case in Sakha, although Crate notes that many residents considered entrepreneurial activities important and hoped in the future to work in small collectives producing food products and other goods.

Democratization and Women's Civic Activism

Women's rights advocates view access to political power as an important indicator of women's empowerment, whereas democratic theorists point to the growth of civil society as central to democratic consolidation. In this volume, "democratization" is viewed as the establishment of competitive elections, the rule of law, and the development of civil society. One of the major points examined in the four chapters in part III of the volume, "Democratization and Women's Civic Activism," is the simultaneous rise of men in formal politics and women in NGOs. Moreover, though NGOs play an important role in offering citizens opportunities to tackle community problems and engage in public advocacy, the fact remains that women find themselves sealed off from other domains of political power. Thus the chapters in this part present important research findings about women's civic activism and how women have made significant contributions to the development of civil society, though not necessarily because it is their avocation but more perhaps because it is the only arena open to them. The chapters also examine the ways in which the international community has reified this position by placing emphasis on gender-sensitive policies that promote women in the NGO arena.

In chapter 7, "Women, Building Civil Society, and Democratization in Post-Soviet Azerbaijan," Nayereh Tohidi presents a succinct summary of the impact of the post-Soviet transition on gender and political activism. She notes that the transition has resulted in two opposing trends for women in politics: a drastic decline in women's access to formal (national and local) government levels on the one hand, and an unprecedented increase in women's participation in informal politics, in building civil society, and in NGOs on the other. With the removal of fixed quotas of representation for women, their share of legislative seats fell sharply, recovered somewhat in the mid-1990s, and then declined over the course of successive elections. Tohidi accounts for women's poor showing by drawing on many factors familiar to Western researchers, such as the domestic burdens associated with child care, but she also points to issues connected to post-Soviet discourses about the role of women. These discourses stress that women should give priority to having large families—subordinating their problems to those of the nation—culminating in Azerbaizhani women finding it difficult to openly declare themselves politicians.

In contrast to women's secondary and marginal role in the formal political arena, Tohidi finds a surge of women's involvement in civil society. Like the other authors in this volume, she contends that a "feminization" of the "third sector" has occurred in Azerbaizan, pointing to multiple factors behind women's strong representation in NGOs: (1) women's exclusion from power centers in government and business; (2) women's networking and linguistic skills, particularly important in linking with foreign and international donors; (3) women's traditional interest in and responsibility for social problems like disabilities, health, and children's issues, all areas that NGOs especially address; (4) women's desire to avoid the taint of corruption, a problem more associated with the formal political arena than the new informal, civic arena; and (5) women's secondary status, a situation that leaves open avenues of participation that lack monetary reward or "prospects" to women due to men's lack of interest (or their preference for the worlds of business and formal politics).

In chapter 8, "Women's Political Activism in Russia: The Case of Samara," Ludmila Popkova relies on interviews with women politicians and NGO activists in the Russian province of Samara to illuminate the subjective world of women who do choose a life of political activism. Women politicians generally do not act as strong advocates for women's rights. The largest group of women politicians denies that women have specific interests and actually avoid accentuating women's themes in election campaigns and political debates. Popkova explains this reluctance as a reaction to the Soviet legacy, which treated women's issues in a paternalistic manner and as low in prestige. Emphasizing women's themes in political life thus becomes associated with undermining one's professional standing. Moreover, these politicians see other issues—such as consolidating democracy or organizing an effective economic system—as more urgent.

Other female politicians do assert that women have specific interests but embrace a subordinate, "woman-housekeeper" role in the political arena, where women take care of the social sphere and routine work and leave other issues to men. Popkova directs attention to the patron–client relations often found between these women politicians and powerful male political figures who play the "woman card" by including a token number of safe, dependable women on their team. Her analysis suggests strong continuity with the Soviet past, particularly with the essentialist approach to gender difference that treats women's secondary position as stemming from natural sexual differences.

In chapter 9, "Two Worlds Apart: The Lack of Integration between Women's Informal Networks and Nongovernmental Organizations in Uzbekistan," Andrea Berg confirms the gendered divisions of political participation in Uzbekistan, with women largely absent from formal politics but dominating the NGO sphere. To a greater extent than other authors in this volume, she emphasizes the socioeconomic gulf between top-down women's NGOs and the bulk of women living in rural areas and poor urban areas. The women who chair women's NGOs are strong, well-educated, urban women who frequently have been pushed out of government or university work. They dominate their organizations and, in their absence, organizational life virtually ceased to exist. They view rural women as "traditional and religious and therefore uninformed." As Berg notes, "target groups are seen as objects of instruction," with rural women often behaving like petitioners. Instead of empowering women, the women's NGOs functioned in a hierarchical manner and showed no desire to mobilize or involve grassroots women.

To be fair, Berg points out that some women's NGOs are learning from their mistakes and appear to be searching for new strategies to contact a broader spectrum of women: reaching out and working with indigenous rotating savings clubs known in Uzbek as *gap,* which rely on informal, grassroots networks of Uzbek women based on kinship or neighborhood. This approach holds some promise of closing the gulf between women NGOs and the bulk of Uzbek women. Nevertheless, Berg's research demonstrates the huge socioeconomic differences found in Uzbek society and the concomitant dominance of elite women in NGO work.

Although many women's NGOs can be described as "works in progress" or have folded their tents, having been unable to amass sufficient financial and human resources, in chapter 10, "Sisterhood versus the "Moral" Russian State: The Postcommunist Politics of Rape," Janet Elise Johnson provides a positive example of women making "use of their new political citizenship." Her research tracks the development of a small antirape movement in Russia, noting the establishment of dozens of crisis centers, of networks and coalitions, and of an ongoing campaign to transform the way the criminal justice system and society at large frames the crime of rape. The success of this movement rests on several factors: the sense of social responsibility felt by educated, middle-aged post-Soviet women, many of whom lost their positions in the 1990s and were searching for new professional opportunities; the strong sense of personal fulfillment many of these activists felt about working with women's organizations; and the presence of foreign funding, particularly since the mid-1990s. Unlike many women's NGOs, the antirape organizations represent women organizing on behalf of women. They have challenged widespread ideas about the "triviality" of women's issues, refuted mythologies about how women are to blame for rape, and have refused to back away from the central principle that women have the right to live without violence. The focus in the chapter is not just on the development of the movement but also on women's ability to influence policy and to change behavior.

Although the overall picture is mixed, these studies do provide considerable evidence that women's NGOs can facilitate active citizenship and that women are coming together to address problems in their communities and in their state; and, in some cases, even developing the kinds of coalitions that carry the potential for policy advocacy in particular policy domains. There is movement and change in the way people think about problems and pursue strategies. We also see problems connected with the tradition of top-down approaches of dealing with the "masses" of women that was inherited from the Soviet and pre-Soviet past. Women's NGOs were not created on a blank slate, but the largest and most active ones often have their roots in the Soviet-era women's councils and/or rely heavily on strong and often well-connected women leaders.

A dearth of financial and material resources emerges as a key theme, rendering a large proportion of NGOs unable to function. But a word of caution is even required with respect to the fundamental issue of money. Scholars have often noted that conducting research on the countries of the former Soviet Union is like hitting a moving target. Clearly, the development of domestic sources of financing, whether from the public or private sector, appears a dreary prospect on the basis of recent experience. The future need not, however, resemble the past. Since 2000, many countries of the former Soviet Union have begun to enjoy economic growth and increases in real wages. There are wealthy people and businesses and thus the potential for philanthropy that could provide domestic support for NGO activity. Currently, however, many women's NGOs compete for and depend on foreign and international sources of aid. The implications of these assistance encounters are explored in the final part of this volume.

Assistance Encounters

Like economists, whose models just a decade ago projected market-based economies throughout the former Soviet states, development specialists envisioned a course of expansive democratization in the new states. In fewer than 10 years of "transition," both assumptions have been shattered. With many good ideas, loads of money, and sincere intentions, international encounters in the post-Soviet states have been more challenging and certainly less understood than in nearly any other region in the world.

The ideological and material shift away from socialism toward capitalism was more difficult than economists or development specialists could have predicted. In a post–Cold War rush to transplant notions of capitalism into the former command economy of the once–Soviet Union, little consideration was initially given to understanding the intricate socioeconomic relationships of the former system, and how to build upon any of its formal or informal institutions. Instead, inherent in the post–Cold War condemnation of most aspects of the former socialist system was the assumption that the destruction of the old Soviet world would invariably lead to something more entrepreneurial and benign, something more like the Western world than like a developing country.[8] Indeed, the assumptions with which Western aid organizations initially approached the post-Soviet states can be more likened to a doctor who attempts to eradicate a disease by cutting off everything below the patient's neck than to a doctor who carefully examines the patient and evaluates what is still functioning and vital, distinguishing what needs urgent versus long-term medical attention.

The four chapters in part IV, "Assistance Encounters," reflect the latter approach to understanding the post-Soviet states. An anthropology of postsocialism in many ways characterizes the entire part, for each chapter offers an insightful critique of the relationship between international aid organizations and recipient countries or projects. The part as a whole provides an exquisite vantage point for reflection about relationships of power and how international agendas influence local priorities in relation to women, and how local groups champion their own agendas in spite of international intentions.

The involvement of Russian women in the post-Soviet world of NGOs were for many a survival strategy, both emotionally and practically speaking, according to chapter 11, "Meeting the Challenge Together? Russian Grassroots Women's Organizations and the Shortcomings of Western Aid," by Rebecca Kay. But what began as a question of personal survival for these women with time became a question of organizational survival. Kay traces the evolution of a handful of women's groups in Russia during the mid-1990s, their leaders and their motivations, their hopes and their disappointments. Common strands quickly emerged, including that of these groups being continuously confronted by the problem of international agendas that often missed the fact that just paying rent on an office or a telephone is a major hurdle toward long-term survival. Nor were these groups looking for handouts from the international community, for Kay provides examples of the type of ingenuity and creativity that these women used to get from point A to point B, including commercial ventures and individual members providing private funding.

In spite of such creative commitment to a cause or a group, most of the groups that Kay studied wrestled with survival issues, partly because, as she argues, the international community of donors lacks an understanding of what is it takes to survive as a NGO in Russia. She traces part of the problem as based on an assumption that the flow of experience and knowledge is unidirectional, from donor to recipient, reiterating "the West knows best," a theme also noted by the other authors in this part, and that there is a need for more dialogue in setting international donor objectives. She points out the manner in which Western organizations have helped to create and sustain a new elite class that possesses the language skills and intimately knows the rules and rhetoric of the donor game. Thus, instead of international institutions assisting in creating networks among women's groups, fiefdoms have resulted. The playing field, or even access to it, is not the same for all Russian NGOs.

Kay draws on interviews that highlight a generally held belief among Russian women's groups, that there are "favorites" as well as preferential treatment by donors of some individuals or groups. The story of her interviewees might be summarized as a field of dreams dashed by the hard ball (and sometimes corrupted) reality of competing for limited funds with many strings attached. With practical recommendations to the international constituency, she echoes what many of her colleagues in this volume support, the need for the dialogue between donor and recipient to be a two-way street; the recognition that knowledge comes in many forms and what is working at the grassroots level should be understood and considered from a local context, not an international one; and that development is not about just the recipient's trajectory but must also include changed attitudes and behavior on the part of the donor.

In chapter 12, "Working at the Local–Global Intersection: The Challenges Facing Women in Armenia's Nongovernmental Organization Sector," Armine Ishkanian offers a detailed discussion on "speaking gender" in the democratization process, the discourse that takes place among NGOs in Armenia. She highlights how women who work in the sector have learned to deploy two different discourses simultaneously; one to communicate with Western organizations using "gender talk" or feminist discourses to secure grants; and the other to utilize traditional discourses rooted in Armenian society when engaged in communications among themselves. The latter aims at legitimating women's NGOs activities in a culture that configures gender from the perspective of women as mothers—more oriented toward family and children than active involvement in politics and social life. Therefore, Ishkanian notes, women's NGOs "cannot address the domestic violence issue in the same way as it is done . . . elsewhere . . . because they must work in the local context, with its own expectations and limitations." She raises the problem of foreign aid as a double-edged sword, because it tends to distort women's NGOs, particularly their agendas and priorities. Confirming the findings of other authors in this volume who work elsewhere in the post-Soviet states, Ishkanian also stresses that Western assistance must take into account the local context and demonstrate respect for local priorities and locally based solutions.

The power dynamics between international institutions and local organizations are intricately examined in chapter 13, "Gender and Democracy: Strategies of Engagement and Dialogue on Women's Issues after Socialism in St. Petersburg," by Michele Rivkin-Fish. She draws upon rich ethnographic data collected over several years of fieldwork in Saint Petersburg to examine the structures of knowledge and action that shape encounters between global and local experts promoting women's issues in the post-socialist context. Specifically, she focuses her critical lens on the distinct approaches that development consultants and anthropologists bring to the process of engaging local communities, highlighting how each seeks to negotiate cultural differences and conflict. In highlighting the collaborative and communicative dimensions of international encounters, she posits that the analysis of women's issues after socialism may "reveal as much, or more, about global activists than about the women targeted for help." To make sense of these distinct approaches to engagement and expose the underlying agendas of the various actors, she offers her own framework of analysis based on the term "stance," which she defines as "global actors' self-conception in the collaborative encounter, as expressed in their assumptions regarding their role and potential contribution to the local setting, and in the practical tasks they undertake (and do not undertake) to pursue their goals."

Rivkin-Fish further distinguishes the development consultants' stance, or "provocateur" stance, from the anthropological stance. The provocateur assumes the role of "expert," armed with knowledge and tools to transfer to the needy local recipient. The anthropological stance, by contrast, begins with the assumption that local actor(s) are experts about their own situation. Such an assumption involves global actors not only in transferring knowledge to local groups but also in gaining knowledge from them. The comparative framework contributes an important model for feminist and development studies regarding how abstract ideals about building democracy can be put into play at the local level of international encounters. Rivkin-Fish works out the dynamics of her model through the case study of a women's health clinic in Saint Petersburg where the World Health Organization (WHO) was training physicians about Western health care practices. She reveals the ways in which the Russian physicians took issue with the WHO consultants, who failed to address the physicians' concerns, in part because their own agenda of reform did not recognize the intricate social processes under way in the clinic. She concludes her chapter by considering how the anthropological stance can be integrated into applied projects.

In chapter 14, "Strategizing Gender and Development: Action Research and Ethnographic Responsibility in the Russian Provinces," Julie Hemment advocates the need for more understanding of the local and more circumspection in critiques of international projects. She situates the story of Western aid in the post-Soviet states not from the position of researcher but from the perspective of a provincial Russian women's group. The complexity of her story is revealed in the ways that the local group strategically uses the rhetoric of what she calls the "democratization apparatus" to achieve their own goals, while still attempting to integrate Western gender concerns into their local context. The story of Zhenskii Svet, a small feminist group in provincial Russia, runs parallel to the stories of many women's groups on which Berg, Johnson, Tohidi, and others comment in their respective chapters—well-educated women, if not of the elite, who find themselves caught between their own self-subscribed mission and the need to address an international agenda that has grant money attached to it. In this case, Zhenskii Svet begins to operate a crisis center, but it is negotiated based on the members' own terms and constructed with their own meanings, although this is not always obvious to the casual outside observer.

What makes this chapter unique, in part, is that Hemment the researcher, formerly an observer, becomes a participant in the process of setting up the crisis center. Hence, her unusual "insider's" perspective allows the reader to witness firsthand how a women's organization that receives international aid in a provincial town has much more ability to make changes in a smaller community than its Moscow counterpart might have in a large urban area. Nevertheless, this local advantage does not ease the tribulations of the members of this nascent group, who begin to feel like they are "chameleons" in the treadmill of international foundations—attempting to devise new ways to meet agendas that are continually being revised. Although once considered a type of career track for Russian women, NGO involvement is being reconsidered by many women who consider NGO work more limiting than creative, and more insecure than secure. Hemment ends her chapter with some larger questions for the development community to consider, including what comes next in the "transition" model of civil society. In spite of the many mistakes in the past decade with the democratization model, she cautions her readers not to throw the baby out with the bath water, and instead she advocates more, not less, Western engagement with the democratization process.

The Fate of Women and the Post-Soviet Transition

Although the rise and fall of communism was one of the defining events of the twentieth century, the twenty-first century undoubtedly will witness the unfolding of a transformation of equal magnitude and importance: the effort of postcommunist countries to survive economic stress and, in some instances, build democratic societies and market economies. Unlike the trajectory of Western history, where democracy and capitalist economies emerged slowly over lengthy periods of time, post-Soviet states are undergoing rapid and fundamental change as they seek to overhaul their societies from above. The stakes are high. For example, will Russia take its place among the democratic countries of Western Europe? Will Uzbekistan succumb to the pressures of Islamic fundamentalists seeking the creation of an "Islamic" state or end up a post-Soviet dictatorship? It is no surprise that Western governments and donors have sought to influence the course of the transition process by advancing democratization and market economies through various types of assistance, ranging from the infusion of money to the delivery of advice, institutional capacity building, and training.

Societal transformation, however, encompasses more than political systems and economies. Social relations between men and women, young and old, rich and poor are also in transition. The formerly predominant Soviet image of women as mother-workers has given way to a welter of competing ideas, from the reemergence of traditional, precommunist ideals of women as mothers and transmitters of national culture to newly voiced feminist ideals of women as full participants in the social, economic, and political life of their countries. Discourse about women's roles figures prominently in contemporary debate over national identities—over what it means, or should mean, to be an Uzbek woman, a Belarusian woman, a Tatar woman, or a Russian woman. Western aid has unwittingly contributed to the minefield of change as it has sought to effect changes in every dimension of life in the post-Soviet states.

Western aid programs that target women have addressed multiple objectives, including gender equality and human rights, the growth of civil society, improved health care and social benefits for women, and the amelioration of specific problems such as unemployment, household poverty, violence against women, and sexual harassment. But these programs do not operate in a vacuum; the domestic context influences how aid programs are received, adjusted, and adapted to distinctive settings. The effectiveness of international aid depends upon the ability of the West to understand and work at the local level and to respond to a diversity of practices, values, and aspirations.

Transitions offer both danger and opportunity. In the post-Soviet states during the past decade, we have seen both. The stories of transition told in this volume are far from finished. In some cases, they foreshadow further difficulties and hardship; in others, possibilities and even hope. In all cases, however, the chapters of this volume illustrate anthropologist Lati Mani's contention about postcolonial India: "The fate of women and the fate of the emerging nation [are] inextricably intertwined."[9]

Notes

1. It is important to note that the term "transition," commonly employed throughout the volume, implies neither a sharp break with the Soviet past nor inexorable "progress" toward such goals as democratization or marketization.

2. Susan Gal and Gail Kligman, *The Politics of Gender after Socialism: A Comparative-Historical Essay* (Princeton, N.J.: Princeton University Press, 2000); Susan Gal and Gail Kligman, eds., *Reproducing Gender: Politics, Publics, and Everyday Life after Socialism* (Princeton, N.J.: Princeton University Press, 2000).

3. See Katherine Verdery, "From Parent-State to Family Patriarchs: Gender and Nation," *Contemporary Eastern Europe: East European Politics and Societies* 8 (1994): 225–55; Katherine Verdery, *What Was Socialism, and What Comes Next?* (Princeton, N.J.: Princeton University Press, 1996); and Mary Buckley, "Victims and Agents: Gender in Post-Soviet States," in *Post-Soviet Women: From the Baltic to Central Asia,* ed. Mary Buckley (Cambridge: Cambridge University Press, 1997); Gal and Kligman, *Politics of Gender;* Gal and Kligman, *Reproducing Gender;* and Lila Abu-Lughod, "The Marriage of Feminism and Islamism in Egypt; Selective Repudiation as a Dynamic of Postcolonial Cultural Politics" in *Remaking Women: Feminism and Modernity in the Middle East,* ed. Lila Abu-Lughod (Princeton, N.J.: Princeton University Press, 1998).

4. Lata Mani, "Contentious Traditions: The Debate on Sati in Colonial India," in *Recasting Women: Essays in Colonial History,* ed. K. Sangari and S. Vaid (New Dehli: Kali for Women, 1989).

5. Gal and Kligman, *Politics of Gender.*

6. Janine R. Wedel, *Collision and Collusion: The Strange Case of Western Aid to Eastern Europe* (New York: Palgrave, 2001), 179.

7. Research on the economic impact of the transition on rural women concentrates on women's involvement in private farming or women's work on private plots. See, e.g., Sue Bridger, "Rural Women and the Impact of Economic Change," in *Post-Soviet Women,* ed. Buckley; and Myriam Hivon, "Rural Women and Agrarian Reforms," in *Women in Post-Communist Russia,* Bradford Studies in Language, Culture, and Society, ed. Sue Bridger (Bradford, U.K.: Interface, 1995). For women's entrepreneurial activity in urban areas, see Z. Khotkina, "Zhenskaia bezrabotnitsa i neformal'naia zaniatnost' v Rossii" [Women's unemployment and "informal" employment in Russia], *Voprosy Ekonimiki* [Problems of Economics] 3 (2000): 85–93; Sue Bridger, Rebecca Kay, and Kathryn Pinnick, *No More Heroines? Russia, Women and the Market* (London: Routledge, 1996).

8. Wedel, *Collision and Collusion,* 62.

9. Mani, "Contentious Traditions."

Part I

Gender and Nation Building

1

Strong Women, Weak State: Family Politics and Nation Building in Post-Soviet Ukraine

Tatiana Zhurzhenko

This chapter addresses the question of how the processes of nation building and economic and political reform in contemporary Ukraine affect the social position of women, particularly by focusing on the family and its changing status, functions, and symbolic role. The chapter examines these processes on two different levels. On the symbolic level, I explore the various discourses about family, reproduction of the nation, and the construction of national identity through the notions of the "Ukrainian family" and the "Ukrainian woman." On the level of the current reality, I examine state policies about the family and the impact of the new family policy on women's status.

This chapter is based on a research project supported by the John D. and Katherine MacArthur Foundation. For the extended version, see my book *Social Reproduction and Gender Politics in Ukraine* [in Russian] (Kharkiv: Folio, 2001).

"Neofamilialism after Communism": Distancing from the Soviet Past, Returning to Europe

The first changes in Soviet family policy started at the beginning of the 1980s, although debate over the compatibility of women's employment with family responsibilities reaches back into the late 1960s.[1] The steady decline of the birthrate forced the political leadership to take pro-natalist measures, first of all, to prolong the terms of maternity leave and to extend social guarantees, especially for mothers with more than one child. Still, the "working mother" remained the main object of this policy. Its declared aim was to help women combine their professional employment with maternal duties.

However, some critical voices questioning the official Soviet egalitarianism were heard on the level of public discourse. Sociologists and journalists started a broad discussion on the problem of the double burden carried by women, which stressed the necessity of having the freedom of choice between their family and professional duties. After 1985, this criticism was combined with the project of market reforms, which were expected to raise the economic welfare of families and to make the "one-earner family" possible. It is not surprising that this discussion coincided with a new discourse about the "crisis of masculinity"—concerning the growing lack of initiative and responsibility among men, the absence of the father in the family, the deficiencies of women's leadership in the education of children, and even "matriarchy" in the Soviet family. From this perspective, it was not sufficient to send women back to their families. Gender roles, especially in the family context, had to be rearranged according to the "natural" order. As is demonstrated in chapter 4 of this volume by Elena Gapova, the emergence of the "new" ideology of traditional gender roles in post-Soviet societies reflected the processes of nation building and the formation of the middle class.

With the collapse of the Soviet system and the abandonment of communist ideology, the reevaluation of family and gender ideology became more radical. The Soviet heritage of gender egalitarianism had lost its legitimacy, but imported Western feminism turned out not to be very influential in affecting mass consciousness. Under these conditions, the rise of neofamilialism became one of the most striking tendencies in the changing gender ideology of post-Soviet societies, though it has appeared in various forms across the post-Soviet spectrum. In Russia for instance, new school courses on the "ethics of family life" and the sexual education of children provoked quite a big scandal.

In Ukraine, neofamilialism has developed its own specific features. Returning to the "traditionally strong" Ukrainian family is usually represented as a basis for national consolidation and renaissance, for maternity is held in high esteem and is seen as a hope for the survival of the Ukrainian "ethnos." The restoration of the "traditional family" is depicted as an important strategy for the "renovation" of Ukrainian society and its liberation from the communist totalitarian legacy. In this type of discourse, the "traditional family" is understood as something between the idealized Ukrainian family of the pre-Soviet past and the American middle-class family of the 1950s. This fluctuation of images between "authentic" Ukrainian and Western is rather typical for contemporary political and academic discourse. But before analyzing the peculiarities of this phenomenon in Ukraine, we focus on six characteristics that it has in common with developments in other post-Soviet societies.

First, in Ukraine as in other former USSR republics, neofamilialism appeared as a critique of the totalitarian communist past and as a reevaluation of Soviet policies of women's emancipation. According to the neofamilialist critique, the decades of Soviet rule resulted in the "destruction of the traditional family," which had negative social effects and even caused the moral degradation of society. The "traditional family" (in this context, the heterosexual nuclear family, which usually consists of two parents and their children, with the man as breadwinner and a nonworking woman) is seen not only as a social norm but also as a moral value, an idealized space of peace and harmony. Returning to family values, the family way of life, family education, and the family business is therefore the main strategy guiding social and economic reforms.

Second, post-Soviet neofamilialism perceives the totalitarian state and its violent destruction of the autonomy of the family as a main cause of contemporary social problems. The elimination of private property and of the freedom of private initiative deprived the family of its economic autonomy and turned its members into the employees of the monopolistic state. The active interference in children's education and the imposition of communist ideology destroyed the moral autonomy of the family. Thus, the main strategy is restricting state interference and paternalism and giving back social and economic responsibility to the family itself.

Third, the characteristic feature of neofamilialism is the focus on the reproductive function of the family, its "children-centric" character. Biological reproduction and the socialization of children are represented as the "meaning" of family life, whereas the conjugal relations between spouses are considered as secondary and determined by the parents' obligations. The "one-child" family is the main object of this criticism, and not only for demographic reasons. This family model is not favorable for the child's education; it causes egocentrism and communication problems. Rejecting "parenthood based on contraception-abortion,"[2] neofamilialists are ready to accept only one type of family as socially desirable: that with two parents and at least three or four children.

Fourth, the restoration of the economic autonomy and high social status of the family requires the extension of its productive activities. Concentration on consumption and dependence on the market, on professional employment, and on state social services undermine the cohesion and unity of the family and turn "natural" gender and age inequalities into a source of conflict. Therefore, the development of intrahousehold production and the encouragement of various forms of family enterprise are considered major factors for economic growth and "informal welfare." Family business and a self-support strategy will help emancipate the family from total dependence on the state but will also contribute to strengthening the parents' authority and improving family education. Naturally, the family enterprise assumes a traditional division of gender roles: Women are responsible for household and children, and men for business and leadership.

Fifth, the neofamilialist critical revision of the Soviet experience is focused on gender relations within the family. The origins of gender conflicts within the family can be found in the social consequences of industrialization and the growing participation of women in the labor force. This caused competition between family members and a growing conflict on the redistribution of housework. The authority of the parents was split into two, with the effect that the father's authority declined, not in the least due to state support for working mothers. The result was a misbalance of gender roles and obligations in the household. The biggest mistake, according to neofamilialists, was the application of principles of democracy (meaning the equality and rights of individuals) to intrafamily relations, which they consider to be unequal by their very nature.

Sixth, though they are very critical of the Soviet experience of state paternalism and though they declare the autonomy of the family, neofamilialists nevertheless are convinced that there is a need for an active role for the state in family politics. They argue that the state has the right to insist on its own preferences concerning the type and form of the family. As a social ideal to be encouraged by the state, they propose the nuclear monogamous family, with two parents and three or four children. Other types should only be tolerated or even discouraged.

As one can see from this reconstruction of the neofamilialist discourse, its starting point is the criticism of the Soviet family policy and the Soviet system in general. The call for the liberation of the family from state domination is one of the strategies of distancing oneself from the Soviet past, of an imaginary return from the failed communist project to a more "civilized" order and a more "universal" set of values. But though the starting point for this transition seems to be clear, the destination is not easy to conceive. Unlike in Russia, in Ukraine neofamilialism is indispensable to the process of constructing the national identity as European; returning to civilized Europe and to the West presupposes the restoration of family autonomy and responsibility. In the context of market reforms and strengthening democracy, the "strong family" is seen as an important institution of civil society. However, Ukrainian neofamilialism (and in this case, it is more like the Russian) is also ambivalent toward "the West."

Although they criticize Soviet patterns of family modernization (forced full employment for women and state invasion into children's education) as opposed to "normal" Western society, neofamilialists also are rather suspicious of feminism, sexual freedom, and the legitimization of gay and lesbian sexuality in the West. If the first attitude was rather popular at the very beginning of the post-Soviet transition, the second prevails today. One can observe a certain shift from "anticommunist" to "antimodernist" rhetoric during the past decade.

The same pattern applies to the idea of a "market economy." In the beginning, in the context of an "anticommunist" critique, the market was seen as an ally of the family in the process of liberation from state domination and the restoration of its economic autonomy. This promarket familialism was based on the image of an idealized Western family, which subsists due to the independent income of its head wage earner. Later familialist rhetoric became more critical of the market, especially of its social consequences: social differentiation and impoverishment of the majority of families, and "antifamily" features of mass culture.

In fact, post-Soviet neofamilialism demonstrates not only an anticommunist critical attitude but, what is more important, also an antimodernist one. Women's participation in the labor force, the undermining of the patriarchal power of the father in family, and the reduction of household production activities are understood not only as the result of Soviet policy but also as part of an inevitable modernization of the private sphere itself. Thus, post-Soviet neofamilianism can be considered a reaction to the consequences of the modernization processes in Soviet society, or more precisely, as a reaction to the obvious crisis of the Soviet pattern of modernization. The process of searching for new patterns and ways of continuing modernization is accompanied by nostalgia for the "traditional family."

Searching for Ukrainian Identity: Images of Women, Family, and Maternity in the Nation-Building Process

Nation building is always based on the mobilization of the cultural resources of society (language, customs, religion, and memories). And according to Nira Yuval-Davis,[3] the images of "women," "family," and "home" are central to every national (ethnic) culture, proving its authenticity, homogeneity, and uniqueness. Women represent the past of a nation by keeping, transmitting, and demonstrating its traditions, and they symbolize a nation's future through childbearing and child care. In Ukraine, since 1991 the contradictory process of national identity formation has involved the construction of images of Ukrainian women and the Ukrainian family through the reinterpretation of historical, ethnographic, and sociological data.

In the media and even in academic publications, the Ukrainian people are often represented as having a traditional, inherent, and unique respect for the family and marriage, even as having a special family mentality. Traditions of having many children, special respect for old people, and valuing peace in the family are depicted as essential features of the Ukrainian ethnos. One of the delegates to the All-Ukrainian Women's Congress in 1998 underlined this idea in her presentation: "Throughout history in Ukraine, it was considered the greatest of sins to kill a child in one's womb; the harshest of God's penalties not to have one's own children; and the most unforgivable crime in the eyes of the people to abandon one's child, to forget one's elderly parents, and to disrespect the father of one's children."[4]

In discussions in the media and in academic writing, a very common statement is that a stable marriage and high birthrates are fundamental peculiarities of the Ukrainian ethnos. The loss of these traditions can be seen as a result of anti-Ukrainian Soviet politics (a radical nationalist interpretation) or of economic hardship during the transition period (a moderate interpretation), but in any case this is viewed as a temporary situation. Ukrainian sociologists stress not the "crisis of family" but quite the opposite: the commitment of the Ukrainian population to family lifestyle and family values. As was mentioned in the official 1999 annual report of the Ukrainian Institute for Social Studies, *On the Position of Families in Ukraine,* "Under conditions of radical changes in the social and cultural environment, of competition on the labor markets and in the professional sphere there is a growing need for the family where one can get emotional support and recognition and find the way out of economic problems by joint efforts."[5] According to this interpretation, "deformations" of marriage and reproductive behavior (the term "deformation" itself presupposes a social "norm") were caused mainly by economic reasons and will be restored as soon as living standards improve.

Moreover, the (traditional) family is often presented as the very basis of the national revival: "The Ukrainian nation must save itself in the family. Home, family, labor, high culture, and civic maturity of the Ukrainian people have to ensure a high standard of living, independence, economic and political stability, the inviolability of borders, and high international authority. Nobody will build the state and create better material conditions for the Ukrainians if the family is disorganized."[6] It is the family where national identity is formed and where love of the native language and culture emerges. The leading role in the family as a spiritual community belongs to the mother. It is she who educates children and transmits national traditions, culture, and language to them. Unlike the Soviet mother, who was represented as a counterpart of the state regardless of the family, the Ukrainian mother acts in her traditional role; she is not "public" but "private."

Ukrainian women in general are often described in essentialist terms—as having a special "nature" and character. They are strong and independent, but at the same time family oriented, committed to their maternal duties, and respectful to their husbands. Typically, they are wiser and more responsible than men and assume real leadership in their families. This hidden leadership of women makes feminism superfluous; there is no need to protect women's rights. Unlike Western egoistic women, Ukrainian women are more interested in the well-being of their family than in gender equality.

The same logic has often been applied at the national level. In principle, Ukrainian women are educated and strong enough to assume male social roles and responsibility, but they prefer their "natural" duties. Professional activities such as participation in politics and business are no problem for women but make sense only as contributing to the "well-being" of their children (or of future generations). Altruism (in contrast to male egoism) is seen as the main motive of women's social and political activities, which is derivative from their primordial role of mother. As an example of how this logic was represented on the All-Ukrainian Congress of Women:

> It is nature itself that imposes the responsibility for the future of humanity on women. Childbearing and the raising of children are the highest goals and ideals in a woman's life. Maybe this was the reason why until a certain time women were not concerned with politics but with the comfort and harmony of their families. However, when these values are endangered, women should become active participants in political life since responsibility for children is responsibility for the contemporary and future society.[7]

This ideology which justifies "gender division of labor" in politics often serves to dismiss women politicians from key problems and decisive positions, to reduce their responsibility to the issues of social protection, education, and health care (see more about similar tendencies in chapter 8 of this volume by Ludmila Popkova).

The popular image of the "strong" Ukrainian woman, an image that only partly follows the old Soviet pattern, is reinforced by the historical myth of the traditional matriarchal character of Ukrainian culture. According to Marian Rubchak, the essence of it is that in the past, Ukrainian women lived in a society in which the sexes had complementary roles of roughly equal value, that they enjoyed "equality in difference," and that their natural female roles were highly regarded.[8] This discourse evokes the ancient image of the Berehinia (a pagan goddess-protectress of the hearth and home), which is widely used today as a female symbol of the Ukrainian nation. The myth of a "Ukrainian matriarchal culture" refers to the pre-Christian origins of Ukrainian culture. This pre-Christian system of values was (according to contemporary interpretations) not structured along the dichotomy of male/female but rather spiritual/material and powerful/powerless. Therefore the "original Ukrainian feminism," which refers to the myth of matriarchy, claims to be universal and holistic by nature. This makes it different from Western feminism, which is interested in "narrow" women's issues.

Discussions about the matriarchal character of Ukrainian culture and empowered womanhood are an important contribution to the process of national identity formation. On one hand, due to the myth of original matriarchy, Ukrainian women's identity has been constructed in opposition to "Western" women and feminism. Ukrainian women are different "by nature"; they are not egoistic, and they care first of all about their families. They are also concerned about the renaissance of the Ukrainian nation and the problems of state building. That is why "gender peace" (a new term coined by several Ukrainian researchers) is a necessary condition for national consolidation. Altruism and the Ukrainian woman's capacity for self-sacrifice—this is what makes this nation different from the West. Ukrainian women do not need feminism because they are already empowered enough—due to their historical tradition.

On the other hand, the myth of matriarchy allows one to construe Ukrainian women as different from Russian women. According to this myth, Ukrainian women were traditionally freer in private and public life, and less restricted by patriarchal norms and institutions, than their Russian counterparts. This corresponds to the image of a "feminist-friendly" Ukraine as opposed to that of a "more patriarchal" imperial Russia. In this type of discourse, cultural decolonization and nation building is implicitly represented as "women's empowerment" by means of referring to the original roots of Ukrainian culture.

Reproducing the Nation: Demography and Nationalism in Ukraine

In her book *Gender and Nation,* Yuval-Davis defines three dominant types of discourse determining nationalist demographic politics.[9] The first discourse ("people as power") determines to some extent the demographic policy of all nation-states and is typical for state-forming nations. In this type of discourse, the future of the nation and sometimes its survival depend on steady population growth. And usually it is the women of the "core" nation who are responsible for population growth; hence, state policy aims to activate their reproductive behavior.

Second is the eugenic discourse, which focuses not on the size of the nation but on its quality. Eugenics as pseudoscience is an attempt to predetermine the quality of the nation by selective breeding and presupposes interference into the reproductive processes to prevent "undesirable" childbirth. The contemporary eugenicist discourse operates with the notions of "genetic pull" and "genetic potential." The preservation and improvement of the genetic potential is crucial for the future of a nation.

Third is the Malthusian discourse, which is connected to the politics of limitation of population growth (mainly in developing countries). In industrial countries, it often serves to rationalize hidden concerns about comparatively higher birthrates of ethnic minorities and the risk of a change in the "ethnic balance."

For the period since 1991, all of the above-mentioned discourses can be found in Ukrainian demographic literature. The new ideology of "demographic development" is not only determined by a nation-building agenda but also sometimes explicitly nationalist. Demographers write about the "development of Ukraine as a new united and coherent social organism," about the "national reproduction of Ukraine" as a political and cultural entity of the people. But as it turns out, they are mainly concerned with the problem of the reproduction of the "core ethnos"—the Ukrainians. The dominance of Ukrainians in the ethnic structure of the population will guarantee, according to these views, the social and political stability of the state. Thus, some demographers consider the change of the ethnic balance in favor of the Ukrainian population (which started in the beginning of the 1990s) as a positive tendency, while disregarding the fact that this change was mainly the result of emigration of members of other ethnic groups. O. Chirkov and I. Vinnichenko stress with satisfaction: "The economic crisis in Ukraine had at least one positive effect—the number of emigrant Russians exceeded the number of immigrant Russians. The numbers of Belarusians also started to decrease. The reduction of the number of Jews, Poles, Czechs, Slovaks, Greeks, Karaim, Krymchaki, and other ethnic minorities is continuing."[10]

According to Chirkov and Vinnichenko's conclusion, these changes of the ethnic structure of the population will favor for the process of national consolidation. Immigration to Ukraine (which includes the repatriation of formerly repressed minorities, e.g., the Crimean Tatars, refugees, and transit migrants from near and far abroad) is also evaluated in this discourse as a negative and even dangerous tendency. Illegal migration from Africa, Southeast Asia, and the Middle East not only causes a growth in the number of crimes but also threatens the very existence of the Ukrainian nation.[11] The same negative attitude can be found with regard to cross-ethnic marriages, which also endanger the ethnic homogeneity of the Ukrainian nation. (Similar concerns about the growing share of cross-ethnic marriages can be found in Tatar ethnic nationalism, as is shown by Katherine Graney in chapter 2 of this volume.)

The "people as power" discourse is popular today in Ukrainian demography. As in other countries facing the same problems, the decline in birthrates and depopulation are a matter of concern of the state because of the worsening situation in the labor market, the aging of the population, and the growing burden of pensions. At the same time, this discourse in Ukraine has some peculiarities. Here the main concern is not depopulation but a more serious threat—"national degeneration," the "erosion of the Ukrainian ethnos." The degradation of the Ukrainian nation is represented as the legacy of Soviet colonial policy. As Chirkov and Vinnichenko put it:

> Mass migration of Russians and members of other Russian-speaking peoples into Ukraine, linguistic Russification of Ukrainians, insufficient development of Ukrainian professional culture, decline of endogamy between Ukrainians on some territories, ideological brainwashing of the population, especially children and youth, open blackening of the history of Ukraine and the inculcation of inferiority complexes, ascribing an archaic character and a lack of perspective to all things Ukrainian—all this has prepared the ground for a total and irrevocable Russification in the near future.[12]

Therefore the "ethnodemographic" situation remains critical, regardless of the growing share of Ukrainians in the ethnic structure of the population. Connections between demography and nationalism are also obvious with regard to the problem of the demographic balance between urban and rural populations. "The inequality between rural and urban living conditions, the underdeveloped industrial and social infrastructure in the countryside caused an intensive migration of the rural population to the cities; the traditional Ukrainian mentality was eroded and the ideal of the rural family with many children lost its popularity."[13] According to this logic, it is the rural population and rural families that are the true bearers of authentic Ukrainian identity, of traditions, culture, religious values, and language. The migration of the rural population to the cities, the social degradation of the rest, and the economic crisis in agriculture undermine not only the demographic potential but also the "spiritual basis" of the Ukrainian nation.

Some examples of the eugenicist discourse can also be found in the demographic literature. The problem of saving the "genetic pull" of the Ukrainian nation is discussed in various contexts—first of all the worsening of health indicators, the general aging of the population, and the growing numbers of congenital diseases and disabilities. The spread of alcoholism and drug addiction, HIV/AIDS, epidemic tuberculosis, and other social diseases threatens the genetic potential of the nation and leads to its physical degeneration. One of the researchers dealing with these problems gives a biological analogy: A population that is 30 percent genetically spoiled is doomed to die out.[14] A pseudoacademic eugenicist discourse, by applying characteristics of biological populations to the human community, offers itself to nationalist ideology. To prevent degradation, the national organism has to be protected from ethnic and racial pollution.

Contemporary demographers refer to Ukrainian scientist Stepan Rudnytskyi, who already in the 1920s tried to demonstrate "the necessity of not only a quantitative, but also a qualitative policy which should aim at the birth of 'genetically healthy and racially normal persons' and should be based on the achievements of a national biology (eugenics)." This discourse considers the nation as an organism to be treated by "scientific" methods. Consequently, some proposed measures to improve the health of the future generation (e.g., compulsory medical genetic investigation before official marriage registration) are discussed more often in terms of the "genetic potential of the nation" and not in terms of the rights and interests of individuals.

Some elements of Malthusian discourse can be found, for example, in relation to the Crimean Tatars. In both the academic literature and in the media, some voices expressed concern about uncontrolled population growth among this group. This growth is caused not only by the repatriation process but also by the Tatar cultural and religious traditions that support active reproductive behavior. In the long run, high birthrates in Tatar families can lead to serious changes in the ethnic population balance in Crimea, and even in Ukraine in general.

Such fears are not only increased by the high population density of Crimea and the growing anthropogenic burden on the environment but also by the threat of political destabilization in the region. As N. Levchuk writes, "The growing number of Crimean Tatars and the gradual ethnosocial modification of the population structure will affect the dynamics of political life in general. The level of their successful integration into Ukrainian society, of their social adaptation will determine the electoral niche they will choose." Having been alarmed by the Kosovo scenario, politicians and bureaucrats see the high fertility of Tatar women as a potential cause of future conflict. Therefore, the reproductive function of women—be it of the "core nation" or of the ethnic and language minorities—is an object of special concern for nationalism.

The Politics of Family: Between Old and New

Due to the specifics of the Soviet political and economic system, the politics of family was not a separate sphere of state interest but primarily a part of labor market regulations. It was derived from the system of measures introduced by the Soviet state to guarantee full employment for women; the object of this policy was the "working mother," not the family itself.

The family as a "cell of the society" was mainly considered in functionalist terms: as a mediator between the individual and the state. The processes of nation building and market reforms in independent Ukraine inevitably raised the questions about the new role for the family and the principles of its relationship with the state. The "politics of family" in contemporary Ukraine combines several types of discourse: still existing relics of the Soviet egalitarian model and of the "protection of motherhood" approach, the conservative ideology of women's natural predestination, the neoliberal discourse of family autonomy and responsibility, and also the introduction of gender-equality agenda initiated by women's groups and by international organizations.

For example, the Labor Code, despite several amendments, has in fact been in force since 1972 and still reflects the Soviet model of the relationship between working women and the state-employer. It contains a significant amount of social guarantees for working women which exceed International Labor Organization (ILO) recommendations in the area of women's labor: prenatal and postnatal leave (56 and 70 days respectively) and three years childcare leave with the right to keep one's position during this period. The Labor Code provides health protection of pregnant women at the work place, employment guarantees and protection against dismissal, restrictions for the usage of women's labor for heavy or harmful work.

The Law on the Employment of Population provides guarantees of resettlement for women with children under 6 years of age or with disabled children and for single mothers with children by reserving for this category 5 percent of all enterprise vacancies. The Law on the Protection of Labor obliges the owner or the management of enterprises to offer free vouchers for health recreation or other services for pregnant women and women with young children, and, if required, to provide them with material assistance. However, under conditions of redundancy and hidden unemployment, unofficial labor arrangements and the difficult financial situation of many enterprises, the enforcement of these rights is rather problematic. For example, many enterprises do not inform the employment offices about existing vacancies. Most enterprises are in financial debt and not even capable of paying salaries on time, let alone providing material assistance or free services.

The "protection of motherhood" originating from the Soviet system made women's labor less competitive under new market conditions, providing the absence of democratic mechanisms of women's rights protection. For example, the Program on the Disengagement of Women from Industries Connected with Heavy Work and Harmful Conditions and on the Limitation of Women's Work during Nighttime, which was approved by the Cabinet of Ministers in 1996, was often used by enterprise administrations as an excuse for the dismissal of women. Meanwhile, the number of women working under unfavorable conditions did not come down but instead increased.

One of the first documents representing state family politics in independent Ukraine was the Long-Term Program for the Improvement of the Position of Women, Family, the Protection of Motherhood and Childhood (1992); but it mainly reflected the logic of late Soviet policy. Having been approved before the beginning of the economic crisis, this ambitious program contained rather expensive measures that required centralized administrative regulation and could not be implemented under the conditions of market reform. It provided enhanced privileges and compensation for working women, the creation of new modernized working places, and encouragement of part-time work. This late Soviet pattern of a "rational combining of women's professional employment with maternity" demonstrated the total absence of any gender equality discourse. Neither problem of equal parenthood nor the question of the distribution of family obligations was discussed.

The National Program on Family Planning, adopted in 1995, shows a growing concern of the Ukrainian state about the worsening demographic indicators: the decline of birthrates, the high level of maternal and children's mortality, and the deterioration of public health, especially the health of children. From the gender point of view, this program had a positive side, because it attracted public attention to the problem of women's reproductive rights and the guarantees and social conditions for their realization (the availability of modern contraceptives, sexual education and information services, and professional medical help), and also to the problem of the high rate of abortions. Unlike in other postcommunist countries, in Ukraine the availability of abortion was not restricted, official regulation was even liberalized, and the main problem became the commercialization of these services. However, the politics of women's reproductive rights in Ukraine were not addressed from the feminist perspective and still are based on the late Soviet approach.

Faced with a worsening demographic situation, the Ukrainian state paid special attention to the problems of young families. It officially recognized the economic difficulties of the majority of young families, especially the problem of separate housing. The Law on the Promotion of Self-Fulfillment and Social Development of the Youth in Ukraine (1993) set up the principles of state youth politics under the new conditions, after the abolition of the Komsomol. According to this law, special social services had to be set up with the support of local authorities, mainly to provide young people with psychological, juridical, and informational assistance. The law included some guarantees for employment but also special measures to solve the problem of housing for young families by offering long-term state loans on privileged conditions for the purchase or construction of apartments or houses. However, the availability of this loan program has been limited by setting a maximum age (28 years), by the requirement of the first rather substantial payment, and also by the condition of having a permanent job.

The Children of Ukraine Program (1996) also reflected concerns about negative demographic tendencies, the increase in children's diseases as a result of an unfavorable ecological situation, and the worsening of life conditions and of the opportunities for children's development due to the deep economic crisis. Besides, it is in this document that the principles of new relations and a new division of responsibilities between family, society, and state were declared officially for first time. According to the preamble of this document, the family is the "natural environment for the physical, psychological, social, and spiritual development of the child"; it is responsible for the child's material provision.

As for the state, it "contributes to the legal and social protection of children" and creates favorable conditions for their development mainly by improving health care and the education system. The state takes direct responsibility only for certain categories of children, mainly those who lack parental care or those who live in "unfavorable conditions." The society (represented by working collectives and nongovernmental organizations) is entrusted with the task "to watch" "unsuccessful" families so as to help their children.

Without a doubt, the World Women's Conference in Beijing in 1995 served as a powerful spur to the introduction of gender equality problems into Ukrainian political discourse. It has activated the growth and development of women's groups and contributed to the emergence of a new feminist language by discussing particular "women's problems" in the context of gender inequality, discrimination, and human rights. The Ukrainian government, bound by international obligations, was obliged to start monitoring the social status of women, to cooperate with women's groups in developing national programs and plans, and to issue special reports.

As a result, in 1997 the *National Plan of Action for 1997–2000 on Improving the Status of Women and the Rise of Their Role in Society* was adopted by the Cabinet of Ministers. It includes informational and educational activities concerning the status of women and their rights. The progressive step was to admit the importance of gender expertise for Ukrainian legislation. Nevertheless, the document still shows some traces of the "protection of motherhood" approach; in fact, it does not differentiate "family politics" and "women's issues." As with previous documents, it leaves the impression that women's problems are only a small part of the more important and universal problems of the family.

In March 1999, the Ukrainian parliament adopted the *Declaration on General Fundamentals of the State Policy in Ukraine Concerning Family and Women.* Like the other documents mentioned above, this document demonstrates the same dualistic approach. On the one hand, it declares the commitment to the principle of equality of men and woman, condemns all forms of discrimination against women, and encourages them to participate in decision making on all levels. On the other hand, it stresses the priority of the family and its rights, the necessity of strengthening the social status of the family, and the importance of the social role of the institution of maternity.

The same approach can also be seen in the *Draft of State Family Policy,* adopted by parliament in September 1999. This document formulates the state–family relationship extensively, in the form of six principles. It declares, first, "the sovereignty and autonomy of the family while minimizing the interference of the state and of self-administration bodies, political parties, public organizations, and religious confessions into family affairs" (which reflexes the general tendency of the emancipation of family from state paternalism).

Second, it assures a differentiated approach to the social protection: State guarantees for a basic income are valid only for disabled citizens; the others have to provide it on their own.

The third principle presumes "parity" and "partnership" between men and women in all social spheres, the provision of equal opportunities and even the "fair distribution of family duties," which illustrates the growing influence of the gender-equality approach.

The fourth principle proclaims the "social partnership between the family and the state" instead of the compromised "state paternalism." It implies, in fact, the reduction of the direct responsibility of the state only to extraordinary circumstances.

The fifth principle guarantees the opportunities for the free development of every child. It appeals to the United Nations Convention on the Rights of the Child and demonstrates the end of the old Soviet approach of the "protection of childhood."

The sixth principle defines the role of the family in the nation-building process, which consists in providing for the continuity of generations, and in passing on national and cultural traditions, values, and customs to offspring. To conclude, the new family policy in Ukraine is a mixture of various ideologies and discourses: the Soviet concept of the "protection of motherhood and childhood;" the post-Soviet "privatization" of the family and the liberalization of state–family relations; the official nationalism with its orientation to the "traditional family"; and finally, the "Western" discourse on women's rights, gender equality, and children's rights, supported by Ukraine's declared "European choice."

From Declarations to Reality: Social Protection of Families in Ukraine

The reality of family policy in Ukraine today is far from official declarations surrounding it. The financial constraints of the state budget do not allow fulfillment of the declared principles and political aims. At the moment, family policy is reduced to the most urgent antipoverty measures (which are usually limited and belated) and certain privileges for special categories of families (the largest group being the victims of the Chernobyl disaster). The state implicitly relies on the informal social welfare: the mobilization of family resources and intrahousehold production, the network of kinship relations, and various small family businesses. (Two case studies of these strategies in other post-Soviet regions are presented by Cynthia Werner and Susan Crate, respectively, in chapters 5 and 6 of this volume.)

According to the Law on the State Assistance to Families with Children, there are the following allowances and payments for families with children: assistance for pregnant women, onetime assistance connected with the birth of child, child care allowances (until the age of 3 years), allowances for parents with three and more children (until the age of 16), assistance to single mothers, help for parents with disabled children, assistance for children from poor families, aid for children without parents, and some others. Most of these payments are calculated as a percentage of the officially established minimum wage (50–100 percent).

In general, this list corresponds to the legislative standards of most welfare states. The problems, however, are (1) frequent nonobservance of declared social guarantees; (2) inadequately small payments; and (3) constant delays in the distribution of payments. The most striking fact is the double calculation of payments. The basis for calculation of most payments is the officially established minimum wage. But until the end of 2000, the local offices of social protection used for their calculations a different, much lower norm (set by the special instruction of the Cabinet of Ministers). As a result of this direct violation of legislation, the real amounts of most social payments were only symbolic. In 2001, the norms for state social assistance to families were officially reduced to 25–35 percent of the minimum wage.[15]

Another serious problem of the recent years has been payment delays of several months, which are now the norm and not the exception. At the end of the 1990s, there was a growing debt with regard to social payments to families with children: in 1996, 20.1 million hryvnia; in 1999, 43.8 million.[16] Until 1999, the calculation and payments of family allowances was a function of the enterprises and companies. Many of them were in a difficult financial situation, under reorganization, or in liquidation, and they could no longer provide these social payments. Since 1999, when these functions were transferred to local offices for social protection, the situation has improved slightly. However, the local offices today still have serious problems with financing social payments—mainly because of the debts of many enterprises to the local budget.

Finally, there are working women in Ukraine who are not entitled to receive these social payments. These are women in small business or who are hired by agricultural enterprises. Due to the liberalization of business legislation (the introduction of the unified tax and trade license), small trade companies and private agricultural firms do not pay money to the social funds. Women in the informal business have even less social protection.

Another example of the shortcomings of recent actions in the sphere of family policy is the document *Measures on the Improvement of the Situation of Families with Many Children,* adopted by a decree of the president in 1999. This document does not provide for the rise of family allowances, as one should suppose, but only for "timely payments and the liquidation of debts." It mainly deals with the collection of information on these families and educational work among them. In fact, this is an attempt to mobilize the relics of the system of nonmonetary privileges and state services for the children from these families (e.g., free school uniforms and breakfasts). In comparison with Soviet times, the motive for special attention to families with many children is not the encouragement of birthrates but the recognition of the fact that the number of children is the main factor in family impoverishment, and that this category of families is the most vulnerable.

Conclusion

Today, the Soviet legacies of the official egalitarianism as well as the state family policy are discredited as a part of the collapsed communist project. Although the relics of the "protection of motherhood" policy in labor legislation and the rather liberal abortion regulation still remind one of the Soviet past, the direct social contract between women and the state has been terminated.

The current discussions about the problems of social protection of the family, the ensuring of social and economic citizens rights, and the guarantees for social and economic equality of men and women reflect the legitimacy crisis of the new Ukrainian state. Because there is no social consensus on the cultural and political identity of Ukrainians, it is not clear what kind of welfare state, or what kind of social and family policy, Ukraine should have. The general shift seems to be in the neoliberal direction; the liberation of the family from state paternalism started with the privatization of the social sphere. But besides the "negative" liberation of the family from the state, what is the "positive" aim of the post-Soviet transformations in this sphere?

The post-Soviet state has terminated the social contract with women, but the new contract with the family has not been made yet. Though emphasizing the role of the family as an institution for the revival of the Ukrainian nation, the state has failed to provide the economic and social basis for the sustainability and autonomy of the family. Under conditions of economic crisis, the family became the site of collective survival thanks to the cooperation and mutual support of its members. It turned out to be an important resource for coping with social transformations. By the very logic of market reform, the costs of social reproduction have been transferred to the households, while the expenses for children's education and health services are increasing due to the cutback of the social functions of the state. The "costs" of post-Soviet transformations are paid to a large extent by changing the balance of paid and unpaid labor, which is one of the factors in rising gender inequality.

Meanwhile, the processes of nation building and state building in Ukraine, as well as the introduction of the institutions of democracy and a market economy, have brought serious changes in the social status and role of the family. Whereas during the Soviet era, the family was interpreted from a functionalist point of view as a socialist "cell of society," under these new conditions, the family has turned into a symbol of national survival and revival, of the continuity of generations, and of the economic and cultural flourishing of the new independent state of Ukraine. The image of the "traditionally strong family" represents not only the commitment of Ukrainians to national traditions and the values of solidarity but also to equality, personal freedom, and high women's status, thus justifying the historical choice in favor of independence and democracy.

In this context, the growing influence of the discourse on women's rights and gender equality strengthens the European image of the Ukrainian state and its openness to the principles of global feminism. At the same time, in Ukrainian society, these principles are easy to instrumentalize for the sake of "national consolidation" (e.g., the recently invented concept of "gender peace").

It is no wonder that numerous programs and legislative acts in the area of family policy and a general "improvement of the position of women" reflect this heterogeneity of political principles, which combines the neoliberal emancipation of the family from state interference, a nationalistically colored nostalgia for the "traditional family," and the discourse on "global feminism." However, in fact, the current situation of state family policy in Ukraine is not so much determined by political principles as by the reality of the economic crisis and difficulties with the state budget. The declared transition from universal social guarantees to selective social assistance to needy families is a forced and belated response to the consequences of market transformation and privatization in the Ukrainian economy.

Although, on the level of the political discourse, neofamilialism competes (and coexists) with the gender-equality approach, in real politics these alternatives are not determinative. In fact, while declaring its commitment to the "European" model of the welfare state, Ukraine continues simply by inertia to follow some Soviet patterns. The rest remains as informal social welfare: the mobilization of family resources and family cooperation, the network of kinship relations, the semilegal small businesses and intrahousehold production. Under the current conditions, the state lacks the financial resources for either the introduction of a gender-equality approach or for the "restoration of the traditional family" and of pro-natalism.

Notes

1. See Gail Warshofsky Lapidus, *Women in Soviet Society: Equality, Development, and Social Change* (Berkeley: University of California Press, 1978), chap. 8; and Mary Buckley, *Women and Ideology in the Soviet Union* (Ann Arbor: University of Michigan Press, 1989), chaps. 4 and 5.

2. A. Antonov and V. Medkov, *Sociologia sem'i* [Sociology of the family] (Moscow: Izdatel'stvo MGU, 1996), 123.

3. Nira Yuval-Davis, *Gender and Nation* (London: Sage, 1997), 43.

4. *Zhinka na porozi XXI stolittya: Stanovyshche, problemy, shliahy social'nogo rozvytku* [Women on the threshold of the twenty-first century: Conditions, problems, and paths of social development] (Kiev: Ukrainian Institute for Social Studies, 1998), 39–40.

5. *Pro stanovysche simey v Ukraini* [On the condition of families in Ukraine], 1999 Annual Report, ed. G. V. Sviatenko, Y. M. Lutsenko, and Y. M. Yakubova (Kiev: Ukrainian Institute for Social Studies, 1999), 53.

6. Yulia Iakubova, "Osobystist ta sim'a v epohu socialnyh transformatsiy" [Personality and family in the period of social transformations], in *Socialna polityka v Ukraini ta suchasni strategii adaptacii naselennia* [Social policy in Ukraine and contemporary strategies of population adaptation], ed. O. O. Yaremenko (Kiev: Ukrainian Institute for Social Studies, 1998), 35.

7. *Zhinka na porozi XXI stolittya,* 36.

8. Marian Rubchak, "Christian Virgin or Pagan Goddess: Feminism Versus the Eternally Feminine in Ukraine," in *Women in Russia and Ukraine,* ed. Rosalin Marsh (Cambridge: Cambridge University Press, 1996), 315–30.

9. Yuval-Davis, *Gender and Nation,* 29–34.

10. O. Chirkov and I. Vinnichenko, "Ethnodemografichny rozvytok Ukrainy: Istoria, suchsnist, perspectyvy" [Ethnodemographic development in Ukraine: History, contemporary times, perspectives], *Suchasnist* [Contemporary Times] 7–8 (2000): 120.

11. N. Levchuk, "Pro doslidzhennia mechanizmu formuvannia demografichnoy kryzy v Ukraini" [On studies of the mechanism of development of demographic crisis in Ukraine], *Demographichni doslidzhennia* [Demographic studies] 19 (1997): 17.

12. Chyrkov and Vinnychenko, "Ethnodemografichny rozvytok Ukrainy," 119.

13. Levchuk, "Pro doslidzhennia mechanizmu formuvannia," 8.

14. Levchuk, "Pro doslidzhennia mechanizmu formuvannia," 15.

15. According to official statistical data, at the beginning of 2000, the average childcare allowance was 15.3 hryvnia per month; allowances for parents with three and more children, 21.8; and assistance for single mothers, 7.2. At the same time, the average wage was 219 hryvnia per month, whereas a basic income was officially fixed at 270.1 hryvnia; for children under 6 years of age, it was set at 240.71; for children, between 6 and 18, at 297. 29.

16. *Socialni indicatory rivnia zhyttia naselennia* [Social indicators of the standard of living] (Kiev: Derzhkomstat, 2000), 145.

2

The Gender of Sovereignty: Constructing Statehood, Nation, and Gender Regimes in Post-Soviet Tatarstan

Katherine E. Graney

Although there is great variation in the overall development of post-socialist states in Eurasia, there are also some important similarities regarding state formation and nation building, which stem from their shared Soviet inheritance and from the fact that all these states face the same twin challenges: negotiating the transition from a socialist command-administrative economy in a neoliberal, globalizing context; and the necessity of establishing new, functional, and democratic nation-states. Several researchers have observed that one of the ways in which post-socialist nation-states seem to resemble one another most strongly is in the nature of their gendered relations of power, arguing that across the board, these states have developed

The research for this chapter was conducted in the summer of 2001 and was supported in part by a grant from the International Research and Exchange Board, with funds provided by the National Endowment for the Humanities and the U.S. Department of State, which administers the Russian, Eurasian, and Eastern European Research Program (Title VIII). None of these organizations is responsible for the views expressed here.

gender regimes that are distinctly more masculinist and more patriarchal than those that existed under socialism. This process has been referred to variously as the "re-traditionalization" of society,[1] the "revival of masculinity,"[2] the "rise of masculinism,"[3] the establishment of "male democracy,"[4] and by Tatiana Zhurzhenko in chapter 1 of this volume as the emergence of "neofamilialism" in the post-socialist world.

For the majority of post-socialist countries, democratization has proven to be a gendered process whereby men and women are granted equal rights in a *formal* political sense (in accordance with Western-style democratic models), while the essentially empty and rhetorical nature of that formal equality is made clear by the virtual "disappearance" of women from positions of power in political life and in civil society.[5] The resulting situation has been referred to as the "empowerment of men and the enactment of masculinity on a grand scale."[6] Simultaneously, the private, domestic sphere has become both increasingly identified with femininity and neglected or devalued by the new states.

In addition, many of the newly "remasculinized" states of the post-socialist world, particularly Hungary, Poland, and Ukraine, have used their newfound political powers to legislate women back into more traditional and restrictive domestic and reproductive roles through the pursuit of a policy of neofamilialism. As Gal and Kligman note in speaking of new anti-abortion legislation in several Eastern European countries, the "ongoing focus on reproduction" across post-socialist nations is "noteworthy and demands attention and explanation."[7]

This chapter explores the case of the Republic of Tatarstan, one of the Russian Federation's twenty-one national homelands. In Tatarstan, as in other post-socialist states, gendered relations of power have helped to shape, and in turn have been partially reconfigured by, the process of state building and nation building. The strong masculinist and neofamilialist tendencies that characterize state building in most post-socialist states, including Ukraine and Belarus (see chapters 1 and 4 by Zhurzhenko and Gapova, respectively, in this volume) are also present in Tatarstan's efforts to build a post-Soviet polity, and yet are somewhat less pronounced than they are in many other cases.

This situation exists because Tatarstan's political elites have been more preoccupied with other aspects of the state-building project, the most important of which is negotiations with Moscow about the shape of Russia's federal system and Tatarstan's place in it, as well as the attempt to carve out new spaces for Tatarstan in the international community in the post-Soviet period. Nation-building efforts in Tatarstan, however—namely, the attempt to use the republic's newly claimed sovereign status to foster a revival of the ethnic Tatar nation—reflect much more strongly a tendency toward neo-familialism and the re-traditionalization of gender roles, a development that has also marked the nation-building process elsewhere in post-socialist Eurasia.

State Gender Regimes and the Gender of Nations

Feminist theories assert that it is necessary to begin any analysis of the state with the assumption that it is "the central institutionalization of gendered power" that exists in most societies.[8] The state's gender regime, as suggested by R. W. Connell, is both constructed by gendered relations of power and relies upon these relations of power for its continued existence.[9]

The key element of the state's gender regime is its "gender division of labor," especially with respect to those who occupy key positions of power in the state.[10] The gender regime of a given state also concerns the state's regulation of gender relations through its wielding of legal and institutional power and economic resources. Legislative and policy initiatives that govern social welfare and benefits, sexuality, reproduction and motherhood, and youth and family issues are the arenas that reveal most clearly this aspect of a given state's gender regime.

In the modern era, to maintain legitimacy, state elites must put forward at least minimally convincing claims that the community populating a given state is a coherent and unique entity, which those elites then claim to represent. The most effective way for elites to make these legitimizing claims is through the discourse on "the nation."[11]

A "nation" is in fact nothing more than "a cultural relation intended to link a state and its subjects and to distinguish them from the subjects of other states."[12] The types of strategies that state elites and state-seeking groups use to create a sense of national identity include creating "national" histories and cultures; elaborating on and supporting national symbols, traditions, and holidays; and creating "national" spaces both literally through the politics of public spaces and metaphorically in the sense of creating "national publics" by establishing common media, educational, and cultural spheres.[13]

The historical and cultural "memories and arguments" that help define a nation may be either ethnic or civic.[14] Often, if not always, civic and ethnic ideas about the nation coexist uneasily in a given state, and in fact the nation must be seen as a fluid and evolving concept that is always deeply contested between state and societal actors in any polity.

In Eastern Europe and the post-Soviet states, an additional variable must be factored into the contentious process of trying to establish a legitimating sense of "nationness" for post-socialist states, namely, the legacy of what Katherine Verdery has called the "socialist nation."[15] Verdery identifies the unique socialist form of the nation as one that is based not on civic or ethnic criteria but rather on an explicitly *moral tie* between the state and its citizens, in which citizens are placed in a position of "quasi-familial dependency on the state," whose moral authority and legitimacy rests in its claim to fairly redistribute wealth and goods in the society.[16]

As with the process of establishing statehood, the process of creating a national community to legitimate the state is profoundly gendered. Though each of the various types of nationhood (civic, ethnic, and socialist) tends to be gendered to different degrees, with ethno-nationalist constructions generally having the most invasive and pernicious affects on women, certain tendencies regarding gender are discernable in *all* nation-building efforts.

First and foremost, because of their reproductive capacity and their traditional association with child rearing, in ethnonationalist discourses women are identified as the primary biological producers and reproducers of the national community.[17] Because women literally bear the burden of ensuring the perpetuation of the national community upon which the continued existence and legitimacy of the state rests, state actors have often found it necessary to control vigilantly women's sexuality and reproductive capacity, which means defining women chiefly if not solely as reproductive beings and mothers. Explicitly ethnonationalist states in particular are concerned that future citizens be born of ethnically pure unions. As Gal and Kligman state:

> In most forms of ethno-nationalist thought, biological reproduction and biological continuity over time are the centerpieces of creation and imagining community. . . . Making members of the nation is not only a symbolic classifying process, but also very much a material, corporeal one: links between generations must, perforce, be reproductive links, embodiments of membership.[18]

Thus ethnonationalist leaders and ethnonationalist states tend to engage in strict endogamous regulation and policing of female sexuality, as well as pro-natalist policies.

Beyond their duty to reproduce for the nation-state, women are also often seen as the ideological reproducers of groups and the chief transmitters of "national" culture, thus bearing an additional moral burden for and duty to the nation-state.[19] Because of this responsibility, the state may demand or encourage certain behavioral patterns from women that it does not demand from its male citizens. These expectations locate women's duties to the state firmly in the domestic, private, nurturing sphere as opposed to the public and civic realm.

Next, because women are assigned the crucially important roles as biological and cultural reproducers of the nation (a "privilege" that carries with it the attendant necessity for strict male control over that power), women are often held up by those seeking to construct nationness as the ultimate symbol and signifier of the nation in question.[20] For this reason, images of women are often used by nation builders to represent the nation, and often the concept of the nation itself is feminized, for example, "Mother Russia." Yet whereas viewing women as symbols of the purity and essence of a national community may seem like a potential source of empowerment for women, it is most often the male leaders of the nation-state who define the parameters within which these "women-as-national-symbols" must act.

Furthermore, when "our women" symbolically represent the essence of a nation, they are made subjects of primarily male agency. Thus, women are not only "protected" by the males of their own national community (a protection that may be unwelcome and oppressive) but are also made the specific targets of males from other national or ethnic communities in times of conflict, to which the sad history of mass rape during wartime attests.

Finally, women do also participate as agents in nationalist-motivated economic, political, and military struggles.[21] However, though women are often welcomed or even recruited into national liberation or state-seeking struggles, and though "traditional" gender roles are often transgressed during these struggles, once a struggle's goals have been achieved, the tendency is to revert back to more traditional, male-defined gender regimes of both nationness and statehood.[22]

Gendering Post-Socialist States and Nations

Although even civic forms of the nation make particular claims on women as agents of biological and cultural reproduction of the national community, the more ethnic a state's conception of the nation is, the more patriarchal and intrusive the gender regime of that nation-state will be. In many post-socialist states, including Belarus, Hungary, Poland, Ukraine, Russia, and the states of the former Yugoslavia, this connection is quite evident among increasing ethnonationalist sentiment, the "disappearance" of women in politics, and the advent of more and more patriarchal and controlling state legislation.[23]

Furthermore, the tendency to allow or recruit women into national liberation struggles but then to "jettison them" once the goals of the independence movement have been achieved has also been visible across the post-Soviet states, particularly in Lithuania and also in Ukraine.[24] In chapter 4 of this volume, Gapova demonstrates how this literally took place in Belarus when women were "ordered home" from the barricades and demonstrations during the presidential elections of 2001.

This rise in ethnic nationalism in post-socialist states coexists with the persistent legacy of the paternalist "socialist nation."[25] Though the paternalist socialist state was itself gendered and patriarchal, saddling women with the double burden while refusing to allow them into the highest echelons of decision making within the "father party," it is also clear that the gender regime of socialism was somewhat less patriarchal than those now being established under increasingly ethnonationalist leaders.

Finally, the influence of international forces on the gendered nature of state- and nation-building projects in post-socialist states must also be noted. For post-socialist states seeking loans or acceptance into international organizations, the expectations of international actors (i.e., a preference for civic conceptions of nationness and a low tolerance for either exclusionist ethnonationalist claims or expensive socialist paternalist claims) also play into nation-building strategies.

The Gender of Sovereignty in Tatarstan

To what degree do Tatarstan's state- and nation-building projects conform to the masculinist and neofamilialist patterns developing in other post-socialist contexts? Though the new "sovereign" Tatarstani state is as intensely patriarchal as some of the others that currently exist, neofamilialist legislation has not yet made the headway there that it has in other places. This relative lack of attention to domestic policymaking seems to be due in part to Tatarstan's preoccupation with negotiating its claim to state sovereignty within the Russian Federation and in the international arena.

Instead, the most gendered aspect of the sovereignty project in post-Soviet Tatarstan has been in domestic nation-building efforts, where there has been an effort to re-traditionalize gender roles among ethnic Tatar women, which is only now beginning to be supported with attendant state policy and legislation. However, these efforts at ethnic Tatar nation building coexist uneasily with the legacy of "socialist paternalist" forms of nation building and the pressure from both Moscow and international constituencies to embrace civic and multicultural forms of the nation.

When *glasnost'* was in full swing during the late 1980s, a group of Tatar scholars and students from Kazan State University and other educational institutions met to discuss the formation of an organized pro-sovereignty movement in Tatarstan. Among this group, which formed the core of what became the Tatar Public Center (TPC), was a small number of female intellectuals.[26] Although this small group of women participated in the first "unofficial congress" of the TPC in October 1989, the organization's leadership was decidedly male.[27]

Indeed, the TPC's founding resolutions did not address gender or women's issues in any particular way, instead focusing solely on the political demand for increased sovereignty and statehood for the Tatar Autonomous Soviet Socialist Republic.[28] In this document, appeals to consolidate and revive the ethnic Tatar nation are treated as purely political issues that could be resolved only by creating a "sovereign" Tatarstani republic, and are not addressed in any way as being private or domestic issues for which women might be given special responsibility.[29]

Some Tatar women were active in the more radical wing of the pro-sovereignty movement in the late 1980s and early 1990s. Most important, as a founding member of the extreme nationalist Ittifak (Unity) and Milli Mejlis (National Congress) parties of Tatarstan, both of which have advocated for full independence for the republic, Fauzia Bairamova became the most outspoken and best known representative of this sovereignty initiative. Though Bairamova herself is an interesting "symbol" of the Tatar nation, she conspicuously wears the Islamic veil as a mark of her commitment to the nationalist movement, despite the fact that very few other Tatar women do.[30] Her political rhetoric has consistently avoided any discussion of the special role of women in reviving the fortunes of the Tatar nation. Instead, she has been a consistent critic of Tatarstan's political leadership, demanding full independence for Tatarstan and supporting the Chechen resistance against Russian aggression.[31]

During the late 1980s, several ethnic Tatar women's organizations emerged and began to propagate the idea that ethnic Tatar women had a special responsibility to help rebuild the Tatar nation, both in the home and in the public sphere. These groups included Apa, the society of Tatar mothers; the Ak Aby (the "White Grandmothers"), a group of elderly Tatar women who are instantly recognizable by their white headscarves; and Ak Kalfak,[32] which is the official state-sponsored ethnic Tatar women's organization in Tatarstan. The Ak Aby became fixtures at the numerous political rallies and protests held in Kazan during the turbulent struggle for sovereignty in Tatarstan.[33] These "honored and pious" Tatar grandmothers were often featured prominently in photographs at pro-sovereignty demonstrations, yet they were rarely called on to speak at these events.[34]

Although ethnic Tatar women participated in the sovereignty movement in the late 1980s and early 1990s, no overt political appeal was ever made to ethnic Tatar women by either the moderate or radical wing of the sovereignty movement urging them to support sovereignty on the basis of their role as the mothers and guardians of the ethnic Tatar nation. However, there were instances of images of ethnic Tatar women being used this way in the press. Because both the moderate and nationalist wings of the sovereignty movement were preoccupied with achieving political goals, it is remarkable that gender was not mobilized and failed to play a significant role in this process.

The Gender Regime of the New Tatarstani State

Since the Tatarstani parliament declared sovereignty in August 1990, the Tatarstani government has largely succeeded in gaining control over the processes of state building and nation building. Under the firm (some say authoritarian) leadership of former Communist Party boss Mintimer Shaimiyev, who was elected president of Tatarstan in 1992 and has since been twice reelected (the second time in March 2001), the government co-opted prominent leaders of the TPC and has effectively marginalized the most radical independence-minded groups, especially Ittifak and Milli Mejlis.[35]

The Tatarstani government's quest to consolidate political authority and create new, supposedly more democratic forms of political rule in the name of sovereignty has in practice led to the creation of a very narrow, male-dominated public sphere. Furthermore, there is a disturbing lack of women's or feminist's political organizations in Tatarstan—not only is the activity of civil society itself increasingly subscribed, women's participation within it is even less visible.

In 1997, according to Tatarstani political scientist Oleg Zaznaev, there were only 5 women within the group of 102 individuals identified as the ruling "political elite" in the Republic of Tatarstan,[36] In the most recent Tatarstani State Council, elected in December 1999, only 6 of 130 deputies were women. The gender division of labor is not much better regarding the leadership of industrial enterprises in Tatarstan. Of the 88 largest enterprises in Tatarstan, which include some of the most important oil, chemical, and automotive industries in all of Russia, only 1 had a female director.[37]

Despite the lack of gender balance in political and economic power structures in Tatarstan, the constitution that was passed in 1992 is a model of gender-neutral democratic governance. This is perhaps because Tatarstan's leadership had one ear cocked toward the international community, whose support they desperately needed in their battle with Moscow over sovereignty. Indeed, the articles of the Tatarstani constitution governing citizenship and family life reflect a *paternalist* state rather than a *patriarchal* state. Thus, in defining citizenship, Article 20 of the Tatarstani Constitution states:

> All citizens of the Republic of Tatarstan shall enjoy equal rights and duties. They shall enjoy equal rights to be protected by the state, without distinction as to their birth, social or property status, race or nationality, sex, education, language, or political views. . . .[38]

Even more interesting is Article 30, which stipulates strict equality within the family:

> The family, maternity, paternity, and childhood shall be protected by the state. Marriage shall be based on free agreement between a man and woman; wife and husband shall be equal in family relations.

Indeed, a unique feature of Tatarstan's new political development seems to be the *lack* of attention paid to issues of family life and reproduction, especially when compared with other post-socialist states. Perhaps this reflects the Shaimiyev regime's preoccupation with pressing its claims to sovereignty within the Russian Federation and in the international arena. In spite of the regime's desire to legitimate the republic's path of sovereignty seeking by claiming to provide a higher level of social welfare benefits than the

Russian Federation overall, little attention has been paid to the *specific* needs of women as mothers or families in general in this regard.

In an interview in June 2001, Rosa Tufitullova, the chair of the Tatarstan State Council's Committee on Family and Children's Affairs, described the difficulties of getting the 124 male members of parliament to listen to pleas for increased attention and funding for women's issues.[39] Tufitullova had called on the government to pass a separate bill or program dealing with issues of maternity and family as early as 1994.[40] However, only at its fall session in 2001 did the Tatarstani parliament even debate Tufitullova's large-scale program, called Families of Tatarstan.[41] Tufitullova herself expressed skepticism that this program would receive the full funding and government support it needs to be effective, though she did note that Tatarstan's politicians "might pay more attention to these issues now that we are in a situation of demographic crisis."[42]

Although the lack of attention paid to issues of women and family policy in Tatarstan may in one respect be seen as benefiting women—in the sense that Tatarstan has avoided the more draconian and coercive types of neofamilialist legislation that Hungary, Poland, and Ukraine have enacted—in other respects it highlights the difficulty that activists lobbying for the needs of women and families in Tatarstan face in trying to influence a closed and patriarchal state bureaucracy. Though the neglectful policy of the Tatarstani government toward its female citizens who are mothers (and their children) might thus avoid the worst excesses of neofamilialism, it certainly also exacerbates their economic and social suffering.

Though failing to enact concrete policy reforms aimed at ensuring the social welfare of mothers and children in the republic, in December 1995 the government created an organization called Women of Tatarstan and organized a Congress of Women of Tatarstan, naming Zilya Valeeva, then–deputy chair of Tatarstan's parliament, as the head of both entities. The chief function of this organization is the sponsorship of apolitical, festival type events that honor women with large families or women with disabled children.[43] It also engages in some intermittent, small-scale charity activities, such as the distribution of clothing and food to orphanages. The group's largest and most public function, hosted by President Shaimiyev, is on the International Day of Women (March 8) and draws a gathering of prominent Tatarstani women.

Although Women of Tatarstan claims to be the umbrella group for all women's organizations in the republic, the most active and independent women's organizations in Tatarstan appear to have made a conscious choice not to join it. For example, the Club of Intellectual Women of Tatarstan, which sponsors public forums on a diverse set of social and political issues in Tatarstan, chose to "preserve its independence" by not joining Women of Tatarstan, which this club believed to be both frivolous and patronizing in its treatment of women and women's issues.[44] The leaders of the club also expressed dismay that Women of Tatarstan did so little to help "make it possible for women to really affect politics" in the republic.[45]

Similarly, the editor of the self-financed Kazan monthly newspaper *Zhenshchina* ("Woman") also complained that despite her repeated efforts to get Women of Tatarstan leader Zilya Valeeva to contribute a piece to her newspaper, she never received any reply.[46] Femina, a self-described feminist organization in Tatarstan that has undertaken some very interesting analysis and activism concerning unemployment and other women's issues in Tatarstan,[47] also has chosen not to join Women of Tatarstan. Yet Femina has not totally removed itself from formal politics in the republic—it has lobbied the national parliament and received a small grant from them, and Femina's leader, Elena Mashkova, was herself named woman of the year by the Women of Tatarstan in its annual competition in March 2001.

The gender regime of statehood in Tatarstan can be characterized as being both patriarchal *and* paternalist, whereby the official state commitment to the equality of the sexes as enshrined in the Constitution is belied by an absence of women in positions of power, a lack of attention to women's concerns, and a pronounced absence of women's voices in civil society. This lack of attention to women's issues reflects both the patriarchal structure of the governing elite and the preoccupation of the government with advancing Tatarstan's "sovereignty project" in other spheres. But it is also partly due to the largely decorative nature of the Women of Tatarstan organization, which has consciously distanced itself from the small number of politically active and independent women who are present in the republic. In essence, the government of Tatarstan has yet to make the jump from ceremonially and paternalistically "honoring" women one day a year (March 8) to seriously addressing women's issues in the republic.

Gendering the Civic Tatarstani and Ethnic Tatar Nations

The government's attempt to construct a legitimating sense of nationness for the new sovereign state of Tatarstan can be characterized as an uneasy mix of elements that reflect the paternalist legacy of the "socialist nation," elements aimed at fostering the creation of a new "civic and multiethnic" *Tatarstani* nation, and elements supporting the ethnonationalist idea that Tatarstan is the realization of the ethnic Tatar nation's 450-year-old dream of recovering the independent statehood it was lost when Ivan IV captured Kazan in 1552. Each of these various discourses on nationness is gendered in different but equally intriguing ways.

Official state discourse about the civic and multiethnic nature of the sovereignty of Tatarstan is enshrined in the founding legal documents of the republic. Both Tatarstan's Declaration of Sovereignty and Constitution state that the republic's sovereignty and authority are derived from the "multinational people of Tatarstan." Beginning with the celebration of Republic Day in August 1994 (the anniversary of the declaration of sovereignty), public officials in Tatarstan began to refer to the collective civic and multiethnic nation in whose name sovereignty was declared as the "Tatarstani people."

References to the Tatarstani people and Tatarstanis have since become omnipresent in official statements and mass media in the republic. In just one example, during his annual address to the republic's legislature in February 1996, President Shaimiyev asserted that Tatarstan was building a "polyethnic and poly-cultural" society based on civic and not ethnic criteria of citizenship, and that the evidence for this was the growth of patriotism toward and pride in Tatarstan "among all Tatarstanis."[48]

A prominent element of the state's efforts to create a civic and multiethnic Tatarstani sense of nationness is the *feminization* of all the peoples of Tatarstan and the location of all Tatarstan's ethnicities in a position of subordination to the paternalistic (and subtly patriarchal) leadership of the state, embodied first and foremost by President Shaimiyev (though also variously by any other high-ranking male officials, most often former prime minister and current speaker of the Tatarstani State Council Farid Mukhametshin).

For example, the most common representations of nationness at such events as Republic Day are folkloric groups that prominently feature young, attractive, conventionally feminine women wearing "ethnic" costumes.[49] When the multiethnic Tatarstani nation is displayed for outside consumption, the images again are invariably of attractive young women, preferably either dancing with or serving bread and salt to one of the "wise fathers" of the Tatarstani nation. These multicultural displays bear more than a passing resemblance to the Soviet-era "friendship of peoples," but with the wise, patriarchal, paternalistic, all-embracing father figure of the Communist

Party now replaced by Shaimiyev, the wise, patriarchal, paternalistic, all-embracing father figure of the new sovereign state of Tatarstan.

Given the government's interest in creating a sense of multiethnic Tatarstani nationhood among the population (chiefly to avoid exacerbating tensions with Moscow and to please such international organizations as the United Nations and the European Union), it is surprising that it has not made a more concerted effort to create a sense of civic Tatarstani nationhood specifically among the republic's women. One could imagine an attempt to use the common bond of gender (and particularly motherhood) both as a way to overcome ethnic differences and as a basis for a new Tatarstani identity. One possible explanation for why the government of Tatarstan has not used gender to pursue intensive civic nation-building projects is that the multiethnic Tatarstani discourse on the nation may be targeted more at external audiences (i.e., the Russian Federation and the international community) than internal ones.

The ethnic Tatar discourse on nationhood propagated by the state in post-Soviet Tatarstan is characterized by a prominent gender discourse that assigns a primary biological and cultural reproductive role to Tatar women, who are to bear both the literal and symbolic burden of the revival and continuity of the ethnic Tatar nation. This is perhaps not surprising; however, what is interesting is that ethnic Tatar women themselves, particularly the Tatar women's organization Ak Kalfak and the official state-sponsored Tatar women's magazine *Syuyumbike* (named after a Tatar national heroine of the sixteenth century), have been among the main proponents of this traditionalist gender division of labor regarding nation building.

In June 1992, the government of Tatarstan sponsored the first ever World Congress of Tatars in Kazan, hosting more than 1,000 Tatar delegates from Russia, the Commonwealth of Independent States, Turkey, and the United States.[50] The Executive Committee of the World Congress of Tatars (the VKT), which was formed to help plan the congress, has since functioned as the main state-sponsored ethnic Tatar organization in Tatarstan, coordinating efforts to revive the Tatar national language and culture both within Tatarstan and for the Tatar ethnic diaspora of nearly 4 million people.[51]

The woman who is both the leader of the ethnic Tatar women's organization Ak Kalfak and who until recently was the editor of *Syuyumbike*[52] is Rosa Tufitullova. Tufitullova, who as mentioned also chairs the Tatarstani State Council's committee on family and children's issues, was the only female founding member of the VKT, and she remains the *only* female on the 37-person VKT executive committee, while simultaneously heading

Ak Kalfak and, until recently, editing *Syuyumbike*. With her new official responsibilities in the government, Tufitullova herself virtually embodies the "official" gender regime of ethnic Tatar nationness in the republic.

Both Ak Kalfak's organizational philosophy and *Syuyumbike's* editorial mission reflect the same basic position on ethnic Tatar women: that the first and most important responsibility for ethnic Tatar women is to their families, specifically, to see that their children are brought up knowing ethnic Tatar traditions.[53] As Tufitullova herself plainly put it in an interview in 1996, "We encourage women to be mothers first—to bring up children is the way to serve the nation."[54] This emphasis on the family as the future of the ethnic nation means that Tufitullova "does worry" about the high rates of intermarriage among Tatars and Russians (43 percent of Tatars are currently in ethnically mixed marriages) but also that Ak Kalfak's official position on the issue is that "we can't and won't say we prohibit it, but we do think assimilation and the loss of national culture is a tragedy."[55]

Although this discourse about the proper role of ethnic Tatar women as first and foremost being mothers and wives may seem limiting to ears used to the equal rights language of Western feminism, it is crucial to note that for Tufitullova, it is through their roles as mothers and wives that Tatar women can and do exercise power in society. As she stated in the same interview:

> Tatar women do not ever come out and make a show of their power, thus we are not interested in getting women elected to parliament or anything like that, but nevertheless, without us, absolutely nothing could happen! Our way is a delicate exercise of power, by protecting and nurturing the family first.

Furthermore, Tufitullova stresses that Tatar women have "always been highly educated, and have always become scientists, doctors, philosophers and historians in large numbers" and that one of the main functions of Ak Kalfak, the VKT, and *Syuyumbike* is to make sure that Tatar women continue to gain access to the education that they deserve and need to fulfill their important roles in Tatar society.[56] Ak Kalfak was very active in the effort to open a Tatar Girls Gymnasium in Kazan, which in addition to Tatar, Arabic-, Russian-, and English-language education and other liberal arts subjects, offers courses in Tatar national domestic traditions and arts. The gymnasium graduated its first class in 2002, and Tufitullova hopes that "in addition to having taught them how to be beautiful and be good mothers," the gymnasium curriculum will have inspired some of them to become "national leaders," much in the way that the Tatar women's icon and historical heroine Syuyumbike herself was.[57]

According to Tufitullova, the ethnic Tatar women that she comes into contact with through her work with Ak Kalfak, the VKT, and *Syuyumbike* themselves have initiated and embraced the return to a more domestic and nurturing role within the family, and they are happy to shed the "proletarian woman worker" image of the Soviet past. As she stated in an interview:

> Before we were called "free" but didn't know why and didn't think we were free at all . . . [a reference to the previous title of *Syuyumbike* which was *Azat Khatyn,* which means "Free Woman" in Tatar]. . . . After perestroika, we were finally able to think about and write about Tatar women as women, to address the things that are the essence of Tatar women, such as preserving family, national traditions and customs and bringing up children. Before we were called free but didn't know why—now we are finally free to pursue our essence, but it is difficult, of course. There have been positive changes, but not enough.[58]

Tufitullova, in her capacity as head of Ak Kalfak and a member of the VKT, and now a member of the State Council, has most recently advocated for the creation of a Fund for the Family to help to "preserve Tatar families and thus the Tatar nation."[59] Her efforts to get the VKT to recognize the importance of women's and family issues as *ethnonational issues* seem to have paid off—in the most recent platform of action passed by the VKT in June 2000, four of thirteen points addressed issues related to the preservation and promotion of Tatar families. They included a pledge to "pay more attention to the problems of Tatar families and demographic issues" (assumedly intermarriage); plans to open a type of Tatar dating service where young Tatars could become acquainted over the Internet and in other venues with the express purpose of "founding Tatar families;" and pressuring the Tatarstani government to pass a program to support Tatar families.[60]

State-sanctioned ethnic Tatar nation-building activities in Tatarstan seem to embody much more *traditionally* gendered goals and ideas regarding social relations than do the rather perfunctory state efforts to create a civic Tatarstani national identity. Yet it is unclear to what extent the government is actually willing to continue supporting the ethnonationalist and gender-sensitive programs of the VKT, Ak Kalfak, and *Syuyumbike.* The appointment of Tufitullova as head of the State Council's Committee on Family and

Children in 2000 suggests both that the government is open to supporting the explicitly ethnonationalist programs of these organizations, and that Tufitullova may have increased leverage in pressing the government to pursue these projects.

The politicization of ethnicity in Tatarstan during the decade-long sovereignty-seeking effort in Tatarstan has deepened the rifts among the country's different women's groups, which also may help to explain the failure of the government to address gender issues or women's concerns in a serious way. Both ethnic Tatar women's activists and ethnic Russian feminist activists decry the lack of attention paid to women's economic and social issues and the lack of women in positions of power in Tatarstan. Similarly, in interviews conducted in Kazan in the summer of 2001, both Tatar and Russian women activists jointly expressed the sentiment that "women's problems"—including poverty, unemployment, worry about the health and future of their children, environmental pollution, and the quest for personal fulfillment—*transcend* ethnicity and affect all women equally.

However, these activists' analysis of why the Tatarstani government does not address such problems differs between Tatars and Russians. Though Tufitullova and other Tatar women activists see the patriarchal nature of post-Soviet states and society as being to blame for the government's lack of attention to women's voices and issues (with gender prejudice trumping ethnic concerns for the revival of the nation), Russian women activists see the politicization of ethnicity in Tatarstan and the "Tatarization" of the republican government as added reasons for the failure to address women's issues (with ethnic concerns trumping potential gender solidarity and gender concerns).[61]

Conclusions

The gender regime of sovereignty in post-Soviet Tatarstan is complex, being informed by the cross-cutting cleavages of gender and ethnicity. The state apparatus of Tatarstan is heavily masculinized, and women's place within the state remains narrowly defined in a paternalist and apparently increasingly neofamilialist way (when it is addressed at all). The main state-building priorities of the Tatarstani elite in the post-Soviet period lean more toward consolidating the claim to sovereignty within the Russian Federation and the international arena than with the recreation of gender relations of power within the state of Tatarstan, though this may change as Russia and

Tatarstan's demographic crises becomes more severe. This is in contrast to other post-socialist states, such as Ukraine, where a neofamilialist agenda has already been pushed forward more vigorously and realized more completely. And yet, with regard to nation-building efforts, the Tatarstani leadership has placed special emphasis on ethnic Tatar women's reproductive and nurturing responsibilities in reviving the ethnic Tatar nation, suggesting that these attitudes may eventually become enshrined in neofamilialist state legislation.

Simultaneously, yet less forcefully, state elites are trying to foster a concept of a new multiethnic Tatarstani people, who exist in a relationship of dependence on and deference to the paternalistic (and masculine) symbol of the Tatarstani state, President Shaimiyev. Thus both international pressures, which favor multicultural constructions of nationhood, and the legacy of socialist paternalism appear to factor into the construction of gender regimes in contemporary Tatarstan—along with ethnonationalist considerations. These findings suggest that the relationship among gender, nation, and statehood in post-Soviet contexts is a complicated one in which multiple pre-Soviet, Soviet-era, and post-Soviet forces interact in unexpected ways. As intriguing as these conclusions may be, however, unfortunately not all the outcomes observed in post-Soviet Tatarstan reflect the interests and needs of women themselves; nor do they necessarily serve to empower women politically, economically, or socially.

Notes

1. Katherine Verdery, *What Was Socialism and What Comes Next?* (Princeton, N.J.: Princeton University Press, 1996), 80–81.

2. Mira Marody and Anna Giza-Poleszczuk, "Changing Images of Identity in Poland: From the Self-Sacrificing to the Self-Investing Woman?" in *Reproducing Gender: Politics, Publics, and Everyday Life after Socialism,* ed. Susan Gal and Gail Kligman (Princeton, N.J.: Princeton University Press, 2001).

3. Peggy Watson, "The Rise of Masculinism in Eastern Europe," *New Left Review* 198 (1993): 71–82.

4. Rosalind Marsh, "Introduction: Women's Studies and Women's Issues in Russia, Ukraine, and the Post-Soviet States," in *Women and Russia in Ukraine,* ed. Rosalind Marsh (Cambridge: Cambridge University Press, 1996), 5.

5. Women's "disappearance" from public life has been attributed in part to the removal of ideologically-motivated female quotas for political structures in post-socialist countries, in part to the fact that women are preoccupied with issues of economic survival and in part as a result of a conscious effort by male actors to "reclaim" the realm of civic and public authority back from the ubiquitous party-state and to deny women a

share of that power. See Marsh, "Introduction," 5; Watson, "Rise of Masculinism," 72. See also Hilary Pilkington, "Can Russia's Women Save the Nation? Survival Politics and Gender Discourse in Post-Soviet Russia," in *Women in Post-Communist Russia,* ed. Sue Bridger (Bradford, U.K.: University of Bradford, 1995); and Valerie Sperling, *Organizing Women in Contemporary Russia: Engendering Transition* (Cambridge: Cambridge University Press, 1999).

6. Watson, "Rise of Masculinism," 72.

7. Susan Gal and Gail Kligman, *The Politics of Gender after Socialism: A Comparative-Historical Essay* (Princeton, N.J.: Princeton University Press, 2000), 16. The debate over the ultimately unsuccessful "Law on the Protection of Family, Maternity, Paternity and Childhood in the Russian Federation," which would have restricted the number of hours women with children under 14 years of age could work, and would have banned women with more than three children from working altogether is another illustration of the kinds of concrete legislative actions common in post-socialist states that have patriarchal and masculinist gender regimes. See Linda Racioppi and Katherine O'Sullivan See, *Women's Activism in Contemporary Russia,* (Philadelphia: Temple University Press, 1997); Elizabeth Waters and Anastasia Posadskya, "Democracy without Women Is No Democracy," in *The Challenge of Local Feminisms,* ed. Amrita Basu (Boulder, Colo.; Westview Press, 1995).

8. R. W. Connell, "The State, Gender and Sexual Politics," *Theory and Society* 19, no. 4 (1990): 519.

9. Connell, "State," 523.

10. Connell, "State," 523–24.

11. Bernard Yack, "The Myth of the Civic Nation," *Civic Review* 10, no. 2 (1996): 193–211.

12. Verdery, *What Was Socialism?* 62–63, 101.

13. Michael Billig, *Banal Nationalism* (London; Sage, 1995); Geoff Eley and Ronald Suny, "Introduction: From the Moment of Social History to the Work of Cultural Representation," in *Becoming National,* ed. Geoff Eley and Ronald Suny (Oxford: Oxford University Press, 1996), 23.

14. Jeff Spinner, *The Boundaries of Citizenship* (Baltimore: Johns Hopkins University Press, 1994), 168.

15. Verdery, *What Was Socialism?* 62–63.

16. Verdery, *What Was Socialism?* 63.

17. Gal and Klingman, *Politics of Gender,* 25–26; Nira Yuval-Davis and Flora Anthias. eds., *Women, Nation, State* (London; Macmillan, 1989), 9–10; Lois West, "Introduction: Feminism Constructs Nationalism," in *Feminist Nationalism,* ed. Lois West (New York: Routledge, 1997).

18. Gal and Kligman, *Politics of Gender,* 25.

19. Yuval-Davis and Anathis, *Woman, Nation, State,* 9–10.

20. Yuval-Davis and Anathis, *Woman, Nation, State,* 9–10.

21. This was the case in Algeria and Iran, where "the fact that women played a crucial role in the [national liberationist] revolts did not prevent them from being discouraged, if not barred from asserting their prominence in the public sphere following victory." In addition to Yuval-Davis and Anthias, *Women, Nation, State* and West, *Feminist Nationalism,* see Kumari Jayawardena, *Feminism and Nationalism in the Third World* (London: Zed Books, 1986), and Valentine Moghadam, ed., *Gender and National Identity: Women and Politics in Muslim Societies* (Geneva; United Nations University Press, 1994).

22. Moghadam, *Gender and National Identity,* 2.

23. See chapter 1 of this volume by Tatiana Zhurzhenko. See also Gal and Kligman, *Politics of Gender,* 26; Verdery, *What Was Socialism?* 78–81.

24. E.g., in Ukraine, the consolidation statehood was achieved with the active participation of women in the Rukh movement, but that state now actively perpetuates "reassertion or invention of myths about the allegedly pure, maternal, self-sacrificial features of the traditional Ukrainian woman." See Marsh, "Introduction," 15.

25. Verdery argues that during socialism, society itself became a type of extended family with the "father-party" at the head, making all important life decisions for and providing all life essentials for the "children-citizens." Verdery, *What Was Socialism?* 64–65.

26. Author's interviews with TPC activists in Kazan, October 1996 and June 2001.

27. Author's interviews with TPC activists in Kazan, October 1996 and June 2001. Also see the newspaper of the Tatar Public Center, *Izvestiya TOTs* (Kazan) from 1989 to 1991 for information about leadership composition, founding documents, etc.

28. The resolution that the TPC adopted at its First Congress is available in an English translation in *Central Asian Review* 9, no. 2 (1990): 155–65.

29. Resolution adopted by the TPC at its First Congress (see n. 28).

30. Although Tatar women did wear headscarves to mark their piety before the revolution, it is quite rare to see women wear them today. However, there is a small but growing number of young medreseh students and even Kazan State University students who have started to wear headscarves, a development that has been received critically by the local press and even by some members of the Tatar intelligentsia. See the Kazan newspaper *Vostochnyi Ekspress,* April 20–26, 2001, 8.

31. For a chronicle of Bairamova's political development, see her speeches in the newspaper of the Ittifak Party, *Alytn Urda,* and in other nationalist publications, such as *Beisez Watan,* the Kazan-based journal/newspaper of the Sovereignty Committee, another nationalist organization in Tatarstan.

32. The *kalfak* is a traditional form of Tatar women's headdress.

33. This is based on the author's fieldwork observations and archival research in Kazan 1996, 1997, 2000, and 2001. The name "Ak Aby" seems to be a play on the term "Ak Sakal," literally, "White Beard," which describes any venerated older Tatar male.

34. In one such case, which appeared in the nationalist journal *Beisez Watan* (Our Free Homeland), the caption under a picture featuring the Ak Aby and other Tatar women at a pro-sovereignty demonstration reads "When such beautiful women turn out to support independence, the achievement of such a paradise on earth in Tatarstan [i.e., an independent Tatarstan], is guaranteed!" See *Beisez Watan* 1, 1995.

35. Damir Ishakov, "Model Tatarstana i Nationalism Tatar" [The Tatarstan Model and Tatar Nationalism], manuscript in author's possession, Kazan, 1996, and Damir Ishakov, "Sovremennoye Tatarskoye Natsional'noye Dvizheniye" [The Contemporary Tatar Nationalist Movement], *Tatarstan* (Kazan) 8 (1993).

36. Zaznayev defined the political elite as including those closest to the President of the republic, including his advisory and administrative staff, all cabinet members and ministers, the leadership of the republic's parliament, and the regional heads of government in Tatarstan. See Oleg Zaznayev, "Respublika Tatarstana" [The Republic of Tatarstan], *Konstitutsionnoye Pravo* [Constitutional Law] (Moscow) 19, no. 2 (1997): 83. There has been an intense consolidation of political power in post-Soviet Tatarstan, evidenced by the fact that out of the 130 deputies serving in the State Council in 1997,

more than 100 were also representatives of the "vertical executive power apparatus" in Tatarstan—i.e., heads of city and regional political administrations, and members of the president's staff and the Tatarstani state ministries. See Midkhat Farukshin, "Politicheskaya Elita v Tatarstanye" [The Political Elite in Tatarstan], in *Politicheskiye issledovaniye* [Political Research] 5–6 (1994); Oleg Zaznayev, "Dinamika Politicheskogo Protsessa v Respublikye Tatarstan" [The Dynamics of the Political Process in the Republic of Tatarstan], *Konstitutsionnoye Pravo* [Constitutional Law] (Moscow) 21, no. 1 (1998). This ruling core elite is are also overwhelmingly Tatar (77 percent) and as aforementioned, male (95.4 percent).

37. Perhaps unsurprisingly, this is a garment enterprise named "kiemnar," which is the Tatar word for "clothes." See *Kto yest Kto?* [Who's Who?] (Kazan; Kabinet Ministrov, 1996).

38. The Constitution of the Republic of Tatarstan is reprinted in English (and Russian) in *Suverennyi Tatarstan: Sovereign Tatarstan* (Moscow; Plenipotentiary Representation of Tatarstan in Moscow and insan Publishers Plenipotentiary Representation 1997), 245, 247.

39. This is from the author's interview with Rosa Tufitullova, Kazan, June 2001.

40. See the interview with her in *Beisez Watan* 1 (1995).

41. One point about "social protection" did make it into Tatarstan's elaborate 1996 "State Program for the Economic and Social Progress," stipulating that the government will provide at least a minimal standard of living for various "socially unprotected" categories, including pregnant women, families with children and "unemployed mothers." Kabinet Ministrov Respublik Tatarstan, *Respublika Tatarstan: Vrem'ya Bolshikh Pereme'* (Kazan: Kabintet Ministrov Respublik Tatarstan, 1996), 262.

42. This is from the author's interview with Rosa Tufitullova, Kazan, June 2001.

43. This is from the author's interviews with Women of Tatarstan staff, June 2001. Also see their brochure, *Zhenzhchiny Tatarstana,* published in Kazan in 1999.

44. This is from the author's interviews with leaders of the Club of Intellectual Women, Kazan, June 2001.

45. This is from the author's interviews with leaders of the Club of Intellectual Women, Kazan, June 2001.

46. This is from the author's interview with editorial staff of newspaper *Zhenshchina,* Kazan, June 2001.

47. See their very interesting collection of survey and other research on women in Tatarstan, *Prava Cheloveka Dlya Zhenshchin* [Human Rights for Women], published in 2001 in the city of Naberezhniye Chelny and funded by the Canadian Program for the Support of Russian Women.

48. *Vremya I Dengi* (Kazan newspaper), February 10, 1996, 1.

49. This is based on the author's fieldwork observations in Kazan 1996, 1997, 2000, and 2001; also see R. A. Mustafin and A. Kh. Khasanov, *Mintimer Shaimiyev: Pervyi President Tatarstana* (Kazan: Tatarskoye Knizhnoye Isdatel'stvo; 1995) for a collection of pictures that illustrate this tendency.

50. At the Congress, President Shaimiyev noted that it marked the first time that Tatars from around the world had been "gathered here in our own homeland, our own state," *Sovetskaya Tatariya,* June 20, 1992, 1.

51. A second, even more lavish World Congress of Tatars was held in August 1997, prompting some commentators to complain about the "waste" of resources on ethnic Tatars instead of the citizens of Tatarstan. See Zaznayev, "Dinamika politicheskogo protsessa."

52. Syuyumbike was a Tatar queen of the Kazan Khanate, who according to legend killed herself rather than be taken prisoner and made wife of Ivan the Terrible when he sacked Kazan in 1552. The revival of interest in Syuyumbike as a symbol of both historic Tatar statehood and as a model of Tatar womanhood is a topic that merits closer attention. The magazine *Syuyumbike* is the former Soviet journal *Azat Khatyn* (Free Woman), which was renamed in 1991 after the fall of the USSR.

53. See the interview with Tufitullova in *Beisez Watan* 1 (1995): 76–79.

54. This is from the author's interview with Rosa Tufitullova, Kazan, October 1996.

55. This is from the author's interview with Rosa Tufitullova, Kazan, October 1996.

56. This is from the author's interview with Rosa Tufitullova, Kazan, October 1996.

57. This is from the author's interview with Rosa Tufitullova, Kazan, June 2001. Ak Kalfak has also sponsored several beauty-pageant type contests for Tatar girls and young, where the criteria for judgment is not swimsuits or displays of talent but rather knowledge of Tatar national history, traditions (including dress), and culture.

58. This is from the author's interview with Rosa Tufitullova, Kazan, October 1996.

59. *Vestnik Mezhdunarodnogo Soyuza Obshchestvennikh Ob'yedinenii: "Vsemirnyi Kongress Tatar"* [Proceedings of the International Union of Social Organizations: "The World Congress of Tatars"] (Kazan: Izdatel'stvo VKT, 2000), 78.

60. *Vestnik Mezhdunarodnogo Soyuza,* 81.

61. Significantly, the editorial page of the women's newspaper *Zhenshchina,* which is one of the few non-state-funded publications in Tatarstan, and which is edited by an ethnic Russian woman, has become a sort of clearinghouse for airing ethnic Russian grievances about living under the "Tatar ethnocracy" of the Shaimiyev regime. This may in part explain Zilya Valeeva and Women of Tatarstan's reluctance to be associated with the newspaper, but it also highlights the extent of self-censorship among state actors and the state-funded press in Tatarstan.

3

Engendering Citizenship in Postcommunist Uzbekistan

David Abramson

> *There is a direct link between the events in Afghanistan and security in Central Asia and Central Asian countries and the radical centres. The centres which are politicizing Islam are pursuing one goal, to stop, to turn back the process which has been chosen by all the people of Central Asia. They want to bring us back to the Middle Ages. To put the paranja on our children, on our beautiful daughters. You see what is happening in Afghanistan. How people are living there.*
>
> —Uzbek president Islom Karimov[1]

Most of the literature on gender in former socialist societies departs from the assumption that nation-states somehow single out and objectify women

The author conducted research for and wrote an early draft of this chapter mostly with the aid of a Policy Research Fellowship from the National Council of Eurasian and East European Research in 1999 and 2000. He is also grateful for institutional support from the Thomas J. Watson Institute for International Studies at Brown University and for suggestions and comments from a number of individuals, including Fred Starr and the participants in the Kennan Institute workshop for which he prepared this chapter.

as embodiments of the nation. Women as symbolic objects become the sine qua non of national distinctiveness. One easily gets the impression that this is a nearly universal phenomenon in the nation-building process. However, we actually know very little about how or why the role of women in society comes to figure so centrally in debates over the definition of nations. The belief that the distinctiveness, and often the survival, of national culture is contingent on the degree to which women live up to ideal representations of femininity must be examined more closely and unpacked.

As the chapters in this volume show, examples abound of nation-state institutions and national discourses that lay the onus of national self-preservation disproportionately on the public presentation of women—their style of dress, their occupations, and their sexual and familial roles. This chapter examines the process through which "women" have become symbolically constitutive of the new nation-state of Uzbekistan. I argue that tensions between the post-Soviet secularist legacy and Islamic revivalism have engendered separate notions of citizenship for men and for women. These separate "citizenships" produce gendered responses, which further undermine the possibility for a rapprochement between secularists and Islamic revivalists. This conflict has a particularly negative effect on women.

I begin with a discussion of the complexities of post-Soviet state "secularism" that have evolved in Uzbekistan since independence and of their impact on notions of citizenship. I then proceed to show how these complexities are reflected in debates over the practice of veiling.[2] Last, I discuss how men and women react and contribute to gendered citizenship in distinctly different ways and the consequences of this for women.

Islam, Secularism, and the Uzbek State

The Republic of Uzbekistan has existed as a sovereign state for just over 10 years, following the splintering of the Soviet Union. Even in this short period, some of the symbols and practices that Uzbeks initially celebrated and understood as givens accompanying national independence (e.g., holidays, ceremonies, and even the right to study and write about the pre-Soviet past) have changed remarkably, both in form and meaning. Of all of these, the role of Islam in state and society is quickly becoming the single most divisive and contentious postindependence issue facing the government and citizens of Uzbekistan.

Islam has been an integral part of Central Asian society for centuries, dating back to the ninth-century Arab invasion. Islam's current revival in Uzbekistan, however, has been more than an attempt by Muslim activists to reinstate the past or inject Soviet style nationalism with traditional flavor. The revival has drawn much of its strength from the perception that there is little of substantive value to what either socialism or nationalism has had to offer. There are myriad reasons for this, not least of which is the widely shared sense that not only did socialism fail but so also did the Soviet nationality policies that were crucial to promoting socialism in a multiethnic society. This twofold disenchantment has been reinforced by the fact that the leadership of Uzbekistan, as well as of the other Central Asian states, for the most part is continuing to operate within the same national-republic structure (even the leaders are the same).

Islam—which was once characterized either as a cultural "survival" of pre-modern Central Asia or as a national cultural trait amid many others in modern Soviet society—has acquired an irrepressible and increasingly pervasive public presence in the building of post-Soviet Uzbek society. This persistence of Islam as an "identity" should be seen, however, not as some ineffable force that has literally compelled people to struggle for or over it—If that were the case, why would there not be more of a consensus?—but rather as a powerful language, or symbolic toolkit, which Uzbeks find indispensable at all levels of social life for conveying moral interests and emotional needs for men and women alike. Islam's political necessity derives from the shared awareness of its social—that is, emotional, spiritual, and moral—appeal.

Under Soviet rule, Islam, like all religions, was anathema to the construction of socialism, whose ideology promoted atheism in both state and society. Islamic practice was therefore officially discouraged to varying degrees of intensity throughout the seven decades of the Soviet period. Nevertheless, the Soviet government did make political compromises in its international relations, especially with developing Muslim countries, and to demonstrate that as long as there were Muslims living in the USSR their needs would be accommodated. Internal compromises were also deemed necessary, especially during World War II and periods when policies of national diversity were preferred to assimilationist ones. Thus, for most of the period the government allowed token *madrassas* (Islamic secondary schools) and other Islamic institutions to function under tight governmental control. At the very least, these gestures enabled state leaders to claim that Soviet society tolerated religious freedom and even played an important regional role as heir to Islam's rich cultural heritage.

From the very beginning of Soviet rule, political strategies that sought to transform Central Asian women from their traditional circumstances into active participants in building socialism were of a high priority. Immediately following the October Revolution, the Bolshevik government organized an aggressive and often violent campaign to eliminate women's veiling (*hujum*), neighborhood religious schools and mosques, and Islamic legal practices.[3] However, the *hujum,* which was an attempt to deprive Central Asian society of its cultural distinctiveness, failed to win over large numbers of Central Asian women during the first two decades of Soviet rule.

Eventually, however, substantive institutional incentives brought future generations of women into higher education, the workforce, and government. This could not have been achieved without the erosion of existing Islamic forms of authority and the institutions that supported them. Primarily for these two reasons, certain practices such as veiling, which had been based on Islamic custom, began to disappear. What remained of these practices was treated as an exception, which the socialist state's discourse of modernization, assisted by the scientific elite, officially isolated and redefined as cultural "survivals."

The near disappearance of Islam from the public sphere contributed to the construction of Uzbek national identity as permanently secular and teleologically in synchrony with the progress of modern (European) history. Women had become full socialist citizens who had liberated themselves from the shackles of tradition when they cast off their veils. So why have many Islamic practices enjoyed a comeback since Uzbekistan became independent from the Soviet Union? To answer this question, one must first examine the Islamic revival in Uzbekistan through its relationship with contemporary nationalism.

Following independence, the Uzbek government (whose leaders also held high offices under Soviet rule) has taken on the difficult challenge of constructing a postindependence nationalist ideology. For example, Russian and Soviet place names were changed to celebrate local heroes, and the government highlighted the *mahalla* (a regional form of urban neighborhood) as a traditional institution where families preserve positive Uzbek values and customs.[4] At the same time, there have been other efforts to celebrate ethnic and regional diversity of the population, despite the fact that emigration of large numbers of non-Muslims from Uzbekistan since 1989 has certainly made the population more homogenous.[5]

An important contributing factor to this climate of politicized Islam in Uzbekistan has been the growth of extremist groups with ties to powerful

Islamist movements in the neighboring countries of Tajikistan and Afghanistan. One consequence of this has been an increase in incidents of violence throughout the region. In December 1997, the Uzbek government escalated its crackdown on Islamic activism by arresting and harassing hundreds of people in eastern Uzbekistan's Farghona Valley after the murder, allegedly by Muslim extremists, of a local state official in the city of Namangan.[6]

Just over 1 year later, in February 1999, six bombs exploded in Uzbekistan's capital city, Tashkent, killing 15 people and injuring more than 100. The government attributed these explosions to Muslim terrorists and subsequently conducted even more massive arrests. Other violent events have occurred since then with the incursions of armed groups into Uzbek territory from across mountainous borders with Tajikistan and Kyrgyzstan. These incidents and analyses of them have occupied numerous pages in the news media and policy papers.[7]

The impact of these events on how and whether women choose to veil as they wish has been considerable in that the government presents unsanctioned forms of veiling as signifying public support for Islamic extremism. It is clear that most people abhor extremist violence and that most women do not veil in ways that are seen as threatening to the status quo. Nevertheless, tensions between religious freedom and Soviet-style nationalism in *contemporary* Uzbek society contribute to passive support for some of the goals of the violence and embolden its perpetrators with the belief that there exists a large, sympathetic constituency within the country.

From an analytical point of view, it makes little sense to ask whether the Islamic revival of a given practice is merely the manifestation of religious freedom or a political act without also considering who is making the claim and why. However, one can distinguish between revivals and movements in the Islamic context. Gregory Starrett uses the term "Islamic trend" to refer to the more disparate, informal ways Islam is (re)introduced into the public sphere, whereas "Islamism," "radical Islam," "political Islam," and "fundamentalism" are terms reserved for self-consciously political and social movements.

This chapter is concerned with the process in which more disparate kinds of Islamic expression find meaning in people's lives before or external to the explicit goals of formal Islamic movements. Moreover, I am also interested in the large gray area where lines between the political and the social are drawn and redrawn. It is precisely in this area where struggles to define Uzbek nationhood and citizenship blur the boundary between religious and political practices.

Embodying Citizenship

Walking around Tashkent these days, one sees more and more young Uzbek women wearing *hijab* (covering their heads with a scarf, or "veiling") in public.[8] It is possible to find veiled women now working in kiosks and restaurants in both semirural and urban settings. Though the majority of Central Asian women have worn headscarves at some point in their lives, there is a new way many Uzbek women are wearing them today.

According to the Human Rights Watch report *Uzbekistan—Class Dismissed: Discriminatory Expulsions of Muslim Students,* university administrators and government officials are enforcing what virtually amounts to a national dress code, in which a distinction is drawn between "acceptable national dress—a patterned scarf worn on the head and tied at the back of the neck, leaving the face open—and what they regarded as 'Arab' or foreign dress—a solid colored scarf that is clasped in front or covers the face. To them [representatives of the state], the latter style was unacceptable because it does not conform with Uzbek tradition."[9] School and university administrators, as well as the police—claiming that such forms of public display are evidence of Muslim "extremist," fundamentalist," or "Wahhabi" sentiment and threaten the state's commitment to secularism in its educational system—have been harassing and expelling female students who do not conform to Uzbek standards of dress.[10]

Those who object to foreign, or non-Uzbek, veiling take their cues in part from public statements like the one made by Uzbek president Islom Karimov (quoted above). Such labels fail to capture the diversity of reasons for veiling this way and overlook the fact that self-described adherents to Wahhabism may be only a small fraction of this population. Moreover, though none of these women veils in accordance with Wahhabi practice in Saudi Arabia, where women must be fully covered, the Uzbek government nonetheless labels them Wahhabis.

Male students with beards have also been harassed and expelled, although apparently in smaller numbers.[11] While I was traveling around Uzbekistan and in the capital city Tashkent with a bearded Uzbek friend, I witnessed widespread suspicion and harassment. In each of many incidents when police and security forces stopped us and asked to see our passports, one of them always mentioned that my friend "looked like a terrorist." Had I, with my U.S. passport, not been accompanying him, he almost certainly would have been detained for much longer. Whenever he wore a tie, he told me, he was rarely harassed. Apparently, Muslim terrorists do not wear ties!

What the Human Rights Watch report does not discuss or explain are the reasons why some Uzbek Muslims insist on wearing *hijab,* growing beards, or engaging in other Islamic practices against the will of the state and for the first time in their lives. Veiling, in a variety of ways, for example, is an opportunity (after several decades) for women to display their newly found commitment to Islam in ways that the Soviet era "Uzbek" headscarf does not. Thus, though the particular banned forms of veiling historically do not carry any national significance, they do constitute innovative ways to reconcile modernity and Islam. Although the official way of veiling might symbolize Uzbek culture's distinct path to modernity, it does not accommodate meaning that is distinctly Islamic.

Veiling, if only in accordance with the national "dress code," has also allowed young women to protect themselves and their dignity in public. In the late 1980s and early 1990s, even before independence, there was a rise in incidents of public harassment by men of women whom they took to be Uzbek. Male youths would shout "Dress like an Uzbek girl" at young women who dressed in miniskirts or wore short hair that might have been died white or with multicolored streaks, according to Russian fashion. It was understood what was meant: longer, colorful cotton or silk dresses that extended to the ankles, and long and naturally colored hair. This harassment, which sometimes led to physical assault, occurred on the streets of Tashkent, a city of 2 million residents, approximately half of whom were members of Uzbekistan's Russian-speaking minorities, as well as in smaller provincial cities.[12]

It needs to be noted that though many Islamic practices disappeared from the public sphere during the Soviet era, people continued to distinguish one another according to national traits. For example, Uzbeks tended to regard Russian and European women as sexually promiscuous and therefore as available for liaisons, extramarital or otherwise, with Uzbek men, whereas Uzbek women were mostly sheltered or even prohibited from entering into ethnically mixed dating and marriage. In reference to the emigration of large numbers of Russians from Uzbekistan that began in 1989 and continued throughout the 1990s, one Uzbek man facetiously lamented, "Who are we going to screw now, our sheep?"

In contrast to the pressure on young women to adhere to a dress code, there was no equivalent for men. In the late 1980s, men began to don the national Uzbek cap (*duppa*) more frequently as an expression of support for Uzbek independence. One middle-aged man shared with me his experience of wearing the *duppa* on a daily basis after having worn it only for special ceremonies such as weddings and funerals. He quickly ceased wearing it when he got tired of friends and colleagues constantly asking him "Who died?" But the issue of how or when to wear the *duppa* never became one of "national" concern as did women's veiling.

In addition to the rather wide range of possible individual motivations for veiling, there is also a collective societal impact. As Starrett points out, "the act of veiling, whatever its individual motivation and spiritual consequences, is a ritual act that contributes de facto to the Islamization of public space."[13] For this reason, the state's nationalist project has involved attempts to render Uzbek nationalism in secular terms. One strategy has been to label and celebrate all practices under the rubric of "national culture." This has involved the manipulation of those cultural practices that after 70 years of Soviet rule continue to have Islamic significance, but in a way that makes them seem uniquely Uzbek. This strategy is predicated on the idea that the more distinctive Uzbek Islam is, the less likely Uzbek Muslims will be to identify with a transnational Islamic authority.

The restoration of an Uzbek national culture in deeper ways than were ever possible in Soviet times, however, has inevitably raised the critical question of how to distinguish between national and Islamic practices. On the one hand, the state leadership has sought to domesticate Islam by relying on it as part of the nation-building process while also putting limits on Islamic forms of expression. Consequently, many women who "veil" in ways that are foreign to Uzbekistan are singled out and disenfranchised because this expression of Islam is understood to privilege symbolically a transnational Islamic community.

On the other hand, it is important not to view transnational veiling only as a deliberate attempt to defy or remake the state. Religious practices have meanings that are not only political but also social. In the current climate, many young women have tried to realize their newfound freedom to practice Islam and apply Soviet values of modern education to succeed in the very difficult economic conditions facing Uzbekistan today. Veiling "transnationally" is also a way for women to show their commitment to Islam in ways that they were unable to do in the past because Uzbek national traditions (which were heavily influenced and engineered during seven decades of Soviet rule) are not meaningful enough to allow for such innovation.

Thus, veiling transnationally can be interpreted as a statement of solidarity with Muslims around the world on issues of common concern. But it also derives its power by symbolizing a rupture with the Soviet Uzbek past in ways the Uzbek style of veiling cannot. The government, having tried to make religious practice conform to an emergent national ideology, tends to interpret any departure as a political, and therefore potentially threatening, act. Given these limitations of "Uzbek Islam," it is hardly surprising that many Muslims would seek to innovate their own versions. Thus, attempts to manage religious practices have only exacerbated tensions between Islam and nationalism in Uzbek society today.

Young women are veiling so that they can both practice Islam and acquire an education so as to survive the post-Soviet transition; yet veiling is also the reason that they are being expelled from school in increasing numbers. Some of the ways in which male administrators have justified the fact that 90 percent of the dozens of university expulsions between 1997 and 1999, and the much larger number of harassment cases, were female students seem to contradict the principles of modern secularism as they are understood in the West.[14] According to an interview with Human Rights Watch, the rector of the Tashkent Pediatric Medical Institute dismissed the suggestion that expulsions of female students is a problem by saying that "the institute is pleased that more men are coming to the university to study now, because all over the world medicine is considered men's work."[15]

That many people choose to use their state offices to insist on the appearance of a secular state and society is ultimately a reactionary position that is legitimated by the mask of modernity. Here, secularism (i.e., the separation of religious and state affairs or the banning of obvious religious symbols and practices from the public sphere) does not coincide with the modern priority of equal social and economic rights for women. The fact that the medical institute rector did not (and could not, given his position on veiling) invoke Islamic principles to expel female students tells us that some interpretations of Islam are more accommodating to women's right to education than are some secular ones.

Thus, not only do these dynamics reveal potentials for tolerance and flexibility within local interpretations of Islam, but they also do not correspond to the dichotomy of "modern" and "traditional" that accompanies the ideology of the secular state and that is reflected in President Karimov's statement on veiling. Nation building, therefore, is not an either/or process but is made up of multiple, overlapping, often contradictory discourses and ways of imagining the nation, which do not evolve in a clear linear direction. Women's socioeconomic and religious rights are often the first to be sacrificed in the resultant inconsistencies. It is ironic, then, that the same educational system that promoted women's emancipation from traditional gender roles is currently stifling attempts to accomplish the same through the integration of Islamic values and practices.

It is important here to distinguish between two simultaneously occurring tendencies. One reflects patterns seen, at the very least, throughout former Soviet society; the other is more specific to Central Asia. In some ways, the Islamic revival echoes or is harnessed to other forms of postcommunist identity politics, such as nationalism. In this sense, Islam is merely one of the many ways people reproduce the structural solidarities that are legacies of the Soviet Union in a post-Soviet context. In Uzbekistan, despite the close monitoring of Islam, people often assert or pressure others to demonstrate their faith in Islam as a public testimony of loyalty to the state, or society. Consequently, words and actions are taken as symbolic of such loyalty much the same as they are imbued with *national* meaning elsewhere in the former Soviet states. The fact that "being" Uzbek and "being" Muslim are generally taken as synonymous reinforces this dynamic. Thus, statements such as "Our women do not travel outside their village"[16] and arguments that women should veil in an appropriately Uzbek way[17] exemplify rhetoric of a typically nationalist mold in reinforcing social norms and in substituting women's individual identities with an imagined national collective.

I have already addressed above the other tendency with respect to women, which revolves around the question of what the present national ideology can substantively offer Uzbeks, in general, in uncertain economic and political conditions.[18] Many Uzbeks are looking beyond national ideology to other frameworks that offer greater promise of material and spiritual rewards. What I refer to as transnational veiling and other practices that push the boundaries of what can legitimately be called "Uzbek national culture" lead more and more to the politicization of Muslim-ness and prompt fierce reactions such as cultural possessiveness (e.g., of women, usually by men). These two lenses are useful not only to distinguish between Islam as a nationalist project and Islam as a potentially transnationalist one but also to explain how both projects, working in concert, lead to the exclusion of women from numerous public domains, as is illustrated by the expulsion of female students.

Women as "Burden of Proof": Islam and Nationalism in Conflict

For Uzbekistan, a country that only recently emerged from 70 years of Soviet rule, the post-Soviet transition has been partly a story of how women have come to be seen as those on whom the "burden of proof" for the distinctiveness of the national culture increasingly rests. For example, the question of whether and how women engage in the Islamic practice of veiling has become significantly more than an issue of individual choice; it is gaining a central place in efforts to define the predominantly Muslim Uzbek nation-state. As President Karimov's statement quoted above implies, the very appearance of women has become a litmus test for the cultural direction that the country will take—framed as a choice between modernity (as progress) and the "Middle Ages."

The study of nationalism has demonstrated again and again the importance of symbols of national "possessions" to the nation-building process.[19] By elaborating on this, one can identify at least three theories that attempt to explain why idealist constructions of women, or womanhood, are included as symbols of national distinctiveness. The first is that nationalist ideologies are universally grounded in metaphors of family and reproduction, and that control over the reproductive process is the only way to ensure the continuation of the nation.[20] Although it is useful for apprehending how people often imagine the nation, this social evolutionist approach to the nation is flawed for two reasons. First, it does not take into account the freedoms that women in some nation-states enjoy, including the freedom to exercise individual control over their own reproductive capacity. Second, if national reproduction is the top priority of a nation's citizens, then why is heterosexual male behavior also not more closely monitored?

The second theory posits that the newly independent states assert their national identity and cultural distinctiveness by overturning Soviet era polices. It explains that the shift toward objectifying women as key symbols of Uzbek national distinctiveness is a reaction to Soviet affirmative action and "modernization" policies that had been implemented on behalf of women. Whether or not Soviet women, when compared with men, enjoyed "an advantageous alliance with the state" is subject to debate.[21] However, even if women had benefited disproportionately from Soviet policies, it does not follow that postindependence rejections of Soviet policies would necessarily seek to rectify this discrepancy.

This "postcolonial" theory, however, does not account for any contemporary disagreements over how Uzbek women really benefited from those Soviet policies. There is no doubt that numerous Central Asian women were given and took advantage of opportunities that Soviet institutions gave them, such as access to higher education, jobs, and the Communist Party (with all its perquisites and privileges). Although nationalists have lamented the "sovietization" of Uzbek women as an indication of the weakening of their national culture, the theory does not provide a link between these laments and kinds of policies deemed necessary to address them. Furthermore, the theory does not explain why secularist policies toward women are not included among those that should be overturned to preserve national distinctiveness. In other words, the theory does not account for the nationalist ideology's selective rejection of the Soviet past in the interest of nationalism.

The third theory regards nationalism as a cover for a more universal pattern of power struggles in gender relations in which men seek to subordinate women. Thus women are expected to serve the nation by serving their fathers, husbands, and sons. Cynthia Enloe, in writing about British masculinized imperialism, suggests that we should see it "not as a crusade to abolish male domination of women but as a crusade to establish European male rule over the men in Asian and African societies.[22] In response, male-led nationalist movements such as that in India sought to control women all the more in defiance of British attempts to emasculate the Indian male. This certainly did not take place in Soviet Central Asia, largely because in the period immediately preceding independence there were no nationalist movements. Only in the late 1980s, when Soviet power was already receding, and in the 1990s, after independence, did a weak form of nationalism emerge in Uzbekistan and the other Central Asian republics.

Even so, this theory does not explain why, for example, the Uzbek state is promoting a model of the modern secular woman over one of the veiled Muslim woman as part of a larger nationalist project, especially given that there is considerable disagreement, among both men and women, about how to define the Uzbek nation. Although both models construct women as national objects, it is at how the tension between them is played out that we need to look.

To address this last, key question, we need to understand how struggles between nationalist secularism and the Islamic revival have affected gender relations and, ultimately, the position of women in Uzbekistan today. The concept of citizenship is particularly useful here for identifying how male and female roles in the nation are defined, negotiated, and contested. As Enloe and others point out, after nationalist revolutions "the concept of 'citizenship' provided the terrain on which gendered struggles were fought between nationalist women and nationalist men."[23] We must remember, however, that the complete absence of a nationalist struggle in Uzbekistan before independence means that the development of a nationalist ideology and a national identity have had to vie with alternatives such as Islam in making a place for male and female citizens. This factor alone justifies an approach to gender in transition that captures the different ways in which

Uzbek men and women struggle to define new roles for themselves in their changing society.

Most analysts consider the concept of citizenship to refer to the relationship among individuals and legal rights, territoriality, and other forms of state sovereignty. Through ethnography and cross-cultural comparison, however, some social scientists have made a powerful case for the need to examine how *plural* notions of citizenship vary and affect social and political behavior.[24] Anthropologists, in particular, have used such nonlegalistic terms as "belonging" and "membership" to examine, comparatively, the cultural logic of rights and claims within the nation-state and other forms of politically and socially organized institutions.[25]

For the purpose of this chapter, I am interested in how this definitional and practical flexibility of citizenship (or membership, or belonging) is often gendered in predominantly Muslim societies such as Uzbekistan. By this, I mean that many struggles over state control of citizenship—both in its legal and substantive forms—take place either in domains (both public and private) where lines of gender difference have been historically drawn or in new situations invested with gendered meaning. These domains include the family, but also men's and women's access to and claims upon social and economic resources in public life given patterns of expectations, moral frameworks, and the like.

Citizenships in Conflict

In his discussion of the relationship between women and the rise of Indian nationalism under colonial rule, Partha Chatterjee traces the emergence of gendered domains of citizenship in which men were invested with the authority of the nation (and, after independence, the authority to speak on behalf of, or invoke, the state), whereas women could only embody it as a model of a traditionalized nation. The tragedy of national emancipation, he argues, is that, by the time it was achieved "it could grant the dignity of citizenship to some only because the others always needed to be represented and could not be allowed to speak for themselves."[26] Although this picture in many ways accurately depicts the current, postindependence situation in Uzbekistan today as seen through the veiling controversy in particular, it fails to capture the Islamic revival's transnational dimension and the extent to which this factor undermines political competency to move beyond transition.

"Theories of citizenship generally include assumptions about political competency," according to Julie Mostov.[27] However, as Arjun Appadurai and James Holston argue, before we can assume anything about political competency, we need to consider the relationship between the theory and practice of citizenship. "In other words, formal membership in the nation-state is . . . neither a necessary nor a sufficient condition for substantive citizenship."[28] Substantive citizenship, they write, refers to the possession and power to exercise an "array of civil, political, socio-economic, and cultural rights."[29] In Uzbekistan today, the kind of Muslim a person professes to be or is accused of being has more and more become the criterion on which substantive citizenship is based. Substantive, or rights-based, citizenship can easily slip away from a theory of citizenship that is encapsulated in a nationalist ideology. For men, Uzbek nationalism equates professional competency with political competency. For example, Muslim clergy fear to deviate from their highly circumscribed role of ministering to a narrowly defined and suspicious community; academics view the academy as a site for the reproduction of, and only of national ideology.

Thus, according to local understanding, political competency means adhering to an unwavering and unmediatable (and therefore undemocratic) party line. This is treacherous terrain for a community whose membership—indeed moral responsibility—is often practically predicated on participation in public purges. To embrace state citizenship exclusively, as it is currently defined, means to embrace isolation from democratic means of moderation, negotiation, and inclusion.

I argue that it is precisely because men are struggling to maintain identities that are separate from the state, while also engaging with the state, that they invest their occupational and head-of-household roles with symbolic meaning. When those roles are difficult to fulfill because of the vicissitudes of socioeconomic transition, men turn to national or transnational ideologies for social recognition of personal merit and group belonging. Uzbek nationalism and Islam are two such available ideologies. One way of seeking such recognition is by identifying closely, and perhaps all too literally, with the imprecise and evolving ideological guidelines that leaders promulgate. In instances of nationalism, this pattern of identification by invoking the state and then reproducing it through social practice contributes to the construction of the state itself.[30] In this way, nationalist discourse becomes a gendered process.[31]

For now, the problem of Islam and secularism in Uzbek society revolves around people's desire to manifest, publicly, their interest in and commitment to an Islamic way of life. This "way of life" is by no means homogenous, but there are certain practices that people generally recognize as Islamic. In addition to modest dressing for women and beards for men, praying five times a day, and attending Friday mosque, making the Hajj pilgrimage to Mecca and fasting for Ramadan are other markers of an Islamic revival in Uzbekistan today. Many government officials and employees of state institutions increasingly engage in these practices as well.

Furthermore, it is not uncommon for academics and state officials, many of whom are erstwhile members of the Communist Party, to intimidate their peers and competitors with the question "Are you a believer?" Rather than using the question to identify "Wahhabis" in their midst, it is instead intended to insinuate that nonbelievers are not Uzbek enough, and therefore are unpatriotic. If this seems to be at odds with patterns of secularization in the public sphere, then we need to rethink what "secular" means in the post-Soviet Uzbek context.[32]

As I have argued above, at the same time that Uzbek leaders are seeking to consolidate their power over the Uzbek nation via state citizenship (and the symbols and policies that constitute it), there is a challenging counter-development of a global form of citizenship, or belonging, that draws on the symbols of a transnational Islamic community. This alternative citizenship draws its strength, in part, from the perception that the Soviet model of Uzbek nationhood has little to offer a population facing increasingly dire economic conditions and a growing awareness of the political inequalities to which they give rise.

This awareness grows all the more apparent in a context where access to the relatively vast wealth of foreign aid, business ventures, and other opportunities offered by overseas sponsors is perceived, correctly, as being out of reach of all but an elite segment of the local population. As in the Soviet period, men continue to dominate positions of power in government and business. The only potentially viable occupation of economic strength in which women play a dominant role is the nongovernmental sector, comprising nongovernmental organizations that are often dependent on foreign funding for their survival (see chapters 9, 12, and 14 of this volume).

Conclusion

This chapter is an attempt to put the study of Uzbek women in postcommunist national and transnational contexts by analyzing how citizenship becomes a gendered process. The arguments in the chapter allow us to look beyond single-factor explanations of gender differentiation in post-socialist societies. As I have argued for the case of Uzbekistan, the growing strength of shared religious belief and the concomitant revival of Islamic practices themselves are insufficient explanations for the gendering of citizenship. Both Islam and secularism are used as discursive frameworks for justifying gender differences; it is the lack of a national consensus and the resultant tension between these two frameworks that serve as an important context for understanding gender relations and the situation for women.

The political culture of Islam in Uzbekistan today can be characterized as one in which state institutions are responding to increasing public displays of Islam by attempting to ascribe "national" and "secular" meaning to them. These displays take a variety of forms, ranging from Islamically meaningful customs and clothing to pervasive Islamic discourse in everyday speech. Attempts to secularize Islam in Uzbekistan involve the recognition that the nation-state is an influential force; they also involve the possibility of successfully casting Islamic practices as national ones. One might expect this to be a relatively simple task, given that the language of secularism and secularizing strategies are readily available from the recent Soviet past. However, the Soviet Union is in the past, or at least the incentives for being secular in a Soviet way are no longer apparent to many people. Freedom of religious expression, including the choice to belong and participate in an Islamic community that transcends strict definitions of national citizenship, is being valued more and more in Uzbekistan.

The Uzbek government's crackdown on Islamism in particular, with ramifications for the more broadly defined Islamic revival, has led to serious conflicts of interest. The vast majority of Uzbekistanis are caught between nationalism and the Islamic revival, valuing both yet unsure how to interpret the authority of the state. Balancing these interests, both professionally and privately, has had a notably negative impact on gender relations to the extent of making citizenship for women contingent on a very narrow ideal of the modern Uzbek woman. The definition of citizenship for women through their objectification is not unique to contemporary Uzbek nationalism. I have noted how the Bolsheviks of the 1920s engaged in objectifications of their own in pursuit of socialism through modernization. However, what is new, and particularly troubling, is the way in which the tensions of transition have engendered separate "citizenships" that foster mistrust for men and severely restrict the opportunities for women to participate in their new society.

The study of gender gives a unique perspective on the interplay between nationalist and Islamic ideals and their influence on notions of citizenship in Uzbekistan. In both private and professional spheres, roles for men and women are being renegotiated in this time of transition. It is in precisely these cultural locations that the uncertainties of economic and social survival in a period of transition are more relevant. The politics of state building and nation building and the relationships they engender are powerful as expressions of these everyday uncertainties.

The studies in this volume all attempt to enrich one's understanding of gender dynamics with respect to the social, economic, and/or political dynamics of post-Soviet nation building. Each examines occupational or symbolic domains that have been masculinized or feminized, yet whose association with one or the other gender continues to be contested. It is hoped that this chapter has contributed to an understanding of why the postcommunist politics of belonging is revisiting the issue of the relationship between gender difference and nationalism in today's Uzbekistan. This revisiting should be understood to be much more than a product of the collective revival of Islamically meaningful practices or as part and parcel of a reactionary process seen to be inherent in nation building after Soviet socialism. It bears a significance that is transnational in essence and raises serious questions about the compatibility of the existing models of national citizenship with Islam.

Notes

1. Kyrgyz Radio first broadcast in Russian, "Uzbek President Rejects Veiling of 'Our Beautiful Daughters'"; <http://www.uzreport.com> (August 20, 2000). The term *paranja* in the last sentence is used for clothes that fully cover a woman's body, including a mesh for the face. The *paranja* was worn in Uzbekistan in the nineteenth and early twentieth centuries.

2. In addressing these issues, I take a bottom-up approach to explain links between the newly emergent structural pressures and potentialities of postcommunist life and the cultural desires and values that give meaning to and are informed by those structuring forces. By "bottom-up," I am not referring to grassroots or informal social organizations; rather, I take the individual as the primary agent of action and examine the range of options available to her for achieving personal and collective goals and desires (getting things done) as well as the cultural values that inform and inspire her. These structuring forces include changing border dynamics and transnational connections, secularist state polices, economic contingencies, and the emerging social pressures within the institutions through which all of the above changes are realized.

3. See William K. Medlin et al., *Education and Development in Central Asia: A Case*

Study of Social Change in Uzbekistan, (Leiden: Brill, 1971); and Gregory Massell, *The Surrogate Proletariat: Moslem Women and Revolutionary Strategies in Soviet Central Asia, 1919–29* (Princeton, N.J.: Princeton University Press, 1972) for studies of Soviet policies and campaigns to reform education in general in Central Asia and to "modernize" women by pressuring them to unveil and bring them into the workplace. See also the excellent historical study by Douglas Northrop, "Uzbek Women and the Veil: Gender and Power in Stalinist Central Asia," Ph.D. dissertation, Stanford University, Stanford, Calif., 1999.

4. David Abramson, "From Soviet to Mahalla: Community and Transition in Post-Soviet Uzbekistan," Ph.D. dissertation, Indiana University, Bloomington, 1998.

5. According to the most recent census figures (1989), the ethnic Uzbek majority makes up more than 70 percent of the population, and an even larger Muslim majority, of Uzbeks, Tajiks, Kazakhs, and other nationalities, makes up close to 90 percent. The percentages for both Uzbeks and Muslims in Uzbekistan must be considerably greater 14 years later, given emigration and population growth for both groups since 1989.

6. Human Rights Watch, *Republic of Uzbekistan: Crackdown in the Farghona Valley—Arbitrary Arrests and Religious Discrimination* (New York: Human Rights Watch, 1998).

7. See Nancy Lubin and Barnett Rubin, *Calming the Farghona Valley: Development and Dialogue in the Heart of Central Asia* (New York: Century Foundation Press, 1999), for one of the only policy-oriented studies of the postindependence conflict in Farghona.

8. I use the term "veiling" in the context of Uzbekistan to refer to a range of ways in which women cover parts of their heads or faces with a scarf for purposes of modesty and in observance of Islamic tradition. Since the early part of the twentieth century, Uzbeks have had no tradition of completely covering the head, as is practiced in Afghanistan and Saudi Arabia.

9. Human Rights Watch, *Uzbekistan—Class Dismissed: Discriminatory Expulsions of Muslim Students* (New York: Human Rights Watch, 1999), 9.

10. The terms "Wahhabism" (from the name of an Islamic movement based on the ideas of an eighteenth-century sheik, Muhammad ibn Abd al-Wahab), and "Wahhabi" (a person who practices Wahhabism) are used in a range of ways in Uzbekistan. Their narrowest usage is in reference to the official, and highly orthodox, form of Islam practiced in Saudi Arabia. They are more commonly used as a synonym for Muslim extremists, or fundamentalists. There exists, however, an even broader, pejorative usage, as a label for anyone who is opposed to or offers versions alternative to state interpretations of Islam or state-sanctioned Islamic practices. Of course, because interpretation is often ambiguous, people have more and more used the label Wahhabi to vilify their opponents in Uzbekistan's secular political culture. This "green baiting," to coin a phrase, has at times effectively resulted in the loss of employment and imprisonment, if not execution.

11. Human Rights Watch, *Uzbekistan: Class Dismissed,* 16.

12. This is based on personal communications. It is doubtful that such incidents occurred in rural areas where few, if any, women dressed untraditionally.

13. Gregory Starrett, *Putting Islam to Work: Education, Politics, and Religious Transformation in Egypt* (Berkeley: University of California Press, 1998), 245.

14. Human Rights Watch, *Uzbekistan: Class Dismissed,* 16. It should be noted that since the report was written, Human Rights Watch has documented only twelve more

cases of expulsions of female students from institutions of higher education. The conclusion they draw is that women who veil in the wrong way are not allowed to matriculate in the first place or, if they enroll, agree not to wear their headscarf the wrong way in school. Among those twelve cases, nine were female students expelled from a state-run Islamic, not secular, school of higher learning for wearing *hijab.* This is based on a personal communication.

15. Human Rights Watch, *Uzbekistan: Class Dismissed,* 16.

16. Billur Gungoren, "Women, Water, and Social Change in the Farghona Valley: Let's Not Call It a Women's Project" (unpublished), Columbia University, New York, 2001, 10.

17. Human Rights Watch, *Uzbekistan: Class Dismissed.*

18. The case of Uzbekistan provides an interesting contrast to those of Ukraine and Belarus (see chapters 1 and 4 of this volume by Tatiana Zhurzhenko and Elena Gapova, respectively). In the latter cases, nationalism and communism are the two predominant and competing political orientations. In Uzbekistan, ruling secular nationalists have both positioned themselves as the heirs to communism and attempted to appropriate a nationalist version of Islam to marginalize extremist nationalists and Muslims. The local concept of Euro-Islam discussed in Katherine Graney's study of sovereignty in Tatarstan (see chapter 2 of this volume) presents yet a third, perhaps synthesized, alternative to nation building with a European point of reference rather than the strictly nationalistic one that is typical of Central Asian states.

19. Not the least among them is Richard Handler, *Nationalism and the Politics of Culture in Quebec* (Madison: University of Wisconsin Press, 1988).

20. For a relevant discussion in the post-socialist context, see Katherine Verdery, *What Was Socialism, and What Comes Next?* (Princeton, N.J.: Princeton University Press, 1996), 69–82.

21. Susan Gal and Gail Kligman, *The Politics of Gender after Socialism: A Comparative-Historical Essay* (Princeton, N.J.: Princeton University Press, 2000), 8.

22. Cynthia Enloe, *Bananas, Beaches, and Bases: Making Feminist Sense of International Politics* (Berkeley: University of California Press, 1989), 49.

23. Enloe, *Bananas,* 54. See also Partha Chatterjee, *The Nation and Its Fragments: Colonial and Postcolonial Histories* (Princeton, N.J.: Princeton University Press, 1993), chaps. 6 and 7.

24. See the collection of symposium articles titled "Citizenship and its Alterities," *Political and Legal Anthropology Review* 22, no. 2 (1999): 41–109.

25. I use the term "cultural logic" to refer to the stuff that makes economic and political actions "thinkable, practicable, and desirable" for the people who engage in them. See Aihwa Ong, *Flexible Citizenships: The Cultural Logics of Transnationality* (Durham, N.C.: Duke University Press, 1999), 5. See also John Borneman, *Belonging in the Two Berlins: Kin, State, Nation* (Cambridge: Cambridge University Press, 1992).

26. Chatterjee, *Nation and Its Fragments,* 154.

27. Julie Mostov, "Endangered Citizenship," in *Russia and Eastern Europe after Communism: The Search for New Political, Economic, and Security Systems,* ed. Michael Kraus and Ronald Liebowitz (Boulder, Colo.: Westview Press, 1996), 39.

28. Arjun Appadurai and James Holston, "Cities and Citizenship," *Public Culture* 8 (1996): 190.

29. Appadurai and Holston, "Cities."

30. Michael Herzfeld, *The Social Production of Indifference* (Oxford: Berg, 1992); and Akhil Gupta, "Blurred Boundaries: The Discourse of Corruption, the Culture of Politics, and the Imagined State," *American Ethnologist* 22, no. 2 (1995): 375–402.

31. See Gupta, "Blurred Boundaries." I use Gupta's conceptualization of the state, in which individuals are agents of state production and reproduction. For Gupta and his colleagues, the state is a translocal institution that is subject to multi-sited ethnographic observation. The approach examines how particular discourses and practices become associated with and thereby legitimated by the authority of the state; how social positions and interactions lend themselves to particular uses of the state for given ends; and the micro- and macro-scale consequences and implications of these actions for the construction of the state and its relation to society. See also Gerald Creed, *Domesticating Revolution* (University Park: Pennsylvania State University Press, 1998).

32. For a theoretical discussion of what the politics of the meaning of "secular" in Islamic contexts, see Gregory Starrett, "Who Put the 'Secular' in the Secular State?" *Brown Journal of World Affairs* 6, no. 1 (1999): 147–62.

4

Conceptualizing Gender, Nation, and Class in Post-Soviet Belarus

Elena Gapova

Woman's place in human social life is not in any direct sense a product of the things she does . . . but of the meaning her activities acquire through concrete social interaction.

—Michelle Rosaldo, "The Use and Abuse of Anthropology: Reflections on Feminism and Cross-Cultural Understanding," *Signs,* no. 5 (1980): 400

On September 9, 2001, Belarus had presidential elections for the first time since Aleksandar Lukashenka became its president in 1994. To stay in power for 7 years instead of the 4 years to which he had been elected, Lukashenka had changed the Constitution. The 2001 elections—which were held in an

The author is indebted to Michele Rivkin-Fish for many valuable comments and suggestions regarding this chapter. Substantial parts of this chapter were published in "On Nation, Gender, and Class Formation in Belarus . . . and Elsewhere in the Post-Soviet World," *Nationalities Papers* 30(4): 639–662.

undemocratic manner, with falsification of voting results and repression of political opponents, with access to most media blocked for the opposition candidates—became the acme point of the confrontation between the country's authoritarian executive power and the opposition, called either democratic or nationalist, depending on who was speaking.

The voting situation and its perception by Westernized urban intelligentsia can best be illustrated by the following submission to the Slavic and East European languages and literatures bulletin board on the Internet (seelangs@listserv.cuny.edu). The message was sent by a list subscriber from Minsk (the orthography is as in the original; the sender's name is omitted):

> Sorry for a bit off-topic, but I want the world to know before I may be switched off. Today we are having presidential elections. It is already completely obvious that they are going to be falsified on large scales. Observers are beaten and thrown out, ballot boxes are opened during the night, many many other things. Security council deleted from DNS server the records for opposition sites: dt.home.by (dzied Talasz), www.bdg.by (live 24hr coverage) www.barcnews.by and many others. Also from inside Belarus we can NOT see www.svaboda.org (RFE/RL), www.charter97.org (live coverage) and a dozen other sites. Beltelecom (the sole state-run [Internet service provider] that controls all other providers) blocks their IP addresses. We are under siege. People get their phones turned off. I hope mine will still be operational. At that same time Russian TV media reports that elections in Belarus are taking place as planned without any falsification. Please, spread the word. There are several trucks with soldiers with machine guns that were unloaded next to us (Rusijanava Street).[1]

On election day, the opposition candidate, Vladimir Goncharik, appealed to his supporters to come in the evening to October Square where his headquarters were situated in the Trade Unions Palace, and to stay there till the voting results were announced in the morning. The idea to bring people to a public space was driven by several goals. One might have been the visualization of people's support by presenting a certain amount of "live bodies" as its evidence (the elections were widely covered by international media), which would present the struggle as a people's cause. A more practical but unrealistic aim was to prevent the falsification of voting results with a threat of a protest strike, which supposedly could spread nationwide from October Square.

By the end of the day, about 3,000 people had gathered at a plaza in front of the Trade Unions Palace. The opposition leaders evidently did not know what to do with them, and after a short meeting it was suggested just to "stay there." Still, the mood of the 24-hour live coverage of the events at the electronic Charter 97 bulletin board (its server is outside the country) was that of reporting from the battlefield. Right after midnight, the following message appeared:

> *00.50.*
> Vladimir Goncharik called the people standing this night in October Square in Minsk to come again at 7 A.M. to find out the voting results. *As for the men (males),* he asked them to stay in the streets till the morning.

Eventually, people began leaving the streets because nothing was happening, and the next message, an hour later, reported:

> *1.45.*
> At the present moment there are about 200 people left at the Trade Unions Palace: women and minors have been driven out from the building after Vladimir Goncharik's request. The men who stayed are now barricading the doors. The law-enforcement contingent is being drawn to the Palace. Vladimir Goncharik left the place but will return there in one hour time. His trustee Mikhail Chigir is there with the protesters.

No action was taken against the protesters that night, while they badly needed some sign from the authorities that they were noticed, that is, that they were political actors:

> *2.45.*
> 200 *courageous men* (*otvazhnyh muzhchin*) who locked themselves this night in the Trade Unions Palace, are currently trying to get ready for a possible police attack: they clasp their hands together with full might, so that if the law-enforcers break in, they couldn't disperse them. The people are regularly brought coffee and food. Vladimir Goncharik is supposed to join their ranks shortly.[2]

"*Quelle noblesse!*" as regards the women . . . who normally supported themselves and their children throughout the twentieth century and generally did what men did. So why suddenly this *noblesse* and courtesy? What are its immediate reasons, and what larger social anxiety does it stand for? What major societal restratification does this dislocation of women from public space signal, and what purpose does it serve?

This chapter intends to go beyond multiple variations of the popular statement that women, potentially, were the greatest losers in post-socialist restructuring.[3] My intention is to make sense of their changing position and of transformation itself as it embraces class, nation, and gender as centerpieces of the post-1991 democratization project. I believe that the major social process in the post-Soviet world is the formation of class distinctions (through income inequality, i.e., through the working of the market), and class necessarily includes the emergence of masculine privilege. National projects serve the purpose of justifying the new social order; national issues, in their various incarnations (whether the demands of autonomy or independence, controversy over disputed territories, or some other argument) are mostly a manifestation of a class issue.

This situation does not imply the absence of national feeling on the part of actors involved, but rather suggests that the roots of the national feeling are in the group (class or "corporate") interests of those disproportionately represented in the articulation of the national cause, that is, intellectuals. National projects, as well as class ones, demand specific gender arrangements and invoke particular symbolic representations of men and women.

Methodologically, the chapter will be focused on analyzing how the post-1991 discourses of gender order have been incorporated into rethinking nationhood not just in terms of contents but also, as Edward Said suggests, in the form of the debate: "how it is said, by whom, where, and for whom."[4] The analysis of the debate as a "symbolic product" built into the cultural semantics of the political moment (which is about reaching democracy through national statehood) reveals that class liberation happens through nationalism; and articulation of a certain mode of gender relations is considered pivotal for the functioning of the national "imagined community."[5]

Though the focus of the chapter is on a particular country, the social and cultural pattern it represents is common to the whole postcommunist space. Other chapters in this volume and other research demonstrate similarities in patterns of social stratification across the region. In this text, I rely on my previous writing on gender and nationalism in postcommunist Belarus; some of the conclusions that I draw here were prepared for in earlier work, and hence the recurrence of some ideas, examples, and quotations.[6]

The Talk of the Nation

Contemporary Belarusian political and cultural discourse revolves around two ideas: of a "return to Europe" as an independent, awakened nation (preached by the opposition); and of integration with Russia, the big Slavic brother (the government plan). Each idea is accompanied by a specific set of economic and political assumptions and claims.

The first idea is portrayed as a nostalgic myth in the national memory, allegedly interrupted but not fully destroyed by the Soviet experience. Patriotic historians looking for a point of departure for a contemporary Belarusian nation-state, view the period of the Grand Duchy of Lithuania—the biggest country of medieval Europe, parts of which were eventually incorporated into different empires—as the "golden age" of Belarusian statehood (this point of view is contested by Lithuania, Poland, and even Russia, which have their own claims on that land and time). They believe that Belarus as a "thing" existed throughout recorded history, for in 1517 Francisk Skorina, a medical doctor and a writer, translated the Bible into Belarusian and published it. In 1588, the Grand Duchy's subchancellor, Leu Sapega, published in Belarusian the third Statut (Law Code) of the duchy, with his own preface, in which he recorded the issues of rule of law and "national" language as of grave importance. Radical literati, searching for the historical continuity of the nation, think of Adam Mickiewicz, the creator of the Polish literary canon, as a Belarusian, or, rather, a Litvan. He began his poem "Pan Tadeusz" with an exclamation "Oh, Lithuania, my fatherland!" (*O* Litwo, *oiczyzna moje*), used local folklore in his work, and in general was conscious of his Belarusian roots—and so also, contemporary intellectuals believe, were many other recognized pillars of other nations' heritage.

Thus, if one wanted to illustrate Ernest Gellner's "Ruritania"[7]—a territory with elites speaking the recognized language of the faraway court, the church (or churches) using another language for liturgy, multiple Jews (this was part of the Pale of Settlement) wrapped in their despised jargon, and the peasantry confined to their vernacular "speak"—the Belarusian-Lithuanian language territory could serve the purpose. Regional culture could, under the processes of modernization, become a kind of raw material for future nation building, if embraced in one package with a clear-cut class issue (inequality) as another resource. Yet for this to happen, for the community of the nation to be imagined, the work of certain human agents is necessary. Intellectuals articulate the cause, and it is fascinating to see how a cultural project and a political project breed on one another.

As with other peasant and subordinate communities, the turn-of-the-century national cultural idea emerged as a means of political empowerment, and its goals were defined as the freedom to use people's tongue in institutions and be educated in it, to get recognition for national culture, to get rid of backwardness, illiteracy, poverty, and to join the project of modernity that other European nations had been enjoying. Teachers, ethnographers, historians, and linguists, many of whom later went into actual politics, sought to awaken the people, to give them a name, to tell them "who they are," and to possibly achieve some autonomy or even create a state. Contemporary promoters of political independence, as well as those politicized intellectuals who at the turn of the twentieth century tried to legitimize the Belarusian nation and its presence in European civilization for the first time in modern history, see Belarusian ethnic lands (i.e., those where the peasantry spoke Belarusian) as "for several centuries an arena of political, national, religious and cultural struggle"[8] between Russia and Poland.

Belarusian statehood—as a republic within the USSR—was achieved in 1921, after several years of a power play between the Russian Provisional Government, Communists, nationalists, Germans who were occupying the country, Poles that were coming and retreating, and Western powers that were attempting to establish "true" ethnographic frontiers in the region after World War I (on the basis of the people's right to self-determination, proclaimed by both Woodrow Wilson and Vladimir Lenin). The 70 Soviet years are now the subject of a major controversy for national historians and a line of political division. Canadian scholar David Marples believes that Communists were both building and destroying the country.[9]

On the one hand, there were tremendous achievements in modernization. By the end of the Soviet period, Belarus had become an urbanized territory with numerous universities and advanced (to a great extent electronic) industries. On the other, patriotic historians argue, the nation's intelligentsia, which had been nurtured on turn-of-the-century ideals, fell victim to the purges of the 1930s, and the new one that emerged did not see itself outside the Soviet context and after World War II almost lost the national language. Educated people speak Russian (except a number of intellectuals promoting the national language cause), and less educated ones speak a mixture of two languages called *trasyanka,* an equivalent of Ukrainian *surzhik.* (There is state supported book publishing and newspapers in the national language.)

If one abandons the idea of an immediate linkage between language and nationhood (which is not necessary), then it is under the Soviet project that a community was formed that views itself as a Belarusian nation. However, the feeling of common belonging was tied—instead of to language and ancient history—to the Soviet modernization experience and even more to World War II. The war's huge casualties, with every fourth citizen killed (the highest rate in the world) and immense common suffering became the national shared past.

This past was inevitably tied to the idea of the Soviet Union as the chief power in defeating fascism, and, in a way, to the idea of socialism as a form of modernity that provides development and economic well-being. A member of a veterans' caucus explains the post-1991 choices of his generation: "We are now voting for the Soviet Union because it was the best we ever saw."[10] The "Soviet Union," in this case, implies closer ties with Russia and support for president Aleksandar Lukashenka, who won the 2001 elections largely by selling unification with Russia in one package with socialist-type welfare and resource distribution.

When, during the *perestroika* period, the national idea (encompassing language, history, ecological disasters, and Stalin's purges) once again emerged, very much as intellectuals' identity politics, they defined it in terms of democracy and of a European comeback through a nation-state. The justification was that the contemporary national revival—pointing toward democratization and creating a life patterned on that of developed Europe—would be based on the discovery of the "true" national history, which places medieval Belarusian statehood in the context of the European renaissance. Thus, the contemporary national movement supposedly established a continuity with the authentic past and suggests returning to a true, European self. The nation that emerged during the Soviet era was not the one anti-Soviet intellectuals would want to see; they refused to recognize it.[11]

But apparently the European idea (and what it encompasses) is not the common (or Soviet) people's project, and they have no "European self" to "recollect"; the Soviet Belarusian nation was the only one contemporary generations remember and have ever known. The Belarusian controversy, however, as well as national disputes elsewhere in the former Soviet Union, is only overtly about different types of nationhood or, as many political scientists, journalists and wider public put it, about *ancienne* nations versus Soviet "denationalization." In essence, it is about different methods of resource allocation—through market or policy.

If one looks into what the two parties preach "economically," one can see that Lukashenka's main point was a nonwithdrawal of the state from the social policy arena. What he really did—at least how he preached it and how it is presented in the government-controlled media—he paid wages, pensions, and allowances, however small; he resisted unemployment by refusing to fire "surplus" workers or close down factories; he insisted on fixed prices (they would rise anyway, but at least he did something); and he preserved free health care and the socialist welfare structure. He distributed resources, and having a need was reason enough for getting at least something. For the proponents of Western-type restructuring, these values look antimarket and antidemocratic. But for those who vote for them, they entail social justice.

The opposition—neoliberal and/or nationalist intellectuals—celebrated national independence, freedom, human rights, the market, free prices, and the competitiveness that they regarded as universal values. They still would not understand why the people who lost most of what they had after the disintegration of the USSR reject the market through which the nation would reach a Western-type prosperity. There is just no other way—see the luxury of the affluent West?

In the post-Soviet world, the opposition between a market economy (and liberal democracy with it) and socialism (and political coercion) as different ways of resource allocation happened to be wrapped up in the discourse on national issues. This discourse serves as a manifestation of a "class discontent"; it is not so much about national belonging as about "class" interests.

What I refer to by "class" here and below is not about one's place in production (as in Marxism) but about the distribution of life chances through the workings of the market (a Weberian perspective); stratification happens, as "the life chances accessible to different groups of the population are distributed unevenly as a collective outcome of the activity of individual economic agents who differ with regard to power in the market."[12] The national discourse is about urban intellectuals (and the language they speak, the version of history they construct, i.e., the symbolic means they use) and the societal arrangement from which they best benefit (or think they do) versus those have-nots (and their "speak") who lost more than they got in the brave new world that was supposed to emerge after 1991. A certain gender arrangement is at the core of these processes, providing the most elementary social stratification for class and nation.

Beyond 1991 and What Women Saw There: Gender, Nation, and Class

Women can be poor; men cannot be. What I mean is that being poor, women still remain women (and even feminine); they are women by the virtue of their bodies, and hardly anything (until it is something very special) can change this perception of what they are. This is not so with men. Manliness is not about their bodies (or not only about their bodies), and those not affluent enough certainly lack a big part of what masculinity is about. I refer here to the social construction of normative masculinity; he is a "man," and that is why he pays for dinner at the restaurant. The reverse would also be true; that is, paying for dinner makes him a man (a woman paying for dinner does not prove her femininity). The Belarusian opposition newspaper *Narodnaya Volya* (People's Will) presents this view of what men should be like as "discontent" with their post-Soviet lack of resources:

> To be a man. And this means, to be a husband, a father, a master in one's house, one's family, one's destiny, after all. But is it easy nowadays . . . to be a man? With a miserable wage of a farmer or a worker? A tiny welfare ration which for some reason is called a salary.[13]

It is not "now," however, but at some point in the Soviet era that masculinity first started to be perceived as somewhat of a problem. Societal concerns over the emasculation of males were first strongly expressed in the 1960s, when the living standards of Soviet people were rising. Overtly, gender debates were spurred by the article "Spare the Men!" in *Literaturnaya Gazeta* (which made a tremendous hit) and never stopped after that. Men were discovered to be physically weak, to be more prone to disease than women, and to have a shorter life expectancy. Besides, they were irresponsible, unable to take care of themselves (they smoked and drank!), and needing supervision and guidance in health and food issues by wives and mothers; these were supposed to "feed" their men with healthy food, arrange regular medical checkups (and in general take care of them).

The skill of arranging appointments with doctors has hardly anything to do with male biology, however, weak or strong as it might be, and the real reason for the perception of men as weak was related to the lack of "opportunities" for traditional masculinity to develop. The famous dissident Anna Natalia Malakhovskaya, who was expelled from the USSR in 1980 for starting the feminist journal *Maria,* recalls that it had published an article on how the Soviet way of life was disrupting the very domains where men could behave in a manly way and was thus channeling them into being unmanly or weak.[14]

Another way of saying this is that the Soviet gender order made it difficult to confirm masculinity as constructed through access to "money" (broadly understood). Thus, masculinity turns out to be part of class. Class is partially about income, and the Soviet "lack of masculinity" was a clear-cut class issue, or, rather, the issue of the absence of such. In that particular (classless) society, men did not have systemic superiority over women in their resources (they had some, of course, but in general women were dependent not on men but on the state for their livelihood), and at some point the society started feeling uneasy about this arrangement.

When Mikhail Gorbachev in one of his early *perestroika* speeches named liberation of women from the dual role (providing them with the possibility of not working so as to be better mothers) as one of the priorities, he was expressing that societal concern. But because other priorities were *glasnost'* and political reform, the "liberation of women" (a euphemism for sending them home) became tied to those and was socially acceptable along with other bourgeois class values (though we honestly did not see them as such then).

This said, a common and visible trend of the past decade in Eastern Europe and the countries of the former Soviet Union—a rise in masculinity[15]—gets a reason in the relationship of power (i.e., in the construction of domination and subordination). Throughout the past decade, quite a number of scholars have registered glorification of a strong male alongside sexualized and caregiving redefinitions of women: the abortion and reproduction debate, the sexualization and objectification of female bodies, the displacement of women from public life (of which sending them home on the election day in Minsk is a perfect example), the relocation of child care back into "women's hands" (from state agencies), and so on.

These redefinitions, being class bound in their nature (i.e., tied to class formation in the sphere of the symbolic and the "practical"), normally are not made overtly but rather within various processes of imagining the nation. The national idea provides a justification for the emerging system of class and gender inequality by "veiling" its true goals with nobler ones—those of "national freedom," and more specifically, of protecting "our women."

A Belarusian opposition thinker, the leader of the independence struggle (who had to flee the country for fear of repression and thus became a symbol of martyrdom for democracy's sake) equates the nation's military casualties throughout history with its losses from abortion and contraception, and he believes that both are parts of the anti-Belarusian genocide, for which Russian imperialism is responsible:

> Russians used the war and even military operations with the goal of genocide of the Belarusian nation. . . . Then, continuing medical genocide, they worked out the harmful policy of restraining Belarusian fertility and

> murdering the human fetus inside the woman's womb. . . . If Belarusian polity does not get rid of the aggression of Russian imperialism and does not do something about the Chernobyl legacy, then in the twenty-first century there will not be a single Belarusian left. The whole nation will be wiped out, to the last man.[16]

The nationalist position (the cited view is still considered extreme) combines patriarchal views on reproduction with liberal, "European" views on overtly political matters. Although freedom of the press is of undeniable value, the discourse disregards any rights to choose women might have as regards reproduction, for a complex (class and national) hierarchy builds on their subordination. Liberty and equality are attributes of the fraternity,[17] from which women are excluded; they are seen as bearers and reproducers of national culture and signifiers of the symbolic boundaries between "us" and "them,"[18] and that is why they need "protection." Thus, men also have obligations within the nation-building arrangement, as the following poem suggests. The poem, which was published in 1993, amid the heated debates on Belarusian independence versus integration with Russia, metaphorically represents Belarus as a suffering woman and powerfully articulates the female body as the national battlefield:

> Song about the Wife
>
> The Russians have slanting sabers,
> The Russians have the eyes of Batyi,
> Horse tails behind their backs,
> The motherland is a sweating mare.
>   Do not get beneath sharp sabers,
>   Do not believe Batyi's eyes,
>   Do not saddle the mare;
>   She will take you to a dark grave.
> And I have my own grave,
> And she loves me.
> She has loved me as a son and a husband,
> Though I beat her with my whip,
>   Asking as the lash falls:
>   Did you sleep with others before me?
>   I slept with the Muscovite;
>   Slept with the Pole,

> But the executioner's block was my bed.
> I slept with your father the Litsvin [Litvan],
> And now I sleep with you—my son.
> Look into the forest rivers,
> Do you have the eyes of Batyi?
> Do you have a horse's tail behind your back?
> Look with whom your motherland slept!
> (*Note:* "Batyi," in the second line represents a Tartar-Mongolian Khan, a symbol of cruelty.)[19]

The emotional impact of this poem is extraordinary (in the original, the verse is absolutely beautiful and leaves no doubt of the author's sincere inspiration), as is the powerful way it engenders national self-definition. The intellectuals' turmoil over proving the nation's legitimacy (neither Poles nor Russians, but people in ourselves) becomes the issue of female purity within the context of the "national mythology." The image of the woman-nation who does not give herself to the rapist-colonizer is related to the outstanding figure in the national pantheon: that of Ragneda, the daughter of the tenth-century prince of Polatsk. When, as the legend goes, she rejected the Kievan prince Vladimir, he captured and burned the town, killed Ragneda's father and brother, raped the girl, and took her away to Kiev. It is believed that Ragneda later returned to her homeland with the teenage son, who was her protector against the brutal father (who meanwhile had turned ancient Rus to Christianity), and founded the town of Zaslaw'je, where her grave supposedly lies (a site with this name really exists).

The story of Ragneda is part of the cultural battle against the idea of Rus as the cradle of Eastern Slavic civilization and, through this, of the Russian empire. So this battle is about today's sovereignty and nation-state. The story is taken as evidence of the equally strong and ancient state in Belarusian lands, which was not willing to submit to Rus, either then or later. In contrast to the term "reunification" used in the historical books of the Soviet period, the writings of the 1990s identify the incorporation of Belarus into Russia at the end of the eighteenth century as invasion and conquest:

> For many years our school textbooks and other publications had it that for centuries Belarusians had been trying to unite with the fraternal Russian people and to live in one state with them. . . . This is not true. . . . Belarusians respected the neighboring people but they never wanted to be under Russian tsars. They remembered only too well how Ivan the

> Terrible killed and imprisoned inhabitants of Polatsk. They also remembered how a hundred years later Russian *voivodes* ordered to kill all the inhabitants of the Belarusian town of Mstislau. . . . It has forever remained in the people's memory that soldiers of Peter the Great exploded the chief temple of our country, Sofia's cathedral in Polatsk.[20]

Thus reads the 1996 book that describes an earlier impossible version of national history for children. The adult vision of the poem eroticizes the conquest and makes the woman crucial for the nation's "honor."

As the "sex and conquest" imagery reveals, the producers of the nationalist discourse construct their collectivity very much by opposing the "colonizing other" (at this time, Russia), who, as the poem above suggests, is threatening to "rape" the woman-nation. The political message given through a sexual metaphor calls for potency and "manhood" as the precondition of independence, for in the cultural constructions of communities that rethink their self-definitions versus powerful others (also colonial and postcolonial communities) emasculated native males are the idiom for disempowerment in relations with the oppressor. Male strength equals the nation's strength, but in the long run it equals male class position.

The workings of post-Soviet society have already resulted in some proportion of strong men or, rather, men never accused of weakness: the "new rich." Popular culture has created a metaphor for their supposed strength; they are often portrayed (in films, anecdotes, fiction, and caricatures) as armed buttheads with huge muscles and heavy golden chains on hairy chests. But in fact, Boris Berezovsky of Russia, whose assets are enormous, does not look physically strong.

The question of whether the rich are really "like you and me" has been a captivating one for many; as social research testifies, they are definitely not the drunken banditry of urban folklore. The new really rich and powerful (who are almost 100 percent male) are usually well educated and connected. In a paper on income inequality in the new Russia, Eric Shiraev mentions that "most young entrepreneurs, bankers, and real estate brokers . . . had a jump-start within the old Soviet social and political establishment,"[21] where they were members of the Soviet *nomenklatura* and Communist Party or Komsomol leaders (which included very few women).

When was it that the Soviet elite and the *nomenklatura* started feeling that for them the Soviet system of resource allocation was too tight? Their power and resources (i.e., their social capital) was due to their status, not to something they "owned"; moreover, that status could not be passed on to their children. They came to believe that with their resources, connections, and education, they would be better off in the market. That was the emergence of a class-based stratification instead of a status-based one. Bulgarian sociologist Dimitrina Petrova mentioned in 1994 that what actually happened in 1991 was not democratization but liberation of class (meaning that it "liberated" itself by breaking the old system of constraints). For the new powerful male class. the market (and liberal democracy with it) symbolizes social justice.

"Mafia" representations of the new class result from their drive for economic accumulation, which "symbolically excludes the new rich from ranks of the cultured, whatever their 'objective' cultural attainments."[22] Even if they are not necessarily physically strong, they are nevertheless seen as manly. Their manliness is also confirmed through "sexual" consumption; it is for them that new men's magazines publish high-end pornography and the whole industry of high-class sexual services emerged.[23] This "was to be expected," because the formation of a Western-style (in terms of possession of resources, opportunities of income, and mode of consumption) middle class and (normative) masculinity go together, and women become objectified in the process. (Emphasizing male sexual potency is a spectacular way to articulate class belonging.)

The subordination of women is a necessary element of both class and nation becoming mature; a certain gender order provides primary social stratification for them. This subordination is not presented as such, of course, and it takes the form of a "redomestication" of women: protecting them, and in general placing them within the private sphere. An opposition journalist believes that "the idea of the necessity, of pleasure, of beauty, finally, of sacredness of housework, of the work for their families, their children, their husbands and, by this, their own happiness."[24] is now most needed for women and that by adhering to it women will best serve the common cause.

But alongside the new rich, post-socialist restructuring produced others. In the journey from status to class, a big part of the intelligentsia (those who are really cultured) was left "outside." Though it had certain status privileges or at least symbolic authority under the Soviet regime, in the new world intellectuals lost their former symbolic status (a poet or a writer stopped being a national oracle), and did not join the ranks of the new rich and the powerful. The highly emotional rhetoric of the nationalist vision is a way to justify a different social hierarchy, to return to the group some of the "old glory," to keep the sense of distinction.

Various national projects serve as a legitimization of the intellectuals' corporate (class) interests, on the one hand, and a justification of middle-class masculinity, on the other. They articulate the nation to bestow themselves, at least symbolically, with the status (this happens to be "masculine" status) they lack under other arrangements. It is at them that a poster was targeted at the Women's March against Poverty in Minsk in 1997, imploring men to fight Lukashenka's antinational regime: "Men! Get off your knees! We love heroes, not slaves!"[25]

During the 2001 elections, the members of the opposition, who were losing them as citizens (the elections were not fair, but the opposition had no chance anyway, for it did not articulate what people wanted), attempted to win as strong males—by "protecting" their women, but in fact silencing them. A "nation" arises in response to the urge to construct a new social hierarchy, which is seen by the community members as fair, but in which redomestication of women is a necessary element, for this is what the assertion of masculine class builds on. The question of what was at the original core of human civilization (or what came "earlier")—class stratification or gender inequality?—has so far not been solved by social science.

Concluding Comments

Several points need to be made to crown the story. The first one is related to the "nationalism as class" generalization and, hence, to the question of to what extent it is legitimate. While recognizing that the actual social tapestry of the transition is more complicated than what has been presented in this chapter—groups, actors, and interests are more diverse—I would still argue that postcommunist nation building is a "class" project. Roman Szporluk, a distinguished scholar of nation building at Harvard University, pointed out in 1991 that in the USSR, economic liberalism went hand in hand with "nationalism" (in the sense of ideas of national independence). The ideal of a market economy was most strongly articulated "at the edges," where nation building resumed (in Estonia, Latvia, Lithuania, and Western Ukraine), whereas adherence to "socialist" administrative methods was characteristic of "the Soviet imperial center."[26]

Szporluk supports his point with the writings of Ernst Gellner himself, one of the founding fathers of contemporary nationalism studies, who also noticed that Estonian nationalists were partisans of economic liberalism and was fascinated by the trend. Everywhere in the former Soviet republics, the "independence" struggle has been initiated by intellectuals (or apparatchiks!) for whom, as Michael Kennedy puts it, the state of the nation is never what it should be and always calls for improvement.[27]

In other words, it calls for a different social hierarchy. And everywhere, in the subsequent process of class formation, elites were eventually better rewarded than those rank-and-file citizens who flooded the streets of Eastern European and Central Asian capitals in the late 1980s. And still more, these democratically elected governments invoke and recreate patriarchal gender systems as a means of creating a "democracy" (much in the same way as Belarusian antiauthoritarian and anticommunist opposition) or, rather, patriarchal gender systems recreate themselves "naturally" under these governments. To put this last point in context, to show how this chapter is about women—who, despite their "absence" (absence in the sense of descriptions of what women per se do or articulate), are absolutely central to it, for it is through women that the whole story builds its meaning and through whom the narrative addresses how different stratification systems (class and nation) are tied together—I must invoke theorizing on the concept of gender.

Gender, as Joan Scott defines it, is "the social organization of sexual difference," the way male/female domination and subordination are constructed and legitimized.[28] She believes that gender is a primary way of signifying relationships of power, and that is why the meanings of sexual difference are contested as a part of many kinds of struggles for power. These struggles, though they build on gender, may not be about gender itself.[29]

Thus, in trying to explain women in postcommunist transitions—their status changes, their gains and losses—we cannot look at gender alone, and certainly not only at women's issues or what women do. We also should look at what societal struggles for power are focused on; these are the positions in new stratification (inequality) systems of class and nation, both of which need to rework gender (but not only, of course) as the most elementary step of human social organization.

Yet it would be too simplistic to think of post-Soviet women as a monolithic group—they also are classed—or to explain the status changes by referring to the economic interest of certain groups alone. There is also the symbolic dimension, the construction of new meaning, an introduction through a discourse of particular images and a repression of others. National projects as well as class ones, first demanding specific gender arrangements, invoke particular symbolic representations (i.e., "strong" males, such as fathers and warriors) "protecting" pure females (the mothers of the nation and its maidens). Or it may be responsible males supporting their wives and children. In this way, the changing status of men is inextricable from the changing status of women, and they are transforming in tandem. They work through each other, need each other, and are intricately tied to the emergence of class and national identity.

Notes

1. The Internet domains home.by, minsk.by, org.by, unibel.by, and nsys.by ("by" stands for Belarus) were blocked.

2. All the messages were at <http://www.charter97.org/r/index/phtml>; translations into English are by the author.

3. Tarja Cronberg, "The Feeling of Home: Russian Women in the Defense Industry and the Transformation of Their Identities," *European Journal of Women's Studies,* 4, no. 3 (1997): 263–81.

4. Edward Said, "Intellectuals in the Post-Colonial World," in *Post-Colonialism: Critical Concepts in Literary and Cultural Studies,* ed. Diana Brydon (Routledge, 2000), 31.

5. Nira Yuval-Davis, *Gender and Nation* (Beverly Hills, Calif.: Sage Publications, 1997), 23.

6. See Elena Gapova, "Open Forum: Women in the National Discourse in Belarus," *European Journal of Women's Studies* 5 (1998): 477–88; Elena Gapova, "National Dreams and Domestic Goddesses," *Translations 15,* no. 1 (1998); Elena Gapova, Almira Usmanova, and Andrea Peto, eds., *Gendernye istorii Vostochnoi Evropy* [Gendered Histories from Eastern Europe], Minsk, Belarus: European Humanities University, 2002; Elena Gapova, "On Nation, Gender, and Class Formation in Belarus . . . and Elsewhere in the Post-Soviet World," *Nationalities Papers* 30 (2002): 639–62.

7. Ernest Gellner, *Nations and Nationalism* (Oxford: Oxford University Press, 1983), 58.

8. Nicholas Vakar, *Belorussia: The Making of a Nation* (Cambridge, Mass.: Harvard University Press, 1956), 109.

9. David Marples, *Belarus: From Soviet Rule to Nuclear Catastrophe* (New York: Saint Martin's Press, 1996), 79–114.

10. *Narodnaya volya,* June 23, 2001.

11. I go into the issue in more detail in Gapova, "On Nation, Gender, and Class Formation in Belarus."

12. Timo Piirainen, *Towards a New Social Order in Russia: Transforming Structures and Everyday Life.* (Aldershot, U.K.: Dartmouth, 1997), 29.

13. *Narodnaya Volya,* no. 166 (1997).

14. Anna Natalia Malakhovskaya, 20 let tomu nazad v Lenigrade zarodilos' zhenskoe dvizhenie [Twenty years ago, the women's movement emerged in Leningrad], *Dialog zhenshchin,* no 9 (1999): 28.

15. Peggy Watson, "The Rise of Masculinism in Eastern Europe," *New Left Review,* no. 198 (1993): 71–82.

16. Zyanon Paz'nyak, "Phyzychnae znishchenne belaruskai natsii" [Physical destruction of the Belarusian nation], *Narodnaya Volya,* July 18, 2001.

17. Carole Pateman, *The Sexual Contract* (Stanford, Calif.: Stanford University Press, 1988), 114.

18. Yuval-Davis, *Gender and Nation,* 39–67.

19. Anatol' Sys, "Vershi" [Verses], *Krynitsa,* [Literary journal], no 9 (1993). The poems are published in the English translation (mine with Bradley R. Strahan) in *Eastern Visions/Visions International* (Washington, D.C.), no. 52 (1996).

20. Uladzimir Arlou, *Adkul' nash rod* [Where do our people come from] (Minsk: Bat'kaushchyna, 1996), 89.

21. Eric Shiraev, "The New Nomenclature and Increasing Income Inequality," in *The Russian Transformation: Political, Sociological and Psychological Aspects,* ed. Betty Glad and Eric Shiraev (New York: Saint Martin's Press, 1999), 110.

22. George Faraday, *Revolt of the Filmmakers* (University Park: Pennsylvania State University Press, 2000), 153.

23. Eliot Borenstein, "About That: Deploying and Deploring Sex in Post-Soviet Russia," *Studies in XX Century Literature,* winter 2000: 51–75.

24. *Litaratura i Mastatstva,* February 13, 1998.

25. *Svaboda,* February 23, 1997.

26. Roman Szporluk, *Russia, Ukraine, and the Breakup of the Soviet Union* (Stanford, Calif.: Hoover Institution Press, 2000), 264.

27. Michael Kennedy, *The Liabilities of Liberalism and Nationalism after Communism: Polish Businessman in the Articulation of the Nation,* Center for Research on Social Organization Working Paper 561 (Ann Arbor: University of Michigan, 1998).

28. Joan Scott, introduction to *Gender and the Politics of History* (New York: Columbia University Press, 1988), 2.

29. Joan Scott, "Gender: A Useful Category of Historical Analysis," in *Gender and the Politics of History,* 28–53.

Part II

Women and Rural Household Economies

5

Feminizing the New Silk Road: Women Traders in Rural Kazakhstan

Cynthia Werner

For centuries, male caravan traders journeyed across the steppes and deserts of Central Asia along the legendary Silk Road. Precious commodities, such as silk, ivory, gold, and fur, exchanged hands numerous times as they traversed distances up to 7,000 miles. After declining in the fifteenth century,

This chapter is based on fieldwork conducted in southern Kazakhstan between 1992 and 2001. The author thanks the following organizations for funding various stages of research that contribute directly to this paper: the Social Science Research Council (SSRC), the International Research and Exchanges Board (IREX), the Wenner-Gren Foundation for Anthropological Research, the National Council for Eurasian and East European Research (NCEEER), the Department of Anthropology and the Center for Global Change and World Peace at Indiana University, and the Lowry Mays College of Business and the Women's Studies Program at Texas A&M University. Some of the funds for the SSRC, IREX, and NCEEER grants were provided by the U.S. Department of State (Title VIII). None of these organizations is responsible for the views expressed here. An earlier version of this chapter was published as "Between Market and Family: Women Traders on the New Silk Road," in *Gender in Economic Life,* ed. Gracia Clark (Lanham, Md.: Altamira Press, 2003).

Silk Road trade was further disrupted in the twentieth century with the formation of the Soviet Union and its nearly impenetrable border with the outside world.[1] Since the fall of the Soviet Union, the bazaars of Soviet Central Asia have once again filled with foreign goods.

On the New Silk Road, the old commodities have been replaced by "modern" global commodities, such as ready-made clothing, packaged foods, and electronic goods. And the earlier forms of transportation—horses and camels—have been replaced by airplanes, trains, and buses. Nevertheless, the nature of this trade is imbued with the spirit of the ancient Silk Road: The trade fills local markets with highly coveted luxury goods, the commodities cross numerous hands before they reach their final destination, and the merchants gain exposure to other lifestyles through travel.

One of the more striking aspects of the New Silk Road trade is the predominance of Central Asian women in the marketplace. In particular, women dominate the exchange of cloth and clothing that are exchanged as gifts, and also of food products that are used to feed families and honor guests. The merchant women who sell these goods spend long hours outside the household, buying and selling goods in public marketplaces. The high visibility of merchant women, including Muslim women, stands in contrast to popular stereotypes of secluded Muslim women. Not only do these Muslim women work in public places; they also travel to markets in distant towns, where their activities are less likely to be observed by kinsmen and neighbors.

On the basis of ethnographic fieldwork, this chapter explores the lives of Kazakh market women in rural Kazakhstan. The chapter begins with a review of the theoretical literature on women and work that addresses the factors that generally affect women's paid employment and the impact of women's earnings on patriarchal social structures. Next, the chapter turns to the village of Shauildir in the Southern Kazakhstan *oblast'* (region) and provides a description of the basic living conditions, the Soviet policies to emancipate women, and the impact of post-Soviet economic change.[2] Finally, the chapter discusses the development of small-scale trade as a household survival strategy, the role of women in the marketplace, and the impact of trade activities on women, their households, and their family relations.

Women, Work, and Theory

All societies have ideal gender roles that influence the activities and occupations of men and women. Although both men and women perform tasks that contribute toward household well-being, female gender roles are typically formed around the practical realities of childbirth and child rearing. Unless alternative options exist for child care, women are responsible for tasks that are less likely to interfere with child-rearing activities. This includes domestic tasks, such as cooking food and cleaning the house, as well as tasks performed outside the household, such as gathering nuts or gardening.

Cross-cultural studies of women demonstrate that female-dominated tasks, such as child care, are rarely accorded as much prestige as male-dominated tasks, such as hunting. In modern industrial societies where individuals work for wages, income-earning "work" is valued more than unpaid "housework," men are viewed as the "primary breadwinners" in two-parent households, and the average income and prestige for occupations dominated by men is higher than those for occupations dominated by women.[3]

In modern societies, at least four factors influence women's prospects for wage employment. First, many societies have social norms that limit women's mobility outside the household and women's interactions with nonkin. For example, in Muslim and Asian societies where family honor is closely linked to women's behavior, women who work outside the home may compromise their family's reputation. Until recently, most Egyptian women perceived work outside the home as undesirable because it took them away from their housework, compromised their reputation, humiliated their husbands (who are expected to provide for their families), and changed the quality of their daily lives.[4] Despite social restrictions on women's mobility in Muslim and Asian societies, women have cleverly managed to earn income without leaving the home.

For many women, earning income is less problematic than working outside the home, especially when the work is "invisible" (and thus does not diminish the importance of male wage earners) and when the work does not disrupt women's housework activities. In pre-Soviet Central Asia, women earned money by selling homemade bread, raising silkworms, sewing clothes, and trading goods. Women traders relied on their husbands or male relatives to serve as middlemen, or more rarely, a small group of women would sell goods on the edge of the bazaar.[5] Similar situations can be found in contemporary Muslim societies. Among the Muslim Hausa of Nigeria, approximately two-thirds of the women earn money out of their homes by using their children as go-betweens to trade food, clothing, jewelry, and perfume.[6] And in urban Turkey, working-class women sell leather and wool clothing, which they produce at home and market with the help of male relatives.[7]

Second, women's opportunities to work are constrained by the practical issue of child care. For many jobs, including factory jobs and most office jobs, women cannot simultaneously care for their children and "work" outside the home. Some women choose to work until they marry and have children, and then again after their children reach a certain age. This has become a social norm among working-class families in Hong Kong, where unmarried daughters work in textile factories until they get married and stop working to become full-time mothers and housewives.[8] In other contexts, women turn to family members, social networks, and day care facilities to provide child care while they work. In the Soviet context, subsidized day care encouraged women to enter the workforce, and post-Soviet structural adjustment policies have reduced these subsidies and thereby hindered women's ability to work for wages.[9]

Third, women's prospects for wage employment are affected by economic and political factors. In the United States, for example, middle-class women were encouraged to work during the World War II when there was a shortage of workers; and when the war was over, they were discouraged from working as their husbands and brothers returned home.[10] In the Soviet Union, women were catapulted into the workforce to increase economic productivity *and* to fulfill ideological goals.[11] In other contexts, household needs, which are often affected by household composition, have a larger influence on an individual woman's decision to work than do national needs. In female-headed, single-parent households, for example, a woman is likely to seek wage employment, unless state welfare programs and/or interhousehold transfers provide sufficient income for her family.

Fourth, women and households are affected by globalization. International organizations, such as the International Monetary Fund and the World Trade Organization, accelerate the pace of globalization by linking international aid and membership status to the reduction of price controls and other government subsidies in developing countries. Several scholars have noted how, in Egypt, these economic reforms have simultaneously raised the cost of living and brought new social attitudes toward women in the workplace.[12] By the early 1980s, large numbers of lower-class and middle-class women were starting to earn money by performing services in other people's homes and by working in factories and offices. New social attitudes do not represent a complete break from the past. When judging the appropriateness of a certain job for women, Egyptians consider whether or not a woman's honor can be protected at the workplace.[13] To diminish concerns about their respectability, many working women have chosen to wear the veil (*hijab*) for the first time in their lives.

Throughout the world, globalization has also increased consumer desires by providing media images of alternative lifestyles and by supplying new consumer goods in local marketplaces. In Kazakhstan, for example, foreign soap operas and foreign consumer goods arrived at about the same time in the early 1990s. Although the soap operas help people imagine new material comforts and new fashions, the marketplace provides opportunities to purchase these things.[14]

Feminist scholars have addressed a number of issues concerning women and work. Cross-cultural studies of gender ideologies have demonstrated that much of the "work" that women perform, although vital to household maintenance, is not even regarded as work, and is therefore devalued in comparison with men's work. This includes housework in most societies, social networking activities in India, the maintenance of kinship ties in the United States, and the home production of clothing in Turkey.[15]

In situations where women start to work outside the home, feminist scholars are still debating whether or not wage employment improves women's lives and/or changes patriarchal gender ideologies.[16] The jury is still out. In her study of working women in Hong Kong, Janet Salaff concludes that wage employment does allow women to enjoy some increased freedom and autonomy, but the benefits of wage employment are limited and temporary.[17] In her study of women in the Soviet Union, Mary Buckley explains how the state went to great lengths to change attitudes toward working women and to increase women's participation in the workforce but did little to change gender relations at home. Thus, Buckley argues that Soviet women were stuck with the "double burden" of doing all the housework *and* working long hours outside the home.[18]

It is somewhat surprising that there have been so few anthropological studies of market women, because they can be found in so many different cultural settings.[19] Market women provide an interesting case for addressing theoretical issues concerning women and work because their work is highly visible, fairly entrepreneurial, and relatively flexible when it comes to child care issues. In her study of women and development, Ester Boserup includes a fascinating cross-cultural look at market women.[20] She finds that women are not very active traders in the Middle East, especially in comparison with Africa and Latin America.[21] As she notes, "In no other field do ideas about the proper role of women contrast more vividly than in the case of market trade."[22]

Although trade may be viewed as inappropriate work for women in many Muslim societies, it is just as likely to be viewed as such for men in other societies. In many (non-Muslim) Southeast Asian societies, for example, the traits of frugality and aggressiveness that are required for successful marketing are perceived to be undesirable in men yet admirable in women.[23] In the present study of market women in Kazakhstan, women are simply perceived to have better trading skills.

Fieldwork in Shauildir Village

This study of merchant women is based on ethnographic research in Shauildir village in Southern Kazakhstan *oblast'*, approximately 180 kilometers northwest of the city of Shymkent. More than 96 percent of the 8,300 residents of Shauildir are Kazakh-speaking Kazakhs.[24] Since 1930, Shauildir has served as the administrative center for Otyrar *raion* (district), which specializes in the husbandry of coat-producing Astrakhan sheep. As an administrative center, Shauildir has more government buildings, small enterprises, schools, and hospitals than the typical village, and thus it provides more diverse employment opportunities.[25]

Most Shauildir residents live in permanent single-family houses made with mud-brick walls, wooden floors, and corrugated tin roofs.[26] For decades, the households of Shauildir have pursued complex strategies to make ends meet. Most households have combined the wages of at least one state employee with the domestic production of vegetables and livestock.[27]

I lived with a Kazakh family in Shauildir while conducting doctoral research in 1994 and 1995, and then I returned for several additional months of research in 1998, 2000, and 2001. While conducting a survey of 100 households, including 25 "merchant" households, I became interested in market women and the ways in which their trade activities affect their family lives and gender roles. Most of the data for this chapter were collected during the summer of 1998, at which time I interviewed eighteen market women in Shauildir.

In the summer of 2001, I conducted follow-up interviews with twelve merchants, including several of the women interviewed in 1998. Some of the merchants interviewed for this study worked in the local bazaars; others sold goods in small street stands or in independent shops and kiosks. Most of the women interviewed for this study work in local marketplaces. Their experiences differ from those of migratory merchant women who regularly sell goods in large urban markets and then send wage remittances home to their village families.[28]

Women's Lives in Shauildir

To explain how trade affects women's lives, it is important to present a picture of women's lives in Shauildir. The recent expansion of market trade is clearly a post-Soviet phenomenon. However, the mobility and freedom that Kazakh women now enjoy should be viewed as an important legacy of Soviet rule. Before the Soviet era, Kazakh women did not receive any formal education, they did not work outside of the home, and their marriages were arranged by their parents. Kazakh society corresponded to Deniz Kandiyoti's notion of "classic patriarchy," which she defined as a situation in which women live in patrilocally extended households where they are subordinate both to all the men *and* the more senior women.[29]

Beginning in the late 1920s, the Soviet state made a zealous attempt to "emancipate" Central Asian women by providing education and employment opportunities. In her study of rural Uzbek women, Elizabeth Constantine argues that Soviet policies were relatively effective in changing women's status *and* women's expectations.[30] Similar observation can be made for the village of Shauildir. With very few exceptions, women under the age of 50 years have completed high school or technical school (*teknikum*).

According to the 1989 census, 48 percent of the women working in Otyrar *raion* had completed high school (as their highest achievement), 25 percent had completed a technical school, and 13 percent had completed an institute of higher education. All education is coeducational, so young Kazakh girls have plenty of social interaction with nonrelated boys. Employment outside of the home is also very common. In 1992, 89.9 percent of the working-age women in Shauildir were employed in the public sector (including those on maternity leave), and women represented 48.5 percent of the workforce in Shauildir.[31]

Although women frequently work outside of the household, their domestic responsibilities reflect more "traditional" gender roles. From the age of 5 or 6 years, girls are socialized to help with the housework. Women's household chores include a number of daily tasks: caring for children, preparing meals, serving tea to guests, cleaning the house, washing clothes, arranging the daily bedding, milking cows and horses, working in the household garden, and assisting men with the care of domestic livestock. Many women also bake their own bread, prepare a variety of dairy products, and sew clothes for their family.

Meanwhile, men also perform several household tasks. They take care of the domestic livestock, the help out with the garden work, and they help with child care. In comparison with men, women have very little leisure time at home. To complete their household chores, many women rely on the help of their children and their daughters-in-law. For children, the boundaries between "female" and "male" household chores is much more flexible. With the exception of preparing food and washing clothes, boys are known to help out with household chores, especially in households that have a shortage of female labor. The expectations for boys' help, however, is lower than that for girls' help.

Women also work hard to maintain household networks by serving guests, helping others serve guests, and preparing gifts for various occasions. With hospitality as one of the central elements of Kazakh culture, households frequently host dinner parties to socialize with friends, and they occasionally sponsor large feasts to celebrate new marriages and male circumcision.[32] These events are enjoyed by women, yet they also burden women with additional responsibilities. Gift exchange is another aspect of women's role in household networking. Different occasions call for different gifts, and women are responsible for selecting and presenting most gifts on behalf of their household.[33]

Concerning marriage, Kazakh women have more control over the selection of spouses than they did in pre-Soviet times, though this freedom has been on the decline during the past decade with the rise of nonconsensual bride kidnappings. In the 1990s, in Southern Kazakhhstan *oblast',* approximately 60 percent of surveyed couples were married through the practice of bride kidnapping, and of those, nearly 20 percent involved minimal consent from the bride.[34] Although some brides are kidnapped with their consent, others are kidnapped with neither their prior knowledge nor consent.[35]

In addition to bride kidnapping, some couples are married through what is being called an "arranged marriage," a tradition that is being revived and recreated in the post-Soviet period. Today, arranged marriages are frequently initiated by young couples yet formally arranged by consenting parents. With few exceptions, marriages take place only after the bride and the groom have finished high school. Village girls typically marry between the ages of 17 and 22 years; boys marry at slightly later ages. Depending on household priorities and family resources, women may or may not live with their husband's parents after marriage.[36]

Upon marriage, a woman takes on several new social roles. In addition to becoming a wife (*ayeil*) and an eventual mother (*sheshe*), a married woman becomes a daughter-in-law (*kelin*). A good *kelin* is expected to respect her in-laws by providing unpaid household services for them. The expectations for daughters-in-law are higher if they are "in hand" (i.e., living in the same household). Nevertheless, expectations exist whether or not the young couple lives with the groom's parents. Further, the English term "daughter-in-law" is somewhat misleading because the social role of a *kelin* is not limited to a woman's relationship with her husband's parents. In other words, the services of a *kelin* can be requested by other relatives on her husband's side. For example, a woman may "invite" her husband's brother's *kelin* to come help her prepare food for guests or to perform other tasks.

This portrayal of women's lives in Shauildir is far from complete, but it should provide some background for understanding the position of market women in Shauildir. The following section describes how village lives have been transformed by post-Soviet changes.

Poverty and the Post-Soviet Economy

Shortly after independence was achieved in December 1991, the leaders of Kazakhstan initiated the transition from a socialist planned economy to a capitalist market economy. In 1993, the government introduced a new national currency and a comprehensive structural adjustment reform program. The structural reforms include the liberalization of prices for consumer goods; the reduction of state subsidies for transportation, housing, and other services; the privatization of some state-owned enterprises; and the downsizing of other state-owned enterprises.

Similar policies were launched throughout other countries of the former Soviet Union as a "shock therapy" approach to economic transition.[37] Although these policies are intended to increase a country's gross domestic product by reducing governmental expenses and liberalizing the economy, they often have the unintended consequence of increasing poverty, especially among women.[38]

Structural adjustment policies have had a definite impact on Shauildir, not unlike other rural communities throughout the former Soviet Union. There has been a sharp decline in the average standard of living, and there is a growing disparity between wealthy and poor households. Throughout the 1990s, villagers complained about extremely high inflation, increased unemployment, and reduced state income. With the dissolution of several prominent state-owned enterprises in the region, including the state farms, the nurseries, and the bread factory, many villagers lost their regular source of income. Until the late 1990s, those still employed by the remaining state-owned enterprises were often paid 6 to 8 months behind schedule. With rising costs, these salaries rarely provide enough to offset basic expenses for food, clothing, and energy.

The transition process has delivered several serious blows to Kazakh women in particular. First, although women have experienced high rates of employment in Soviet Kazakhstan (up to 49 percent of the registered labor force), women lost more jobs during the initial transition years.[39] Second, as Tatiana Zhurzhenko explains in chapter 1 of this volume, the post-Soviet state has terminated its social contract with women and transferred the costs of social reproduction to households. In Kazakhstan, this is vividly illustrated by cutbacks to the heavily subsidized day care programs.[40] As a result, working women have to become more dependent on social networks for child care and/or find jobs, such as trading, that allow them to bring their children to the workplace.[41]

Kazakh households in Shauildir have developed new strategies to cope with these new post-Soviet strains on household economies. Before the transition, most households were already pursuing complex survival strategies, by combining the wages of at least one state employee with the domestic production of vegetables and livestock. Similar to the Viliui Sakha described by Susan Crate in chapter 6 of this volume, most Kazakh households have increased the production of food for domestic consumption in the post-Soviet period.

In addition, many households have turned to new sources of income from private farming, handicraft production, or small-scale trade. Both men and women have become more entrepreneurial. Though men may earn money as videographers at wedding feasts or truck drivers for private livestock sale, women may earn money as seamstresses or weavers. Small-scale trade, the focus of this chapter, is an entrepreneurial activity pursued by both men and women.[42]

Patterns of Trade on the New Silk Road

The expansion of bazaar trade signifies a sharp break with the Soviet period when the state controlled the production and distribution of most goods. Although small neighborhood and village bazaars did operate in the past, they were primarily limited to fresh produce, livestock, and secondhand goods. There was also an active "black market" for coveted goods, including banned imports. Anyone who was involved in the black market trade was either profiting at the expense of the state or illegally selling goods from abroad. In contrast, many Kazakhs today view small-scale trade as one of their most viable options for survival.[43]

In rural areas, this is especially true for the towns and villages that have central marketplaces and easy access to railways and larger cities. For these reasons, Shauildir is ideally situated. As an administrative region, there were already two semiweekly, state-run bazaars in place, one specializing in livestock and one in food products and household goods. A third privately owned daily bazaar was opened in 1994 to accommodate the increased volume of trade. Shauildir also benefits from its relative proximity to several cities with large trade centers. Turkestan, Shymkent, and Tashkent are 2, 3, and 6 hours away by bus or train.

Because the marketplace attracts individuals from various backgrounds, it is somewhat difficult to characterize the new class of village merchants. Some of them are displaced shopkeepers with sales experience, whereas others are displaced workers from other fields, such as nursing and teaching. In Shauildir, one can find merchants in three local bazaars, dozens of independent kiosks, and numerous street corners. Some merchants work daily, and others resort to trade on those occasions when they need some extra cash. Many of the part-time merchants in particular are still full-time employees in other sectors. Some merchants sell home-produced goods, such as fermented horse milk, and others exclusively buy and resell consumer goods. Most village traders buy goods in nearby cities within Kazakhstan, but a few travel across national borders to buy goods in Uzbekistan or Iran.

With the exception of the semiweekly livestock bazaar, which is dominated by men, women outnumber men in the local marketplace, especially when it comes to older and elderly merchants. On one day in 1998, I counted seventy-five merchants working in the daily bazaar where food products, clothing, and household goods can be purchased. Fifty-six percent of them were adult women, 16 percent were girls, 19 percent were adult men, and 9 percent were boys. Although merchants typically specialize in either food or clothing, most merchants sell a variety of goods. On that particular day, 40 percent of the merchants were selling fruits and vegetables, 32 percent were selling clothing, 30 percent were selling rice and pasta, 28 percent were selling candy and cookies, 20 percent were selling home-produced goods, and 4 percent were selling meat. Unlike some marketplaces, the merchants are not organized into any association or organization. Prices are set informally by each trader, depending on initial cost, local availability, and local demand. Though merchants do not work together to establish prices, they do cooperate informally, for example, by watching a neighboring merchant's goods while she runs an errand.

The gender differences in the marketplace can be explained from both economic and cultural perspectives. From an economic perspective, there are more women in the bazaars because more women have been laid off in the post-Soviet period, especially during the early transition years.[44] Alternative, cultural explanations for women's dominance in the marketplace emerge in interviews with both men and women. According to some informants, Kazakh men just do not handle money as well as women. They are more capricious when it comes to cash, either spending it on alcohol or loaning it to undeserving friends. They say that this is why women usually manage the household income and why women belong in the marketplace. From their perspective, men simply do not have the patience to sit at the bazaar for long hours. Some explain this lack of patience in connection with the "fact" that men are better suited for "hard" manual work, and others suggest that men are just too lazy to sit at the bazaar.

One female informant believes that Kazakh men simply do not have the ability to be aggressive or pushy with customers: "You can't sell things without talking to your customers. You need to say something to get people to look at your goods and you must be able to convince customers that a product has certain desirable features. The men who work in the bazaar can't do this as well as the women." Some of my informants provide another explanation for why there are fewer men in the bazaar. They explained that men are involved with bazaar trade, but they work behind the scenes doing the tasks that require less time but more physical effort. For example, in some family-run operations, the men go to buy goods in other bazaars and they help carry goods to the marketplace, while the women sit in the bazaar and sell things.

Case Studies of Merchant Women and Their Businesses

Portrayals of four merchant women are presented here to explore the nature and dynamics of the bazaar trade in Shauildir. The first, "Zhanar," a 56-year-old wife and mother of four, provides an example of a full-time merchant woman who has expanded her business as a way to compensate for reduced income in the post-Soviet period. She sells a small assortment of home-produced and retail goods in front of the central bazaar. She was trained as a nurse, and she is now on an extended maternity leave from the local hospital, where she is still officially employed. She started working as a merchant in the Shauildir bazaar in 1995 with the sale of homemade dumplings.

For a while, Zhanar received a lot of business from local offices that would contract her services for special events, such as birthday parties and holidays. By 1997, local organizations could no longer afford such luxuries. Now her business is limited to the sale of eggs, candy, soap, socks, tea, and *kozha* (a chilled drink made by boiling corn, sour cream, and other ingredients). She produces the *kozha* herself and buys the eggs from a neighboring family, but the other goods come from the nearby city of Turkestan.

Because her volume of trade is so small, Zhanar generally relies on her merchant friends to purchase goods for her. They do not charge her for this service. Her children also help out with the business by helping her carry things by foot from her house to the bazaar and by running home for extra goods when necessary. Zhanar works at the bazaar 7 days a week, unless she has a social obligation, in which case one of her older children will sit at the bazaar for her. In comparison with other merchants, her expenses are relatively low. She has no transportation costs because she lives so close to the bazaar and does not travel herself to the other bazaars. She also does not have to pay for a license because of the small volume of trade. Like the other merchants, however, she does pay a daily fee to the bazaar manager and a retail tax to the tax collector. She claims that her business is successful, although her profits only cover a small percentage of her household expenses.

The second woman, "Gulnara," a 55-year-old mother of eight, provides an example of a temporary merchant woman who turned to trade to pay for unplanned expenses. She works full time as a schoolteacher and part time as a merchant. In addition to receiving her income from the school and her husband's income from the Department of Culture, her family manages to save money by producing its own fruit and vegetables. Gulnara started to engage in trade shortly after her first daughter eloped with her boyfriend in 1994 and the family found themselves unprepared to pay for all of the gift and dowry expenses.

Following the lead of neighbors, Gulnara decided to try her luck selling things at the bazaar. In her first effort, she bought a sheep in town and she had her husband slaughter it. Then she got on an overnight train to Tashkent, where she sold the meat in the central bazaar. In one day, she managed to make about $10. This amount represented one-quarter of her monthly salary, a salary she had not received for several months due to government delays. The profits were great, but the work was difficult and time consuming, so she decided to change tactics. Using a portion of the profits as capital, she traveled to the nearby city of Turkestan and purchased an array of inexpensive clothing. She recruited her teenage daughters to sell these items in the town bazaar, while she continued to work in the school.

Gulnara's profits, however, were only trickling in. So she eventually decided to turn to a third strategy. She decided to travel with several other merchant women to Almaty and then to Baikonyr, two cities that are each a full day's train ride away. She borrowed money from friends and relatives and then used this capital and reliance on informal exchanges of knowledge to buy goods that were known to sell at favorable prices in these distant bazaars. She was gone for more than a month. Unfortunately, after subtracting expenses for housing and transportation and paying back her loans, Gulnara only received a small profit (about $25). Her participation in the bazaar economy ended after her daughter's wedding.

The third woman, "Raikhan," a 66-year-old wife and mother of six, provides an example of an elderly merchant woman who makes a vital contribution to her household's income by working as a merchant. She sells a wide array of goods 7 days a week from an isolated stand that is situated across the main street from the central bazaar in Shauildir. For decades, she was a full-time mother and housewife. She started her business in 1995 by selling rice in the bazaar. By 1998, her business had expanded to include tea, preserved fruit, butter, cigarettes, matches, soap, and laundry detergent. Her husband helps her with the business by purchasing goods at the wholesale bazaar in Turkestan and by driving her and her things to work everyday. She lives with her husband, her grown son, his wife, and her six grandchildren.

Unlike some of the other women, Raikhan has the advantage of having a daughter-in-law "in hand," which means that she can pass much of the housework off to her daughter-in-law. In fact, she admits that the merchant lifestyle is much more peaceful than her home life, because the young children are always fighting with each other and running underfoot. At work, she enjoys gossiping with friends and passersby while making a decent amount of money. Her business income, however, only makes up a portion of the household income, which also includes her husband's salary, her pension, and her son's income as a private taxi driver. Like most merchants, she was unwilling to specify her net profit, yet notes that her trade income provides her household with enough money to buy food and coal (used to heat houses in the winter), two of the most crucial expenses for basic survival.

The fourth woman, "Maira," a 17-year-old girl, provides an example of a younger girl who works together with her mother in the local bazaar. She sells fruit, vegetables, and toys with her mother in the daily bazaar.[45] As an unmarried girl, she still lives with her parents and siblings, where she helps with household chores. She has been working with her mother as a merchant for 2 years. Her mother goes to Shymkent or Turkestan twice a week to buy products, while Maira sells things 7 days a week in the village bazaar. In addition to paying taxes and bazaar fees, she and her mother pay a small fee to store their products in a locker every night.

In general, Maira is satisfied with her job, especially on the days that she sells a lot of things, but she gets bored sitting at the bazaar day after day. In the future, she hopes to attend the university, but for now her family cannot afford the "bribe" that is necessary for admission. Because both of her parents are now unemployed, the only source of household income is the profit from market trade. Her family manages to reduce household expenses by producing some vegetables, but they no longer provide their own meat because they gradually slaughtered all their livestock for food and cash.

The Impact of Trade on Women and Their Families

Taken together, the stories of these four merchant women illustrate the nature and scope of small-scale trade in post-Soviet Kazakhstan. Each of these merchant women is bringing in significant amounts of income, which they generally contribute to the household pool. All of the women with whom I spoke started their businesses because their household needed more money for basic survival. Some households rely exclusively on the income derived from small-scale trade, whereas others receive income from multiple sources. Regardless, the income from small-scale trade represents a significant portion of household income, especially at a time when state salaries and state pensions are delayed for months.

I turn now to some of the ways in which this trade is affecting gender roles and family relationships. I have borrowed several insights from the literature on "working women" and "working daughters" in Asia and the Middle East. Scholars in the field have examined the extent to which wage employment improves women's position within the household and transforms patriarchal gender roles.[46] As these researchers cautiously point out, women's income may benefit other household members, but income alone does not necessarily transform women's status within the household. In the case of rural Kazakhstan, the majority of merchant women rely on other household members to help them with their work. Their husbands and children provide assistance in purchasing, transporting and selling goods. Thus, although the women who sit daily in the bazaar do the most time-consuming aspect of the job, the business itself is viewed within the family as a collaborative venture.

Although trading is a time-consuming and tiring job, Kazakh merchant women do report three perceived benefits. First, many of the women enjoy the social atmosphere of the bazaar. The social isolation of nonworking women varies from family to family. Although some women socialize regularly with friends and relatives and share household tasks with daughters and daughters-in-law, others are much more socially isolated at home. In particular, young wives who grew up in different towns have fewer social contacts. In contrast, merchant women are anything but isolated. During nonpeak hours, there is plenty of time to catch up on gossip with other merchants and their customers.

A second perceived benefit is that merchant women have fewer responsibilities at home because of their responsibilities at work. This is also the case for women who are employed in other sectors, in nuclear family households with older children, and in extended family households with other adult women. In these types of households, the nonworking women and older children do the bulk of the cleaning, cooking, and child care. Though nonadult sons are unlikely to perform certain "female" tasks, they do help with child care and general housecleaning. Adult men, however, are much less willing to cross these gender boundaries, even if they are completely unoccupied with other tasks and there is no one else to do these things.

Third, some merchant women relish the travel and shopping opportunities involved with this line of work. This is especially true for those women who have traveled across national borders to purchase goods in Russia, Uzbekistan, Turkey, and Iran. Just as international tourists boast about their experiences, these transnational traders gain social capital from their firsthand knowledge of distant places. Even those who do not travel so far can benefit socially from their knowledge of and frequent access to consumer markets in nearby cities. For example, merchant women often have the opportunity to gain social credits by purchasing consumer goods for their nonmerchant friends and relatives. Depending on the relationship, they may provide these goods at reduced or no cost. Because merchant women have less time to devote to these traditional exchanges, supplying friends with consumer goods provides them with an alternative means to maintain their social networks.

In addition to these perceived benefits, women's involvement in small-scale trade sometimes comes with social costs. In particular, as women spend long hours outside the home, this trade can have negative effects on children, who may receive less supervision, and on marital relations, which may become strained. To illustrate both of these social costs, I will now turn to the case of Jazira, a 35-year-old mother of four.

Jazira started to engage in small-scale trade when her household lost its primary source of income due to the dissolution of the state farm. After earning small profits for a few months, Jazira decided to move temporarily to Almaty, where she could earn greater profits. Although Almaty was a 12-hour train ride away, she made arrangements to share an inexpensive apartment with friends who were also involved in trade. Her husband and her in-laws were not sure if this was a good idea, but her mother-in-law agreed to take care of her grandchildren.[47] Every few weeks, Jazira returned to the village to visit her family and to bring home a portion of her profits. Then, one day, her husband unexpectedly showed up at her bazaar stall in Almaty and harshly announced that he knew she was having an affair with another man. He yelled at her in front of her friends and then beat her for the first time ever.

As Jazira retold these events, she insisted that the accusation was a lie and that she pursued a divorce because she refused to live with a man who did not trust her and who beat her after hearing such a rumor.[48] This example demonstrates that the costs of trade, most notably the time away from the family, occasionally outweigh the perceived benefits, such as the exciting social atmosphere, reduced responsibilities at home, and the opportunity to travel outside the village.

Conclusion

In the post-Soviet period, the number of Kazakh merchant women has increased dramatically. Most have been catapulted into the marketplace due to the rising cost of living. Some market women have lost their public sector jobs; others combine public sector employment with trade. In addition to providing income for food and clothing, some women turn to trade in order to afford household networking activities, such as the exchange of gifts and the entertaining of guests.

There is no single demographic characteristic that defines Kazakh market women; the market is filled with young and old, married and unmarried, rich and poor. Some women manage to make large profits, but others barely break even. In Kazakhstan, the trade in certain goods (cloth, clothing, and packaged goods) is dominated by women. Although men are reluctant to sell these goods in the bazaar, they do help their wives and mothers by providing transportation and purchasing goods in other bazaars.

Despite traditional values that limit women's mobility, the idea of Kazakh women in the marketplace is not so farfetched given Soviet policies to emancipate women. As the result of Soviet emancipation campaigns in Central Asia, Kazakh women have already been visible in the workplace for decades. However, compared with other occupations, market women do put themselves in slightly compromising positions by traveling to other cities to buy goods. One of the ways they mitigate this potential problem is to travel in small groups, or to travel with male relatives.

Finally, the impact of the New Silk Road trade on women and their families varies greatly. The benefits for women include greater social interaction, reduced household chores, and increased physical mobility. In some families, the cost of trade extends as far as family dissolution. For most families, however, the income that a merchant woman brings into a household to pay for basic foodstuffs outweighs the strains that these activities place on family relationships. As market women continue to occupy a central position in the marketplace, future researchers might want to consider the long-term impact of this work on gender relations within the household, on the extent to which women's income contributes to overall income, and on the degree to which this work is redefined as women's work.

Notes

1. The Silk Road Trade decreased in the fifteenth century, when the decline of the Mongol empire brought political instability to the region and technological advances in shipbuilding encouraged alternative routes.

2. In previous publications, I have referred to this village with the pseudonym "Kyzylkum." I now use its actual name, Shauildir.

3. Nancy Bonvillain, *Women and Men: Cultural Constructions of Gender,* 2d ed. (Upper Saddle River, N.J.: Prentice-Hall, 1998), 1–12, 160–76.

4. Andrea Rugh, "Women and Work: Strategies and Choices in a Lower-Class Quarter of Cairo," in *Women and the Family in the Middle East: New Voices of Change,* ed. Elizabeth Fernea (Austin: University of Texas Press, 1985).

5. Vladimir Petrovich Nalivkin and M. Nalivkina, *Ocherk bita zhenscheni osedlogo tuzemnago nacelniia fergani* [Essay on the daily life of the women of the settled indigenous population of Ferghana] (Kazan: Tipografiia Imperatorskago Universita, 1886), 110–12. I would like to thank Elizabeth Constantine for referring me to this source.

6. Catherine VerEecke, "Muslim Women Traders of Northern Nigeria: Perspectives from the City of Yola," *Ethnology* 3 (fall 1993): 217–36.

7. Jenny White, *Money Makes Us Relatives: Women's Labor in Urban Turkey* (Austin: University of Texas Press, 1994).

8. Janet W. Salaff, *Working Daughters of Hong Kong: Filial Piety or Power in the Family?* (New York: Columbia University Press, 1994).

9. This is one of the factors that affects the lives of working women in the Former Soviet Union. See Jeni Klugman, Sheila Marnie, John Micklewright, and Philip O'Keefe, "The Impact of Kindergarten Divestiture on Household Welfare in Central Asia," in *Household Welfare in Central Asia,* ed. Jane Falkingham, Jeni Klugman, Sheila Marnie, and John Micklewright (New York: Saint Martin's Press, 1997).

10. Stephanie Coontz, *The Way We Never Were: American Families and the Nostalgia Trap* (New York: Basic Books, 1992).

11. Mary Buckley, *Women and Ideology in the Soviet Union* (Ann Arbor: University of Michigan Press, 1989).

12. Rugh, "Women and Work"; Arlene MacLeod, *Accommodating Protest: Working Women, the New Veiling, and Change in Cairo* (New York: Columbia University Press, 1991); Homa Hoodfar, *Between Marriage and the Market: Intimate Politics and Survival in Cairo* (Berkeley: University of California Press, 1997).

13. Rugh, "Women and Work," 282–83.

14. In a recent article, Kathleen Kuehnast examines how these new global images and market opportunities affect the identities and attitudes of young Kyrgyz women. See Kuehnast, "From Pioneers to Entrepreneurs: Young Women, Consumerism, and the 'World Picture' in Kyrgyzstan," *Central Asian Survey* 4 (December 1998): 639–54.

15. Ursula Sharma, *Women's Work, Class, and the Urban Household: A Study of Shimla, North India* (London: Tavistock Press, 1986); Micaela di Leonardo, "The Female World of Cards and Holidays: Women, Families, and the Work of Kinship," in *Families in the U.S.: Kinship and Domestic Politics,* ed. Karen V. Hansen and Anita Ilta Garey (Philadelphia: Temple University Press, 1997); White, *Money Makes Us Relatives.*

16. Salaff, *Working Daughters;* Hoodfar, *Between Marriage and the Market;* Diane Wolf, *Factory Daughters: Gender, Household Dynamics, and Rural Industrialization in Java* (Berkeley: University of California Press, 1992).

17. Because parents control the bulk of their daughters' income and working daughters return to subordinate positions upon marriage, Salaff argues that women's participation in wage employment has not changed patriarchal gender relations in any fundamental way. See Salaff, *Working Daughters.*

18. Buckley, *Women and Ideology.*

19. Gracia Clark's study of market women in Ghana and Florence Babb's study of market women in Peru represent two of the more detailed case studies in anthropology. Gracia Clark, *Onions Are My Husband: Survival and Accumulation by West African Market Women* (Chicago: University of Chicago Press, 1994); Florence Babb, *Between Field and Cooking Pot: The Political Economy of Marketwomen in Peru,* rev. ed. (Austin: University of Texas Press, 1998). A recent volume, edited by Linda Seligmann, provides additional resources for studying women traders; see Seligmann, ed., *Women Traders in Cross-Cultural Perspective: Mediating Identities, Marketing Wares* (Stanford, Calif.: Stanford University Press, 2001).

20. Ester Boserup, *Women's Role in Economic Development* (New York: Saint Martin's Press, 1970).

21. In Ghana, the country with the highest percent of women traders, women represent 80 percent of all workers in trade and commerce. In comparison, the proportion of

traders who are women is 1 percent in Turkey, 2 percent in Iraq, 18 percent in Hong Kong, 13 percent in Taiwan, 29 percent in Mexico, 56 percent in Thailand, 59 percent in Nicaragua, and 65 percent in Jamaica.

22. Boserup, *Women's Role,* 87.

23. Robert Hefner, *Market Cultures: Society and Morality in the New Asian Capitalisms* (Boulder, Colo.: Westview Press, 1998), 24; Boserup, *Women's Role,* 92. Hefner's volume shows that these perceptions of male market activity are changing in some regions of Southeast Asia.

24. This is high compared with the national average in Kazakhstan of about 50 percent Kazakhs, many of whom do not speak Kazakh well. The minority ethnic groups include Russians, Tatars, and Uzbeks.

25. Shauildir has several administration buildings, a post office, a police station, a fire station, a library, a pharmacy, three 10-year schools, two specialty schools (for sports and music), two nurseries, a technical institute, a central department store, a produce bazaar, a livestock bazaar, several bread and vegetables shops, a bread factory, an all-purpose hospital, a tuberculosis hospital, two museums (for history and literature), a cultural palace (with a large auditorium), a movie theatre, a hotel, and several restaurants.

26. Basic living conditions vary from household to household. A typical house has four to six rooms, including an indoor kitchen, a wide hallway, and a formal guestroom. Most houses are situated within a fenced compound that typically include livestock and poultry pens, a vegetable garden, an outdoor kitchen, one or more wooden platforms (for sleeping and eating outside during the hot summer months), an outhouse, and a bathhouse. The homes have electricity but no running water. Some homes have telephones. A small percentage of families live in the two-story apartment buildings that line the central village roads.

27. Throughout rural Kazakhstan, livestock and poultry have been an important indicator of household wealth and well-being. In addition to providing food, livestock can be sold for cash and exchanged in the gift economy. At the end of 1993, the average household in Otyrar *raion* had 8.73 privately owned sheep and goats, 1.45 cows, 0.33 horses, 0.03 camels, and 5.82 chickens. The average vegetable garden consists of tomatoes, cucumbers, green onions, peppers, and eggplant. Some households also produce grapes, apples, and melons.

28. I approached all of the women in the workplace, and asked them if they would be willing to answer some questions about their work. A few women declined to be interviewed, including one woman who belligerently asked how she could possibly benefit from the study. The majority of women I approached were more than willing to help me with my research. I quickly learned that they were much more willing to talk to me during the weekdays, when the mornings and afternoons passed slowly with little trade activity. During each interview, I asked the women to describe how and why they started their businesses, how they deal with the costs and difficulties associated with trade, who helps them with their market activities, and how their work affects their family life.

29. Deniz Kandiyoti, "Bargaining with Patriarchy," in *The Women, Gender, and Development Reader,* ed. Nalini Visvanathan, Lynn Duggan, Laurie Nisonoff, and Nan Wiegersma (London: Zed Books, 1997).

30. Elizabeth Constantine, "Public Discourse and Private Lives: Uzbek Women under Soviet Rule," Ph.D. dissertation, Indiana University, Bloomington, 2001.

31. Women dominate the occupations of day care workers, bread factory workers, state shopkeepers, secretaries, nurses, and janitors. Meanwhile, both men and women

work as doctors, teachers, economists, state farm employees, shepherds, and cultural palace employees and performers. Finally, there are a few positions that rarely if ever are filled by women in Shauildir: policeman, fireman, state farm administrator, and village administrator (at the highest level).

32. With few exceptions (such as funerals), Kazakh social events are not gender segregated. Men and women sit together and women actively participate in the conversation and toasting.

33. Gift exchange may seem like a trivial task, but it is not when one considers the number of gifting occasions and the financial constraints on household budgets. See Werner, "Household Networks and the Security of Mutual Indebtedness in Rural Kazakhstan," *Central Asian Survey* 4 (December 1998): 597–612.

34. For more information on bride kidnapping, see Werner, "Women, Marriage, and the Nation-State: The Rise of Non-Consensual Bride Kidnapping in Post-Soviet Kazakhstan," in *Reconceptualizing Central Asia: States and Societies in Formation,* ed. Pauline Jones Luong and John Schoberlein (Ithaca, N.Y.: Cornell University Press, 2003). In this paper, I argue that nonconsensual bride kidnapping has been on the rise since the late 1980s because young men have less financial security to offer potential mates. In addition, men do not fear legal repercussions in the context of post-Soviet nation building, which emphasizes the re-traditionalization of Kazakh women. Chapters 1 and 2 of this volume by, respectively, Tatiana Zhurzhenko and Katherine Graney similarly discuss the re-traditionalization of women. For a comparative case of bride kidnapping in Kyrgyzstan, see Russell Kleinbach and Sarah Amsler, "Bride Kidnapping in Kyrgyzstan," *International Journal of Central Asian Studies* 4 (1999): 185–216.

35. In the middle, there are bride kidnapping cases that involve the boy's perception of *implicit* consent from the bride. E.g., a girl may express interest in a boy either by going on dates with him or appearing to be interested; although the boy senses that the girl might want to marry him and he gets the approval of his parents, he does not ask her if she wants to marry him and he does not announce when he plans to kidnap her.

36. Most families prefer to have at least one daughter-in-law at home, but in households with many sons, families prefer to limit the number of sons living at home.

37. For a critique of these policies and the role of international development agencies, see Janine Wedel, *Collision and Collusion: The Strange Case of Western Aid to Eastern Europe* (New York: Saint Martin's Press, 1998).

38. Lourdes Benería and Shelly Feldman, eds., *Unequal Burden. Economic Crisis, Persistent Poverty, and Women's Work* (Boulder, Colo.: Westview Press, 1992).

39. Between 1990 and 1994, the number of jobs occupied by women decreased by 22.7 percent, compared with only 10.2 percent for men. Approximately 700,000 women were laid off during this period. This figure does not even include the number of women who have been placed on part-time status or who have difficulty returning from maternity leave. See Armin Bauer, Nina Boschmann, and David Green, *Women and Gender Relations in Kazakhstan* (Manila: Asian Development Bank, 1997).

40. From 1989 to 1994, the total enrollment in Kazakhstan's nurseries has declined from 52 to 28 percent of preschool children. See Klugman et al., "Impact of Kindergarten Divestiture," 188.

41. Zoya Khotkina's work provides a parallel account of how the transition to a market economy has affected Russian women. Zoya Khotkina, "Women in the Labour Market: Yesterday, Today and Tomorrow," in *Women in Russia: A New Era in Russian Feminism,* ed. Anastasia Posadskaya (London: Verso Press, 1994).

42. Chapter 8 of this volume by Ludmilla Popkova mentions that the percentage of women in politics decreases as the level of power increases. The same can be said for women in trade—women are active traders in local bazaars, but there are few women who own large-scale trade businesses.

43. This phenomenon is not limited to rural Kazakhstan. For a discussion of woman entrepreneurs in urban Kazakhstan, see Bauer et al., *Women and Gender Relations,* 35–42. For Ukraine, see Tatiana Zhurzhenko, "Gender and Identity Formation in Post-Socialist Ukraine: The Case of Women in the Shuttle Business," in *Feminist Fields: Ethnographic Insights,* ed. Rae Anderson, Sally Cole, and Heather Howard-Bobiwash (Orchard Park, N.Y.: Broadview Press, 1999). For Siberia, see Alexia Bloch, "Global Capitalism and Fallen Socialists: Women Traders Reflect on New Meanings Around 'Work' in Russia," paper presented at the American Anthropological Association Annual Meeting, Washington, D.C., November 28–December 2, 2001.

44. Bauer et al., *Women and Gender Relations,* 21–28.

45. I use the word "girl" rather than "woman" here in accord with Kazakh usage where the word for girl is used to describe all unmarried females, regardless of age.

46. Salaff, *Working Daughters;* Wolf, *Factory Daughters;* Hoodfar, *Between Market and Family;* White, *Money Makes Us Relatives.*

47. This was not out of line with Kazakh cultural norms, whereby parents frequently rely on grandparents and other relatives for long-term child care.

48. She thought seriously about all of the consequences of this divorce. She would have to move permanently to Almaty. She could only afford to take her school-age child, because the cost of day care was too high to take the others. And given her "family situation," she knew she would have some problems getting remarried. For these reasons, her parents were giving her a very hard time. Despite the beating, her husband was a good man, they argued, and besides that, he was the son of their close friends and this would put a strain on their friendship.

6

The Gendered Nature of Viliui Sakha Post-Soviet Adaptation

Susan A. Crate

At the 1993 New Year's celebration in Elgeeii village, located in western Sakha Republic, Russia, amid the evening's fare of dances, songs, and skits, one act in particular captured my attention. At first, the stage is empty of all but a single table and chair. In staggers a man who appears to have trouble aligning himself to sit in the chair, but after a few attempts, he makes it into a seated position. He is wearing the typical garb for the subarctic winter—a fur hat, boots, and layers under a heavy quilted jacket. After seating himself,

The author acknowledges the people of the villages of Elgeeii and Kutana, Suntar region, Sakha Republic, without whose help her ongoing research would not be possible. The research described in this chapter was funded by a National Science Foundation Dissertation Improvement Award, a Fulbright-Hays Doctoral Research Abroad Award, a Social Science Research Council International Dissertation Field Research Fellowship, and an International Research and Exchange Board Individual Advanced Research Award. The writing was funded by an American Association of University Women fellowship and a Social Science Research Council Write-Up Fellowship. The author gratefully acknowledges and thanks each of these organizations.

he lays his head and arms on the table and begins to sleep. Just then, in comes a woman in her housedress. She flits about for a few seconds, focusing here and there, and then notices the man. She looks distressed and concerned and proceeds to take off his hat, boots, and coat, during which time he appears half-awake yet oblivious, allowing her to pamper him. After he is in his house clothes, she rushes offstage to return with a bowl and spoon and feeds him. He eats like an infant, and she cleans up his sputterings accordingly. Once he has been fed, the woman holds her head in distress and looks about to locate and position a footstool for him. He then passes out on the table, at which point she drags him offstage to put him to bed. The audience laughs guardedly throughout the skit.

At first I thought the skit was someone's idea of a bad joke—after all, what was funny about alcoholism? After a few more years of field experience, I realized that the skit portrayed the bittersweet and common experience of most of those attending. It reflects the harsh reality of male alienation and female overaccommodation emblematic of the late Soviet and post-Soviet periods. Alcoholism was a problem in the Soviet period, especially after the state farm consolidations of the 1950s, when traditional rural economies were augmented into agro-industrial operations.[1] The problem of alcoholism only increased due to the economic downturn of the 1980s and the dissolution of the Soviet Union in the early 1990s. Through its public venue, the skit worked to confirm the common scenario in many of the village households. It made a joke out of the villagers' shared reality, namely, the unprecedented rise in alcoholism, which acts as the central indicator in these villages of unemployment and overall social alienation.

The discussion of women's roles in post-Soviet adaptation includes an understanding of the prevalent tendency of their male counterparts—husbands, brothers, fathers, sons. The post-Soviet female tendency to "keep the household together" through overwork and the maintenance of social networks compensates for male irresponsibility. The central role of women and the alienation of men is the same picture in many post-Soviet settings.[2] However, due to variation in employment opportunities, resource and market access, and environmental constraints, women in different contexts respond in unique ways to their post-Soviet predicament. For example, in chapter 5 of this volume, Cynthia Werner demonstrates that rural Kazakh women are developing new strategies to contribute to household economies. In her context, women have access to markets, where they can profit from the sale of food and clothing. Viliui Sakha do not have such access to markets, and thus they find their survival "niche" by setting up their own system of in-house food production.

Similarly, the Viliui Sakha case differs from the mainstream with regard to the severe increase in unemployment in the post-Soviet context. For rural Viliui Sakha, it was not the women who disproportionately suffered from lost employment, as was the case in most of the post-Soviet states. The disbanding of centralized state farms especially generated unemployment among men. As a result, rural Viliui Sakha women are slightly more likely to be employed as wage earners than their male counterparts, in 2000 bringing home 56 percent of household income.[3] Women also perform the majority of work in the home, juggling child rearing, food preparation and production, and cattle husbandry. In addition, many women are single mothers and heads of households, factors that make their workload even heavier.

This chapter explores the role of gender in the post-Soviet transition for Viliui Sakha, with a particular focus on how gender affects survival strategies. My research demonstrates that economic challenges generated change in gender roles, as families sought to adapt to new conditions. I begin with an orientation to the field site and an explanation of the central research findings regarding survival strategies, and I illustrate those findings with two case studies. Next I explore the evidence of a nascent trend toward greater gender role flexibility, with women and men increasingly taking on activities formerly associated with the opposite sex. An additional theme involves the emergence of village-level women's organizations and their efforts to improve women's lives.

Cows-and-Kin: Contemporary Viliui Sakha Survival

For the inhabitants of the Elgeeii and Kutana villages,[4] the fall of the Soviet Union and the introduction of structural adjustment policies meant the dismantling of the Elgeeii State farm and massive unemployment, especially for the male population.[5] Also, meat and milk, the staple foods of Viliui Sakha, were no longer available through state farm affiliation. This increased the pressure on households to keep cows and to produce much of their household's needs themselves. This turn toward subsistence production represented a common survival strategy across the rural post-Soviet states.

The focus on local household-based subsistence strategies as adaptations to change draws on the work of Robert Netting. In *Smallholders,*

Householders: Farm Families and the Ecology of Intensive, Sustainable Agriculture, he explores agricultural practices and how they are linked to household organization and land tenure.[6] He argues that in times of transition the household is the most efficient and enduring unit, because it is both a repository of intimate ecological knowledge and a highly integrated, gender-based labor force rooted in implicit contracts that provide for the care of children and the elderly. This research examines such household resiliency in the context of post-socialist Russia, or, more specifically, in the case of two former Elgeeii state farm villages located in western Sakha.

From the 1950s to the breakup of the USSR in 1991, the inhabitants of the Elgeeii state farm territory had a serflike relationship with regional industry. In the 1950s, geological expeditions discovered diamonds in the Viliui regions. The government redrew regional boundaries to designate the diamond-rich areas as an industrial region and mandated that the outlying agricultural regions produce food for the nascent mining center. In Elgeeii, the process of consolidating nearby collective farms was already well under way. It culminated in the establishment of the Elgeeii state farm, an agro-industrial enterprise the size of Indiana, with the sole purpose of producing meat and milk to feed the immigrant work populations of the diamond region. The Elgeeii village population increased from several hundred to several thousand as adjacent collectives and entire villages were relocated to work at the center. The farm was fully subsidized by the government, and materials and consumer products flowed freely through the villages to the inhabitants.

In the mid-1980s, the USSR sought greater links with global markets. For the diamond industry, this meant finding cheaper sources of meat and milk not only in other areas of Russia but also in southeast Asian countries. This was the beginning of the end of the Elgeeii state farm. In 1992, after 7 years of struggle, local officials voted to disband the farm and divide its assets among the workers. Farm officials and their relatives appropriated the bulk of the property, leaving the majority of the population without access to productive resources. The farm's demise eliminated most of the jobs, removing the main incentive to live in Elgeeii. In addition, the end of the Elgeeii state farm cut off access to many commodities formerly secured through the work place.

Data describing the contemporary economic characteristics of surveyed Elgeeii village households provide insight regarding the change from full employment and product availability during the late Soviet period to the unemployment and lack of products in the post-Soviet context. Figure 6.1

Figure 6.1
Breakdown of Employment, Income, and Pensioners across Surveyed Households

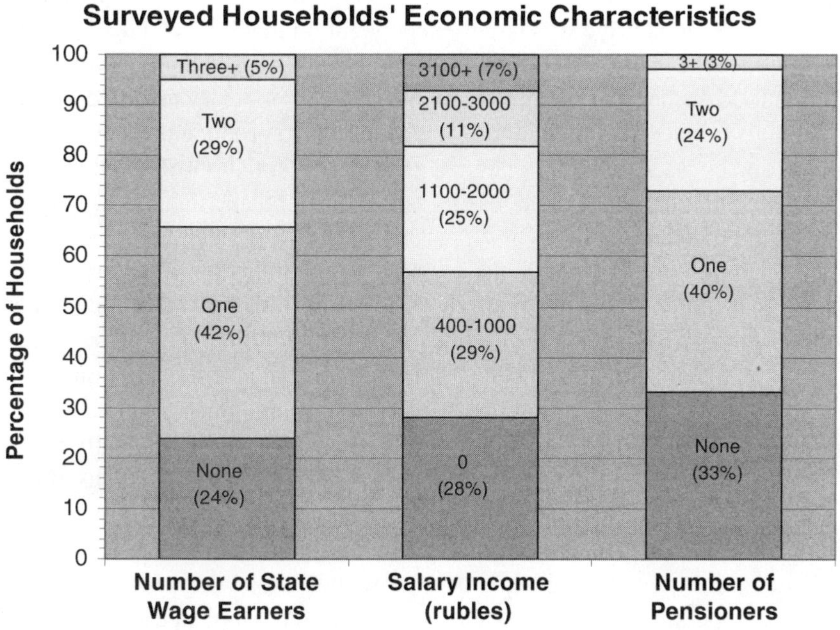

gives a sense of the impoverished economic state of village households, showing the percentage of surveyed households that have state salaried workers, the amount of state salary income that goes toward household expenditures, and the percentages of households with pensioners.[7]

It is important to note that state salary makes up about half of a given household's monetary resources, with the remainder coming from pensions, child subsidies, and money made through informal sales of products or services. On the basis of the 2000 survey results, involving a random sample of 30 percent of all Elgeeii households ($n = 210$, $N = 700$), the average monthly breakdown of total household income was salary = 1,200 rubles ($43); pensions = 880 rubles ($31); child subsidies = 140 rubles ($5); and informal sales of products or services = 211 rubles ($8).[8] This gave a total average monthly income of 2,431 rubles ($87).

The official minimum monthly income per household member set by the state was 1,400 rubles ($50) as of February 2000. To meet this minimum, a household of four, the average size of surveyed households, would need to make 9,724 rubles ($347) per month, or four times the average income of surveyed households. Local village officials argued that the state minimum level was irrelevant in the rural villages, because how much any given household needed to survive was largely dependent on that household's capacity to produce its own food. In fact, most households are actively involved in home food production to supplement insufficient monetary resources. More than half keep cows and other domestic animals to produce their own meat, milk, and eggs. Similarly, 70 percent grow a substantial portion of their own food, and 65 percent of the households forage, hunt, and fish to supplement domestic food production.

Since the Soviet breakup, the focus of Viliui Sakha survival has shifted from dependence on the socialist infrastructure for employment and consumer goods to dependence on a household production system called cows-and-kin. Whereas in 1992 only 10 percent of all households kept one milk cow, in 2000, 55 percent held three or a herd of six. On average, a household of four needs two milk cows or a herd of six to supply its daily needs for meat and milk. Each household must harvest an average of 2 tons of hay per cow and new calf for fodder during the 9-month subarctic winter. The main way that households negotiate this high labor demand in summer is by maintaining reciprocal dependencies with non-cow-keeping kin household members who provide extensive summer hay labor in exchange for a year-round supply of meat and milk. Due to these kin interhousehold kin dependencies, an additional 35 percent of all households are supplied with their milk and meat needs, making a total of 90 percent of all households self-sufficient. The remaining 10 percent earn enough money to buy their meat and milk.

In the post-Soviet setting, cows-and-kin represents Viliui Sakhas' local response to Russia's economic dilemmas. To illustrate, I will discuss two household cases, both based on cows-and-kin relationships, but one geared toward subsistence and the other toward entrepreneurial activities.

Cows-and-Kin in Case Studies

The most common cows-and-kin pattern is characterized by a young family dependent on a parental household for meat and milk in exchange for supplying labor during the haying season. Yelli and her husband, Vlad, both have full-time jobs, she as a dance choreographer at the village culture center and he as a firefighter.[9] They have three small children; two attend preschool, and the other elementary school. Although they have a new house on the village's perimeter, Yelli and her family spend most of their time, when not at work or school, at their kin households, either Yelli's or her husband's mothers' houses. Both their mothers live in the village center, convenient to day care, school, and workplaces. These mothers not only supply the young family with all the meat and milk products they need but also provide child care and regular meals.

Yelli and her family eat most of their meals at Rozalia's, Yelli's mother's house. Rozalia keeps five milk cows. One belongs to her, three belong to each of her three children, and the last one is owned by her brother-in-law, whose wife, the former cow tender of their family, died several years ago. The brother-in-law provides Rozalia's year-round tractor needs in exchange for her daily care of his cow. The cows owned by Yelli, her brother, and her sister were all received as gifts from their mother when each married. The mother continues to give her children the gift of daily care for the cows. Each cow produces a calf annually, which is slaughtered in 2 to 3 years to provide a continuous, ample meat supply for each household. With the meat from an average cow slaughter at 160 kilograms, this represents 526,400 kilocalories. For Yelli's household, this is one-fifth of their annual total kilocalorie requirement. But the mother also supplies daily meals, which supply most of the rest of their total kilocalorie needs; the remaining balance comes from Vlad's mother's household, where they eat on occasion.

From late May until the end of August, Rozalia lives at her *sayylyk* or summer house, located several miles from the village. At the *sayylyk,* Rozalia tends the family cows and chickens and grows all the potatoes and vegetables for her children's families. In exchange for the mother's year-round labors, Yelli and her family, along with her sister's and brother's family, cut all the hay needed to overwinter the "family" cows.

Yelli and her family also frequent Yelli's mother-in-law's household. However, resources are scarce because the mother lives with three of her five adult children. They also keep five cows but only produce meat and milk for the consumption of their immediate household and for one daughter and her family, who live in a separate household in the village. Yelli's family mostly relies on this household for child care and occasional meals. The degree to which resources and labor flow through this extended family network is the same for the majority of village households.

Within this context of reliance on cows-and-kin, Sakha are undertaking new entrepreneurial activity. Tania and Nikifor, both retired teachers in their late 50s, grow vegetables, raise cows and chickens, fish, and forage, all in excess of their immediate needs, to sell and barter products in local markets.

Nikifor takes a bus or buys a seat in a private car 15 miles to the regional center, Suntar, to tap the market there. He goes straight to the regional administrative buildings, where he enters each office to peddle his wares, including *sobo,* a popular lake fish; curds; cow stomach and intestines; and *kymys,* fermented mare's milk. He takes the remainder to local stores to sell. He averages about ten trips a year and generates the equivalent of 6 months average village household income, before costs, from these commercial expeditions.[10]

Producing these products for sale requires a major time investment. Nikifor is an avid fisherman and leads village fishing brigades. Winter ice fishing takes an annual average of 150 hours away from home and brings in a half a ton of *sobo.* In the temperate months, he net fishes and annually averages 116 hours away from home to produce another half ton of fish.

Tania sells a lot of their products out of their Elgeeii home. One of her most successful products is a traditional Sakha milk food, called *khayakh,* which she dyes pink with natural colorings from homegrown beets and red cowberries and forms into festive shapes for the New Year's holiday. Sales from this specialty item garner income equivalent to 4 months of the average village household income.

Of their total production, be it fish, garden produce, or dairy and meat products, Tania and Nikifor sell approximately one-third, use one-third in barter transactions, and the rest goes directly to their own and their kin's consumption. Commercial sales give Tania and Nikifor an income substantially higher than that of most Elgeeii households. They share these monetary resources freely with their kin and mostly to supplement their children's households. Several years ago, they completely financed the materials and building of a new house for their son, and this past year they bought their daughter her own apartment in the regional center. Local entrepreneurial activities remain, not unlike the cows-and-kin adaptation in general, focused on providing assistance to family and kin.

In 2000, about 10 percent of all Elgeeii households relied on such entrepreneurial activities to support themselves and their relatives. In every case, the foundation of these entrepreneurial efforts involves household-level, cows-and-kin-based knowledge to either produce traditional foods in excess for sale and/or collaborate with kin households to develop goods for the marketplace. It is noteworthy that profits flow freely to relatives. Overall, these nascent entrepreneurial efforts reveal household resiliency based upon implicit kin labor contracts and intimate ecological knowledge.[11]

Field research suggests that the 90 percent of households not engaged in entrepreneurial activity nonetheless consider these activities important for the future of their village. They stress the need to create local opportunities and markets. Some want to work in small collectives to produce meat, milk, grains, and vegetables for market. Others would like to begin a village-based cottage industry that could provide jobs and produce needed goods. A few want to develop local tourism. Still others, like Tania and Nikifor, are well on their way to developing niche markets.

Gender in the Contemporary Setting

Viliui Sakha's contemporary reliance on cows-and-kin relationships and nascent entrepreneurial endeavors is based on intimate ecological knowledge and implicit labor contracts. Households are a repository of ecological knowledge, allowing members to make the most effective use of their small land holdings. Viliui Sakha depend on a familiar landscape and on centuries-old knowledge pertaining to horse and cattle husbandry in their subarctic environment. Household members possess a strong work ethic and provide dependable labor for daily chores and seasonally specific demands. On a daily basis, family members care for their herds and engage in food production tasks; seasonally, they harvest hay, forage for wild foods, and slaughter animals.

Specialization of work by gender contributes to household efficiency and, in many ways, reflects more traditional gender roles (see the discussion below). This is exemplified in Viliui Sakhas' labor specialization during the intensive summer period, when males spend their waking hours cutting and stacking hay while women rake and stack the hay into smaller piles. Men hunt and fish while women forage for wild berries and plants, tend home gardens and greenhouses, and see to the herds when they return from daily pasture at night.

Given the extreme climate of this subarctic environment, households with at least one adult male have an easier time securing both domestic and wild sources of food. However, in Elgeeii, 10 percent of all households have only a single head, including twenty-six single-mother, five single-father, and twenty-seven divorced households.[12] Additionally, during the past decade, inhabitants have reported major changes from the traditional Sakha gender roles. These changes are perhaps a response to both the increase in single-head households and to the higher employment of female heads, who traditionally performed the majority of domestic duties. The historical literature describes the strict delineation of gender roles in the past and provides a baseline to gauge the extent to which gender roles are changing in the contemporary context.

Traditional and Contemporary Gender Roles

Until their exposure to Christianity in the late eighteenth and early nineteenth centuries, Sakha practiced polygamy. It was most common among *toions,* who were the local clan heads and members of the wealthy class. I. Ides and A. Brandt, who explored the region in the late seventeenth century, documented that approximately one-third of all Sakha men had more than one wife and concluded that "Sakha take as many wives as they can feed."[13] Notes from the expedition of F. I. Langas listed these reasons for taking many wives: (1) Sakha marry off their children at an early age and so when the men grow up they fall out of love and take a second wife; (2) they also take a second and a third wife, if the initial marriage(s) do not produce children; (3) they then can increase their herds by having each wife tend cows based at different homesteads; (4) they replace wives who prove to be poor herd keepers; and (5) by having a child-bearing wife at every homestead, they maximize the chances of having many children who can work and carry on their herds.[14]

The central reason for having many wives stemmed from women's role in caring for the herds. Thus the wealthier a Sakha man was, the greater his herds and hay land areas, the more wives he needed. According to folklore materials, the wealthiest *toions* had from seven to nine wives. The first wife was the head female in the household, if they all lived together. She and her children had the first rights over all other wives and their children.

After polygamy waned, women continued as the main keepers of the household herds. In the harsh Siberian climate, with average winter temperatures of –50 °F, gender roles were clearly defined, with women confined to the inside environment. Their work was varied and consisted of maintaining the living area; preparing and preserving food; making and repairing the family's clothing; making containers and utensils of hides, hair, birch bark, and clay; caring for children; and tending the herds in barns throughout the 9-month winter.

Men were responsible for the outside tasks. The list was equally long, and it entailed harvesting the hay to overwinter the herds, tending to all the daily outside work for the herds, hunting and fishing, daily gathering firewood,[15] procuring drinking water, building all the living and other structures on the homestead, managing the fences for the hay fields, and slaughtering animals.

In the brief months of summer, both sexes worked and toiled in the warmth of the long subarctic days. Men cut the hay while women raked it into small piles. Men hunted and fished while the women foraged for berries, roots, and herbs. Soviet policies worked toward gender equality to the extent that women were as likely to be employed as men on the collective and state farms. However, women still carried the double burden of domestic chores.[16]

Are these gender roles changing during the post-Soviet transition? During the past 10 years of ongoing research in the Viliui regions, I have heard repeatedly about how men's work was being done by women now and vice versa. Field research in 2000 provided quantitative data to verify those inhabitants' comments. On the basis of my analysis of time allocation data,[17] I created an activity calendar by charting observations specific to main Sakha seasonal activities. Table 6.1 shows these food production and resource management activities and defines the range of dates over which I observed each activity, the number of times I observed each activity, the range of ages of participants involved in an activity, each activity's gender breakdown, and the number of households where I observed each activity.

This table shows that certain traditionally gender-specific activities remain so today. Women in general perform the activities that are either inside or close to the household, and men do work that requires travel into the outlying areas.[18]

I further analyzed the time allocation data to measure the proportion of male and female adult participation in given activities.[19] Out of the 587 observations of people at work at a regular job, half were male adults and half were female adults, coinciding with the fact that women hold slightly more than half of the available jobs in the village. I next recorded all "unobserved" activities or those that were reported by household members regarding where absent household members were at the time of my time allocation spot check. These fell into two broad groups, either working at a salaried job or not. Of the observations in which inhabitants did not have

Table 6.1

Time Allocation Observations of Sakha Seasonal Activities

Activity	Date Range[a]	Number of Observations	Age Range (years)	Percent Female	Percent Male	Number of Households
Food production						
Berry picking	7/22–9/25	36	4–68	72	28	21
Hunting (duck and game)	9/6–11/6, 5/12–5/24	27	17–65	0	100	23
Fishing (lake and sylyhar)	Year round	14	7–76	0	100	13
Fishing (riverfish)	5/31–7/24	3	12–35	67	33	2
Sayylyk[b]	4/10–10/12	131	0.1–84	49	51	21
Haying (main haying)	7/19–9/6	151	3–73	22	78	73
Haying (preparation and hauling)	6/11–1/7	11	25–71	0	100	7
Horse tending	11/6–4/10	6	24–72	0	100	3
Cow tending, overall	7/19–6/11	287	4–84	47	53	96
General	7/19–6/11	208	4–84	46	54	83
To pasture or milking	9/30–6/11	26	6–78	58	42	22
Feeding	9/6–5/31	30	4–75	47	53	20
Watering	10/6–4/29	4	37–77	0	100	4
Khoton[c] and hay preparation, manure management	9/18–5/18	24	35–78	51	49	19
Pig and chicken tending	7/28–3/4	7	11–68	55	45	6
Gardening, overall	5/24–9/25	45	2–78	55	45	18
Greenhouse, overall	4/29–8/18	26	10–73	54	46	13
Food storage, overall	7/22–6/11	46	14–88	70	30	33
Putting up food, duck cleaning	8/12–10/19	8	14–65	100	0	6
Fish cleaning	8/12–6/5	11	28–70	82	18	10

Resource Management						
Firewood harvesting, away	7/24–5/31	42	9–68	0	100	25
Firewood in home use, other fuel management	8/6–6/11	64	3–78	40	60	49
House and out building—own	7/19–11/12	8	28–69	38	62	6
House building—other's	6/5–12/1	16	22–65	0	100	11
Water harvesting, away[d]	10/30–4/16	13	14–72	0	100	10
Water, overall	8/1–6/11	49	8–85	41	59	39

[a] This range reflects the date range of the author's time allocation observations, which started July 19, 1999, and ended June 11, 2000.
[b] *Sayylyk* is the Sakhas' summer home.
[c] A *khoton* is a barn for cows.
[d] The Sakha use ice for water from November through May.
Source: Author's observations.

a salaried job but were away from the household, males were gone twice as often as females and were reportedly involved in haying, firewood harvest, hunting, fishing, and horse care. This also supports the traditional role of men.

I also found some blurring of traditional gender roles. When I looked at the frequency of male versus female involvement in housework, I found that women are doing 70 percent of the housework,[20] and that men are performing the rest, representing a break from the traditional gender roles in which women did all the housework.[21] Similarly, in contemporary times, males and females equally share all activities involved in keeping the household's herds, which traditionally were done only by women. Another sign of the blurring of traditional gender roles is the proportion of males and females doing outside work, including raking, shoveling, firewood management, and water hauling, formerly all male activities; but, in a contemporary context, women perform 28 percent of these acts. Before discussing more fully these blurred gender lines, I want first to describe village-level efforts to relieve women's burdens.

Village-Level Efforts to Relieve the Burden on Sakha Women

In 1994, the former Soviet-era Zhenski Komitet or Women's Committee director established the Mother and Child Center, a village-based, state-funded organization established to provide social services for all village women and children. In its early years, the center mainly focused on providing support by forming arts and crafts clubs. Since 1998, the center has begun working mainly with families that are struggling because they have an income below the minimal level, one or both of the parents are alcoholics, and/or they do not keep cows and gardens, one of the keys to post-Soviet subsistence survival in Viliui Sakha villages.[22]

The center's greatest success so far has been to help these households by sending the children of alcoholic parents to boarding schools. Another service they provide involves counseling for alcoholics and their household members, but they have had little success in reducing the problem. Because of a marked rise in female alcoholism in late 1990s, the center started a program to employ fifteen alcoholic women. It pays them a nominal 280 rubles ($10) per month to sew, run the center's tea and pastry café, and maintain its facility. The results have been mixed. The women show up for work only half the time.

Clearly, the center is making efforts to deal with a harsh reality among village inhabitants, namely, the ubiquitous problem of alcoholism and the recent rise in female addiction. However, local women whose households do not meet the center's criteria for services complain that the center no longer serves its original purpose of assisting all village women and children. Whether it is a lack of funds that limits the center to assisting only the most needy or a misuse of allocated funds is not clear. What is clear for the purposes of this analysis is that village-level efforts, although apparently making strides to affect some women's lives, do not serve the majority of burdened females, the original protocol of the organization.

Contemporary Trends: Are Changing Gender Roles a Wave of the Future?

There are at least two reasons why Viliui Sakha women are more highly employed than men as wage earners.[23] First, the majority of remaining village jobs after the state farm disbanded involved female-dominated positions, in the fields of education, medicine, and administration.[24] Second, men, due to widespread alcoholism, constitute an unreliable and irresponsible workforce. In addition, male alcoholism fostered a rise in single-mother households; women claim they would rather carry the burdens themselves than live with an alcoholic—a situation that can quickly deplete a household's financial resources.

These single mothers must manage all the inside and outside domestic work of their households. In the Soviet period, they could get the outside and traditionally male-oriented tasks done either for free or a nominal fee through the communal services. Today, they do it themselves, pay for a man to do it for them, or, as frequently happens, a male relative performs these duties.

As was stated above, women bear the brunt of household duties. They account for 85 percent of the time spent cooking, 93 percent of clothing and footwear manufacture and repair, 85 percent of dishwashing, 89 percent of clothes washing, 82 percent of general housecleaning, 77 percent of food preservation, and 85 percent of child care.[25] In the context of the high demands on contemporary Sakha women, one trend appears to bring some relief. Male heads have taken up many of the traditionally female roles of cooking, cleaning, caring for children, and tending the household's herds and gardens.

This relaxation of gender-specific economic roles is juxtaposed with rigidly defined traditional Sakha gender roles. In the village, it is common knowledge that these gender role blurrings are operative, and most inhabitants accept them as one more way to cope with the contemporary socioeconomic changes. When I inquired as to why they are taking on "women's work," men commented that they had no salaried work and to them it only made sense to help maintain the household while their wives worked for wages. In Elgeeii in 2000, I witnessed 10 households out of my village sample of 210 whose unemployed male heads had taken on primary responsibility for running the household.

Although this nascent trend is still a minor one, it does provide some relief for over burdened women. Could this be a wave of the future? Several factors suggest that it could be. First, post-Soviet village-level efforts to assist women only include a fraction of those households in need, and the effectiveness of these efforts is marginal.[26] Moreover, there do not appear to be any foreseeable changes in women holding the majority of the wage-earning jobs. Where gender role flexibility is operative, households function as a sound and egalitarian approach to post-socialist village survival. If further research can verify this, the next step will be to introduce policy to support education and other local activities to facilitate this trend.

Conclusion and Thoughts on Policy

The lives of Viliui Sakha generate unique patterns with respect to gender roles, with relationships undergoing transformation in response to the challenges posed by the post-Soviet transition. Women hold slightly more of the available regular wage-paying jobs than men. Women also perform the majority of household duties. This "overwork" of women is one way to mask male irresponsibility.

Although many activities are still, as they were traditionally, male or female dominated, some traditionally sex-role stereotyped activities are now shared by both sexes. This includes many of the duties involved in household food production, which after the end of the state farm system became the major source of food for rural inhabitants. Village-level efforts earmarked to address women's plight are only working with a special sector of the population. In some households, men are taking on women's roles as housekeepers and herd tenders. This nascent trend, provided it is amenable to all involved, could bring relief for many overworked women during the post-Soviet transition.[27]

The hope is that over time, the quality of life will improve for rural Viliui Sakha with the introduction of sustainable local economic plans to increase employment, create markets for entrepreneurs, improve the effectiveness of local social services, and introduce other improvements that would make life less labor intensive, that is, provide gas for heat, good-quality drinking water, and more regular shipments of basic consumer goods.

These measures could result in a very different ending to the skit at the 1993 Elgeeii New Year's celebration. It could begin with the same stage, empty except for a single chair and table. This time the wife enters, returning home after a day at work. She takes off her coat and then goes to change into her house clothes. While she is gone, the man enters with two half-filled buckets of fresh milk. He begins to separate the milk. The wife reenters, and they finish up the milk work and then sit down to dinner prepared by the father and children. Their conversation about their day is interrupted by the telephone, with news that the man has been offered a job at the new small business cooperative in the village.

Some Viliui Sakha and others in my audience may think that such a scenario is farfetched. I argue the opposite. If the nascent trend toward greater gender role flexibility continues, and sustainable economic plans can be introduced to support other improvements in village life, then the latter scenario may well be a vivid preview of the future to come.

On a broader scale, the Viliui Sakha case underscores the particularities of one part of the post-Soviet world, thereby emphasizing the diversity of local realities across the post-Soviet states. Paying attention to the variation and diversity of local realities is the key to developing effective policy. I recommend that policymakers collaborate with social scientists working in anthropology, sociology, and other applicable fields to understand local diversity and to ensure that the policies they generate are sensitive to micro-level cultural variation.

Notes

1. Male alcoholism plays a highly negative role in the context of Viliui Sakha household systems and their overall social structure, not unlike the general trend documented in most indigenous communities of the Russian Arctic. The late Soviet period phenomenon of "lumpenization," resultant of the diminishment and reorientation of traditional

rural economies, the extrafamilial socialization of young people, and the rampant unemployment in the traditional economic spheres, has been cited as the major source of increased male alcoholism in northern communities. For more about this, see Aleksandr Pika, ed., *Neotraditionalism in the Russian North: Indigenous Peoples and the Legacy of Perestroika* (Seattle: University of Washington Press, 1999), 128–29. I argue that a similar phenomenon has precipitated the problem of male alcoholism in Viliui Sakha communities.

2. This assertion is based on our discussions as a group preparing this volume.

3. Women hold most of the state jobs that include work as teachers, administrators, medical professionals, and in social services.

4. These are the names of the two Viliui Sakha villages I studied during my 1999–2000 research on household-level adaptive strategies.

5. For a discussion of structural adjustment policies, see chapter 5 of this volume by Cynthia Werner.

6. Robert Netting, *Smallholders, Householders: Farm Families and the Ecology of Intensive, Sustainable Agriculture* (Stanford, Calif.: Stanford University Press, 1993).

7. The majority of unemployed and wageless households depend on the monthly pensions from elderly kin for their monetary resources.

8. Ruble-to-dollar conversions are based on the 2000 exchange rate of 28 rubles to the dollar.

9. All names are pseudonyms used to protect my consultants' privacy.

10. See above for details on average monthly household income.

11. Netting's theories were a close fit in most ways for Viliui Sakha adaptation. This research also extends Netting's theories, originally focused on intensive agricultural households to include agro-pastoralist peoples.

12. In these cases, the couple is still registered as a household but one parent lives outside the household and provides little if any support—in all cases but one the absent parent is male.

13. E. Ides, A. Brand and M. Kazanin, *Zapiski o Russkom Posoltsve v Kitai (1692–1695)* [Notes of the Russian Consulate in China (1692–1695)] (Moscow: Glav. red vostochnoi lit-ry, 1967), 288.

14. Langas's observations are considered accurate by scholars at the Institute of Humanitarian Research in Yakutsk and are published in P. A. Sleptsov, *Traditsionnaia Sem'ia i Obriadnost' u Iakutov: XIX–nachalo XX v.* [Sakha Family Traditions and Rituals: Nineteenth and beginning of twentieth centuries] (Yakutsk: Yakutsk Book Publishers, 1989), 12.

15. In the pre-Soviet period, the Sakha did not harvest firewood annually but gathered it daily from the woodlots adjacent to their single-family homesteads.

16. The concept of "double burden" that is commonly cited in reference to Soviet women was first introduced by Mary Buckley. See her *Women and Ideology in the Soviet Union* (Ann Arbor: University of Michigan Press, 1989).

17. Time allocation is a quantitative methodology used to measure the time expenditure to various activities. I made spot checks of my random sample of households every 6th day. This resulted in 5,932 observations over the course of my research year.

18. This food production and resource management data can further be analyzed to understand what, if any, age ranges the activities are specific to. Children are involved in many of the same acts as women, and their contributions start at an early age. Boys shift to the adult male pattern at about the age of 16 years. Around the home, it is not

uncommon to see children helping with cow care, such as general tending, leading the herd to water or pasture, and feeding, as well as helping with gardening and greenhouses and learning splitting, stacking, and carrying firewood from an early age. Children are also taken along to participate in berry foraging, haying, and some forms of fishing.

19. I defined adults as those of age 19–55 years, inclusive. Fifty-five is the general age at which village inhabitants no longer participate fully in the activities described.

20. In this context, housework includes all the duties associated with housekeeping, maintaining household supplies of water and wood, and domestic animal and garden care.

21. Men's contribution here is not limited to assisting with women's work in progress, i.e., helping with cooking or dishwashing. Men were observed in the same range of activities as women. Similarly, children do help as they are able, mostly with washing dishes.

22. The Mother and Child Center claimed there were 90 such households out of 700 total households in Elgeeii in 2000. However, 2000 research revealed a higher percentage of households in Elgeeii that claimed incomes below the poverty level of 1,400 rubles ($58) per household member per month. Accordingly, 40 percent or 260 households were below the poverty level, yet the Mother and Child Center only counted 90, or 14 percent of their 650 households as *kimmat* (poverty stricken) on the basis of income.

23. Although the Soviet state acted to increase female employment and many women entered the workforce at that time, male employment still was proportionally higher. With respect to the workload of contemporary Viliui Sakha and income, the Elgeeii village women hold 54 percent of the wage-earning jobs and bring home 56 percent of the income.

24. In the 2000 context, men's work was limited to a very small percentage of the jobs in administrative work, teaching, and medicine, and as night watchmen or seasonal furnace attendants.

25. These data are based on my year-long time allocation study of 210 randomly sampled households.

26. This is true if need is based on the minimum or welfare level (40 percent of households) versus the center's classification (14 percent of households).

27. I suggest further areas of research, including interviewing men and women, to find out if they perceive the changing of male/female gender roles a viable answer, soliciting opinions from youth about contemporary conditions and future perspectives, and tracking macro policy to the local level to see how large-scale initiatives are "lost in local translation."

Part III

Democratization and Women's Civic Activism

7

Women, Building Civil Society, and Democratization in Post-Soviet Azerbaijan

Nayereh Tohidi

As a woman politician, you have to first prove yourself as loyal to your homeland and national cause; then you can push for women's rights.

—Maraym Orujova, Azerbaijani woman activist, 2001

In the wake of the disintegration of the Soviet Union, Azerbaijan was among the first Soviet republics to declare its independence in 1991. But even before the USSR's disintegration and Azerbaijan's formal declaration of independence, the Parliament of Azerbaijan Soviet Socialist Republic under its chair,

The author thanks Erin Trouth for her assistance and Janet Elise Johnson, Kathleen Kuehnast, and Carol Nechemias for their useful comments on the drafts of this chapter. Special thanks go to Azade-Ayse Rorlich whose work on Azeri women (1986) was one of the earliest sources for this author's work on Azerbaijan. The author is most grateful to Azerbaijani women activists in nongovernmental organizations and political parties as well as women in Parliament and government offices whose generous cooperation made this research possible. This chapter was in part supported by the Title VIII–sponsored grant through the Kennan Institute.

Elmira Gafarova (a woman), passed a Constitutional Act on State Sovereignty in September 1989. This indicates both a strong sense of nationalism and the presence of women's voices in nationalist processes from very early on.[1]

Unlike the democratization processes in the Middle East, South Asia, Southeast Asia, Africa, and Latin America, where demands for women's rights and gender equality are *new* elements recently entered into the discourse on democracy, in Azerbaijan the demands for women's rights and equality smack of Communist rhetoric—and hence the *former* regime—and thus have been received, for the most part, with suspicion.[2] This chapter thus addresses a unique predicament: how gender issues are situated in the post-Soviet states, more specifically, in Azerbaijan. I examine how women's political and civic activism in post-Soviet Azerbaijan is evolving from a gender-neutral nationalism toward a gender-sensitive prodemocracy and equal rights movement.[3] I argue that the interplay between two main influences—the domestic/local and the international/global has contributed to the changing orientation in women's response to and role in the democratization of Azerbaizhan. Domestically, women face the post-Soviet conservative and regressive challenges to women's rights, whereas at the same time they are influenced by global feminism, gender-sensitive international United Nations.[4]

Challenges to Women's Rights: Regression in the Gender Regime?

Although post-Soviet changes have had both positive and negative implications for Azerbaijan, the overall impact of the transition on women, particularly on the older and middle-aged women in rural and provincial areas, has been predominantly negative.[5] Women make up the majority of the newly unemployed. This negative trend coincides with the nationalist criticism of the Soviet regime for overemploying and abusing Muslim women in jobs disrespectful of women's feminine qualities, undermining their primary duty as mothers and guardians of home and hearth. But even those women worn down by the "double burden" of the Soviet times cannot afford to stay home without some source of income.

In the realm of education, the universal literacy and high educational attainment of Azerbaijani women under the Soviet system has been jeopardized. Following the privatization of education, changes in the job market, and increases in the cost of higher education (even in public universities), the proportion of students who are female dropped from 58.9 percent in 1993 to 45.5 percent in 1997,[6] and to 41 percent (36,600 women and 51,900 men) in 2000.[7]

The mental and physical health statuses of women and children, the quality of maternity and child care, and reproductive rights have all deteriorated not because of legal barriers but because of the disintegration of the public health care system, the high cost of new private medical institutions and hospitals, increasing rates of violence, trafficking in women, prostitution, drug abuse, and poverty.

Despite constitutional guarantees of equal rights with regard to marriage and family, the enforcement of these laws has become more difficult. The rise of the cult of motherhood and domesticity, the revival of some traditional customs, the increase in the practice of *nikah* and *kabin* (sharia-based marriage, which follows a male-biased conventional Islamic law), and increasing rates of women as single family heads due to increasing numbers of men searching for employment abroad, have jeopardized women's rights and constrained their options as wives and mothers.

Women's role in the realm of politics and leadership—the focus of this chapter—has also been going through significant changes, which will be discussed below. Historically, women in Azerbaijan have been more socially and politically active than women in Central Asia. This difference is related to the geopolitical and geocultural situation of Azerbaijan, its relatively high level of industrialization and urbanization, and its more intense identity politics—the result of conflict over the Karabagh region and over the large population of ethnic Azeris living in Iran.[8]

In the late 1980s and early 1990s, both women's and men's political activism in Azerbaijan focused on issues of national sovereignty and territorial integrity in the face of Russian domination and the Armenian invasion of the Karabagh region. Women, however, gradually noted that an overall decline in well-being accompanied specific threats to the Soviet legacy of social entitlements and to their equal rights as *women* in various capacities: as paid workers, partners or wives, mothers, caretakers, and citizens. It was this gender-asymmetrical adversity that opened the eyes of many women and turned them from gender-blind activism to an increasingly gender-sensitive attitude toward the nature of postindependence development policies, nationalism, marketization, and democratization.

A New Era of "Genderquake"?

Between 1991 and 1997, gender and feminism were rarely discussed in Azerbaijan. But in recent fieldwork (done in the summer of 2001), gender appeared to have gained new credibility among many intellectuals, academics, and activists from nongovernmental organizations (NGOs). Although the use of the term "feminism" is still avoided, "gender" has become so trendy that even some male activists have been trying to form gender-related NGOs and several universities have been developing curricula aimed at offering courses in gender studies. A few new journals covering gender issues have also emerged; the sustainability of such journals, however, remains to be seen.[9]

This new trend stems from the interplay between both local interests (domestic dynamics) and global or international interventions. As was noted above, the deteriorating status of women's health, education, and employment, the increasing constraints on women's rights in both public and private realms, an increased sense of insecurity in the face of violence, poverty, narcotics, and prostitution, and the increasing popularity of traditional and Islamic models of gender relations have convinced many activists of the urgency and significance of women's concerns and gender issues. Conversely, recent contacts with transnational feminist networks and encouragement from some foreign donors—especially the conferences and projects supported by the United Nations—have certainly fostered the recent increase in gender sensitivity among activists in Azerbaijan.

The changing views and actions of leading women activists in the Musavat Party (or MP, a major opposition party) illustrate this change in the perception of gender issues. Maleke Hoseinli, a 46-year-old civil engineer and a member of the central committee of the MP, commented:

> We noticed that despite women's pioneering role in the national liberation movement (*milli–azadlik herkati*) since February 1988, and their various activities in support of the Popular Front, women remain on the margin, since it is only men who hold the leadership positions in the political parties. To specifically deal with this problem, we embarked on setting up the organization Mosavatchi Qadinlar Birliki [Unity of Pro-Equality Women, UPEW].[10] We became convinced that to speed up the process of democratization, we have to mobilize women.[11]

Hoseinli's statements, along with those of her colleague, Maryem Orujova (a 42-year-old historian, member of the MP central committee, and vice chair of the UPEW), represent the latest mindset among a number of women activists in the present stage of democratization. Orujova states:

> Many women do not have the necessary understanding of the issues as they have given in to inequality and believe their role in politics is limited to giving support to this or that male politician. When Maleke khanim said; "What is the difference between Isa bey [chair of the MP] and me? Like him, I too am a politician;" most of them were amazed and said, how can a woman be a politician?

On the basis of such observations, Orujova concluded that "it is women themselves who have to change their subordinate positions, but they cannot do this without self-consciousness, self-esteem, and political empowerment." When asked how other women received UPEW's pro-equality initiative, she indicated that women have come to accept the group as a political entity.

This points to the fact that in nationalist and postcolonial projects, women's rights are intertwined with the broader national cause, the latter usually overshadowing the former, because the question of national independence and the Armenian–Azerbaijani war have overshadowed all other issues. It is only recently that some women have begun to raise concerns and demand their share from the "free market and open society." I turn now to a discussion of how this demand is taking shape in the emerging arena of women and politics.

The Current Role of Women in Politics

In Azerbaijan, as in other post-Soviet states, the transition has generally resulted in two opposing trends for women's role in politics: a drastic decline in women's share of representation at the formal (national and local) government levels, on the one hand, and an unprecedented increase in women's participation in informal politics, civil society building, and NGOs, on the other hand.

Women and the Government

The Soviet pattern of one or two women ministers in the cabinet (usually in the ministries of health and/or education) and a few women deputy ministers has been maintained in post-Soviet Azerbaijan. As of 1998, the level of female representation (10 percent) in ministerial and other high offices of the executive branch of government had not changed much since the transition. This level of representation is below the present world average (13.2 percent) but higher than that in other post-Soviet states and Eastern Europe (see table 7.1). At the subministerial, district, and local levels, however, women's presence in governmental positions has considerably declined in post-Soviet times. The Soviet-era requirement that women should hold political positions at the local and district (*raion*) levels, at least as deputy administrators, has been abandoned.[12]

Women's inadequate representation and small share in political power is a worldwide problem and not unique to Azerbaijan. However, given the Soviet legacy of egalitarian laws and rhetoric, the post-Soviet political ac-

Table 7.1

Women in Government, Eurasia, and Selected Other Countries, 1998 and 2000

Country	Percentage of Women in Parliament, 2000	Subministerial World Ranking	Percentage of Women in Government as of 1998		
			All levels	Ministerial	Subministerial
Azerbaijan	10.5	63	6.0	10.0	4.7
Georgia	7.2	88	5.3	3.8	5.9
Armenia	3.1	107	3.5	0.0	4.9
Kazakhstan	10.4	64	2.3	5.0	1.5
Kyrgyz Republic	10.0	67	3.4	4.3	2.8
Tajikistan	12.7	52	6.2	6.5	6.1
Turkmenistan*	26.0	17	2.5	4.0	0.0
Uzbekistan	7.2	88	5.3	3.3	12.5
Russia	7.6	85	4.7	7.5	4.3
Turkey	4.2	102	13.3	5.0	19.0
Iran	3.5	106	0.4	0.0	0.5
United States	14.0	49	33.0	26.3	33.4
Average for Eastern Europe and CIS	8.4		10.34	7.6	11.6
Average for OECD member countries	15.1		13.5	16.4	12.7
Average for world	13.9		11.1	13.2	11.1

Note: CIS means Commonwealth of Independent States; OECD means Organization for Economic Cooperation and Development.

*Figures on Turkmenistan are still reflective of the Soviet quota system.

Sources: United Nations Development Program, *Human Development Report 2000* (New York: Oxford University Press, 2000). Inter-Parliamentary Union, "Women in National Parliaments"; <http://www.ipu.org/wmn-e/classif.htm> (November 28, 2001). United Nations, *The World's Women 2000: Trends and Statistics* (New York: United Nations, 2000).

tivism of women in the national liberation movement, universal literacy, and women's high level of economic participation, one would logically expect a much stronger representation of women in political power.[13] How can this gap be explained?

In postindependence history writing and national narratives of Azerbaijan, loyalty to the family and clan, modesty, bravery, honesty, and heroism in defense of the homeland are extolled as the qualities necessary for patriotism. The loss of 20 percent of Azerbaijan's territory to Armenians in the conflict over Karabagh and the misery of 1 million internally displaced people or refugees (one out of every seven people in the country) have made taking back the lost land and resettling the refugees a central moral and political concern for male and (especially) female activists. The feminine metaphor of homeland, denoted as the "motherland" (*ana vatan*) whose honor (*namus*) is to be defended by all possible means, remains strong in Azerbaijani culture and associates patriotism with the sexually loaded cult of honor.[14]

The dynamic of national honor was revealed in the following exchange, which took place during the first post-Soviet presidential elections in the early 1990s, when the war with Armenia was in full force. "Who is your favorite international role model for a strong woman?" I asked Zamfira Verdiyeva, a prominent administrator, scholar, and political figure during the Soviet period, and chair of a leading post-Soviet women's organization, the Azerbaijan Women's Association. She identified Margaret Thatcher of the United Kingdom. When I asked why she or other women in Azerbaijan were not running for the presidency, she said that Azerbaijani society was not yet ready for a woman president, or even a woman candidate:

> If I nominate myself as a presidential candidate, men may see it as an insult to their manliness. When a woman steps forward to lead as a president, it may imply that in this nation there is no competent enough man to do the job of building a strong state. Such implications are not good for the image of our nation, especially when its territory and land are under threat.[15]

It is instructive to note that the impact of war on Armenian women, as demonstrated by Nura Dudwick, has been similar to its impact in Azerbaijan. Both Armenian and Azerbaijani women have been expected to give priority to raising large patriotic families and to subordinate their problems to that of the nation and thereby their political ambitions to that of men in a "gesture of sacrifice that may never be rewarded."[16]

In Azerbaijan, as in many other societies, then, the relationship between nationalism and feminism has been problematic. As discussed by Tatiana Zhurzhenko, Katherine Graney, and Elena Gapova in post-Soviet Ukraine, Tatarstan, and Belarus (respectively in chapters 1, 2, and 4 of this volume), identity politics, ethno-nationalist and religio-nationalist projects, and especially interethnic warfare can instrumentalize and objectify women or may homogenize them and deprive them of their status as full citizens.[17] Despite their active role in nationalist struggles, women may remain secondary and marginal by being relegated to the role of the "guardians of the family and transmitters of culture within the domestic sphere."[18]

In the early 1990s, women, though expected to be patriotic and actively supportive of the independence movement led by a male elite, rarely played leadership roles in the Popular Front of Azerbaijan (PFA). The PFA government led by Abolfaz Elchibey replaced many women in various positions of government service with its own male cadres. President Elchibey stated that men should be given priority in employment, particularly in the face of increasing unemployment rates. Other than Leila Yunesova, who for a short time was a deputy in the Defense Ministry of Elchibey's government, he appointed no new female politicians to his cabinet. Lidiya Rasulova, the only woman minister in Elchibey's cabinet, was hardly a product of recent nationalist transitions. Rasulova, a mild yet strong and shrewd administrator, led the Ministry of Labor and Social Security, and then the Ministry of Education, under both the Communist and nationalist governments, losing her position in 2000.

Heydar Aliyev, who succeeded Elchibey in 1993, though far from being a democrat, became popular thanks to his image as an experienced, competent, and strong leader who could bring stability and serve as a "father figure" for a nation in turmoil. His image fit well with the patrimonial and clan-oriented political culture of Azerbaijan.[19] In terms of gender policy, there have been some positive changes during Aliyev's reign. Aliyev began his term with a strong woman, Lala Shovkat Hajieva, as his chief of staff, supposedly the second highest political position. There were also two women ministers (of education and justice).

In fewer than two years, however, Shovkat Hajiyeva resigned from her position in the cabinet and also from her membership in the ruling Yeni Azerbaijan Party.[20] Later, she established her own party (the Liberal Party of Azerbaijan) and ended up running as the only woman candidate against her former boss during the presidential elections in 1998. The relative visibility of women in Aliyev's government has declined, and as of 2000 there were no remaining women ministers, and the ratio of females to males in Parliament also had fallen from 12 to 10.5 percent. Nevertheless, Aliyev's women supporters adore him, insisting that he has always promoted women in many ways. As a matter of fact, Aliyev endorsed the Convention for the Elimination of All Forms of Discrimination against Women (CEDAW; Azerbaijan ratified CEDAW on July 10, 1995).[21] He issued a Presidential decree on January 14, 1998, that established the State Committee on Women's Problems.

Women in Parliament

Immediately after the collapse of the USSR, Azerbaijan, like all other post-Soviet states, experienced a drastic decline in women's representation in the national Parliament, from 40 percent in late 1980s to 2 percent in 1992. This initially very low rate has changed slowly, reaching 12 percent in 1995 and 10.5 percent by 2000. The present figure is still below the world average (13.6 percent). The vice chair (deputy speaker) of Parliament is a woman, one of the parliamentary commissions has a female chair, and several other commissions have a female vice chair. It is interesting to note that the percentage of Azerbaijani women in Parliament is higher than in many other post-Soviet states, including Russia, Georgia, and Armenia, and also higher than many Muslim countries, including neighboring Turkey and Iran (see table 7.1).

The removal of the quota system of representation used in the Soviet Union can explain only part of the decline in female representation. As in most other societies, many factors, including the strain of the "double burden," gender role socialization and lower self-esteem, lack of experience among women candidates, traditional gender stereotypes and sexist discrimination in society at large, and finally the state's policy have all contributed to the small numbers of women in public office and low levels of women's participation in politics.

In terms of gender sensitivity and democratic orientation, the competence of the women in the present Parliament of Azerbaijan is encouraging. Opposition activists are critical of the undemocratic nature of the latest parliamentary elections and claim that the current deputies, women and men, are only those who have passed Aliyev's screening. Nevertheless, some of the anti-Aliyev women activists have spoken highly of a number of women deputies and have found opportunities for collaboration with them on women's issues. Among some of the deputies, there appears to be a similar sense of solidarity and willingness to collaborate with women in NGOs and the opposition parties on issues concerning women and on broader national issues.

A significant change in post-Soviet parliamentarians (male and female) concerns their class background. Ranging in age from 27 to 65 years, women in Parliament include one singer, one movie star, and one "chess master." The others (more than 76 percent) are academics, physicians, lawyers, and engineers. A similar pattern can be seen among male deputies. According to an explanation offered by Goltakin Hajiyeva, a 27-year-old woman deputy with training in law and philology,

> Under free competition, people would naturally elect more qualified and better educated professional people who can be good legislators. They have rejected the Soviet idea of electing peasants and workers as representatives. How can a worker or peasant be a good legislator?

She chose to run from her birthplace, the village of Granboy, because her family, especially her father as a *katkhoda* (village head), is very well known in the region, an indication that "who you know" is crucial to political office. Hajiyeva stated that, "qualified candidates are elected regardless of gender." Why, then, is the number of women in Parliament so small?

> The reason is not the lack of votes for women. It is rather easy for a qualified woman to become a politician. But we had few women candidates. We are still in a transitional stage; our women have not gained political skills and self-esteem.[22]

In contrast, another woman deputy, Rabiyat Aslanova, a 50-year-old academic who ran from Balakan, located near the border with the Dagestan republic, strongly disagrees with Hajiyeva:

> No, it is not easy for women to become politicians. Hajiyeva is young and has reached this status rather easily. She will learn later whether or not our society takes women politicians seriously; whether or not men are pleased to lose their seats to women. In Azerbaijan, a woman cannot openly declare herself a politician.[23]

Aslanova admits that there are many Azerbaijani women activists involved in politics, but they have a long way to go to become "a real politician like Tansu Ciller of Turkey, Benazir Bhutto of Pakistan, and Margaret Thatcher of England." She thinks women are also disadvantaged because they do not generally begin their political careers until after age 40 years of age, when child care and family responsibilities have diminished, whereas men begin their careers much younger. Asiya Manafova, a 60-year-old woman deputy who chairs the Parliamentary Commission on Ecology and the Environment and who has extensive political experience in the Soviet and post-Soviet times, points to additional constraints faced by women politicians:

> In democratic elections, you have to compete. Political competition and campaigning are much harder for women as they do not have the same opportunities that men do. For instance, one has to meet with the voters. As a woman, one cannot sit next to any man, shake hands with him, and talk to him about her qualifications. She cannot go to distant villages and knock on the doors.[24]

Aside from some aspects specific to post-Soviet states, the above statements made by Azerbaijani women deputies testify to the commonality of the challenges for women's political empowerment in many parts of the world.

Women and Political Parties

Azerbaijan has a multiparty electoral system, and as of 2001, there were thirty-eight officially recognized political parties (registered by the Ministry of Justice). Women lead only two of the thirty-eight parties, and eighteen of them have a women's council.

Generally, since its independence, three political trends have become prominent in party politics, and each has different gender implications: Turkism (Turkchilik), Islamism (Islamchilik*)*, and Azerbaijanism (Azerbaijanchilik). The Popular Front Party of Azerbaijan, a carryover from Elchibey's PFA,[25] has adopted an ethnocentric Turkism.[26] Many other parties, including the ruling Yeni Azerbaijan Party, have pursued a more pragmatic multiethnic "Azerbaijanism," balancing all three tendencies while maintaining the secular nature of the state and politics. The primary representative of the third trend, Islamism, is the Islamic Party of Azerbaijan.

Among the secular parties, women make up 10 to 25 percent of the membership. For instance, the MP (led by Isa Gambar) represents democratic and liberal tendencies and emphasizes civil and inclusive nationalism by recognizing human rights and equal citizenship regardless of ethnicity, gender, and religion. Women make up 13 percent of the MP, including two women on its central committee (out of twenty-three). These two women (Hoseinli and Orujova, introduced above) succeeded in proposing a gender quota (25 percent female) in the MP, which, following some heated debate, was approved during the Sixth Congress in April 2001. Before this, women made up 5 percent of the parliamentary candidates on the MP's list.

There have been a few smaller parties, such as the Social Democratic Party and the Liberal Party of Azerbaijan, which are led or co-led by such women as Arzu Abdollayeva and Lala Shovkat Hajiyeva. Besides partisan activity, Abdollayeva (who is in her 40s) has been a hardworking and sincere advocate of peace, dialogue, and conflict resolution with her Armenian counterparts, a cause quite risky for herself and her political party. She has been leading the activities of the Helsinki Citizen's Assembly of Azerbaijan. Shovkat Hajiyeva, a 50-year-old physician, Chairwoman of the Liberal Party of Azerbaijan, and among the country's most charismatic and maverick woman politicians, was the only woman candidate among those running for president in the September 1998 elections. According to a number of pre-election polls, Hajiyeva ranked among the five leading candidtates.[27] Leila Yunesova, a historian in her 40s and another strong and intelligent woman political figure, was among the founders of the PFA. She split from it early on and founded the Independence Democratic Party, splitting again later to join the Vahdat Party. In 1996, she broke away from partisan politics to establish the Peace and Democracy Institute, an NGO.[28]

Another small but active party with three women as deputy chairs is the Azerbaijan Democratic Party of Independence. The original leader of this party, Rasul Quliyev, is known as one of the richest men in Azerbaijan and was second only to Aliyev in his political power before open animosity developed between the two and he left the country for the United States. His party calls for the overthrow of the present government and, according to one of its women leaders, Mirvari Gahramanli (an oil engineer in her 60s) and the chair of the Azerbaijan Democratic Party of Independence's Youth Council, Zarifa Zeinalova (a student in her late 20s), their party has been in the forefront in mobilizing women and students to protest against human rights abuses, poverty, and the occupation of Karabagh by Armenians. They have founded the "women in black scarves movement," a group of 50 to 100 women who occasionally demonstrate outside the Taza Pir (a central mosque in Baku), holding empty pots as symbols of poverty and unemployment.

The third trend, Islamism (Islamchilik), which is much smaller than the other two, has been represented mainly in the Islamic Party of Azerbaijan (IPA), which represents the Shi'a branch of Islam.[29] As an opposition party, IPA challenges "official" Islam and the government. In the view of IPA, religion—that is, Muslimhood (Musalmanlik), rather than ethnicity or nationality—is the basis of Azerbaijani identity. IPA's reputation among many Azerbaijanis, especially most women's groups, has remained negative because of its close ideological and financial connections to the conservative Islamists in Iran and because of its intellectually low caliber and antidemocratic, sexist, and sectarian views.[30]

In recent years, some of the more enlightened women members of IPA have become disillusioned with the segregationist practices of its leadership and have joined more moderate Islamic groups. The most prominent among them is Esmat Mamedova, a professor at Baku State University, who is an Islamic, but not Islamist, woman activist.[31] As an active member of IPA, she led its women's council before leaving that party and running for a seat in Parliament as an independent candidate. She is now the only woman member of Parliament who covers her head. She also leads a women's NGO called Kamillik (perfection) Women's Charity Society, which strives to enhance moral development among women and youth, protect national traditions, and disseminate information and research.

The Islamic trend in Azerbaijan, however, is not limited to Islamism of the kind advocated by IPA. The growing prominence of moderate Islamic groups in neighboring Turkey and the decreasing credibility of the fundamentalist Islamists in Iran have contributed to a "new Islamic thinking," which is akin to the *jadid* (modern) movement of early twentieth century among Muslims in Azerbaijan and Central Asia.[32] The gender implications of such moderation and secularization of Islam in the Caspian Sea region, along with the interaction between Azerbaijani women and the growing feminist movements in both Iran and Turkey, are clearly encouraging.

Building Civil Society and NGOs: Women's Active Role

Although the public at large still knows little about the meaning, functions, and significance of NGOs, the so-called Third Sector in Azerbaijan is gaining prominence among intellectuals and activists. The recent surge of interest in building civil society, especially among nonpartisan NGOs, may reflect a new dynamism toward democratization in the country.[33] The widespread misunderstanding and resentment against NGOs, especially on the part of government supporters in the period 1994–96, seems to be changing, as many activists and officials, both proponents and opponents of the Aliyev government, show a relatively good understanding of and mixed attitude toward NGOs.

In Azerbaijan, women have been active, often playing leading roles in the Third Sector from very early on, but women-focused NGOs did not form until a few years after the collapse of the USSR, when women began to fear that they were losing social status. As has been pointed out by Valerie Estes, it is necessary to separate the role of women as actors in NGOs from the role of NGOs in addressing women's and gender issues. Many women work in NGOs that do not address women's concerns, and many NGOs that are not identified as women's NGOs deal with problems specific to women or gender issues.[34]

Why have women in Azerbaijan, as in other post-Soviet states, been so active in NGOs?[35] According to Irada Kulieva, one of the founders of Gulyum (my flower), an NGO aimed at strengthening environmental education for preschool children throughout Azerbaijan,

> The Third Sector suits women, because NGOs are busy addressing many of the social problems that women have been left to address for years—disabilities, health, children's issues, and education.[36]

There are more reasons behind women's activism in NGOs. As has been argued by Estes (and confirmed by Armina Ishkanian in the case of Armenia; see chapter 12 of this volume), in the face of the exclusion of women "from the power centers of government and big business, NGOs offer women one of the few avenues currently available to them to promote broad-scale socioeconomic change, not just change connected with women's issues."[37] Estes also suggests that, compared with the traditional positions of power, NGOs are new and relatively devoid of corruption and hence less liable to damage the reputation of women and their families. In addition, one should consider that Azerbaijani women (compared with men) have better communication skills, more foreign language proficiency, and stronger informal networking abilities. This can facilitate their contacts with foreign donors as well as grant writing and resource mobilization.[38]

The main barriers to the growth of NGOs continue to be related to economic hardships and lack of resources and philanthropic institutions, exacerbated by the fact that the issues concerning Karabagh refugees draw away most of the available resources. Despite some improvements in NGO–

government relations and communication, legal and governmental barriers, long waits for registration, and a lack of transparency continue to interfere with the proper and free functioning of NGOs. Due to a scarcity of resources, NGO activism (for both men and women) is confined primarily to the capital. There are very few NGOs addressing gender issues in the provinces.

Generally, the initially fierce competition to establish contacts with donors and secure grants is slowly giving way to a realization of the necessity of cooperation among NGOs. As of 2001, about ten coalitions of NGOs had emerged. One of the largest and most active coalitions is the National NGO Forum (Milli QHT Forumu), which was formed in 1998. The NGO Forum brings together and coordinates 262 NGOs, including a number of women's NGOs, and it has recently established branches in five regions. It is encouraging to see that one of the forum's main sectors of activity is gender (the others being human rights, development, ecology, peace, and democracy). Women make up 40 percent of the forum's administrative body (six out of fifteen), 37.5 percent of its working staff, and 10 percent of its experts.[39] The forum's member organizations hold monthly meetings to share their concerns, experiences, and ideas. It was due to such coordination and cooperation that NGOs were able to bring more serious pressure on the government for legislative reform.[40]

Presently, women's NGOs are of various types (see table 7.2). Although these NGOs usually claim political independence, a number of them are directly or indirectly active in partisan politics as well as women's rights issues. For instance, the Azerbaijan Women's Majlis (Sevil) claims to be the largest women's association (with chapters or representatives in seventy-two regions of Azerbaijan) and is led by the president's daughter, Sevil Aliyeva.

The D. Alieva Society for the Protection of Women's Rights initially emerged as the women's wing of the PFA, and up to 1995 it engaged actively in nationalist politics with no clear gender perspective. However, as stated by its chair, Navella Jafarova, in recent years, this organization has become "more inclusive, less militant, and more concerned with and active on women's and gender issues":

> We practice what Ibrahimbeyova [coordinator of Gender in Development, or GID] preaches and theorizes. For example, after a seminar in a village in Khachmaz region, we taught 40 women how to punish a man in that village who was battering his wife. We have been the first to address the issues concerning prostitution and trafficking in women. We teach women *and* men how to use contraceptives.[41]

Table 7.2

Examples of Women's Nongovernmental Organizations (NGOs) in Azerbaijan, 2001 (with contact person)

Organizations Focusing on Gender Issues *24 percent of all women's NGOs*	Organizations Promoting Peace *8 percent of all women's NGOs*	Professional Organizations *19 percent of all women's NGOs*	Ethnic- and Faith-Based Organizations *11 percent of all women's NGOs*	Charitable and Humanitarian Organizations *38 percent of all women's NGOs*
Association of Women of Azerbaijan (Zemfira Verdieva)	Azerbaijani Women for Peace and Democracy in the Caucasus (Rena Safaralieva)	Association of Creative Women (Afag Guseynova)	Azeri-Turk Women's Union (Tanzila Rustamhanli)	Charitable Center for Mothers of Victims of War (Rafiga Askerova)
Baku Association of Women of Azerbaijan (Zarifa Salahova)	Society of Soldiers' Mothers (Elmira Buniyatzadeh)	Association of Women Journalists (Sabina Iskenderli)	Fatima Zahra Muslim Women's Society (Zemfira Isaeva)	Charitable Society for Pregnant Women and Infants (Museyib Aliev)
Center for Women and Development (Elmira Suleymanova)	Women's Society for Peace (Rugiya Gambar)	Association of Women Managers (Gulnara Zamanova)	Humanitarian Association of Jewish Women (Larisa Reykhrudel)	Charitable Society for Single Mothers and Orphans (Parvana Sadigova)
D. Alieva Society for the Protection of Women's Rights (Novella Jafarova)		Business Women's Association (Svetlana Kasumova)	Society for Pious Intellectual Women (Durdana Shabanova)	Disabled Women Society (Mehluga Rahimova)
Gender and Human Rights Research Union (Rena Mirzazadeh)		Society of University Women (Tamam Jafarova)		Havva Charitable Center (Solmaz Yusifova)
International Association for Family and Society (Faiza Alieva)		Society of Women in the Oil Industry (Solmaz Gadjieva)		Kamillik Women's Charitable Society (Asmet Mamedova)
"Noble Women" Cultural Union (Arifa Mamedova)		Union of Intellectual Women (Sevil Mamedli)		Merciful Women's Society (Rena Velieva)
Sevil Azerbaijan Women's Mejlis (Tarana Guseynova)				Mother's Cry (Dilara Orudjeva)
Symmetry Azerbaijan Gender Association (Kamilla Dadasheva)				Mothers and Children of Victims of War, Nasimi district (Zemfira Tagizadeh)
				Society for Single Mothers and Children (Natig Babazadeh)
				Tomris Society for Mothers and Sisters (Nushaba Mamedova)
				Umid Society of Mothers (Susan Akhmedova)
				Women's Charitable Center for the Arts (Sudaba Shiraliyeva)
				"Without You" Charitable Society (Zemfira Ragimova)

Source: Author's research and *Directory of Women NGOs in Azerbaijan,* published by the GID unit of Azerbaijan, UNDP, Baku, 2001.

One of the positive recent developments concerning women's NGOs has to do with the establishment of a GID unit in Azerbaijan (in September 1997) under the auspices of the United Nations Development Program. Under the directorship of Rena Ibrahimbeyova (a capable, gender-conscious Azerbaijani woman with training in psychology), this center has embarked on a series of impressive and unprecedented educational and capacity-building programs among women. Among the center's innovative and timely activities in Baku, it has organized national and regional conferences on issues, such as "Women's Rights are Human Rights" and "Women in Conflict Resolution" (Baku, May 1998); disseminated brochures on such taboo issues as violence, rape, and sexual harassment[42]; and produced educational and empowering television programs dealing with gender relations.[43]

The growing transnational feminist networks, gender projects of such UN agencies as UNICEF and the United Nations Development Program, and United Nations–sponsored regional and world conferences on women, along with the activities of gender-sensitive international foundations—such as the Initiative for Social Action and Renewal in Eurasia, the Soros Foundation's Open Society Institute, and the National Democratic Institute—have together responded to the urgency of Azerbaijani women's needs for information, resources, and gender education. Despite some undesirable consequences of intervention by foreign donor agencies in post-Soviet Azerbaijan (similar to those in Russia, discussed by Michele Rivkin-Fish in chapter 13 of this volume), the interplay between domestic and international factors has contributed to an incremental shift toward gender sensitivity in the views, orientations, and goals of women's NGOs.

Unfortunately, however, before such initiatives can have a wider impact on society, projects such as GID are terminated due to a lack of funding. This underlies a serious concern over the sustainability of NGOs, because donations from international sources make up more than 95 percent of financial sources of support for most NGOs. "Donors give birth to the child and leave it out there with no support to grow," according to Allakhverov.

Due to the efforts of GID (led by Ibrahimbeyova), women's NGOs such as the Center for Women and Development (led by Elmira Suleymanova) as well as women in the government, such as Fatma Abdollahzadeh, Dilara Saeedzade, and Zahra Quliyeva (head of the State Committee on Women's Issues), Azerbaijan ratified CEDAW and has officially adhered to several UN conventions concerning human rights and women's rights. The success or sincerity of Azerbaijan's authorities in the implementation of these conventions, however, remains to be seen. Since the creation of the above-mentioned state committees and especially since preparation for the Beijing conference began, a renewed sense of enthusiasm has emerged among women activists, especially those close to the government. Although still limited to a small number of elite women and some political activists, this has set in motion a more gender-focused, systematic, and sustained engagement of women's groups, which may pave the way for the emergence of a more popular and grassroots women's movement in the future.

Another encouraging development is increased cooperation between Armenian and Azerbaijani NGOs. Women activists and NGOs, such as the Society of Azerbaijani Women for Peace and Democracy in the Caucasus (directed by Rena Safaralieva), have been playing a particularly important role in peacemaking. Arzu Abdullayeva, the head of the Helsinki Citizens Assembly of Azerbaijan (and a leading member of the Social Democratic Party of Azerbaijan), has been harshly criticized by Azeri ultranationalists for her increasingly bold peace initiatives. With the help of international donors, a number of Azeri and Armenian women have paved the way toward conflict management and peacemaking efforts by holding meetings and establishing dialogue between Armenian and Azerbaijani NGOs (also including Georgian NGOs) in Baku, Yerevan, and Tbilisi.[44]

The State Committee on Women (created in January 1998) is supposed to "oversee and coordinate" all programs and activities, including those of the women's NGOs dealing with women's status in Azerbaijan. The extent of this oversight is not yet clear, nor is its relationship with women's NGOs. The independence of NGOs from state control, however, is necessary for the emergence of civil society. Conversely, certain aspects of the NGO movement, such as total dependency on foreign donors and orientation of issues and projects toward grant-giving external and foreign donors rather than internal and domestic needs and priorities, may increase the potential for bureaucratization, corruption, and homogenization of women's activism similar to that seen in the Soviet Union and other authoritarian regimes. Such a state-centered, foreign-dominated, or grant-dependent "feminism" is bound to diminish women's grassroots initiatives and overshadow diversity and genuine agencies working for change toward real needs, equality, and democracy.

Conclusion: Emerging Feminism?

Although the overall impact of the post-Soviet transition on women's status and their economic and social rights has been negative so far, many women are taking advantage of recently introduced civil rights and new opportunities. Many women—alarmed by the retrogressive gender agenda of the post-Soviet nationalist, conservative, and Islamist forces—have begun to redefine the gender parameters of national independence, the market economy, and democracy. Through their political and civic activism many women, especially those with higher education, professional experience, and language skills, are taking part in civil society building and democratization. They are fighting unemployment, political exclusion, and social marginalization by asserting their presence in both formal politics and the informal civic arena, especially in NGOs.

Women's social activism, which was initially dominated by charity and promotion of nationalism, is gradually gaining gender consciousness. Azerbaijani women presently avoid identifying themselves with feminism, especially "Western feminism," which is associated (in their minds) with hostility toward men and the family. But many aspects of their social activism would serve a long-term feminist strategy.[45] For example, their fight against unemployment and poverty—and more recently also against domestic violence, sex discrimination, regressive attempts to reverse egalitarian family law, and trafficking in women—as well as their support for implementing the Beijing Platform for Action and for promoting women's representation in Parliament and the political parties all are indicative of a growing gender sensitivity in women's civic activism in Azerbaijan.

Regardless of whether they categorize themselves as feminist or not, many women have begun to assert their rights by incorporating a gender-conscious approach into a struggle toward gender-sensitive socioeconomic development and democratization. The activism of many may evolve into a "national feminism"[46] containing a nationalist undertone, or it may grow in line with the "difference" feminism as observed in Latin America.[47] But it seems unlikely that well-educated, professional, and economically active Azerbaijani women will passively submit to a loss of their civil and human rights.[48]

Notes

1. The prodemocracy movements in Azerbaijan and other post-Soviet states in the Caucasus and Central Asia can be seen as part of the global trend of the "democracy century," but some of the characteristics of the "national liberation movements" of the early twentieth century have overshadowed their prodemocracy aspects. Azerbaijanis, along with the rest of Central Asia, were colonized by the Russian Empire in the 1820s and were among the last Muslim communities to become independent (1990s).

2. For a comparative discussion on the gender aspects of democracy movements, see

Jane Jaquette and Sharon Wolchik, eds., *Women and Democracy: Latin America and Central and Eastern Europe* (Baltimore: Johns Hopkins University Press, 1998).

3. Thanks to an academic-year Fulbright scholarship in 1991–92 and then several UN assignments as a consultant, I was able to do extensive fieldwork in Azerbaijan during the 1990s.

4. In Azerbaijan, and throughout the Caucasus and Central Asia, issues of national sovereignty, decolonization and nation building took precedence over issues of individual liberty and equal rights. Immediately after the collapse of the Soviet Union, nationalist discourse, identity politics, and economic concerns were dominant in these new states, while democratization, civil rights and equality were peripheral issues.

5. For elaboration on the impact of post-Soviet transition on women in Azerbaijan, see Nayereh Tohidi, *Situatsionniy Analiz Polozheniia Zhenshchin v Azerbaidzhane* [An Analysis of Women's Position in Azerbaijan] (Baku: UNICEF, 1994). For similar patterns in other post-Soviet and post-Communist states, see, e.g., Mary Buckley, ed., *Post-Soviet Women: From the Baltic to Central Asia* (New York: Cambridge University Press, 1997); Gillian Pascal and Nick Manning, "Gender and Social Policy: Comparing Welfare States in Central and Eastern Europe and the Former Soviet Union," *Journal of European Social Policy* 10, no. 3 (2000): 240–66; and Susan Gal and Gail Kligman, eds., *Reproducing Gender: Politics, Publics, and Everyday Life after Socialism* (Princeton, N.J.: Princeton University Press, 2000).

6. Reported by the Human Rights Center of Azerbaijan, "Comments on the Government Report on CEDAW Compliance," 1998 (numbers are based on state statistics), 4.

7. *Azerbaycanda Qadinlar ve Kisiler 2000* [Women and Men in Azerbaijan], State Statistical Committee of Azerbaijan Republic and GID unit of UNDP (Baku: Sada 2000), 91–92.

8. For discussions of women's role and gendered aspects of nationalism and identity politics in Soviet and post-Soviet Azerbaijan, see Nayereh Tohidi, "Soviet in Public, Azeri in Private: Gender, Islam, and Nationality in Soviet and Post-Soviet Azerbaijan," *Women's Studies International Forum* 5, no. 19 (January–April 1996: 111–23; Tohidi, "Gurdians of the Nation: Women, Islam, and the Soviet Modernization in Azerbaijan," in *Women in Muslim Societies: Diversity within Unity,* ed. Herbert Bodman and Nayereh Tohidi (Boulder, Colo.: Lynne Rienner, 1998); and Tohidi, "Gender and National Identity in Post-Soviet Azerbaijan: A Regional Perspective," in *Gender and Identity Construction: Women of Central Asia, the Caucasus, and Turkey,* ed. Feride Acar and Ayse Gunes-Ayata (Leiden: Brill, 2000).

9. Due to financial pressure, one such journal, *Qadin ve Jamiyat,* ceased publication after only four issues, and the two other journals, *Genderology and Samavi,* faced with financial difficulties, cannot publish on regular basis. There are also some more conventional papers or magazines dealing with women issues that are either government supported or commercial, including *Azerbaijan Qadini* [Azerbaijani Women] and *Mir Zhenshchin-Qadin Dunyasi* [Women's World].

10. It is interesting to note that *mosavat* means equality, hence gives a double meaning to the title of this women's group, pro-equality as well as pro-Mosavat, the party to which many of the members of this Unity belong.

11. This is from an author's interview, August 1, 2001, Baku.

12. One of the strengths of the Soviet system was that it institutionalized the social and economic aspects of civil rights—namely, guaranteeing full employment, public education and health care to both male and female citizens. However, these societies were

weak in terms of legal and political rights, leaving a society with economic rights but lacking a comprehensive civil society. The post-Soviet transition has jeopardized the social and economic rights of women, but it remains to be seen whether an improvement in their political and civil rights is on the horizon.

13. I have met many of the women ministers, deputy ministers, and other women officials in the executive branch of the government in post-Soviet Azerbaijan, and they seem to be not token symbols but women of strength and influence. Perhaps only a few of them are genuinely interested in democracy and representing the interests of the ordinary women of Azerbaijan, but this pattern applies equally to male government officials as well.

14. One of the questions I posed to my women respondents during a recent field visit to Azerbaijan (summer 2001) was the following: What do you see to be the three most urgent national concerns and primary barriers to economic development and democracy in Azerbaijan? Almost all (98 percent) of the respondents (both governmental officials and nongovernmental activists) ranked the "occupation of Azerbaijani lands by Armenian invaders," the problem of refugees, and the resolution of the Karabagh conflict as the first or second most important issue. In the context of widespread sense of defeat and humiliation, the urge to restore national honor and the desire to build a strong army may have reinforced patriarchal norms and ideas of masculine patriotism nourished by women in their role as wives and mothers.

15. This is from an author's interview, Baku, 1992.

16. Nora Dudwick, "Out of the Kitchen into the Crossfire: Women in Independent Armenia," in *Post-Soviet Women,* ed. Buckley, 245.

17. See, e.g., Carole Pateman, *The Sexual Contract* (Stanford, Calif.: Stanford University Press, 1988); Nira Yuval-Davis and Floya Anthias, eds., *Women, Nation, State* (Hampshire: Macmillan, 1989); Deniz Kandiyoti, *Women, Islam, and the State* (Philadelphia: Temple University Press, 1991); V. Spike Peterson and Anne Sisson Runyan, *Global Gender Issues* (Boulder, Colo.: Westview Press, 1993); Simona Sharoni, "Gender and Middle East Politics," *Fletcher Forum of World Affairs* 17, no. 2 (summer 1993): 59–73; Valentine M. Moghadam, ed., *Identity Politics and Women: Cultural Reassertions and Feminisms in International Perspective* (Boulder, Colo.: Westview Press, 1994); Barbara Einhorn, "Links across Differences: Gender, Ethnicity, and Nationalism," *Women's Studies International Forum* 19, nos. 1–2 (1996): 1–3; and Uma Narayan, *Dislocating Cultures: Identities, Transitions, and Third-World Feminism* (New York: Routledge, 1997).

18. Tohidi, "Gender and National Identity in Post-Soviet Azerbaijan."

19. The nation is usually perceived as the family writ large and Heidar Aliyev, the "big father" of the nation who is occasionally called "Heidar baba" (papa Heidar) or simply "kishi," (the man) in a double meaning by both critics and admirers of his personality cult. In the second congress of his party, Yeni Azerbaijan, held in November 2001, Aliyev's son, Elham Aliyev (presently in control of the oil industry) was nominated as the successor to his 83-year-old ailing father. This may indicate the persistency of the clan-oriented and patrimonial polity.

20. In a press conference several years later, Hajieva spoke out about the reasons for her resignation from the president's office. She claimed that she could not stand the "corruption and bribery in the governmental bodies and also in the ruling Party." *Ayna* (Baku), September 19, 1998.

21. CEDAW, passed by the UN General Assembly, first went into effect in 1981.

22. This is from an author's interview, Baku, July 31, 2001.

23. This is from an author's interview, Baku, August 5, 2001.

24. This is from an author's interview, Baku, July 23, 2001.

25. The Popular Front of Azerbaijan, established in 1989, represented the leadership of the anti-Soviet and independence movement in Azerbaijan. The Karabakh conflict with Armenia served as a catalyst for the creation of this front and its subsequent mobilization of the population against the Communist Party and its eventual takeover in 1992.

26. For many in this group, the aspiration and struggle for a unified or single (*vahid*) Azerbaijan (unifying more than 25 million ethnic kin inhabiting Iran with more than 7 million Azeris of the Azerbaijan Republic) has become part of their "national idea" Hikmet Hadjy-Zadeh, *A New Identity for a New Azerbaijan* (Baku: Far Center, 1998), 4.

27. Reported by the Women's Rights Monitoring Group, the Center for Human Rights in Azerbaijan, *Information Bulletin* 9, part 1 (September 1–10, 1998).

28. For elaborate analyses and sociopolitical portraits of these and other contemporary elite women, see my book *Gender, Islam, and Democracy in Post-Soviet Azerbaijan* (in progress).

29. According to some estimates, more than 70 percent of Muslim Azerbaijanis are Shii, and about 30 percent are Sunni.

30. Four leading members of the IPA were imprisoned in 1997 for allegedly spying for Iran. A few years later, they were released upon a presidential pardon.

31. A distinction should be made between "Islamic" and "Islamist." "Islamism" refers to those who use Islam as a political ideology (as an "ism") to take the state power and establish a religiously based authoritarian government, whereas "Islamic" refers to those Muslims who either adhere to or are influenced by Islam as a religion and culture.

32. For elaboration on this and other historical background, see Tohidi, "Gurdians of the Nation." See also Tadeusz Swietochowski, *Russia and Azerbaijan: A Borderland in Transition* (New York: Columbia University Press, 1995), 223; Audrey Altstadt, *The Azerbaijani Turks: Power and Identity under Russian Rule* (Stanford, Calif.: Hoover Institution Press, 1992), 55, 59, 61; and Adeeb Khalid, *The Politics of Muslim Cultural Reform: Jadidism in Central Asia* (Los Angeles: University of California Press, 1998).

33. For an informative overview of NGOs in Azerbaijan, see Azer Allakhverov, "The Third Sector in Azerbaijan: Theory and Practice," and "The Report on the Development of the Third Sector in Azerbaijan (2000)" by Society for Humanitarian Research, Baku, August 22, 2001 (<http://www.mg.klever.net/~shr/>). Some information is provided by Azay Guliev, head of the NGO Forum during author's interview, August 8, 2001, Baku.

34. V. Estes, "Lessons in Transition: Gender Issues in Civil Society Development," *Give & Take* (a journal in Civil Society in Eurasia) 3, no. 2 (summer 2000): 5–6.

35. As of 2001, about 1,500 officially registered and nearly 1,000 unregistered public organizations existed in Azerbaijan. However, only about 200 of them are actually active. Of these 200 active NGOs, 37 of them are women-focused groups and 30 are aimed at youth. The most active and strongest NGOs (numbering 50-60) are the ones concerned with Karabagh refugees and internally displaced persons, health and children's issues, human rights and women's rights, and environmental and ecology issues.

36. See Charmaine Bickley, "Gyulum: Azeri College Friends Found NGO, Find New Opportunities," *Give & Take* (a journal in Civil Society in Eurasia) 3, no. 2 (summer 2000): 8.

37. Estes, "Lessons in Transition," 5–6.

38. As observed also by Dudwick, "Out of the Kitchen into the Crossfire," 243, in

the case of Armenia, higher rates of female students in philology and foreign languages has become a special asset for women in transitional context.

39. Figures calculated based on the information in the report *2 Illik Hesabat: Iyun 1999–May 2001* [A Two-Year Assessment Report] (Baku: Milli QHT Forumu, 2001), 9–11.

40. Coalition building among women's NGOs has been much slower, however, and it has been only through the State Committee on Women's Issues and such international agencies as the United Nations–supported GID, ISAR [Initiative for Social Action Renewal in Eurasia], and the Soros Foundation's Open Society Institute that women's groups have established some degree of contact and cooperation. A related obstacle is the strength of the cult of personality. Many NGOs, including women's NGOs, are formed around a strong person rather than a vision, program, and plan of action. Personality and ego friction often limits the potential for solidarity, collaboration, and coalition building.

41. This is from an author's interview, Baku, August 7, 2001.

42. See "Azerbaycanda Qadinlarin Veziyyeti" [Women's Status in Azerbaijan] in *Me'lumat Bulleteni* [Information Bulletin] 1, part 1 (January 1–15, 1999), published by the Center for Defense of Human Rights in Azerbaijan.

43. See "The Gender in Development Unit in Azerbaijan: A Growing Experience," UN Development Program Regional Bureau for Europe and the Commonwealth of Independent States, February 1997; available at <http://www.undp.uz/gid/eng/azerbaijan/index.html>.

44. As a member of the Advisory Committee for the Armenian–Azerbaijani Peace Initiative, I have been a participant observer to at least one of these efforts that began in 1993 with the support of the Stanford Center for Conflict and Negotiation and the Foundation for Global Community.

45. Maxine Molyneux correctly distinguishes between women's strategic (antipatriarchal) and practical (welfare and immediate) interests in her "Mobilization without Emancipation? Women's Interests, the State and Revolution in Nicaragua," *Feminist Studies* 11, no. 2 (1985): 227–54.

46. See Lois A. West, ed., *Feminist Nationalism* (New York: Routledge, 1997).

47. On the basis of an "ethic of care" as opposed to an "ethic of rights" proposed by scholars such as Carol Gilligan, "difference feminism" suggests that "women have something unique to bring to the content and practices of political life." See Jaquette and Wolchik, *Women and Democracy,* 26.

48. For policy recommendations toward a more effective and gender-sensitive international intervention in Azerbaijan, see Nayereh Tohidi, *Woman, Democratization, and Islam in Post-Soviet Azerbaijan,* Policy Papers Series on Women in Transition, published by The Kennan Institute of the Woodrow Wilson International Center for Scholars, July 2002.

8

Women's Political Activism in Russia: The Case of Samara

Ludmila Popkova

The inclusion of women in politics poses a controversial issue for the democratic transformation of post-Soviet Russia. The political transition allowed women's rights activists' to demand official action rather than mere declarations about women's equality. There is an acute interest in conducting analyses of women's political leadership and civic activism, with the aim of increasing women's involvement in political decision making. This chapter furthers that effort by exploring women politicians' perceptions of their own "place" in politics, their priorities and values, and their views of women's roles in postcommunist development.

Political representation of women at both federal and regional levels remains low. As Russian and foreign researchers note, commonly accepted world structural and situational barriers are in use here. First, they name gender differences in political socialization, which cause weak motivation for women in this activity. Second comes unevenness in the distribution of the various resources that may be used by men and women, and this unevenness limits the political possibilities of women in politics. To the above-mentioned structural factors, researchers add the existence of discrimination, displayed both through unwillingness to give key positions in party organizations and government bodies to women and through the predominance of traditional gender stereotypes, which cause distrust toward women in politics.[1]

The third situational factor includes the particular features of women's course of life that demand individual women's responsibility for raising children and housekeeping. Judging by global experience, we may say that the extent of the development of a country's women's movement is of specific importance in this situation. For that reason, the weakness of the independent women's movement in Russia in practice not only excludes recruiting women politicians out of the sphere of social activism but also does not give women an opportunity to articulate the problem of their rights in public discourse.

My research is based on interviews conducted with women politicians and nongovernmental organization (NGO) activists in Samara, a city in the Volga River Valley. The research raised several principal questions: What kinds of motivation and objectives of activity of women in politics can be traced? And what are the political priorities and social interests of women? The research was carried out on the basis of specially arranged focused interviews with women—leaders and participants of social organizations, deputies and candidate members of different legislative bodies, and representatives of the regional administration elite. In addition, documents and public speeches were analyzed.

Framing Women's Activism: The Legacy of the Soviet Gender Order

Analysis of objective facts is not enough, however. Researchers need to should pay more attention to the subjective and discursive constraints on women's political choices from a perspective of post-Soviet cultural transition. In this context, it is crucial to explore the influence of past norms of gender and culture. The Soviet state institutionalized a distinctive order in which the roles of men and women were defined according to the needs of the communist state. The state-prescribed Soviet gender order had a significant impact on the subjective perceptions of Soviet men and women.

Many researchers have shown that the gender identities even of the younger generation are still strongly influenced by Soviet values. There are certain common themes in their perception of women's roles. These include the acceptance of supposedly natural sexual differences, which leads to perceiving a woman's secondary position in all spheres as natural. Sociological surveys show that despite negative assessments of their chances in the labor market in politics, women rarely claim that they face discrimination. This acceptance can be seen as a form of self-limitation on the part of women, which reinforces their subordinate position. Yet what is more important is that the most Russian women do not challenge the existing post-Soviet gender order. During the transition period, there has not been a focus on gender relations in a way that could be compared with the process that took place in Western Europe and the United States during second wave feminism. Instead of conscious reflection on gender, we could instead call the post-Soviet ideological process one of adaptation to social and economic necessities.[2]

According to the social movement theory, the transformation of civic conscience is a necessary condition for social and political activism. The important consequence of constructing the collective political identity is the mechanism of group mobilization. Mobilization could play an effective role in galvanizing a group's participation in the political process. Some scholars stress the particular importance of mobilization in a society experiencing a transition to a democratic system. Mobilization helps citizens gain access to new political roles and become political agents.

Social and political activity requires a critical mass of individuals who recognize that the discrimination or oppression they are experiencing is a systematic or political problem, not a personal one, and that the rectification of the injustice they experience is possible. This process is diversely referred to as "framing," "cognitive liberation," and the "transformation of consciousness"; social movement activists, by definition, have begun such a transformation of consciousness. These activists regard the injustice or set of injustices by a given societal group or class as a systematic problem. Social attitudes toward women help enforce sex-role stereotyping in Russia's current transition period, thereby creating another set of attitudinal obstacles to the expansion of the contemporary women's movement.[3] It is important to recall that a person may perceive injustice as a shared political phenomenon yet doubt that any public actions to alter the situation would be effective or—especially in the case of a repressive regime—even feasible.

During the transitional period, the emerging women's movement is speculating that women will lose the state's "protection." However partially, they will have to learn to fend for themselves and their families even more than they do at present. This reflects the dilemma of actually being both a woman (in need of "specific" rights and politics) and an individual. When policies assist women only as mothers, they reinforce the existing gender code. It is also true that these policies can lessen discrimination as they can potentially lessen women's sole responsibilities for children and domestic work. Russian women fear that new post-Soviet legislation will misrepresent the complicated reality of women's specific needs and their equal rights.

According to recent cross-national studies on gender culture in Hungary, the former East Germany, Poland, and Russia, women in Russia are less sensitive to male domination than in other post-socialist countries.[4] They deny any kind of gender conflict in their professional and private life. But at the same time, they are much more critical and even hostile toward men in their interpersonal relations. This hidden and unrealized gender conflict could be considered one of the main obstacles to creating women's rights activism and reforming the gender norms.

In the lower chamber of the Russian parliament, the Third State Duma, elected in 1999, there are 34 women among the 450 elected deputies (i.e., 7.6 percent). The representation of women on party lists and the share of women among electoral candidates to the State Duma in single-member districts is 12 percent. There were two women's political organizations among twenty-eight registered for participation in parliamentary elections. The dynamics of women's political activity in the Samara region in the late 1990s confirms a Russia-wide tendency toward civic and political "demobilization." The proportion of women elected to the Second State Duma in 1995 was 11 percent; the proportion of women elected to the Samara Gubernskaya (Regional) Duma in 1997 was about 7 percent. In 1997, two out of the eleven women candidates became deputies of the Gubernskaya Duma (out of twenty-five members); in 1999, only one out of the three Samaran women candidates won election to the State Duma from a single-member district.

At the local authority level in the city of Samara, official indices of women participating in the decision-making process are more impressive. Of the eighteen deputies to the City Duma elected in 2000, eight were women. Political representation of women at all levels of the Samaran regional power reflects a Russia-wide pyramid: the higher the level of power, the fewer women.

As far as civil society is concerned, statistical data also give some perspective. Among 2000 NGOs registered in the Samara region, 17 were referred to as women's NGOs in 1998. The above-mentioned numbers of organizations, as well as 600 other women's NGOs registered all over the country in the Russian Ministry of Justice, would not mislead a Russian reader. The fact is that some of these organizations existed only on paper from the very beginning, others were dismissed long ago, and some of regional organizations, being branches of other organizations, never pursued their own policies.

In beginning to conduct research on women's political activity in the Samara region, we managed to find only five actually existing and functioning women's NGOs by the autumn of 1999. The women's NGOs articulate various ideologies—democratic, communist, social-reformist, and nationalist—and they can hold social "protectionist" ideas in the political sense and a combination of traditional and egalitarian ideas with regard to gender. New social movements in Russia's post-socialist development raise an important issue: What strategies of social and political activities can facilitate the actual advancement of the country in developing a civil society and consolidating democratic policies?

Political Participation: Gender-Neutral Strategy

Research on the political and social activity of women at the regional level made it possible to distinguish two groups of regional women politicians. The division into these two groups is based upon their understanding of the problem of women's representation in governmental structures as well as their attitude toward decision-making processes in general. The subjective interpretation of one's own political participation reflects in many ways two possible approaches to women's political strategies and estimation of their effectiveness.

The first approach, which can be called the *gender-neutral* approach, is ideologically connected to the liberal direction of women's movements worldwide. It is based on the recognition of principles that comprise gender equality of rights and an absence of gender distinctions in the political sphere. Overcoming structural and situational barriers leads (in its supporters' opinion) to overcoming women's marginalization in politics and gives them the opportunity and right to take part in governing processes on a par with men. For this reason, political attention should be directed toward professionalism and the search for allies in party and politics. The second, *gender-sensitive* approach, has the objective of finding out gender differences in preferences, values, and priorities of the electorate and politicians as well as that of determining specific women's roles and interests in decision-making processes.

The first group of politicians, those upholding the neutral-gender approach toward understanding their own activity, appeared to be the most numerous in our research. In their opinion, in politics there cannot and should not be any specific women's interests or women's type of leadership (nor, correspondingly, any specific roles for women in politics). As the chair of the Regional Duma Legislative Committee put it:

> There are not any specific feminine or masculine interests, there are only problems common to all that should be solved. The differences between men and women in politics must be as little as possible—just as there doesn't exist any feminine or masculine style in politics.

This denial of the necessity to pursue a specific policy with regard to gender distinctions is expressed in many cases as an unwillingness to lower the level of one's own political pride. Because "specific" women's interests are associated in the public's consciousness either with the experience of Soviet state paternalism or with women's exceptional responsibilities in the "unprestigious" social sphere, a policy with "a woman's face" is considered in their opinion as rather weak, somewhat defective, inferior, and secondary.

The politicians in this group explain that they would not like to accentuate women's themes in political debates, especially during election campaigns, for fear of meeting condescending and skeptical attitudes toward their civic and professional standing. In this connection, it is important to remember the words of the famous female politician Galina Starovoitova: "The 'floor' (which means 'the starting level of her activity') of a woman politician shouldn't become her 'ceiling.'"[5]

These politicians consider fundamental problems of democratic consolidation and organizing an effective economic system to be more urgent for Russia nowadays. Therefore, they find the fields of common civic interests more important than those of group interests for their political career. They claim to be guided by a desire to cater to the educated, progressive-minded, advanced part of electorate, who expect power to be in the hands of professionals able to design both social and economic strategies. That is the reason they took part in the elections as independent candidates.

Because of the political position of this group, the problem of women's political participation does not seem urgent to them. The pace of Russia's advancement on the way to democratization and organizing a civil society is slow. This is caused, in the opinion of "neutral" and "independent" women politicians, by a lack of "intelligently educated people of principle who would have a developed civic consciousness." The increase in numerical representation of women does not change the nature of power, according to their assumption, because women themselves do not introduce any particular positive perception of problems and do not facilitate the process of making significant decisions. As the woman who chairs the Samara City Budget Committee stated,

> I consider that gender initially doesn't include any positive or negative aspect. The City Duma of Samara is quite a rare phenomenon, where at its starting point half of the elected members were women. However, quantity doesn't always turn into quality. What it is guided by is important. When there were quotas for women, a woman often tended to mold her behavior according to men's behavior instead of introducing her own positive perception. Russian women are easily influenced after they have been elected; they feel thankful. Many of these women easily agree or are easily bought. There is another problem with politicians in our country: Having gained some definite political level, they cease listening to anybody.

The fact that six women came to the Samara City Duma from what are traditionally women's spheres—health protection and education—may serve as proof of this statement, as this respondent herself sees it. In spite of this fact, all of them except this deputy voted for the reduction of expenditures on medical services and a simultaneous increase in expenditures on bureaucratic personnel offered by the mayor. Actually, for the whole period of the Duma's work, only one of the eight tried to oppose the head of the city, who had usurped both branches of power. The remaining obedient deputies of both sexes turned the local self-government institution into a kind of "pocket" organization attached to the body of executive power.

Political Participation: Gender-Sensitive Strategy

In contrast, the second group of politicians—to counterbalance the first—insists upon the assumption that women do have specific interests and, owing to their "nature," are supposed to change the character of political power in the country. The gender-sensitive interpretation of women's political leadership in this case is based on the essentialistic concept of specific, biologically determined female features.

In an election campaign, the key expressions widely used by this group include such word combinations as "a mother-woman" and "a housekeeper-woman." Their political strategies are based on this ideology. Correspondingly, a specific "mission" of women in politics is understood as a traditional responsibility of the women's sphere, specifically social and family politics. Assigning personal responsibility for the problems in this sphere only to women, "feminine women" declare men to be unable to solve these problems because of their "nature." As a woman candidate for mayor put it:

> I'm sure if the city fell into the hands of women, it would make it possible to start things going. Every home should have a housekeeper. The fact that we are not satisfied with our life nowadays, in the first place, is our fault. Women haven't informed men that they don't feel comfortable in such a society and in such a city. The city and our country are parts of a big household, and we should do exactly what we are used to doing in our home. Women can arrange life better. A woman will never send children to war to be killed by tanks, will not step over a helpless old man, will never pass by a crying child or a stray dog. The reason for it is the feeling of sensitivity and understanding of other people's sufferings, which is inborn with us.

This "housekeeper's" strategy functions rather successfully in regional and city elections. Sociological studies have shown that these images of "a firm manager and defender," of "the chief of the city" or of a "housekeeper," regardless of the sex of the candidate, "fit" mass political expectations in provincial Russia.[6] In interviews, the only woman mayor in the Samara region constantly stressed her managerial experience, while being, in her words, "absolutely politically independent": "I don't claim to be a member of the political elite in our region, because you have to do something of merit to deserve it." As analysts have observed, the fact that women were active in district social security bodies facilitated and determined the victory of women in elections to the Regional Duma.

One of the distinguishing features of "a woman housekeeper's" rhetoric is her readiness to accept the "secondary nature" of both her sphere of influence and her role in society: "Let women put everything in order in a social sphere and let men, if they want, take up defense, space, oil and gas," stated a Third State Duma deputy from Samara.

The social policy priorities associated with women's political participation have been demonstrated in worldwide politics. In supporting this idea, the politicians of this second group try to meet traditional expectations and even insist on not laying claim to more power than is provided by the gender system. Their strategy for pre-election behavior is "a submissive style" that is "not irritating" to either the male members of the electorate or their party colleagues. As a Regional Duma deputy put it:

> A woman politician shouldn't be too proud. You needn't dream of wide scale actions, you must do routine work. You can win the respect of all only doing specific deeds. We enter the realm of politics not to fight men but to help them to look at problems with our eyes. Can men really be disappointed if we put everything in order in our country?

As these politicians see it, drawing public attention to their dependence represents a rather successful election strategy given Russia's traditional gender culture. It is interesting to note that this second group recognizes the professional career of a politician for a woman as "nontypical," and this feature is characteristic of their rhetoric. In popularizing a specific image and role for "a politician with a woman's face," they find it necessary at the same time to confirm the stability of stereotyped gender norms for the rest of women. Because women's political participation may be considered rather an exception to the rule, this model can hardly be suggested to other women. As one woman politician expressed it,

> joining the idea of women's and men's equality in political and economic spheres, I'm inclined to be perceive a woman as a mother. This is her natural predestination. I can't imagine a woman in the post of the president of Russia or the post of Samaran governor. Women are more emotional. They are prone to feel failures keenly, they are inclined to be subject to introspection. Such behavior is unacceptable for a politician.

On the one hand, this stereotyped position cannot be applied to the representatives of a new post-Soviet elite. Most members of the regional elite have come into post-*perestroika* politics from former Communist Party and Komsomol *nomenklatura* bodies. One can dare to say that double moral standards (one standard applied to common citizens and quite another applied to themselves) are more characteristic of these people. On the other hand, such claims—which were repeated throughout a number of interviews—

prove the conclusion about the particular complexities of the gender identification and socialization of women in Russia.

Many Russian scholars have shown that this specific Soviet Russian lifestyle called for an "impossible mission" for women. It was necessary for women both "to suit" an untraditional model of behavior (i.e., being professionally employed outside the home was considered to be a part of a typical lifestyle) and at the same time to "match" a quite patriarchal system that included specific ideas of femininity and women's predestination.[7] In many cases, "successful women" try to use these patriarchal ideas to secure themselves against accusations of "nonfemininity." If the reality does not correspond to a privately oriented model of women's behavior, a woman ought at least to justify her "invasion" of politics and government structures with the necessity to introduce "women's care" of socially unsecured citizens.

The Effectiveness of Women's Strategies

Women politicians from the first professional group deny the specific gender character of their own participation. In the end, they call for a change of the existing gender system and reject traditional models of lifestyles assigned to women. According to their logic, an effective strategy for political success excludes an emphasis on sex distinctions and on outlining specific women's problems. Women politicians from the second professional group hold the view of a biologically determined "natural" gender role. For women, leadership—widely acknowledged as an exceptionally masculine quality—should be either disguised in the public sphere or must be forgotten for good, and one should surrender and take up the "defense" and patronage of stronger politicians.

The politicians of the first professional group won their seats in local authority bodies as independent candidates. The political strategies of the second group, with their traditional gender roles of mother and housekeeper, appeared to be successful in using the resources of stronger parties. For instance, Vera Lekareva's victory in a single-mandate electoral district at the election to the Third State Duma was ensured, in the opinion of many regional observers, by the Samara governor's support. The governor's team was staking out a "woman playing card" against the most influential candidate in this electoral district, the notorious Communist deputy of the Second State Duma A. Makashov.

In addition, Lekareva's use of the rhetoric "I am as a woman and a mother" to acknowledge her dependence on the support of the governor, Konstantin Titov ("the governor invited my participation at the election and I agreed") caused her to be included in Titov's team, to its advantage. Titov supported Lekareva despite the fact that, before December 1999, she had shared the ideological position of the Communist Party. The firm belief that a future deputy should be trustworthy, devoted, and thankful became more important for the choice of a "suitable" candidate. In contrast, another candidate from the same electoral district, a deputy of the Samara City Duma, Alla Demina, was not equally advantageous for the governor, in spite of her identification with the Union of Right Forces, the electoral alliance supported by Titov at that time. This was the case because she was famous for her active independent and liberal political stand as well as for her opposition to the authoritative regime of the mayor of Samara.

The fact that women candidates from the second group fully recognize their dependence and also emphasize their "destiny" to carry out routine work that is "unprestigious for men" makes this group a more convenient choice for stronger parties. Their lack of electoral resources makes women weak competitors in the struggle for power. Taking this lack of support into consideration, women have to find an opportunity to be nominated by parties (to a larger extent than men). It will enhance their chances to win. Yet weak candidates are useful for strong parties because in case of victory, the latter can count on their deputy's discipline, loyalty, and subordination. Moderate political views, which actually mean ideological indistinctiveness, becomes an inevitable part of the electoral strategy concerning women politicians.

The identification of women with social policy in general and family policy in particular becomes their only trump card. Underlying this interpretation is the worldwide public opinion, which is accepted in Russia as well, that the accession of women to power is proof of the success in strengthening social policies and forming "a welfare state." The paradox of applying this rule to Russia is the fact that although "housekeeper-deputies" aim at solving problems connected to the status of women in society, they are not ready to extend the traditional range of issues by raising questions concerning employment and professional career discrimination, violence at home, advancement of women into government structures, and so on.

Meanwhile, "independent professionals" in turn direct their attention toward general democratic and civic ideals and do not single out "women's" policy. However, in the course of their political activity, the latter become aware of gender discrimination problems and of the need to stand for women's rights in making decisions concerning fundamental problems. None of the regional women politicians identified herself with a women's social organization.

Women's Social Activity: Formal Women's Nongovernmental Organizations

We can classify women's organizations in the Samara region, as well as women's movements in Russia in general, according to a number of characteristics: the declared sphere and objectives of their activities, the type of organizational structure, ideology, political orientation, social base, and so on. In studying the problem of women's social and political activities in post-Soviet Russia, it is important to note that in addition to classifying women's organizations according to their ideological affiliation, they can be divided into formal social institutions (officially established) and informal ones (grassroots institutions).[8]

Perhaps, the oldest and most numerous (with more then 300 active members) formal organization is the Samara Union of Women, which was organized in 1987 on the basis of *zhensovety,* the former structural units of the Soviet Women's Committee. From the moment of its organization until the present day, it has been headed by the woman who is vice chair of the Samara Regional Trade Union Federation Council and who is also a member of the Russian Communist Party. This organization does not have individual membership and is supported by its network of district committees. These district committees, in the early 1990s, had to "invite for participation" (it was obligatory) women who were leaders in different professional spheres. They were "invited" because they could use their subordinates (the female fraction at least) to fulfill the obligatory demonstrative action.

By the end of 1990s, the majority of these women leaders had to resign, and some of them were able to become engaged in social activities, working in the committees willingly and not because they were obliged to. Although the Samara Union of Women has the juridical status of a regional social organization, its members also consider themselves to be a part of the Russian sociopolitical movement Women of Russia.

The same "top-to-bottom" scenario was used to organize the second formal *nomenklatura* organization, the Samara Branch of the Women's Movement in Russia. This organization is also very proud of its numerous members and "demonstrative actions." As is generally known, after the failure of the electoral bloc Women of Russia at the parliamentary elections of 1995, the "women's" party divided into two groups: Women of Russia (chaired by Alevtina Fedoulova) and Women's Movement in Russia (chaired by Ekaterina Lakhova).

The vice chair of the Samara Regional Duma, Ludmila Dourova, having won election as an independent candidate, at Lakhova's request formed a regional branch of the Women's Movement in Russia. The Constitutive Congress of the Samara branch of the Women's Movement in Russia was held in the spring of 1998. Women leaders from local executive and legislative bodies, female leaders of Samara NGOs, and "influential and famous" professionals all participated in it.

Both Women of Russia and the Women's Movement in Russia formed collective structures as their ruling bodies. They are the Council of the Samara Union of Women and the Coordinating Committee of the Samara branch of the Women's Movement in Russia, and they include only women with a political "status" who are leaders of different professional and business structures.

The government roots of women's movements are not an exceptionally Russian phenomenon, and the government does not determine the content of ideology, political strategies, and the extent of their involvement and effectiveness. Likewise, in the United States in the 1960s, the most influential and active NGOs were formed on the basis of the U.S. Department of Labor's Women's Bureau and the Presidential Commission on the Status of Women. Members of federal and state commissions introduced women's problems into public discourse long before informal and grassroots women's organizations emerged. For this reason, the question about the development of political platforms and activities for such organizations is considered to be of the utmost importance.

Women's organizations in Russia as well as the majority of NGOs and political parties do not have written platforms and define their ideological priorities mostly through interviews, newspaper publications, and election campaign documents. In stating the ideological strategy of the Samara Union of Women, its chair stressed its adherence to traditional gender roles:

> The Statutes of our organization state: Our main priorities are family, women, and children. It's the preservation of our nation that is our most important goal, that is, the preservation of women's ability to give birth.

Women's interests are left to be determined exclusively within the family, the private sphere.

The most striking and important fact here is that a women's NGO puts women's interests within the framework of the state's demographic interests. These priorities can be traced through the electoral discourse. Even the well-known truism used by a women's organization—"unemployment has a women's face"—does not promulgate individual human rights but rather serves the state's objectives. The chair of the Samara Union of Women put it this way:

> Full employment is our priority; we received some financial aid due to a decree at the gubernatorial level to solve the problem of women's unemployment. Women are a specific category of the labor force, which is determined by their ability to give birth. We are now a nation, which is dying out; if we don't create proper working conditions for our women they will not give birth to children. The birthrate in our country dropped the moment the reforms started. Young girls are not ready to perform the functions of a mother; are not ready to sacrifice themselves to meet traditional requirements. To live like a great nation—that to a large extent depends on women. The assurance of women's group rights is included in nation building.

Both the ideological closeness of the Samara Union of Women to the left-wing opposition and its Soviet *nomenklatura* roots can help to explain why it is more concerned about the break-up of the Soviet Union than about current women's problems. It argues for the necessity to return to the main Soviet gender contract of "working mothers," the reason for this being that giving birth is not women's "natural predestination" (this is the point of view that is being revived by the mass media nowadays) but a "civilly prescribed obligation and civic duty of women." Its approach to women's citizenship is limited by women's traditional responsibility for family in the interests of solving the state's problems. The vice chair of the Samara Women's Union expressed this view:

> Traditionally, a Russian family was referred to as a productive, federal, and military unit because it was from the family sphere that children were recruited to participate in wars. And what now? Do we give soldiers to our Russia? Young people are not ready—physically and morally—to

> serve in the Army. And for this reason, our task is to draw social attention to the change in family functions.

Thus, the individual rights of a woman, her autonomy, and her independence are supplanted by traditional concerns for the "collective good," which is said to be equal to state interests.

An ideological postulate about the subordination of women's interests and family interests to the interests of the state underlies the activity of social organizations and facilitates interaction with the authorities that provide resources for NGOs. The close collaboration between the Samara Union of Women and the Regional Administration confuses the left-wing party allies of the women's organizations. Some active members of the Samara Union of Women complained about the "lack of understanding on the part of their Communist comrades," who accuse them of "strengthening the existing power." So to justify themselves, the interviewed women put forward the idea of "unselfish" care for the good of the motherland and personal disinterestedness in solving of those women's problems, which they support. A member of the Samara Union of Women stated that

> personally we need nothing, we have everything—children, grandchildren, husbands; thank God our families have already been formed.

The political plan of this organization therefore bases its appeal on archaic layers of collective consciousness and on gender politics that has a "moral" and maternal face. The Samara branch of the Union of Women is oriented, as are many contemporary Russian social movements, toward the "negative social project," which is formed under the influence of conservative motives—"to preserve, to guard, to survive."

For the Samara branch of the Women's Movement in Russia, there is no necessity to justify themselves before the left-wing opposition. This movement stands apart from both left- and right-wing groups making moderation, centrism, and compromise its priority. Functioning independently since 1996, the Women's Movement in Russia, contrary to Women of Russia, called for the modernization of the gender system in Russia. Its main political slogans are a demand for "parity democracy, the assurance of women rights, state policy of equal opportunities for men and women."

At the same time, this modernist rhetoric includes an emphasis on the archetype of "women's mercy and motherly care." Emphasis on the specific "nature"' of women politicians and "women's policy" is quite successful at the regional level. This is the basis for the mobilization of women in Russia, a country going through a transformational period from a traditional gender system. The political activity of the Samara branch of the Women's Movement in Russia, unlike that of the Union of Women, is limited.

On a regional level, the Samara Women's Movement abstains from public political activity. The leaders of the organization find it to be disadvantageous to advance their own candidates publicly or articulate "women's questions" during election campaigns. At the same time, the task of increasing women's representation in government structures is regarded as a priority. To reach this goal, one may use the great potential of the informal contacts with state officials, which has been preserved from the Soviet era and could be used to advance women in legislative and executive bodies.

Grassroots Women's Social Activity

The second group of NGOs includes the ones that have been formed at the grassroots level as a result of women's initiative and self-organization. The most active in the Samara region since mid-1990 have been the organizations whose aim is to ensure the rights of soldiers, young men due for enlistment, and their parents. All these organizations have included mostly women members and leaders. From the very early formation of these organizations in the first half of 1990s, they have claimed and proved to be women's rights–ensuring organizations aiming at "teaching the basics of civic rules and democratic participation in country's life."

The most numerous and influential such organization, which is a part of the Association of Soldiers' Mothers Committees, has functioned in Samara since 1990 and has, as its leader states, 300 active workers. This organization has the name Synovia (Sons). Its aim, as its platform states, is "to teach mothers to defend their own civil rights and their sons' rights." According to the leader of the organization, its main problem, except for the endemic financial one, involves the sociopolitical passivity of women. As the leader of Synovia explains, not only the population's total illiteracy concerning legal matters hinders Russia's advancement to a democratic state and civil society but also (and perhaps to a greater extent) the belief that "we can do nothing, nothing depends on us":

> Nobody can help those who don't want to help themselves. We teach moms to defend their rights and to demand that the authorities act according

> to the law and their promises. But those who are afraid of military registration offices, who are lazy and don't bring their cases to the court, can hardly expect any success.

To gain resources and to raise the problem of human rights in public discourse, Synovia made good use of one of the sacred Russian maternity symbols; their appeal to defend mothers' rights provided for collective actions committed to social change.

These collective actions included addressing the authorities and the mass media, consulting with parents on the rights of military men, organizing civil control over the armed services, and holding meetings of protest against the first war in Chechnya. The first active volunteer members were mostly the mothers who were worried about the violation of their sons' rights during their term in the army. Gradually, it came to pass that the nucleus of the organization consisted only of the members whose mission had been fulfilled as their sons finished up their military service. As a result, by the late 1990s, Synovia's defense of human rights position was undergoing some considerable evolution in its strategic and ideological direction.

Being organized to defend citizen's interests in the face of state authorities, at the time when the second war campaign in Chechnya began in autumn 1999, Synovia declared a new objective: "to raise the prestige of our Army, to fight slander against it." So, in the mid-1990s, Synovia collaborated mostly with the Chechnya organizations, which included the mothers and widows of soldiers killed in the first Chechen war.

In the late 1990s, a new partner appeared: the Samara Oblast (Region) Administration and military officials. Antiwar appeals to stop the first Chechen war were replaced with special demonstrative actions organized along with the Volga Military Okrug Headquarters. The meetings and concerts for soldiers' mothers and a distribution of gifts appealed to notions of "civil service of mothers and their sons to their Motherland." All activity was provided according to a popular Soviet song: "You should first think of your Motherland and only then of yourself." This stepping back to traditional and state-oriented values has caused the decline and neglect of democratic principles critical of governmental structures. No wonder then that Synovia did not react to the beginning of a new campaign (by the Union of Right-Wing Forces) calling for a referendum on having a professional army in Russia.

The majority of organizations of the second type, which were created on the initiative of different women's groups, are aimed at solving a single problem. They are formed as self-help organizations and have the objective to compensate for the drawbacks and deficiencies in the socioeconomic policy of the state. These organizations are Parents Against Drugs, the Association of Mothers of Large Families, and the Business Women's Club. Notions such as "discrimination, women's rights, inequality" are not found in their rhetoric and platforms. They do not strive to influence decision-making processes; therefore, they stay away from any political participation.

Women's Citizenship in Russia

The indistinctiveness and discrepancies of ideological principles among women's NGOs prevent them from recruiting new members—young, educated women, capable of achieving their own goals, enhancing their personal growth, independent, and opposing the traditional gender system. The leaders of these NGOs often explain their lack of support by pointing to the passivity and "unrealization" of their own interests in power on the part of women.

In partial agreement with this explanation, one must take into consideration the slogans and ideas offered by the organizations and women politicians themselves. They complain that the women's faction of the electorate does not vote for them, but their archaic idea of a woman's "destination" in a new wrapping does not seem attractive to Russian women. One would like to agree with another interpretation of women's political indifference: "A Russian woman keeps silent not because she does not know what she wants, but because she wavers between a socially approved women's mission and the desire to find her own niche in her everyday routine." The problem of self-determination, including sociopolitical self-determination, is the most complicated issue, especially in the current period of radical transformation.

Analyzing the forms of collective actions of NGOs, one can find out that they are guided not by the concept of the independent civil society but by that of the third sector that can help the state pursue its social policies. They realize that their objective is to organize support for clients and improve thereby their living conditions. According to the character of their activity, women's organizations can be referred to as so-called service organizations. The content of their work includes, first, the accumulation and redistribution of resources and, second, the implementation of projects for social assistance. Here the leaders of formal organizations suppose that well-organized demonstrative action can be of greater importance than any routine work in giving women more means to help them in their everyday life, contrary to the point of view of informal organizations.

"Harmony" between official women's organizations and Samara region governor Konstantin Titov is praised by both sides. The governor claims to be a politician of national importance and creates an image of the Samara region as industrially developed and the most advanced region, and therefore rather favorable in the social sphere. He extends this "advancement" to "women's questions" and often attends local women conferences.

In May 1998, at the Second All-Russian Conference on Women's Position, Women and Development: Rights, Reality, and Perspectives, Titov was the only male politician to give a speech on gender politics. Along with a well-thought-out family policy and the decrease in women's unemployment by half, he mentioned the success in gaining representation by women in the political sphere of the region: 35 percent in executive bodies, 50 percent in the Samara City Duma, and dozens of women's NGOs. The conference participants found Titov's speech to be an "enormous qualitative leap in the interrelations between men's power structures and women's nongovernmental organizations." In their opinion, the integration of women's interests into the region's politics is taking place thanks to the "openness and enlightenment" of regional leaders. These leaders make it possible for the region to gain a high position in every sphere.

For this reason, the political strategies of Samaran NGOs appear to be successful. One should mention that of all known actions of group influence (legal actions, lobbying, events of protest, formation of concurrent structures), women's organizations are inclined to use lobbying and prefer to act through informal contacts. The third sector in Russia, as has been mentioned, does not have the opportunity to legitimately represent group interests through any formal legislative mechanism. The existing "patron–client" relations offer more opportunities to be successful in making decisions through executive power structures, where there are more possibilities to use informal contacts. It is easier for women's NGOs to take such steps because post-*perestroika* leaders at all the levels are still connected to their Soviet *nomenklatura* past.

In May 2001, Governor Titov established the Commission on Gender Policy, which should inform legislation in light of its potentially differential effects on women and should also ensure that all legislative and executive measures guarantee women and men equal rights and opportunities to exercise them. Even though some critics consider this decision only a propagandistic one in the governor's public relation and image-making campaign, it is a very important step in introducing gender expertise into public and political discourse.

Active citizenship means participation in democratic processes aiming at self-governance in society. In this way, the boundaries between the public sphere of society and the private life of individuals are broken down. Women as citizens have tended to participate in local politics, taking care of everyday activities and contributing togetherness in ways that can be seen as deeds of everyday heroism.

The terms and ideals for political mobilization are embedded in discourses that provide the ground on which they are understood and from which they gain their power to move people. Political solidarity cannot be assumed on the basis of shared "womanhood." The cultural category of "women" as a practical, everyday form of subjectivity, is called up by innumerable mundane activities and practices. It is not the same as the politically significant category of "women" as a mobilized identity, a self-conscious social collective. For social categories such as "women" to serve as the basis for mobilization, they must first be constituted as politically relevant. This is done through public discussion and by social movements. It follows that a commitment to advance women's interests—and the definition of such "interests"—is never merely the reflex of politicians or a group's subjectivity as women, or even their experience of discrimination and oppression. Politicized identities are themselves a result of public arguments and activities that allow individuals to redefine both their own sense of self and also events and social processes.[9]

Many scholars see the main contradiction of the discourses on women's identities and women's interests in the fact that most post-socialist women's organizations center on women's collective interests—that is, on women as a "category" rather than as individuals entitled to basic rights. Women's claims may be framed in terms either of rights or of entitlements and social benefits. The danger in not attending to these differences is that viewing women only as potential beneficiaries of the welfare system may in fact, and even unwittingly, reinforce traditional women's roles and perpetuate inequalities. Thereby, issues of women's identity and professional and personal self-realization are marginalized in public discourse.[10]

The absence of a coherent women's electorate, its obedience, and its consequent inability to defend women's interests is connected to the image of gender-sensitive politicians as nonaggressive, centrist, moderate, and eager to compromise. The outcomes of the 2000 Russian presidential elections confirm such perceptions. The one female among nine candidates for president—the famous politician, former minister, and State Duma deputy Ella Panfilova—during her campaign accentuated not her professional experience and leadership skills but rather traditional female qualities and her devotion to the state's social protection of "new poor Russians." But the role of "social motherhood" has transformed her into a marginal political figure, who received only 1 percent of electoral support.[11]

Another paradox of "feminine" politicians involves their appeal to the restoration of the Soviet gender contract of the "working mother" as the only model role for women. This is a dangerous situation for gender democracy in Russia; what one sees is an essentialist understanding of women's roles combined with traditional Russian rhetoric about self-sacrificing women who turn away from a concern with their individual interests and rights for the "benefit of the family" and their predestination as mothers. In the context of the post-Soviet gender order, a more important basis for women's political activity is individual-centered orientation toward democratic values.

The political activity of women at both regional and federal levels gives way to various interpretations by researchers. The "optimistic" point of view is based on the positive evaluation, given to any manifestation of women's activism, including the theme concerning preserving traditional women's roles. Any "display" of the "woman question" in public discourse is assumed to be a basis for raising the question of gender system reorganization in the future. "Moderate" researchers, to which group the present author herself belongs, agree with this opinion. However, they also find the activity of women's organizations and women politicians important in facilitating Russia's advancement on its way to democratization and to strengthening civil society values and gender equality.

The research presented here shows that the female proportion of elected officials may have only a loose correlation with the advancement of women's issues. This research explores the fact that one of the reasons for women's exclusion from the political discussion is the very problematical notion of women's and gender politics in postcommunist Russia. I think it is reasonable for educated young Russian women to be suspicious of all political "feminine" strategies that emphasize gender differences and women's special political and social obligations in a context where individual identities are submerged in the collective—whether that collective be the nuclear family or the nation-state. The articulation of the real needs and interests of women in a radically changed economic, political, and social situation is a complex, difficult, and slow process.

In this situation, introducing feminist and civic consciousness discourse has become the most influential tool for creating women's independent political activism at both the personal and political levels. Thus, the transitional period gender studies centers and university programs that emerged in Russia in the 1990s are in some sense more important for promoting women's rights agenda than is the increase in the number of women politicians in legislative and executive bodies. Since the beginning, the gender studies academic community has been involved in feminist education and training for women's activists. Without the civic consciousness-raising process of learning to perceive their real interests, it is impossible, in my view, for women to articulate their group rights, create solidarity, and increase their political role in decision making at all levels of power.

The social and political views of the majority of women politicians, as well as the ideology of women's NGOs in the Samara region, on the whole, stay within the traditional gender system. The task of empowering Russian women to actualize their personal, individual potential and of enabling them to understand their own political behavior seems to be the most important one in the sociocultural context of post-Soviet Russia.

The next task will be to design common strategies for Russian women's political activities and participation in the decision-making process. Their gradual deliverance from the syndrome of "full dependence on the state" should be accompanied by encouraging each woman to develop an independent, active personality aware of her civil standing. Women's specific views on general problems in politics, economics, and culture, as well as new proposed decisions, will be able to ensure the involvement of women in the process of reorganizing the gender system and reforming the democratic institutions of Russian society.

Notes

1. Anna Temkina, "Entering Politics: Women's Ways, Gender Ideas and Contradictions of Reality," in *Russia in Transition: The Case of New Collective Actors and New Collective Actions,* ed. Anna Temkina (Helsinki: Kikimora Publications, 1997); Mary Buckley, "Adaptation of the Soviet Women's Committee: Deputy's Voices from Women of Russia," in *Post-Soviet Women: From the Baltic to Central Asia,* ed. Mary Buckley (Cambridge: Cambridge University Press, 1997); Peggy Watson, "Civil Society and the Politics of Difference in Eastern Europe," in *Transitions, Environments, Translations,* ed. J. Scott, C. Kaplan, and D. Keates (New York: Routledge, 1997); Nanette Funk and Magda Mueller, *Gender Politics and Post-Communist: Reflections from Eastern Europe and the Former Soviet Union* (London: Routledge, 1993); Valentina Konstantinova, "Women's Political Coalitions in Russia 1990–94," in *Women's Voices in Russia Today,*

ed. A. Rotkirch and E. Haavio-Mannila (Aldershot, U.K.: Dartmouth, 1996); Carol Nechemias, "Politics in Post-Soviet Russia: Where Are the Women?" in *Democratizatsiya* 8, no. 12 (spring 2000): 199–218; Linda Racioppi and Katherine O' Sullivan See, *Women's Activism in Contemporary Russia* (Philadelphia: Temple University Press, 1997).

2. Sarah Ashwin, *Gender, State and Society in Soviet and Post-Soviet Russia* (London: Routledge, 2000).

3. Valery Sperling, *Organizing Women in Contemporary Russia: Engendering Transition* (Cambridge: Cambridge University Press 1999).

4. Olga Zdravomyslova and Marina Arutyunyn, *Rossiiskaia sem'ia na evropeiskom fone* [The Russian family against a European background] (Moscow: Editorial URSS, 1998).

5. In Russian the world "floor" sounds the same as the word "sex." So G. Starovoitova's words can be interpreted like this: "Neither her starting point nor her sex/*gender* should restrict the advancement of a woman-politician in politics."

6. Elena Meleshkina, "Otnoshenie zhenshchin Samary k obchestvennym organizatciyam" [Women's relationship with public organizations: The case of Samara], in *Socialnaia feminologia* [Social feminology], ed. Eugenie Molevich (Samara: Samarskii gosuniversitet, 1997).

7. Olga Zdravomyslova-Stoyunina, "Obshchestvo skvoz prizmy gendernykh predstavlenii" [Society through the prism of gender], in *Zhenshcshina, Gender, Kultura* [Women, Gender, Culture], ed. Zoya Khotkina (Moscow: MCGI, 1999), 43.

8. Anna Temkina, *Russia in Transition: The Case of New Collective Actors and New Collective Actions* (Helsinki: Kikimora Publications, 1997), 26; Olga Lipovskaya, "Women's Groups in Russia," in *Post-Soviet Women,* ed. Buckley; Elena Zdravomyslova, "Civic Initiatives: Soldiers Mothers Movement in Russia," in *Politics of Civil Society: A Global Perspective on Democratization,* NIGD Working Paper 2, ed. Heikki Patomaki (Nottingham, U.K.: Network Institute for Global Democratization, 2000), 2; Racioppi and See, *Women's Activism.*

9. Susan Gal and Gail Kligman, *The Politics of Gender after Socialism: A Comparative-Historical Essay* (Princeton, N.J.: Princeton University Press, 2000), 105–6.

10. Krasimira Daskalova, "Women's Problems, Women's Discourses in Bulgaria," in *Reproducing Gender: Politics, Publics, and Everyday Life after Socialism,* ed. Susan Gal and Gail Kligman (Princeton, N.J.: Princeton University Press, 2000), 360–61.

11. Svetlana Aivazova and Grigoriy Kertman, *Muzhchiny i zhenshchiny na vyborah: Gendernayi analiz izbiratelnyh kampanii 1999 i 2000 v Rossii* [Men and women at the polls: Gender analysis of the 1999–2000 election campaign in Russia] (Moscow: Eslan, 2000).

9

Two Worlds Apart: The Lack of Integration between Women's Informal Networks and Nongovernmental Organizations in Uzbekistan

Andrea Berg

When I began studying nongovernmental organizations (NGOs) in Uzbekistan, a new type of organization that appeared after national independence in 1991, I questioned whether NGOs arose from preexisting informal social networks or depended upon them for support. Because these informal networks are highly prevalent in neighborhoods, it was surprising that only one of the NGOs with which I worked made an effort to contact women via their informal networks, although all NGO-affiliated women know of the existence and importance of such networks. This discovery led me to begin investigating why there is such a limited overlap or cooperation between women's informal networks and NGO activities.

Thus, this chapter analyzes women's involvement in both informal and formal institutions in Uzbekistan, namely such informal networks as *gap*

This chapter was prepared with editorial help from Richard Gardner. All translations are by the author.

(Uzbek: conversation) and NGOs. It discusses how the socioeconomic and political changes during the past decade has had an impact on the access to and the nature of informal networks and the emerging formal NGOs. Further, it offers an ethnographic perspective in relation to Uzbekistani women and NGOs in light of the local and historical context of Uzbekistan as a former Soviet republic, and it illustrates the types of problems that women encounter.

The chapter is based on data collected during field research trips in 1997, 1999, and 2000. Though I studied neighborhood networks in 1997, in 1999 and 2000 I was primarily interested in the activities of local NGOs. The data consist largely of material on how directors of NGOs discuss their organization. Another primary source of information on NGOs were the various leaflets, brochures, and documents published by Uzbekistani NGOs. Additional information was obtained through participatory observation during seminars hosted by NGOs, training for the administrative staff of NGOs, and participatory community appraisals in local neighborhoods.[1] Integral to my research was the participant observation data that I gleaned from residing with various Uzbek, Russian, and Tajik families in rural and urban Uzbekistan. This granted me immediate access to, and insight into, daily life, neighborhood networks, and social problems.

Informal Social Networks of Women

During my first research trip to Uzbekistan in 1997, I lived with an Uzbek family in a traditional-style neighborhood in Tashkent. One day my hostess asked me if I would like to play *gap,* and I agreed. We went to a neighbor's house, where the hostess welcomed us. A group of women were sitting around a well-spread "table" in the parlor (*mexmonxona*) offering a prayer to every newcomer. We sat down, ate, and chatted. At the end of the evening, the participating women pulled money out of their dresses and bras and gave it to one of the other guests, who noted each amount in a small notebook and handed the sum amount over to the hostess.[2]

This kind of indigenous socioeconomic network is very popular in Central Asia, because *gap* is not only a social gathering but also a rotating savings association.[3] The phrase "playing *gap*" is used because the participants draw lots to determine the order within one cycle. The woman with the first number has a good lot, because she receives the money before paying in.

The woman with the last number has to pay in the whole cycle before receiving any money.

In the neighborhood I researched, many women were participants in several different *gap* groups. In the neighborhood itself, there were two women's *gaps*. The older group was composed of fourteen women between the ages of 48 and 75 years, some of them having played *gap* with their neighbors for 30 years. There is a fixed number of participants per cycle. All participants meet each other once a month in the hostess's house. They eat together, chat, and exchange information. Everybody gives a fixed amount of money (1,000 so'm in the autumn of 1997) to the treasurer. The hostess is given the money. The younger group was composed of eleven women between the ages of 29 and 48. It was established by the youngest member of the older group, who participated in both groups. *Gap* and other informal networks in Uzbekistan are an expression of local needs, experiences, and mutual aid.

In addition to their "original" function, these informal networks often provide emotional and financial support during times of difficulty. This holds true for such networks in various regions of the world. In their book on social networks, Kathryn March and Rachelle Taqqu write: "Members usually participate because they want the services that the informal association organizes. Because many informal associations respond to several needs and perform several functions simultaneously, this rather obvious proposition can be easily obscured. Even neighborhood gossip circles, friendship groups, and visiting networks can be mobilized to serve important social and economic needs."[4] Furthermore, informal networks are potential resources of political participation as well as political agents themselves.[5] Because formalized political activities are often dominated by men, this is especially important to women. Some contend that women in particular train their civic skills within informal networks.[6]

Social and Economic Aspects of *Gap*

During the past several centuries, *gap* in Uzbekistan consisted of a collective meal for men at the village or neighborhood level during wintertime.[7] They ate together in the mosque or the public guesthouse (*mexmonxona*) and discussed religious issues and neighborhood problems. Furthermore, they sang, played musical instruments, danced, and performed theater. In some regions, all men contributed food to the collective meal; in others, one individual was responsible for the meal at each meeting.[8] According to R. Rachomov, men's gatherings in public places were widely held from the end of the nineteenth century until the 1930s. Afterward, *gap* took place in private parlors more and more.[9]

Little information is available about the participation of women in *gap* until the beginning of the twentieth century. Although the preparation of the Central Asian dish *osh/plouff* is male work, Snesarev writes that in the region of Khorezm the women of the host's family prepared the food. Either they sent it with their husbands to the *gap* or they prepared the entire meal when their husband's turn took place at home.[10] Though Snesarev explains that all women left the house and that doors and windows were closed when a *gap* was held, Rachimov notes that women invited female neighbors and relatives when a men's *gap* took place in their house.[11] Furthermore, he reports on independent *gap* groups of women in the Samarqand and Buchara regions, but without any details.

Gap existed before and during the Soviet period, and it still exists across Central Asia. There is no doubt that the function of *gap* has changed over the time. In the course of Soviet collectivization, *gap* lost its original function as an opportunity to discuss and manage various problems in a village or neighborhood. During the Soviet period, evening gatherings with people of different age, sex, and profession and even meetings or seminars with colleagues came to be called *gap.*[12]

During that time, women began to participate more actively in *gap.* Because there is little information about the process of women's inclusion, one can hypothesize that the declining administrative importance led to the transformation of *gap* into a social event, thereby increasing access for women. Snesarev writes that women and girls were among the participants in the intelligentsia's *gap* groups, such as those of teachers in the early 1960s.[13] Probably, women's inclusion in Russian-style gatherings called *vecher* (Russian: evening) assisted this development. Since the 1960s, money has been introduced into the *gap;* before this, Sattor argues that food was the primary item exchanged.[14] Another possible explanation for this development is the Russian *chernaia kassa* (similar to club-money), which became popular at about the same period.[15]

The amount of money contributed varies between different *gap* groups, depending on gender, income, and living standard. In rural areas, they give less than in urban areas. For the most part, men give more than women. Sometimes participants buy goods for the host during one cycle, for example, a carpet. Most of the women I spoke with said that the money is less important for them than social aspects, because they are happy to see the others, to have some fun, to dance, and to spend time with others without any family obligations. Because Uzbek girls normally leave their parents' house and neighborhood to live with their family-in-law, they mostly start to develop their networks after marriage. This is very important for establishing one's own self in the social environment. Though men often play *gap* with classmates or colleagues, women play with neighbors and kin. A women's *gap* in a neighborhood can be of high importance for her individually as well as for common activities.

To be a member of a *gap* group gives one many opportunities and enables people to survive in an extremely vague environment characterized by various socioeconomic changes in the wake of national independence. Despite the somewhat high financial demands, many people are participants in several *gap* groups. Whether it is men or women, a rural or urban setting, gatherings of a *gap* group serve as an important information exchange and discussion circle. Moreover, participants in one *gap* group have very close relations. They trust each other, and they help each other in difficult situations.

Changing Patterns of Informal Networks

Gap is only one among various kinds of informal networks in Uzbekistan. These networks, which are based on kinship, neighborhood, or regional affiliation, form the lifeline of Uzbekistani society. The networks are established and confirmed through gift exchange or mutual aid at life-cycle events. Through reciprocal labor cooperation, called *hashar,* a household is able to build a new house or to realize other work intensive activities. In short, from the networks one can receive support, exchange information, and improve the social or economic level of his or her family.

Women make use of various networks in different ways. The *gap* gatherings are fun for them. Most of them told me that they spent the money on weddings and for their children. The money from their *gap* group enables them to contribute gifts to events in their family or in their neighborhood and in that way enables them to participate in other networks. Only two of the thirty-one women I interviewed in the neighborhood did not take part in *gap* due to financial problems. One said that she receives only a small pension. The household of the other woman was building a new house—a task that requires the cash of all household members. This leads to another aspect of informal networks: the costs associated with "belonging."

Due to their dominance in the public sector, women are extremely affected by transition. They were laid off or their (low) wages have not been paid for months. With regard to informal networks, this means that (1) women lost one part of their radius of activities and the access to networks linked to their workplace; (2) and women lost their individual disposable income, and therefore their participation in other networks was at risk. This development takes a course opposite to the importance of informal networks that bridge gaps arising from transformation. Because the closing of day care centers and schools, increasing work in the household, and additional activities in part-time jobs put a load on women, more than ever they need mutual support.

Although mutual aid and gift exchange among relatives and neighbors was taken for granted during the Soviet period, problems have mounted during the past 10 years of economic transition and declining living standards. Investments and participation in informal networks are no longer realizable for all parts of society. Women of one *gap* group are able to counter financial problems for a while; they can extend the time between the gatherings or minimize the cash dues. A woman can decide to play only in one group instead of two or three. But these are only short-term strategies and do not solve the basic problem, which is the lack of money. On the one hand, poor households are sometimes confronted with unsolvable problems either to contribute their limited resources into informal networks or to meet their own basic needs (e.g., food, clothes, and fuel). On the other hand, wealthier households are able to do without informal networks because they can pay for goods and services. Victoria Koroteyeva and Ekaterina Makarova call this development "a classic pattern of the disintegration of the egalitarian spirit of community."[16]

Despite these problems, women's informal networks are very active. The networks are among the few "places" where women can discuss their private and public needs. Common themes at such women's gatherings are not only family problems—such as the alcoholism of husbands, unintentional pregnancy, financial problems—but also economic developments, especially rising prices and unemployment or distress about the future. Although they may not solve these problems, they learn to discuss, to debate, and to develop an opinion with familiar persons. Women's informal networks have persisted for a long time and are well embedded into the social environment.

Another domain where women are working actively are NGOs. These organizations have a certain similarities to women's informal networks. NGOs are often dominated by very active women and are characterized by a focus on women's issues. In addition to informal networks, NGOs constitute a platform for women's civic activism. Nevertheless, women's NGOs are often formed in hierarchical ways with few links to their target groups. The following sections will discuss the structures and ideas of local NGOs and will show that the Soviet legacy still has an influence on women's public activities.

The "Feminization" of NGO Work: New Tendency or Soviet Heritage?

Nongovernmental organizations (Uzbek: *nodavlat notijorat tashkilotlari*) are a new type of organization in Uzbekistan. The activities of a few NGOs go back to the late 1980s and early 1990s, but the majority of today's NGOs were established only after the mid-1990s, when foreign businesses, as well as aid organizations, appeared in Uzbekistan.[17]

Because of the expectation linked with the role of NGOs in democracy building and in the development of a vital civil society, one can find great activity by donor agencies in Uzbekistan. It is because of this situation that the number of NGOs has increased rapidly during the past several years. According to the statement of a staff member of the Organization for Security and Economic Cooperation in Europe, only 40 of the approximately 400 local NGOs in Uzbekistan are working actively.[18]

Indeed, this reflects my own experience, for it was difficult to find the NGOs from a database or telephone lists. In several cases, I spoke with NGO representatives who explained that they were not working because of a lack of resources including time, money, and labor power. Many NGOs that exist as registered organizations apply for grants because they are not able to start any activities without this financial support. A significant number of NGOs are involved with women's issues and problems, including reproductive health, children's disabilities, and craft activities. Women-centered NGOs provide services, especially information. They host seminars, for example, on health, small business, and women's rights. Some of these NGOs have even established telephone hotlines.

The high number of women managing NGOs is notable in Uzbekistan. These women are well educated and have been working since the Soviet era in various capacities, including at universities, in government administration, and for the Communist Party. Furthermore, the majority of the staff, trainers, and members of NGOs are also women. The literature on NGOs in Eastern and Central Europe, Russia, and Eurasia also has this women-oriented tendency. Among others, Armine Ishkanian states in chapter 12 of this volume that in Armenia, the NGO sector has become a "feminine" sector in which more than two-thirds of the organizations are led by women.

This feminization is due to men's lack of interest in such "nongovernmental" organizations, women's exclusion from the governmental sector, and international donor agencies privileging of women's organizations and gender-related projects (see chapter 3 of this volume). All of these reasons are in keeping with developments in Uzbekistan. Men are not very interested in NGO work there while they dominate formal political activities. As in many other former Soviet republics, the number of women in political parties and the national parliament in Uzbekistan declined rapidly after the disintegration of the Soviet Union. At present, only one woman (the chair of the National Women's Committee) is represented in the Uzbek cabinet council.

But the gendered division of political participation is not a new phenomenon in the post-Soviet states. Although women were very active in several kinds of public organizations, they were mostly excluded from key positions in the Communist Party and in politics. Susan Bridger reported in the 1980s "that rural schoolgirls are considerably more active in Young Pioneer and Komsomol activities than are boys. Until marriage, young women often form the majority of activists in social and political work (*obshestvenno-politicheskaya rabota*) and predominate in leadership positions in, for example, rural Soviet and Komsomol committees."[19] Although women were, by quota, included in the Communist Party, the real power was almost solely in the hands of men.

The feminization of today's NGO work has its harbinger in this long and forced tradition of honorary social activities by women during the Soviet era. In a Western context, honorary social activities are voluntary. But in the Soviet Union (and in other socialist countries), it was expected that everybody bears his or her share to the development of society. Behind this policy stood the economic and ideological requirement to mobilize especially women to mitigate social hardness.

Due to their position at that time, today's women NGO chairs are familiar with campaigns focusing on the "emancipation" of women. Furthermore, they know how to adapt to the given odds—whether a Soviet ministry in former times or a foreign donor agency today—and achieve their own aims. The attention paid to women's issues in Central Asia seems to have been undiminished during the past decade and will be continued due to priorities of foreign agencies launching projects there. It is because of the Soviet legacy that educated women in Uzbekistan can adopt easily the new language and definitions that have arrived with the appearance of foreign organizations. The opinions put forward by several informants make clear that they combine arguments from both periods.

Evegeniy Abdullaev, of the National Human Rights Center, offers the following explanation for the dominance of women in NGO activities:

> In their early days, family and children are most important to women in Uzbekistan. Even if they hold a university degree they take care of their family in their 20s and 30s. When they reach their 40s, the children have grown up. They have more time and still enough strength. It is because of this fact that they go into NGOs.

NGOs are seen here as a useful occupation for women after they have fulfilled their obligations inside the family. This occupation is compatible with female role models in the Uzbekistani society—business or politics are not. In addition, Saodat stresses the financial aspect:

> Men think that NGOs do not leave a margin. Therefore this is no occupation for men. In addition, they are more interested in politics. . . . Men do not see a prospect in the work of NGOs.

This statement shows that the work of NGOs is not linked with prestige in men's eyes and is not regarded seriously by men. For men, NGOs seems to be a "playground" for women distinguished from the male world of "serious" issues like politics. On the contrary, women see the possibilities of working in NGOs to improve their economic and social position. The fight for political influence and power seems to play no role.

Several women who were interviewed referred to differences in male and female nature when explaining the dominance of women in NGO work. They were of the same opinion that women on the one hand are more affected by the results of the political and economic transformation and on the other hand react more flexibly to a situation than men do. During a coffee break at a seminar, we discussed the role of women in Uzbekistani society with Nigora and Sulfia. Nigora explained:

> Many people did not find a place for themselves, no orientation [to the new situation, annotation by the author]. Many intelligent people who are able to work could not switch. They are not flexible. For that reason women are more active. Men would like to work, but they are not able to switch.

Sulfia went on:

> Nigora is right. As a result of the last years, women took even more upon themselves, because the men became unemployed. Men are not able to switch. They become addicted to alcohol and drugs. These are all economic problems. If there is no work, men fall into decay—what shall I say, they degenerate.

Ruqia argued that women tend to work together, but men are loners:

> Men are isolated, they want to solve all problems on their own. They do not even change their opinion with friends. Women are very quick in contacting each other. I think this is a gender difference. To establish an organization is easier for women. First, one woman knows her worth, then somebody trusts her and somebody else would like to support them. In the end, you have a small heap of people. Without such a small heap, you are not able to establish an organization, just on your own. But men are very conservative in this respect. First, they will think ten times if they need an organization or not.

Altogether, the interviewed women regarded NGOs as a kind of "natural" association and occupation for women. In my opinion, this is the result of a synthesized use and processing of Soviet and Western ideas. Due to their age, education, and working position during the Soviet period, they are used to incur the responsibility for their family as well as for colleagues, friends, and other women. Foreign donor agencies focus on these arguments favoring the role of women's NGOs in stabilizing society. In the same way these women tried to counter problems during the Soviet period, they now try to "compensate for the drawbacks and deficiencies in the socioeconomic policy of the state," as Ludmilla Popkova puts it in chapter 8 of this volume. In chapter 10 of this volume, Janet Johnson calls this the sense of "social responsibility" among many educated, middle-aged post-Soviet women.

Life Histories of Women NGO Chairs

When we look at the life histories of women NGO chairs in Uzbekistan, it is obvious that their involvement in the NGO sector is not the beginning but the result of years of professional and personal activities and experiences with social or economic affairs. There are several notable patterns. Most women who are NGO chairs belong to the educated, urban middle class. All the women chairs I interviewed hold a university degree. Among the interviewees are biochemists, psychologists, teacher, textile engineers, philologists, and philosophers. They speak at least Russian and Uzbek, and in some regions Tajik. In addition, a few are learning English to improve their access to the donor community. Half of the women chairs studied in Mosow or Leningrad, where they came into contact with the idea of grassroots organizations or lobby groups for the first time.

During the Soviet era, today's NGO women chairs were to be found in two main occupations. Either they worked for many years in government administration or at universities. The turning point in the shift of their activities was not national independence in 1991 but the appearance of foreign organizations beginning in 1994 and 1995.[20] Their work experience and academic background enabled them to meet the requirements of the current situation.

The women chairs were in their mid-30s to mid-50s. That means that all of these women at least grew up and finished their education during the Soviet era. They are familiar with Soviet campaigns for (Central Asian) women's emancipation as well as with Soviet women's identities. De facto, these women personify the Soviet ideal of a successful woman. Today's women chairs are used to giving instructions to subordinate or less educated people. Due to their age (as well as to their position), they are respected by the people in their environment. Some of them are mothers of adult children or teenagers contributing the special skills of a new generation to the work of the NGOs. Let us look briefly at the experiences of several of them.

Delia

Delia, who is 48 years of age, is typical of a woman managing an NGO.[21] She studied in Moscow and worked for 20 years in the government administration. In June 1996, she was invited to work in the regional branch of the Business Women. There she gathered her first experience with NGOs. After 6 months of work, she left the association and established her own NGO in March 1999. The NGO has three different projects, all supported by grants. Delia's office is equipped with four computers, email and the Internet, and a photocopying machine. Six paid trainers and several volunteers are working in the NGO's projects.

Delia's daughter is one of the trainers. Her son, who works in the regional branch of the administration of justice, takes care of the computers. As Delia told me, her husband supported her to finance the registration procedure. Delia is in many respects a typical example of an Uzbekistani woman NGO chair. She is familiar with the local administration, has friends and relatives at her disposal who support her, is financially secure, and has built up strong relations with international donor agencies.

Saodat

Saodat worked in the reconnaissance unit for 14 years. After the collapse of the Soviet Union, she was dismissed. For a while, she worked as a teacher. Then she took office as vice chair of the Board of Trade. It was because of conflicts with her colleagues and her chief that she quit her job:

> I worked there for 2 years. In the last 6 months, my chief did not come to work when I was there. He called the office before he came there. In principal he did not come to work for 6 months or he only came at night. I left and started my own business.

With the establishment of her firm, she became a member of Tadbirkor Ayol (Businesswomen) and a friend of its woman chair, with whose help Saodat got her first information about NGOs. As of the time of the interview, Saodat was a businessperson as well as an NGO chair.

Delia also started the narration about her NGO activities with Tadbirkor Ayol:

> In the very beginning I was invited by the *oblast'* branch of Tadbirkor Ayol to work as executive director. I worked there for 6 months. During this time, I took part in various seminars hosted by the Center of Market Strategies. And Counterpart Consortium hosted seminars. I knew nothing about NGOs. And then my eyes opened to the very existence of an institution like NGOs and its possibilities.

The Tadbirkor Ayol organization seems to play an important role in certain regions. Many women had their first experience with NGOs in projects of this organization before establishing their own NGO. Probably, this is explainable by its very extensive structure. Tadbirkor Ayol is one of the oldest NGOs in Uzbekistan. In several towns, the local branch of Tadbirkor Ayol was the only NGO for many years. It is difficult to get away from or avoid this organization, and this has led to quarrels in certain cases.

A few women worked not only at Tadbirkor Ayol but also in the Women's Committee before establishing their own organizations. Manzura started her business in 1996. For that reason, she got in touch with Tadbirkor Ayol. In 1998, she started to work in an education center of the Women's Committee. At the time of the interview, she was both chairwoman of her own NGO as well as board member of Tadbirkor Ayol.

Nargiza

Nargiza worked in the city hall (*hokimiyat*) from 1982 until 1995. In 1994, a new *hokim* (Uzbek: mayor) took office. First, he fired her. Then he hired her again after a while. She explains her entrance into NGO work as follows:

> Here we had illegal dismissals, my dismissals. In 1995, I was put into office again. Maybe it is not very nice to tell such things. These are internal affairs. But all this resulted in my involvement in the third sector.

Although she disagreed, in 1995 she was transferred into another department, the Women's Committee. About her further personal history to NGO work she says:

> In 1996, the question was whether to establish a branch of Tadbirkor Ayol. Because I was the specialist of the Women's Committee of the *hokimiyat,* I invited all the women. Until that time nobody was in contact with businesswomen. In case of need, I organized exhibitions and seminars. I knew how to gather them and how to talk to them. I invited all the women to this meeting to establish a branch of Tadbirkor Ayol. And of course they nominated me as a candidate.

Comments

Some of the interviewed women got their first information about NGOs while traveling or studying abroad. A woman working in a crisis center said about her boss: "During her study in Moscow and Leningrad she saw organizations giving aid to people." When international donor agencies appeared in Uzbekistan she started immediately to apply for a project. The woman chair of an ecological organization took part in a conference in Russia in 1989. Then she established her organization in Uzbekistan.

All the women have been very much affected by the transition. Several of them lost their position in the government administration. They were excluded from decision-making processes and the public sphere. Some of them were "pushed" from their former position into the Women's Committee. Academics either lost their jobs or were confronted with a situation of declining income as well as a declining reputation of their work. Although they did not fare well in the transition, these women were able to adapt to the new circumstances and possibilities because they are well educated and have access to information, and therefore have better conditions. NGO work seemed to them very interesting and gave them the feeling of making something useful and that someone needs them.

The Relationship between Women Chairs and NGO Staff

Inside the NGOs chaired by women, one can often find hierarchical structures. The chair is at the head, followed by the paid staff of various programs, and at the bottom by the so-called volunteers. The volunteers are mostly students or younger family members of the chair or her staff. In general, one can say that in Uzbekistan, one woman often writes an organization's statute and organizational mission. She then asks her friends and relatives to sign the registration documents. Within this particular NGO, the chair then controls most functions. Some of the chairs are able to use their private connections to the local administration to better conditions for their respective NGOs. The concepts of NGOs are mostly worked out by the chairs. They hold all the strings in their hands, distribute the functions, and hire the staff.

Foreign aid supports the hierarchical structures within NGOs. Because foreign organizations like to have fixed partners, they tend to work with persons they already know. Once a woman reaches that point, she will be invited again and again. Work-related journeys to Tashkent and Almaty, or even London and Washington, strengthen her position. Women NGO chairs do not always pass on their new knowledge and experiences to the staff of the organization.

Because the chair personalize contacts with the donor organizations, the staff depends financially on her. Many staff members also work in a second and even third job. Delia's statement shows the dependence of the staff on the woman chair:

> Our staff is good. When I hired them in the beginning, they did not know what an NGO is. I explained it to them. Now they are working, but the program will soon be finished. They asked me to please do something to continue the program. Please find sponsors. We have experience, we know the methods. Everything was fine. The staff is sorry for the program.

An illustration of the authority of an individual woman chair is the experience I had when I arrived in a town to interview one of the NGO leaders. A few days before my visit, I had called the chair, announced my coming, and asked for her help. She told me to come to her office when I arrived. After a 5-hour taxi trip and with all my luggage, I went to her office, happy to know a person and place in an alien environment. When I entered the office, which was situated in her private house, about twenty women waited for me and were prepared to answer for their activities. Among these women were not only staff members of her organization but of other organizations as well.

The entire situation was overwhelming. I wrote down all the names and organizations' addresses and promised to visit them within the next few days. As I recognized later, there is a board near the entrance of the office where the NGO chair publicly lists active and inactive members and draws up a list of those who did not come to certain events. Both observations are typical for the hierarchical relation within NGOs and showed part of the sphere over which prominent women NGO chairs have influence. On the one hand, they distribute the resources to which their staff have access. On the other hand, they expect support and subordination for this.

Although I was alarmed by this procedure, the staff members I talked with did not see a problem. Although they often realize their chief's ideas and orders, most of them are proud of their work. One interviewed psychologist at a crisis center was very proud of her specialist knowledge. She told me that the woman chair of the center where she was working took part in a workshop in the United Kingdom before establishing the NGO:

> When she came back, she hired specialists (*kadry*). And of course she was right to hire only the most competent specialists: psychologists, lawyers, gynecologists. These are exactly the best specialists. They have a good knowledge of their work and they want to help other people.

This estimation already bears witness to the private relationship between certain women chairs and their staff members. Due to her position, age, and experience of life, a woman chair is not only a chief but also an adviser on private issues. Younger staff members are especially proud to belong to the NGO and regard the chair as a role model. Their statements and behavior are mostly determined by this loyalty. For instance, Djamila's narration underlines her private attitude toward the woman who chairs the organization where she is working:

> My husband and I got a divorce and I came back to Kokand. . . . I started to work but I needed a kind of moral support. Somebody told me to contact Tadbirkor Ayol, a women's NGO.

The case of Djamila illustrates some of the problems with which women in post-Soviet Uzbekistan are confronted. Because she lived with her husband in another region, Djamila lacked social networks in Kokand. Her parents were not able to support her. Their generation is faced with a different set of problems. She does not receive financial support from her former husband. To keep herself and her two sons, she works at the city hospital as well as at an NGO. The organizations and its woman chair provide her with a friendly place and help her to overcome her private problems.

For an individual woman, support from an NGO, and particularly from its woman chair, can be very helpful in an emotional as well as financial sense. Conflicts occur when former staff members not only establish their own NGO but also avoid their former chief. In one town, one women's organization claimed a crisis center as a part of it. Although the crisis center was a former project of the women's organization, it is now registered separately and acts independently. Furthermore, the woman who chairs the crisis center had broken with the other organization's woman chair. When one of her staff members told me that they had received a grant, she asked me not to tell this to the other women's organization. Though the crisis center established its own relation to the donor community and left the sphere of the women's organization, the latter launched a new crisis center with a woman as chair who is friends with the organization's chair.

The subordinate role of staff members became evident when in several cases they were not able to answer my questions about their organization. They just gave me brochures or flyers and asked me to come again another time. I am not sure if that happened because they did not trust me or because they did not know anything. Yet I wonder how NGOs are able to work when no one is able to give information during the absence of the woman chair. Visitors, including both me and people really needing help, stand in front of closed doors or are asked to come back another week. This occurs most of all when women chairs take part in seminars in Tashkent or even go abroad. One time, nearly all the chairs of well established Uzbekistani women's NGOs traveled to the United Kingdom at the same time. During this week, it was very hard to get in contact with these NGOs.

The Relationship between NGOs and Their Target Groups

The relation between NGOs and their target groups includes two levels: the reciprocal perception and the mutual contacts. Because the women who chair these NGOs see themselves as the center of their organizations, huge gaps exist between them and their target group. The chairs are representatives of the urban middle class. Their activities are mostly aimed the rural population or poor sections of the urban population.

During the interviews, an immense distance was expressed. The women chairs characterized the rural women as traditional and religious and therefore uninformed. Zoreh Ghavamshahidi stated that "most of the women's NGOs share the Soviet as well as the Western view that Islam is responsible for the regression of women and the absence of development."[22] Furthermore, most of the chairs stressed their own activity as opposed to the inactivity of the target group. How the chairs assess rural women is revealed by the following statements:

> The girls know neither the Islamic law or the new law. Their parents just give them in marriage. Because of this reason I wanted their knowledge to increase. I wanted to improve their knowledge. The girls must understand that they must have their own opinion. . . . I know that in the rural region they give birth to many children who are ill. The nutrition is bad. And all this comes together. It is very hard for those women. . . . In my opinion our mission, the mission of women's NGOs is to teach women how to work. I think all our women's NGOs try to teach women how to work under modern conditions.

These statements are explainable by urban—rural differences in Uzbekistan in general and the representation of rural women in particular. Women who chair NGOs appear to draw an unbalanced picture of rural women. They persist in their bias instead of considering local forms of survival strategies. Rather than relying on the strategies and ideas of their target group, the chairs monopolize the valuation of its needs and wants. Put bluntly, target groups are seen as objects of instruction. This trend is not only to be found in Uzbekistan. Sarah Henderson wrote about her observations in Russia: "Groups' activities were surprisingly insular—groups were beginning to network with each other, but the idea that there was a public out there that could be mobilized—seemed of little or no interest to many groups."[23]

Most of the seminars I observed in Uzbekistan do not train rural women to take care of their own interests. The relation between NGOs and their target groups is determined by a high degree of hierarchy. The target group is not included in decision making. The NGO staff conducting seminars in the villages are seen as an authority and in some way linked to the administration. In several NGOs I observed, consulting rural women behaved themselves like petitioners.

Such findings also hold true for the "Consultations with the Poor" study contribution for *World Development Report 2000/2001.* It quotes some statements of participants who had never heard about NGOs or had bad experiences with NGO representatives. The study summarizes: "In the former Soviet countries poor people expressed ambivalence and suspicion toward NGOs because of their lack of accountability."[24]

Another problem is how NGOs get in contact with their target group. What many of the NGOs women do is to use their own networks to contact the local administration to bring women's groups together for seminars. Partly for this reason, women in the target group, such as the rural women, react with great caution to NGO activities. Generally, they have no idea of the very existence of NGOs before such seminars. Manzura explained to me her strategy for gathering women for a seminar:

> First of all we went to the *hokimiyat* and told them about our program. The vice *hokim* supported us to bring a women's group from different districts together. We are not able to do this. There are many firms, factories, and *mahallalar* [Uzbek: neighborhoods]. In our region we have a lot of *mahallalar.* And he asked everyone to send representatives. He brought fifteen women together.

One staff member of a women's center earlier worked in the registry office. Her former colleagues now send young couples to her. In the women's center, they receive an introduction to family issues. Another organization hosts its seminars in the *mahallalar* where staff members live. There are several other examples.

Because of bad cooperation with the local administration, Ruqia started to contact women via their networks:

> We went to the *mahalla* committee and told them that we will conduct a seminar on reproductive health for the women of their *mahalla.* Please bring the women together. If you have a teahouse, bring them together there. We will come and conduct the seminar. They agree. Then we arrive, and he completely forgot about us. He neither brought together women nor told anybody about our seminar. And then he is in a hurry to find some women. One time we arrived and a grandmother was sitting there. Does she need contraceptives?

After such disasters, they started to contact women in a more private way. At the time of the interview, NGO members took part in two different *gap* groups in rural areas. They got in touch with these *gap* groups with the help of staff members' relatives. Due to this means of access, the rural women feel more comfortable and rely on the relationship of their neighbors. The private atmosphere of a *gap* is much more relaxed than an official meeting in the teahouse or in the school.

In addition, the organization's members use weddings and other events to talk about their activities. In several cases, they were able to gather a group of women and to organize a seminar a few days later. By working in that way, the NGO is able to rely on patterns of trust and reciprocity among a certain group of women. Their seminars are not a one-term or short-term event but a long-term process. Perhaps these women's groups, in cooperation with the NGO, are able to train woman in new skills and in how to enter new realms of activities and influence.

Summary and Conclusion

Ten years after national independence, one can find two areas in which women are very active: informal networks and NGOs. Although informal networks existed for a long period in Uzbekistan, NGOs are a new type of organization. Nevertheless, public organizations existed during the Soviet era, and women were working actively in those organizations.

Urban and rural women in Uzbekistan have taken more and more divergent development paths since national independence. During the Soviet period, the government was eager to eliminate urban—rural differences at least in education, infrastructure, and communication. After the disintegration of the Soviet Union, these efforts were discontinued. If we ask about what advances women have made and what setbacks they have experienced, I agree with Nancy Lubin's statement: "While some women have flourished, overall, women have suffered greatly."[25]

Although urban women are by no means the winner of the transition, some of them were able to adapt to the donor agencies' focus on women's issues and women NGOs. The lack of information and knowledge prevent rural women from taking part in NGO activities. At the moment, NGOs are relatively exclusive islands in an urban environment. Huge differences exist between them and their target groups. The main strategy used by rural women to deal with their private and public needs and problems is to pursue activities within informal networks.

In addition to a continuous dialogue with the government and fund-raising activities directed toward donor organizations, NGOs ought to take into account the actual needs of the rural population and rely on their informal networks. In that way, they could obtain the trust of rural women as well as support local forms of activity. Such cooperation between informal networks and NGOs could lead to indigenous and effective strategies to achieve economic as well as political goals to better the situation of women in Uzbekistan. Donor agencies hinder the development of local activities if they work only with the most visible and best-known NGOs. On the contrary, they should encourage and enable local NGOs as well as citizens' groups to develop locally acceptable and understandable activities.

Notes

1. Participatory community appraisals use a participatory research process to identify communities' needs and interest from the perspective of their members.

2. The total was 13,000 so'm—1,000 so'm by each member. In the autumn of 1997, $1 was worth 150 so'm on the black market. At that time, one loaf of bread was 10–15 so'm and 1 kilogram of tomatoes was 20–25 so'm. The minimum pension was 850 so'm and a child's allowance was 375 so'm.

3. According to Shirley Ardener's definition, rotating savings associations are "formed upon a core of participants who make regular contribution to a fund which is given in whole or in part to each contributor in turn." Shirley Ardener, "Women Making Money Go Round. ROSCAs Revisited," in *Money-Go-Rounds: The Importance of Rotating Savings and Credit Associations for Women,* ed. Shirley Ardener and Sandra Burman (Oxford: Berg, 1995), 1.

4. Kathryn S. March and Rachelle L. Taqqu, *Women's Informal Associations in Developing Countries: Catalysts for Change?* (Boulder, Colo.: Westview Press, 1986), 8.

5. See Heidi Wedel, "Informelle Netzwerke und politische Partizipation von Frauen in informellen Siedlungen in Istanbul" [Informal networks and the political participation of women in informal settlements in Istanbul], in *Die islamische Welt als Netzwerk: Möglichkeiten und Grenzen des Netzwerkansatzes* [The Islamic world as a network: Possibilities and limitations of network analysis], ed. Roman Loimeier (Würzburg, Ergon 2000).

6. Wedel, "Informelle Netzwerke," 390ff.; March and Taqqu, *Women's Informal Associations;* Diane Singerman, *Avenues of Participation. Family, Politics, and Networks in Urban Quarters of Cairo* (Princeton, N.J.: Princeton University Press, 1995), 270.

7. In some regions, *gap* is called *gashtak* (Tajik: *gashtan,* stroll about, pass over) or *soubat/suhbat* (Persian: conversation). See: G. P. Snesarev, "Traditsiia muzhskikh soiuzov v ee pozdneishem variante u narodov Srednei Azii [The tradition of male groups and its latest model among the peoples of Central Asia]," in *Materialy Khorezmskoi ekspeditsii: Polevye issledovaniia Khorezmskoi ekspeditscii v 1958–1961 gg. Vypusk 7* [Materials of the Chorezm expedition: Field research of the Chorezm expedition of 1958–1961], ed. Akademiia Nauk SSSR (Moscow: Akademiya, 1963), 171.

8. See Rachmat R. Rachimov, *"Muzhskie doma" v traditsionnoi kul'ture tadzhikov* [Men's houses in the Tajik traditional culture] (Leningrad: Nauka, 1990), 24.

9. Rachimov, *"Muzhskie doma,"* 8.

10. See Snesarev, "Traditsiia muzhskikh soiuzov," 159.

11. See Snesarev, "Traditsiia muzhskikh soiuzov," 159, 163ff. and Rachimov, *"Muzhskie doma,"* 53ff.

12. See Snesarev, "Traditsiia muzhskikh soiuzov," 204ff.

13. See Snesarev, "Traditsiia muzhskikh soiuzov," 205.

14. See Mahmud Sattor, *Uzbek udumlari: Millatning kenja bo'g'iniga* [Uzbek traditions: For the younger generation of the nation] (Tashkent: Fan, 1993), 125.

15. "Chernaia kassa" is a rotating savings association without social aspects such as a collective meal. It is usually played at the working place by mixed ethnic groups. Khatib-Chahidi highlights the fact that the financial element in social gatherings of Northern-Cypriot women was introduced by the wives of Turkish soldiers after 1974. Rotating coffee and tea-parties became the *altin-günü* (Turkish: gold day). See Jane Khatib-Chahidi, "Gold Coins and Coffee ROSCAs: Coping with Inflation the Turkish Way in Northern Cyprus," in *Money-Go-Rounds,* ed. Ardener and Burman, 253.

16. Victoria Koroteyeva and Ekaterina Makarova, "Money and Social Connections in the Soviet and Post-Soviet Uzbek City," *Central Asian Survey* 4 (1998): 592.

17. See: Oliver Roy, *The New Central Asia: The Creation of Nations* (New York: New York University Press, 2000), 133. See: David Abramson, "A Critical Look at NGOs and Civil Society as Means to an End. Uzbekistan, A Case Study," *Human Organization* 3 (1999): 243.

18. This is from an interview with the author on March 8, 2000.

19. Susan Bridger, *Women in the Soviet Countryside: Women's Roles in Rural Development in the Soviet Union* (Cambridge: Cambridge University Press, 1987), 187.

20. E.g., the Soros Foundation in Uzbekistan was registered in October 1996. The Konrad Adenauer Foundation (Germany) started its activities in July 1994, and Counterpart Consortium (United States) in the spring of 1995.

21. All interviewees' names have been changed. All personal data were valid at the time of the interview.

22. Zoreh Ghavamshahidi, *Die Entstehung des Nationalstaates und die Geschlech-*

terideologie in Usbekistan [The emergence of the nation-state and gender ideology in Uzbekistan], in *Feminismus, Islam, Nation: Frauenbewegungen im Maghreb in Zentralasien und in der Türkei* [Feminism, Islam, Nation: Women's movements in the Maghreb, Central Asia, and Turkey], ed. Claudia Schöning-Kalender, Ayla Neusel, and Meethild Jansen (Frankfurt: Campus Verlag, 1997), 163.

23. Sarah Henderson, "Russia's Virtual Civil Society. Foreign Aid and Civic Development"; <http://pro.harvard.edu/papers/013/013013hendersons.pdf> (June 18, 2001).

24. Deepa Narayan, "Voices of the Poor: Crying Out for Change," in *World Development Report 2000/2001: Attacking Poverty,* World Bank (New York: Oxford University Press, 2000), 228.

25. Nancy Lubin, "Central Asian Women: Observations over the Past Twenty-Five Years," in "Women in Central Asia. A Turn of the Century Assessment," Women's Series of the Middle East Project, ed. Haleh Esfaniari, Andrea Bertone, and Kathleen Kuehnast (unpublished), Woodrow Wilson International Center for Scholars, Washington, D.C., 2000, 21.

10

Sisterhood versus the "Moral" Russian State: The Postcommunist Politics of Rape

Janet Elise Johnson

In 1998, two high school students, "Olga" and "Irina," were out with a group of classmates and friends, enjoying the late summer daylight in a small Russian city.[1] They met up with other classmates, the groups merging and dividing until Olga and Irina were left with two young men, "Sasha" and "Alyosha," who were friends of friends. The foursome wandered around, laughing, drinking, and smoking, until they found themselves in a quiet corner of the city. The men turned on the women, held them down, and raped them both.

The author thanks, especially, Indiana University's Russian and East European Institute for the Mellon Endowment Fellowship, the Institute of State and Law at the Russian Academy of Sciences, the International Research and Exchange Board, Miami University's Havighurst Center for Russian and Post-Soviet Studies, the Moscow Center for Gender Studies, and the National Security Education Program, as well as Gabrielle Fitchett-Akimova, Irina Khaldeeva, Dianne Post, Jean Robinson, and Natalia Sereda for their various expressions of generosity. All translations and interpretations, except where noted, are by the author.

Olga's and Irina's experiences are typical of the kind of sexual violence that face women in Russia. According to the Ministry of Internal Affairs, there were 14,073 registered or reported rapes in 1991, 12,515 in 1995, and 10,888 in 1996,[2] constituting approximately 10 percent of all reported crimes. According to a 1998 report, the ministry suggests that there are many more rapes, perhaps one rape every hour, and that 30 percent of female high school students are victims of sexual violence every year.[3]

Olga's and Irina's stories also illustrate the challenges facing women who want to report rape. When Olga came home, she told her mother what happened, and her mother went to the police. On the basis of her written statement, the police referred Olga to a medical expert and took her underwear as evidence. The next day, her mother returned to see if the police had opened a criminal case against the two young men. The criminal investigator refused to talk to her. While at the police station, Olga's mother saw her daughter's underwear lying in a open box under the table.

Irina told her mother what had happened the day after the rape. Her mother went directly to the police station to file a complaint. However, when she tried to give the statement to a clerk, he refused to accept it, asserting that because a statement had already been filed on behalf of Olga, there was no need to file another. He said that she needed to speak with the criminal investigator, who was out of the office that day. When Irina's mother came back to the police station the next day, the criminal investigator told her that he was busy and to come back later. After a week of this kind of evasion, the investigator took the statement but told her that, at this late date, it was not possible to collect evidence.

Both mothers, frustrated by the police treatment, appealed to a lawyer associated with one of the new women's crisis centers in Russia. This lawyer filed a complaint against the investigator with the city prosecutor. The prosecutor refused to check into the statement, stating that he did not want to work on this "garbage" and that the young women were themselves at fault. The lawyer then filed a statement with the *oblast'* (regional) prosecutor, who ruled that no laws had been broken. The lawyer then took the story to a (woman) journalist at the local newspaper, who wrote an article about the mishandling of the case.

Yet the crisis center lawyer could provide only limited help. While Olga and Irina were working with the crisis center to deal with the trauma of rape, Sasha and Alyosha started threatening the young women and offering them a large sum of money to retract their statements. The young women decided that it was better to take the money rather than experience further humiliation from the criminal justice system or be afraid of the young men for the rest of their lives. Olga and Irina read the signals that Russian law enforcement was sending about the level of regard for their bodily safety and assumed that they would get little protection from future harm.

With this kind of response from law enforcement, why would a woman who had been raped even attempt to file a statement? On the basis of their several years of experience working with survivors of rape, the Russian Association of Crisis Centers for Women estimates that only 5 to 10 percent of rape victims file a report with the police.[4] Research in Saratov in 1995 by a women's organization found that 8 percent of women who viewed themselves as victims of rape had reported the rape to the police.[5] In contrast, the Ministry of Justice estimates on average that for every one crime reported, at least two are not filed.[6] The low reporting rate for rape puts a sinister twist on the decreasing number of officially reported rapes. That 14.1 percent of all reported crimes were rapes in 1991 and only 8.7 percent in 1995 may not suggest that there are fewer rapes but rather that rape victims increasingly doubt that the Russian criminal justice system will help them and thus do not even bother reporting their rapes.[7]

However, another type of sex-related crime dominates the Russian imagination, that of the serial murderer-rapist. For example, in the summer of 2000, Barnaul, a midsize Siberian city, was rocked by the disappearance of five young women.[8] Although the disappearances were at different dates, all of the women disappeared while taking the required entrance exams to enroll as students at the local State Technical University.

The Russian police respond quickly to these kinds of crimes. In Barnaul, they set up checkpoints and conducted widespread searches. The police response was supplemented by community involvement. Though a few residents of Barnaul questioned whether this had been some kind of suicide pact, the community engaged in the campaign to find the young women and the perpetrator. Flyers were printed and posted on mass transportation. One local newspaper established a website to centralize the available information. The father of one of the missing women even established his own website to plead for more information and to encourage other parents to protect their children.

Coordination between law enforcement and the community facilitated finding evidence. In October, the police discovered two bodies 25 miles outside the city limits. They identified one of the bodies as that of one of the missing young women. In February, another young woman came to the police, asserting that she had just escaped from a 22-year-old man, Aleksandr, who had tied her up and sexually abused her. The police responded quickly by arresting the man and confiscating 300 pornographic photographs they found in his apartment. The city prosecutor explained, "As is customary when a man is accused of sexual violence, we check whether he had anything to do with all unsolved rape and murder cases. We will know whether he is the man by the end of the week."

According to a local newspaper reporter, the suspect had been suspected of rape twice before but had never been charged. Aleksandr fits the model of a typical convicted rapist in Russia: male, under the age of 24 years, no prior convictions, and most likely drunk during the rape.[9] In contrast to the first narrative, in which the police and prosecutors delayed and blamed the victims, this narrative suggests that the criminal justice system responds with both alacrity and resolve (although not necessarily accurately or justly).

Examining the Postcommunist Politics of Rape

This chapter examines the postcommunist politics of rape—the contestation over what constitutes rape and how the state should respond—as a case study of how women's citizenship in Russia has been renegotiated during the post-Soviet transition. Because research on women and politics establishes the importance of women's movements in this type of politics,[10] my analysis relies on social movement theory, especially that of Sidney Tarrow, which seeks to explain how social movements emerge and succeed at changing policy.[11] Tarrow holds that the crucial factors are the political opportunity structure, the way policy claims are framed, and mobilizing structures.

By political opportunity structure, Tarrow refers to the "consistent—but not necessarily formal, permanent, or national—signals to social or political actors which either encourage or discourage them to use their internal resources to form social movements."[12] In practical terms, the political opportunity structure includes the state, elite alignments, the availability of influential allies, and the state's capacity for repression. By frame, I refer to the way that people come to understand a problem or even identify something as a problem worthy of state response (as opposed to an idiosyncratic misfortune). Through a process of frame alignment, movements can recruit constituents and help persuade the state to change policy. Valerie Sperling has shown that key mobilizing structures in the development of the Russian women's movement are the availability of financial resources and a group of women with the need to get involved.[13]

Shedding light on the two narratives of rape given above, I examine the development of a small antirape women's movement, one dimension of a larger women's crisis center movement, has emerged, seeking to institutionalize the state's responsibility to treat all nonconsensual sex as a violation of women's rights.[14]

The antirape women's movement has attracted activists who have a sense of social responsibility as well as foreign assistance. As these women (and some men) have become agents of democratic change by becoming politically engaged and by responding to people's needs, the emergence of an antirape movement is a small success amid the glut weaknesses of Russia's civil society.[15] Unfortunately, public attitudes severely limit the movement's political prospects and reinforce a government policy of responding only to what are perceived as "real" rapes, such as the serial rape-murders in Barnaul, but not to the "unreal" rapes, such as those of Irina and Olga.

This study is grounded in an 8-month research trip to Moscow and the regional capitals of Orel and Saratov in 1999.[16] Because these are all cities in Western, or European, Russia, my research findings do not reflect experiences in the Russian Far East or rural areas. I gathered my data through participant observation, structured interviews, attendance at conferences, roundtables, and parliamentary hearings, and by working with lawyers providing legal aid to victims of violence. I began with the larger, more established, more centrally located women's organizations and made use of their networks and contacts to look for other, less visible branches of the loosely connected women's movement.

The Antirape Movement

Mikhail Gorbachev's liberalization in the late 1980s created the political opportunity for a wide variety of groups in society to form social organizations and movements. Organizations could exist independent from the influence of the Communist Party and even challenge aspects of Soviet-style communism. There were not many women's groups, especially feminist groups, until the 1990s.[17] But by 1998, members active in several women's organizations were estimating that there were up to 2,000 such organizations in Russia.[18]

One of the new women's organizations, Syostri ("Sisters"), was most likely the first Russian crisis center specifically for victims of sexual assault when it opened in 1994 in Moscow. The idea for Syostri came from Natalia

Gaiderenko, who had been the first to translate an English-language book for survivors of sexual assault and who became the executive director of Syostri, and Martina Vandenberg, who brought her experience working at rape crisis centers in the United States and the United Kingdom.[19] Syostri's original and primary focus was and is the hotline (*telefon doveriia* or *goriachei linii*), which provides "urgent psychological help and medical and legal information."[20] By the end of 1998, Syostri had received almost 20,000 calls. The center has been staffed with ten to twenty mostly young women, ranging in occupation from psychologists to engineers.

From the beginning, Syostri's agenda included consciousness raising. Syostri holds workshops on the problems of sexual violence and conducts assertiveness training and self-defense programs for young people.[21] The center also launched a media campaign, complete with television advertisements and articles in newspapers. Acting on their own and in cooperation with the American Bar Association Central and East European Legal Initiative (ABA-CEELI) Gender Issues Program in Moscow, Syostri activists work with agents of the criminal justice system and participate in research conferences and seminars on sexual violence.

Since 1993, the number of nongovernmental crisis centers for women has multiplied. Common estimates of the number of crisis centers that focus on violence against women as well as sexual assault, range from 30 to 40, but there are probably many more. In 1999, the U.S. Agency for International Development–Russia began a 3-year small grants program for crisis centers for women in Russia, with the goal of supporting their crisis counseling and legal services.[22] The $600,000 program, which is administered by the International Research and Exchange Board (IREX), received 84 applications for the first round, about 20 of which were not actual crisis centers. In the third round, IREX received 125 applications. In total, the program has funded 35 crisis centers across Russia (see figure 10.1). It is likely that there are even more organizations without the Internet resources necessary to learn of the IREX program and without the resources or desire to register with the Ministry of Justice.

In Saratov, Nadezhda Kuznetsova founded the Interregional Association of Women Lawyers in 1994 to facilitate the collaboration of women lawyers.[23] Their original organizational focus was on violence against women. For a fee, lawyer members provided legal aid to victims of sexual and domestic violence as part of their legal practice. This in itself was a major step, because lawyers during the Soviet period rarely advocated on behalf of victims. In addition to this private service, Kutznetsova argued that mem-

Figure 10.1
Map of Russia Showing the Thirty-Five Crisis Centers for Women Sponsored by the International Research and Exchange Board

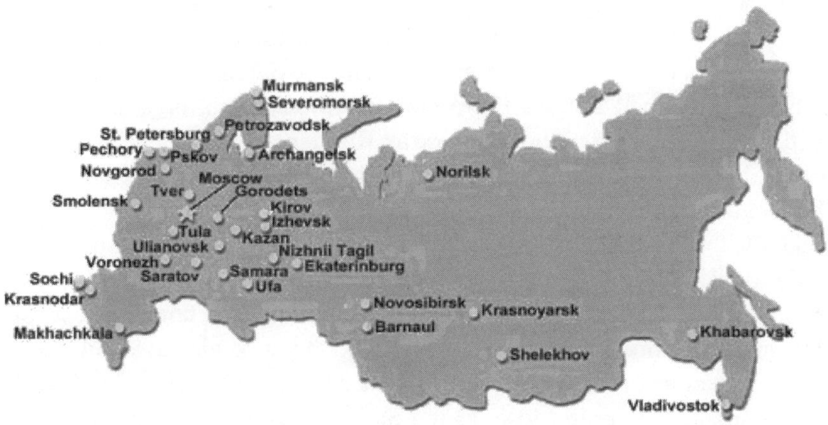

Source: <http://www.irex.org/programs/wcc/recipients.htm> (March 31, 2001).

bers felt a "social responsibility" when the enormity of the problem of rape became apparent. They established a hotline and a support group for young women who had suffered sexual violence and produced a television program on violence against women. They also ran a campaign, "16 Days without Violence," in 1995 in cooperation with local law enforcement agencies and other city nongovernmental organizations.

In addition to Kuznetsova's organization, a second women's organization in Saratov, the Saratov Crisis Center founded in 1996 by Irina Khaldeeva, more closely resembles Syostri with its hotline and advocacy programs. The main difference is that the Saratov Crisis Center addresses both sexual and domestic violence.

The fusion of services for both sexual assault and domestic violence found in Saratov is typical of crisis centers across Russia. Of the thirty-five different organizations funded by IREX, only one, ANNA, a domestic violence crisis center in Moscow, makes explicit its primary focus on one issue to the exclusion of the other.[24] This fusion makes practical sense in these regional cities. Because the primary service of almost all the crisis centers is a hotline and the hotlines are often quiet, fusing the services can save valuable resources, especially the time of volunteers or nominally paid telephone consultants. Partially because of these practical reasons, Kutznetsova's organization, when faced with competition from the Saratov Crisis Center, chose not to continue to focus on violence against women.

Syostri and the Saratov Crisis Center are members of an umbrella organization, the Russian Association of Crisis Centers for Women (RACCW). Syostri was a founding member in 1994, and the Saratov Crisis Center was founded through RACCW. There are also international organizations directly involved in providing help to the Russian crisis centers. In the late 1990s, both Syostri and the Saratov Crisis Center received assistance with their legal aid projects through the Russian Women Legal Advocacy Project run by Gabriel Fitchett-Akimova from Women, Law, and Development International.[25] This program has helped train Russian lawyers to work with crisis centers, supporting them so that they can work pro bono for rape victims and as community activists. Legal guidance was also available to the crisis centers from the ABA-CEELI Gender Issues Program in Moscow.

The crisis centers in Moscow and Saratov share the belief that sexual violence poses a serious problem that requires public attention. Syostri challenges the status quo, confronting the "myths" about sexual violence in Russian society with the "facts" in their written materials and workshops.[26] They reject the myth that "men rape because they cannot restrain their passion or strong sexual desires," claiming instead that "rape is a crime against a person. The purpose of the rapist is to subjugate the victim and/or to demonstrate his power." Syostri contends that if Russian society and culture did not hold women responsible for many of their own rapes, fewer rapes would occur.[27]

The Saratov Crisis Center, like many of the crisis centers that address both sexual and domestic violence, explicitly frames sexual violence as part of the larger category of violence against women. For example, the Saratov Crisis Center's main bulletin in 1999 was titled "The right to live WITHOUT VIOLENCE." This frame was imported from radical feminists, such American Catharine MacKinnon, who claim that a government's failure to respond to violence against women ensures women's subordination. Placing rape as a category of violence against women makes a political claim about the government's responsibility to protect women's right to live free from all sexual violence.

In contrast to this explicitly feminist stance taken by both Syostri and the Saratov Crisis Center, Kuznetsova's Interregional Association of Women Lawyers sought to categorize its work on rape as part of the "protection of women's and children's rights,"[28] rhetoric recalling the problematic Soviet approach to the "woman question." Though Kuznetsova's response is more maternalist, focusing on the protection of women and children, she also calls for a broader understanding of rape, especially for the explicit inclusion of marital rape in the criminal code.[29]

The existence of several dozen women's crisis centers across Russia, some of which are linked under an umbrella organization, and their collective call for a more expansive understanding of and more vigorous response to rape resembles a small social movement. This is a remarkable achievement, especially because it has been reached within a decade of the USSR's collapse.

Key factors accounting for this success involve a sense of "social responsibility" (*obshchestvennaia otvetstvennost'*) coupled with the availability of educated women who had been marginalized by the labor market. Kuznetsova highlighted the central importance of a widespread sense of social responsibility among educated, middle-aged post-Soviet women, a legacy of Soviet community-oriented education. As these women became aware of the sexual violence around them and the failure of the criminal justice system to provide meaningful remedies, they became more politicized. Many women lost their jobs in the mid-1990s,[30] and they stood little chance in a labor market geared toward men and young, sexually available women. They were forced to search for and to create new professional opportunities, and nongovernmental organizations held tremendous appeal, a phenomenon of the feminization of civic activism that is examined by several chapters in this volume. For the activists with whom I talked, working with women's organizations was the most rewarding employment they could imagine.

Foreign assistance was also crucial to the development of this network of crisis centers. Though much of Syostri's support came from individuals volunteering their time and energy (or being paid small salaries), their external funding comes from the West, such as from the Canadian Embassy in Moscow, the International Women's Club in Moscow, a women's shelter in Santa Monica, California, and from women at a hotline in Berlin. The Saratov Crisis Center has similarly benefited from Western funding, including the IREX-administered moneys.

In some instances, entrepreneurial activities provide additional revenues. For example, Khaldeeva and her sister established a small business to subsidize the center. The studio designs and publishes bulletins and posters for a wide range of clients, including the broader women's crisis center movement. However, as discussed in part IV of this volume, foreign assistance can create problems for Russian women's groups.

Drafting Rape Policy in New Criminal Codes

As democratization fostered the development of an antirape movement, it also created opportunities to reform rape policy, specifically in the criminal and criminal procedural codes. As early as 1985, legal scholars at the Institute of State and Law proposed reform, but discussion in the State Duma occurred only after 1994. The best opportunity for women's organizations to influence legislative activity was through a potential ally, Women of Russia, an electoral association that had garnered enough votes to become one of the five largest parties in the State Duma in 1993 but was defeated in the next election in 1995.[31]

Nevertheless, Women of Russia's political agenda did not include addressing the issue of rape. Liudmila Zavadskaia, a Women of Russia deputy, served as chair of the subcommittee on individual rights and federal legislation (1993–95). Although Zavadskaia did pursue women's rights in other policy areas, she did not address issues related to sexual violence in the criminal code.[32] Rape was not on Women of Russia's agenda. When I spoke with Zavadskaia, she explained to me that the "criminal code already gives the possibility to deal with violence [against women]."[33] Although she later became an advocate for women against gender violence with ABA-CEELI in 1999, she told me that I should be studying the feminization of poverty.

Sexual violence was, however, on the policy agenda of independent women's organizations. A report from RACCW, written by a working group under the leadership of Marina Pisklakova of ANNA, critiqued the definition of rape in both the Soviet period and in post-Soviet draft codes.[34] First, they pointed out that the law excluded psychological coercion—forcing a woman to have sex by means of coercion other than physical violence or the threat of physical violence.[35] The official commentary on the Soviet-period criminal code defines "psychological violence" as requiring physical threats that are immediately actionable—for example, the brandishing of weapons such as a "knife" or "razor" or other threats of severe bodily harm or death.[36]

As explained by Aleksei Ignatov, a professor of criminal law and member of the advisory council for drafting the new criminal code, for a crime to be rape, there must be "physical threats."[37] RACCW wanted a broader definition of coercion, including threats to discontinue economic support or threatening to hurt the victim's children.

RACCW also tackled the legal codes' failure to refer to the body parts and the act of penetration involved in rape. The codes resort to describing rape as "natural" sexual intercourse that is "perverted" by violence.[38] As Ignatov elaborates, rape is distinguishable from other forms of sexual violence because rape is

> intercourse between the sexes, intended for reproduction, that can cause a woman to become pregnant. All of the rest are different ways to satisfy sexual needs, but they are not sexual intercourse . . . if it's not sexual intercourse, that means it's not rape.[39]

Resorting to the construction of rape as the perversion of the "natural" form of sexual intercourse that can result in pregnancy suggests a quite different frame for rape than that sponsored by the women's groups, which makes no categorical distinction between the bodily sites of sexual violence. Ignatov's need to make this distinction suggests that regulating rape under this second frame is not about protecting women from bodily harm but rather about protecting men's right to the wombs of "their" women.

In the end, legislators crafted a new section in the 1996 Russian Federation Criminal Code to address sexual violence, the "Crimes against Sexual Inviolability and Sexual Freedom of the Person" (chap. 18). Significantly, this chapter codified the decriminalization of consensual homosexual intercourse and criminalized coerced homosexual intercourse (article 132), signaling progress toward constructing rape as a crime of the infliction of bodily harm regardless of a person's sex and the site of penetration.[40] However, the code keeps separate penile-vaginal rape (article 131) and, according to the new commentary, restricts psychological coercion even further as "psychological violence" is defined as the "application of force."[41] Repeating Ignatov's comments, the official commentary explains that rape is the "perversion" of the "natural—taking form in nature—sex act" ("*estestvennogo, slozhivshegosia v prirode, polovogo akta*").[42]

In addition to reforming the criminal codes, legislators tried to reform the Soviet-period criminal procedural code, but because the Procuracy wanted to keep its Soviet-period powers, a new procedural code could not be passed. Instead, the Duma passed transitional amendments to the Soviet-period criminal procedure code to bring it in line with some of provisions of the new criminal code. An important problem is that this revised code continues to distinguish "simple rape" (1996 Russian Federation Criminal Code, article 131.1) from other types of violent crimes by stipulating that this kind of rape case is initiated in no other circumstances than when a victim brings a complaint.[43]

Because the antirape movement emerged only in the mid-1990s, it had limited opportunity to raise public consciousness about the problem of rape before crucial legislative decisions were made. The parliamentary debate and the resulting legislation indicates that even if there had been more time, reform of rape policy would have been unlikely. Duma deputies, including those from Women of Russia, have fundamentally different understandings of rape than the Russian antirape movement. The antirape movement framed rape as part of the broader category of violence against women, invoking women's human rights, countering the tendency to blame women for their own rape, and rejecting biological justifications for rape. In contrast, the policymaking process suggests frames for rape that are more skeptical and that link rape to biology and morality.

The Criminal Justice System and "Real" Rape

These skeptical frames are reiterated in the responses to rape by the criminal justice system. To analyze the postcommunist rape policy, I return to the narratives with which I began.

Olga's and Irina's Stories

The first obstacle that Irina encountered was the reluctance of the police even to accept her written statement, the first step in initiating a criminal case.[44] In their 1997 report on violence against women in Russia, Human Rights Watch (HRW) found that police in all their data-collection sites were routinely rejecting sexual violence statements without any investigation.[45] Persistence does seem to pay off in terms of getting the statement accepted. For example, a 15-year-old gang rape victim said that after telling her story twenty times, the police finally accepted her statement. According to HRW, victims of sexual violence usually had to tell their stories at least four times to different police officers.[46] One of the major achievements of victim advocates, whether attorneys or crisis center volunteers, is that they have been able to help persuade the police to accept their initial statement.

Reluctance to investigate crimes may be common in post-Soviet Russia, but in the case of rape, the police recognize and justify their behavior by asserting that most rape claims are not legitimate. HRW found that almost all the police with whom they spoke mentioned cases where they believed that woman had used rape accusations to exact revenge or to blackmail men for money—or even to coerce men to marry.[47] In a study by the liberal Moscow-based weekly, *Argumenty i Facty* (Arguments and Facts), reporter Elena Shesterina found that "many police detectives" believe that young men are often victims of false allegations made so that the "rape victims" can extort them.[48] The police in this report even go so far in their skepticism that they claim that 70 percent of the men who are convicted of rape in Russia are "essentially not guilty."

In other cases, the police allege that the victims provoke their own rape.[49] For example, one 16-year veteran of the Moscow police and former director of the All-Soviet Association of Policewomen described her only rape investigation this way. The victims were two women who were deprived of their freedom, beaten, and raped over the course of several days. Because they had been drinking with the four men who became their rapists, she blamed the women.[50] Like others in the criminal justice system, this woman police officer confused what some might consider bad judgment with legal responsibility.

As in Olga's and Irina's cases, because a "simple rape" case is only initiated by the complaint of the victim, delaying and refusing complaints can empower the rapist. The rapist can coerce or bribe a victim into dropping her complaint before the criminal investigator makes a decision to pursue a case. The dynamics of this policy are similar to the phenomena encountered by woman battery victims in the United States before the adoption of "no drop" policies, when the de facto policy was to automatically drop a woman battery case if the victim changed her mind. In Russia, the more a rapist intimidates the victim, the more likely he can protect himself from criminal charges.

Delaying the complaint can have other serious consequences. Because the police appear specifically to delay rape statements, the delay signals that the police believe that rape is somehow the fault of the victim. Why else would a victim have to tell her story over and over? At times, the police explicitly state that this is their purpose. According to Zoia Khotkina, a researcher at the Moscow Center for Gender Studies, the police took 8 days to be persuaded to take the complaint of a 22-year-old who had been raped and badly beaten.[51] The police had told her, "It is shameful. . . . There will be a court hearing. It will take too long. It is shameful." I wonder, shameful for whom?

As in Irina's case, the practical consequence of delaying the acceptance of the complaint is that victims are prevented from getting the referrals necessary for the collection of forensic evidence.[52] A week after a rape is often too late to collect evidence. Under the law, rape victims could go to a private doctor because there is no explicit preclusion against using medical evidence obtained privately. However, private doctors do not have the proper equipment (e.g., "rape kits") or the knowledge to deal with evidence collection, and the crisis centers did not think that, in practice, such evidence would be accepted.

Even when women are given referrals, the police often act irresponsibly, scheduling the appointment several days after the complaint is accepted. The police also fail to inform rape victims that by washing themselves and their clothes, they may be destroying the only evidence they have. The founder of Syostri, Natalia Gaidarenko, argues, "We can regard these cases as sabotage because it is hard to imagine that the police do not know how to proceed."[53]

Both Olga and Irina encountered a second set of obstacles from prosecutors who often refuse to begin a preliminary investigation or to prosecute. Prosecutors doubt the legitimacy of rape claims with the same justifications given by the police: Rape victims either make false allegations for their own gain or provoke the rape themselves. A Saint Petersburg prosecutor, Tatiana Nikolaeva, claimed that one out of ten women who report rape is making false allegations.[54] Research in Saint Petersburg, Murmansk, and Moscow shows that prosecutors blame the victim for drinking or meeting with the future rapist, especially in his apartment or car.[55]

As in Olga's case, most rape cases do not get beyond the initial consideration of whether to open an investigation. And if an official preliminary investigation is begun, it is frequently halted without prosecution. According to a member of the General Prosecutor's Office, the majority of cases that are closed during the preliminary investigation stage are rape cases.[56] In Saratov, the lawyer working with the Saratov Crisis Center through the Women Lawyers Advocacy Project reported that she had not had a single case in which a woman wanted to go through with prosecution for sexual violence.[57]

Similarly, Nadezhda Kuznetsova reports that, of the 104 rapes registered in the Astrakhan *raion* (district) in 1994, only 8 cases resulted in the rapist being sentenced to prison, and these cases were "especially aggravated" forms of rape.[58] With so much resistance from the police and the procuracy, and if the rapists are offering money and issuing threats, the "rational choice" for most rape victims like Olga and Irina is to take the money and run.

The Rape-Murders of Five Young Women in Barnaul

In contrast to Olga's and Irina's stories, the case of the rape-murders of the five young women in Barnaul suggests that the Russian criminal justice system can and does respond to at least some forms of sexual violence against women. In this case, the police and prosecutor's office responded immediately to the first disappearance, expending tremendous resources to set up checkpoints and to search the city and surrounding regions. Law enforcement was coordinated with the community residents, establishing a climate in which even a woman who had chosen to go to a man's apartment (as the witness had done) could get her claim of sexual assault heard.

This story is an example of the kind of case that results in the historically high conviction rate for rape trials in Russia. If a rape case gets to the trial stage, conviction rates for rape are nearly 90 or 95 percent, higher than the average for most crimes (which is about 84 percent).[59] It also sheds light on the severity in Russia of punishment for rapists in comparison with that for other crimes (although not in comparison with the United States). For example, in 1990, 54 percent of adult convicted rapists were sentenced to between 5 and 10 years imprisonment.[60] Another 33.9 percent were sentenced to 3 to 5 years. The average sentence in 1990 was 7.5 years, slightly higher than the average sentence for all crimes of 7.4 years. From 1990 through 1993, approximately one rapist a year was sentenced to die.

Russian law enforcement officers have created a complicated schema to distinguish between "real rapes" and "false claims." For example, a Muscovite who had been raped orally and anally and beaten in her own apartment reported the assault 5 days later. The police initially refused the statement, claiming that she had waited too long to report the crime. A police officer from Saratov echoed the sentiment that "real" rape victims hasten to the police station. "As a rule, women who are [really] raped come to the police immediately."[61] For Margarita Paniflova, a Moscow prosecutor, the key is whether the victim behaved appropriately during the incident and at the police interview. A "real" victim of rape must appear distraught. These sentiments were even repeated by a former Moscow prosecutor with 17 years of experience who had chosen to work with the crisis center ANNA through the Russian Women Lawyers Advocacy Project.[62]

In other cases, the distinction is about whether the victim was a virgin or not.[63] According to Zoia Khotkina, a senior researcher at the Moscow Center for Gender Studies, when she tried to help a victim of sexual violence, the police "would say that people are murdered on the street, but here it is just rape. And what was so terrible? . . . She was not a virgin, she was not a child."[64] According to Natalia Gaiderenko, the police initially rejected a statement from a woman who had been raped and beaten, asking why she was distraught because she was not a virgin.[65]

The criminal justice system does not recognize rape within marriage.

When members of the women's movement asked Saratov prosecutors at a roundtable on domestic violence about marital rape, the prosecutors claimed that marital rape is an impossibility.[66] When presented with the proposition that a wife could experience rape by her husband, a young police officer at Syostri's training on sexual violence exclaimed, "Why would she get married if she didn't want to have sex?"[67] Another officer connected the issue to prostitutes who, he asserted, cannot be raped by anyone after they have taken money from a client.

Thus, the criminal justice system sponsors frames for rape distinct from those of the women's movement, which construes rape as a violation of a woman's right to live free from bodily harm. Reproducing the understanding of rape that dominated the debate over criminal rape statutes, the reluctance to accept complaints or begin an inquiry, the tendency to blame women, and the relevance of virginity indicate that morality is at stake and that only "moral" victims deserve protection. The denial of the possibility of marital and prostitute rape—suggesting a belief in sexual contracts in which consent, once given, cannot be retracted—indicates that the protection of some men's access to some women is at stake.[68]

The serial rape-murder avoids this skepticism because it triggers concerns about disorder. Stories of serial murders fixate Russians as much as they fixate Americans, dominating both the press and mass culture accounts of violence against women. Criminologist Alison Young suggests that some societies "need" these narratives of extraordinary, horrific crimes to maintain a sense of community.[69] Serial killers and rapists are the "outlaws" who help us make sense of right and wrong, innocence and guilt. Elena Lvova, a former Moscow prosecutor turned defense lawyer, asserted that 100 percent of stranger rapes, if reported, would result in conviction.[70] The criminal justice system fosters the fantasy of its effectiveness against the most horrific of crimes by instituting "popular justice." It is not unusual in these kind of high-profile cases for courts to travel to bigger venues to meet the demands of the public.[71]

Conclusion

Women's organizations have seized the post-Soviet opportunity to establish dozens of crisis centers across Russia, building coalitions to make political claims about the need to respond to all forms of sexual violence. Antirape activists across Russia have been persuading the police to at least accept rape statements. The success of these activists in creating networks and achieving some policy change on the local level illustrates that women in Russia can and will make use of their new political citizenship.

However, as is indicated by the negotiations over the rape statutes in the criminal code and by current practices, women face political and criminal justice systems that imagine rape in limited ways, allowing only some rapes to be seen as "real." Other forms of sexual violence—such as acquaintance rape, marital rape, and rape with little additional physical force—are invisible or seen as the woman's fault.

Both transition theorists and Russian politicians contend that the country's primary task is to establish the foundations for procedural democracy and capitalism. Women's issues are often dismissed as trivial distractions. This sentiment was echoed specifically for the case of sexual violence by Alevtina Aparina, the chair of the Duma's Committee on Women, Family, and Youth (May 13, 1996):

> When there is war, when there are moral tragedies in the country, there is no time to think about sexual violence. Because there are more important problems now, sexual violence does not deserve much attention. Women have other concerns. Russian women are strong, and men know that.[72]

Unfortunately, there are serious consequences for women when questions of violence are put off until later. In the short run, rape victims face a second victimization when they find no validation of the criminality of their rapes from the criminal justice system. When rapists remain unpunished, there is no de-legitimation of the violence of rape, leaving all women in Russia more vulnerable.

More significant for the long run, women's fundamental right to live free from bodily harm is relegated to some indeterminate future. Instead of creating an unbiased democratic system that can provide opportunities for inclusion of citizens not equally included in the initial transition—transition theorists' justification for deferring women's concerns—citizenship is stratified by sex, creating institutionalized inequalities that are hard to eradicate.

Postscript

In December 2001, a new criminal procedural code was passed by the Russian parliament. After the first reading of the draft legislation, the leaders of

Syostri wrote letters to the Duma committee charged with reforming the code.[73] They expressed their concern that the new code's presumption of innocence, unmitigated by any new provisions countering the institutionalized skepticism toward rape, would give the police and medical examiners even more opportunities to avoid helping women. They received no response and were closed out of the Duma debate. Thus, unsurprisingly, the new criminal procedural code maintains the unjustified distinction between simple rape and all other forms of violence crime.[74] And, according to Syostri's director, the criminal justice system, in practice, is even more unresponsive to women who have been raped.

In addition to the setback at the state level, the crisis center movement's focus on sexual violence—and the organizations specifically focused on the issue of rape—has declined.[75] The primary reason is that the target of foreign assistance has shifted. The same small grants from the U.S. Agency for International Development that allowed the crisis centers to proliferate also produced powerful incentives to shift the direction of the movement away from sexual violence because the funds were earmarked only for domestic violence. Since 2001, the target has shifted again to sex trafficking. The unintended consequence may be a decline in the effectiveness of the crisis centers in dealing with both sexual and domestic violence. A political opportunity for change appears to have been lost.

Notes

1. This narrative is based on a real case in a midsize Russian city. I have given pseudonyms to the participants and have changed some specifics about the rapes to protect the young women.

2. Human Rights Watch, *Russia—Too Little, Too Late: State Response to Violence against Women* (New York: Human Rights Watch, 1997), 17.

3. Russian Women Lawyers Advocacy Project, *O chem my molchim?* (brochure) [Women against violence] (Moscow: Russian Women Lawyers Advocacy Project, 2000), 1, 3.

4. Human Rights Watch, *Russia—Too Little, Too Late.*

5. Nadezhda Kuznetsova, "Prava zhenshchin: Real'nost' i perspektivy" Zhenshchiny protiv nasilia [About what do we keep silent? Women's rights: Reality and perspectives], *Vy i My: Dialog Rossiiskikh i Americkanskikh zhenshchin* [You and We: Dialogue of Russian and American women] 1, no. 13 (1997): 16–18.

6. Gennady M. Danilenko and William Burnham, *Law and Legal System of the Russian Federation* (Yonkers, N.Y.: Juris Publishing, 1999), 454.

7. Human Rights Watch, *Russia—Too Little, Too Late.*

8. Unfortunately, this story of the rapes in Barnaul is true. The details come primarily

from several articles in *The Moscow Times,* February, 8, 2001; <http://www.altapress.altai.ru/special/agtu/> and <http://www.biysk.ru/~mvg/> (which are the two websites I mention).

9. A. D'iachenko and I. Koloskova, "Iznasilovaniia: statisticheskii aspekt" [Rape: statistical aspect], *Voprosy statistiki* [Statistical questions] 2 (1995): 84.

10. E.g., see Najma Chowdury and Barbara Nelson, eds., *Women and Politics Worldwide* (New Haven, Conn.: Yale University Press, 1994). Their multinational study shows that disruptive, sustained, multi-issue action from women's groups is the most effective, common avenue for woman-friendly change around the world.

11. Sidney Tarrow, *Power in Movement: Social Movements, Collective Action and Politics* (Cambridge: Cambridge University Press, 1994).

12. Sidney Tarrow, "States and Opportunities: The Political Structuring of Social Movements," in *Comparative Perspectives on Social Movements: Political Opportunities, Mobilizing Structures, and Cultural Framings,* ed. Doug McAdam, John D. McCarthy, and Mayer N. Zald (Cambridge: Cambridge University Press, 1996), 54.

13. Valerie Sperling, *Organizing Women in Contemporary Russia: Engendering Transition* (Cambridge: Cambridge University Press, 1999).

14. For a discussion of the domestic violence dimension of the women's crisis center movement, see Janet Elise Johnson, "Privatizing Pain: The Problem of Woman Battery in Russia," *NWSA Journal* 13 (2001): 153–68.

15. See, e.g., Sarah E. Mendelson and John K. Glenn, eds., *The Power and Limits of NGOs: A Critical Look at Building Democracy in Eastern Europe and Eurasia* (New York: Columbia University Press, 2002).

16. This project is part of my dissertation. Janet Elise Johnson, "State Transformation and Violence against Women in Postcommunist Russia," Ph.D dissertation, Indiana University, Bloomington, 2001.

17. Carol Nechemias, "The Prospects for a Soviet Women's Movement: Opportunities and Obstacles," in *Perestroika from Below: Social Movements in the Soviet Union,* ed. Judith B Sedaitis and Jim Butterfield (Boulder, Colo.: Westview Press, 1991).

18. N. I. Abubikirova et al., *Directory of Women's Non-Governmental Organizations in Russia & the NIS,* trans. I. Savelieva (Moscow: Aslan Publishers, 1998), 9.

19. Tatiana Zabelina, "Syostri" [Sisters], *Violence against Women* 1, no. 3 (1995): 266–71.

20. Syostri, *Syostri: 5 Years!* (bulletin available at the fifth year anniversary press conference) (Moscow: Syostri, 1999).

21. Marina Mironova, interview with the author, Moscow, 1997.

22. U.S. Agency for International Development, "Press Release: USAID Grants $100,000 to Fund Women's Crisis Centers in Russia"; <http://www.usaid.gov/press/releases/pr991006> (1999).

23. Nadezhda Kuznetsova, interview with the author, Saratov, Russia, 1999.

24. International Research and Exchange Board (IREX), "Program to Support Crisis Centers for Women in Russia"; <http://www.irex.org/programs/wcc/index.htm> (2001). Syostri did not receive U.S. Agency for International Development money in this IREX-administered distribution.

25. Gabrielle Fitchet-Akimova, interview with the author," Moscow, 1999.

26. Syostri, *Syostri.*

27. Mironova, interview with the author.

28. Abubikirova et al., *Directory,* 9.

29. Nadezhda Kuznetsova, "Violence against Women" (unpublished), Interregional Association of Women Lawyers, Saratov, Russia, 1996.

30. Mary I. Dakin, "Women and Employment Policy in Contemporary Russia," *Demokratizatsiya,* summer 1995: 252–61.

31. For a discussion of the political faction "Women of Russia," see Wendy Slater, "'Women of Russia' and Women's Representation in Russian Politics," in *Russia in Transition: Politics, Privatization, and Inequality,* ed. David Lane (New York: Longman, 1995); Mary Buckley, "Adaptation of the Soviet Women's Committee: Deputies Voices from 'Women of Russia,'" in *Post-Soviet Women: From the Baltic to Central Asia,* ed. Mary Buckley (New York: Cambridge University Press, 1997); and Mary Buckley, "From Faction Not to Party: 'Women of Russia' in the Duma," in *Women and Political Change: Perspectives from East-Central Europe,* ed. Sue Bridger (New York: Saint Martin's Press, 1999).

32. Liudmila Zavadskaia, "Seksual'nye Domogatel'stva na Rabote" [Sexual Harassment], in *Zakonadatel'stvo i prava zhenshiny,* ed. Zoia Khotkina [Legislation and the rights of women] (Moscow: American Bar Association Central and Eastern European Law Initiative, the Women's Consortium, Moscow Center for Gender Studies, 1996).

33. Liudmila Zavadskaia, interview by the author, Moscow, 1999.

34. Russian Association of Crisis Centers for Women, "Violence against Women in Russia: Research, Education, and Advocacy Project" (unpublished), Russian Association of Crisis Centers for Women, Moscow, 1996.

35. Under the Russian Soviet Federative Socialist Republic Criminal Code (hereafter, RSFSR CrC) as updated to 1995, "simple rape" was defined as "sexual intercourse by use of force or threats or by taking advantage of the helpless state of the victim."

36. Iu. D. Severin, *Kommentarii k ugolovnomu kodeksu RSFSR* [Commentary on the criminal code of the RSFSR] (Moscow: Iurisdicheskaia Literatura, 1984), article 117.

37. Aleksei Ignatov, "Voprosy razvitiia ugolovnogo zakonadatel'stva ob otvetstvennosti za prestipleniia na seksual'noi pochbe" [Questions on the development of criminal legislation on the responsibility for sexual offenders], in *Seksual'nye Domogatel'stva na Rabote* [Sexual Harassment], ed. Zoia Khotkina (Moscow: ABA-CEELI, the Women's Consortium, Moscow Center for Gender Studies, 1996), 45. This book documented a seminar on sexual harassment at the Moscow Center for Gender Studies in May of 1995.

38. Severin, *Kommentarii.*

39. Ignatov, "Voprosy razvitiia ugolovnogo."

40. A. V. Naumov, *Kommentarii k ugolovnomu kodeksu Rossiiskoi Federatsii* [Commentary on the criminal code of the Russian Federation] (Moscow: Iurist', 1997). Article 133 of the 1996 CrC establishes another form of sexual violence which might be construed as covering broader forms of coercion, such as taking advantage of the economic dependence of a person.

41. The new rape statute defines rape as "sexual intercourse with the application or threat of the application of force against the victim or other persons or by taking advantage of the helpless state of the victim" (1996 RF CrC., article 131).

42. Naumov, *Kommentarii.*

43. RSFSR Criminal Procedure Code (hereafter, CrPC), article 27, first promulgated in 1960.

44. Refusing this written statement (or complaint) is not legal; article 109, 1960 RSFSR CrPC.

45. Human Rights Watch, *Russia—Too Little, Too Late,* 21–24.

46. Human Rights Watch, *Russia—Too Little, Too Late,* 21–22.

47. Human Rights Watch, *Russia—Too Little, Too Late,* 22.

48. The original article was "The Rape Game," reprinted in *World Press Review,* February 6, 1996.

49. Human Rights Watch, *Russia—Too Little, Too Late,* 19.

50. The police sometimes also blame their limited resources or their desire to have a low official crime rate. In a period of increasing crime rates and limited resources for law enforcement, these statements make some sense. However, they do not explain why the police are more skeptical of rape claims than other types of crimes.

51. Human Rights Watch, *Russia—Too Little, Too Late,* 23.

52. This is also illegal. According to article 20 of the "Fundamental Legislation of the Russian Federation on the Protection of the Health of the Citizens," citizens have a right to an expert medical opinion. Further, refusal by doctors or the police to provide medical treatment is a crime if this refusal leads to harm to her health (Russian Federation Criminal Code, article 124).

53. Human Rights Watch, *Russia—Too Little, Too Late,* 25–26.

54. Human Rights Watch, *Russia—Too Little, Too Late,* 31.

55. Human Rights Watch, *Russia—Too Little, Too Late,* 20.

56. Human Rights Watch, *Russia—Too Little, Too Late,* 30.

57. Iuliia Isaeva, interview with the author, Saratov, Russia, 1999.

58. Nadezhda Kuznetsova, "Prava zhenshchin," 16–18.

59. Danilenko and Burnham, *Law and Legal System.*

60. D'iachenko and Koloskova, "Iznasilovaniia."

61. Human Rights Watch, *Russia—Too Little, Too Late,* 22.

62. Zynaida Batrakova, interview by the author, Moscow, 1999.

63. Human Rights Watch, *Russia—Too Little, Too Late,* found that the Russian criminal justice system has a fascination with the state of a women's hymen.

64. Human Rights Watch, *Russia—Too Little, Too Late,* 22.

65. Even for the handful of cases that Human Rights Watch found that made it through to the final stages of the preliminary investigation and to a trial, legal mechanisms were often used to verify that the rape was "real." Some procurators used criminal procedure statutes (articles 162–63) that allow the confrontation of the witnesses including the victim (*ochnaia stavka*) (Human Rights Watch, *Russia—Too Little, Too Late,* 23). At trial, defense attorneys still used a Soviet handbook for sexual violence cases in which they are urged to "tak[e] into consideration the possibility that the woman claiming she was raped in some way provoked the act or had engaged in provocative behavior prior to the sex act" (p. 20).

66. Russian Association of Crisis Centers for Women, "Violence against Women, 3.

67. Observed by the author, Moscow, June 6, 1999.

68. For a discussion of the sexual contract, see Carole Pateman, *The Sexual Contract* (Stanford, Calif.: Stanford University Press, 1988).

69. Alison Young, *Imagining Crime: Textual Outlaws and Criminal Conversations* (Thousand Oaks, Calif.: Sage, 1996).

70. Elena Lvova, interview with the author, Moscow, 1999.

71. E.g., in 1990, Kazan authorities decided to conduct a rape trial in a soccer stadium so that more people could observe; Gordon B. Smith, *Reforming the Russian Legal System* (Cambridge: Cambridge University Press, 1996), 155. Today's idea of popular justice may be different. *The Sharpshooter,* a popular 1999 Russian film, is about a

grandfather of a young girl who was raped by three men. The grandfather, with the tacit approval of the police, exacts revenge on all three, hitting them where it hurts them most. The granddaughter's experiences, other than the rape itself, shown in graphic detail, appear irrelevant. Within the mafia, rape of rapist's wife or woman lover appears to be "popular."

72. Human Rights Watch, *Russia—Too Little, Too Late,* 19.

73. This is from an interview by the author with Maria Mokhova, Syostri director, Moscow, 2002.

74. Russian Federation Criminal Procedure Code, promulgated July 1, 2002, article 20.3.

75. These observations are based on 2-month research trip to Russia in the summer of 2002, including to the Siberian provincial capital of Barnaul.

Part IV

Assistance Encounters

11

Meeting the Challenge Together? Russian Grassroots Women's Organizations and the Shortcomings of Western Aid

Rebecca Kay

Immediately following the demise of the Soviet Union, in January 1992 the leadership of the newly independent Russian Federation embarked upon a program of accelerated and full-scale, pro-market reform. From the onset of this process, Russian women saw previous securities and certainties eroded, the career paths they embarked upon diverted or interrupted, the material comfort of their families undermined, and, in the most extreme cases, their physical survival threatened.

Millions of women have met these challenges with great courage and ingenuity, developing and sustaining survival strategies for themselves and their

The major period of fieldwork upon which the findings of this chapter are based was conducted in 1995–96 with the support of a travel grant from the Harold Hyam Wingate Foundation. Supplementary fieldwork in 2000 and 2001 was supported by the Department of Central and East European Studies of the University of Glasgow. Thanks go to Sue Bridger, Julie Hemment, Armine Ishkanian, and Michele Rivkin-Fish for their helpful comments on the drafts of this chapter.

families, many of which fly in the face of prevalent attitudes toward gender and post-Soviet expectations of female roles. These strategies might involve embarking on new and previously unconsidered forms of work, retraining, engaging in informal-sector activities, entering the world of commercial enterprise and small business development, or falling back on home-based activities and subsistence farming either as a means of income generation or as a way of economizing and reducing expenditure.[1]

For some women, engagement in activities of this nature drew them together with other women from similar backgrounds or with women facing similar struggles. Some chose to formalize their support networks and resource pools by establishing grassroots women's organizations. Others established women's groups and organizations for a particular female constituency, often finding that issues of practical and emotional support become the driving force behind the organization and the primary motivation of those involved, whether or not it was a key consideration from the outset.

Both these paths to organizational activity were described by the women involved in a study of grassroots women's organizations in Moscow, Saratov, Tver', and the small provincial town of Tarusa in Kaluga *oblast'* (region).[2] This chapter illustrates some of the problematic encounters between local understandings of the purposes and priorities of women's grassroots organizing and the aims, design, and implementation of programs of foreign assistance. This analysis draws on the experiences of these organizations and the women who were their members. The arguments that follow are based primarily on data collected during a 6-month period of fieldwork in 1995–96 that involved the in-depth, semistructured interviewing of more than 100 women in the four centers mentioned above, as well as extensive participant observation at women's organization events, meetings, and seminars. Additional information was gathered during shorter visits to Moscow, Tver', and Tarusa in May 2000 and to Moscow and Tarusa in September 2001.

The specific focus and constituency of the organizations studied varied, ranging from professionally oriented groups such as the Saratov-based Club for Business Women and the Moscow branch of the Russia-wide Association of Women in Aviation, Aviatrisa, to groups based on local constituencies such as the Tarusa Association of Women and to those focusing on specific female life experiences such as the Moscow-based organization for single mothers Tol'ko Mama (Just Mom). Yet what each of the sample organizations had in common was a determination to provide tangible, practical support to members and to help the women involved overcome the challenges and hardships of post-Soviet life by pooling both material and emotional resources and offering a sense of solidarity and shared experience.

The leader and founder of Tol'ko Mama described the original motivation for establishing her organization as rooted in a recognition that help for single mothers would not be forthcoming from the post-Soviet state. She therefore determined to set up a "self-help group so that people could help themselves." Similarly, the organizers of a Club for Women's Initiatives, nominally attached to the local employment service in Tver', pointed to the lack of any "state mechanism to deal with specifically women's problems" as the raison d'être of their group and its activities. Other groups, including the Tarusa Association of Women, formed more gradually as women gravitated toward one another in search of mutual support and comfort and around those displaying strong leadership skills, whereas some groups originated in leisure-oriented, shared-interest organizations until the more pressing realities of daily life took over. As the leader of one such group explained, "The point is, it is not even about a struggle for change, it is about survival!"

Feminism and Gender Equality: Legitimate Goals or a Waste of Precious Time?

This focus on survival shaped the activities and priorities both of the majority of the grassroots organizations studied and of many of their individual members. Frequently these activities challenged the most rigid definitions of appropriate female behavior and roles propounded by contemporary Russian media discourses and public rhetoric.

These women—far from retiring quietly from the public arena into primarily home-based and family-oriented roles and responsibilities—actively sought employment and demanded recognition of the value of their skills. Many of them were confronting local authorities and struggling to keep "women's issues" on local political agendas. They were also actively displaying abilities and forms of behavior not deemed "naturally female" by currently popular definitions of biologically determined differences between male and female roles and aptitudes: leadership skills, strategizing, and autonomous decision making, to name but a few.

For many individuals and organizations, challenging the post-Soviet version of publicly acceptable attitudes toward gender was not seen as a legitimate and recognized goal in its own right but rather as a means to an end—

namely, the practical improvement of women's lives through increased security, better living conditions, and opportunities for "personal development." In keeping with this perspective, it was perfectly acceptable for women to pursue improved living conditions via a husband's family wage and to see motherhood and domestic concerns as the primary source of well-being and personal development.

Rather than wishing to develop an alternative worldview in direct contradiction to mainstream post-Soviet discourses of gender difference, these women stressed the importance of each woman's right to choose her own style of living, relationships, and identities. This emphasis on individual freedom of choice was explained by many of the women interviewed as part of a rejection of the Soviet version of "enforced" emancipation, which they described as an extremely oppressive experience. By the same token, they were unwilling to accept any new ideological stance that they perceived as rigidly imposing a particular version of liberation on all women.

Although some women were convinced of the need for equal opportunities, others subscribed more strongly to a view of crucial and inalienable differences between the sexes. Those supporting the latter point of view frequently claimed that these differences were the key to defining separate spheres of opportunity and areas of activity as appropriate for men and women. From this perspective, many of the activities in which women were engaged as part of a struggle for survival, which contradicted a narrow definition of "appropriate" female abilities and "feminine" roles, were characterized as unfortunate symptoms of economic insecurity and social upheaval. As such, these activities were viewed as a temporary necessity rather than as a long-term goal. Thus, the pursuit of gender equality per se was often perceived as irrelevant or inappropriate, whereas "feminism" was viewed by many either as a concept alien to their culture and experience or as a theoretical pursuit for privileged (Western) women enjoying the luxury of spare time, financial security, and material comfort.

In contrast, some members of the grassroots organizations studied, particularly those in leadership positions, expressed some sympathy for feminism, especially if it could be adapted to suit what they viewed as the cultural and social specifics of post-Soviet Russia. Yet even the strongest advocates of a feminist perspective were highly sensitive to the importance of addressing women's most pressing needs and concerns first and foremost and absolutely convinced that this would be the only means of subsequently convincing members of the value of concepts such as equal rights and equal opportunities. An example of such an approach was demonstrated by Stupen'

(Step), an organization for young women based in Tver' and established with the specific aim of attracting more young women to the feminist-oriented women's movement developing around the Independent Women's Forum in Moscow. The two young women who had founded this organization were convinced that the only way they would be able to attract their contemporaries was by offering practical resources and activities within a framework that might then develop consciousness-raising activities and educate young members about feminist principles and values.

With this in mind, they were planning a drop-in center with dress-making courses, possible commercial outlets for the garments produced, and information on sexual and physical health—as well as feminist slogans, leaflets, and discussions. Clearly this was an ambitious project, one that in May 2000 had still not come to fruition in any tangible way. One problem was that though delivering lectures and even distributing books and leaflets might be organized on a relatively low budget, the drop-in center and the more practical projects, which the organizers believed were a necessary prerequisite for attracting members, required both initial and long-term funding.

"Bread and Butter Issues" and the Survival of Grassroots Women's Organizations

The question of funding and lack of material resources to support the functioning of small scale, grassroots organizations preoccupied the leaders and many of the rank and file members of virtually all the organizations studied. Without exception, these groups had no premises, little if any office equipment, and no paid staff.

This set of circumstances placed a considerable constraint on organizations' scope of activities and was particularly problematic for those groups placing the highest emphasis on pragmatic goals and activities. With no other resources available, each grassroots women's organization studied relied heavily on the voluntary work, enthusiasm, and goodwill of its members in agreeing to help organize events, offering the use of their restricted living space for meetings, and allowing their private addresses and telephone numbers to be used as points of contact to the organization. The predicament of two groups, Tol'ko Mama, and the Tarusa Association of Women, illustrates the immense strain that a lack of funding imposed on individual members, especially those taking on leadership responsibility, and on the sustainability of an organization.

In Moscow, the single mothers' organization Tol'ko Mama, set up in 1990, was becoming entrapped in something of a vicious circle by 1995. By their very nature, groups such as Tol'ko Mama attracted women in particularly difficult and strained sets of personal circumstances with very few reserves of time and energy and still less money to contribute to the organization. Ironically, for this group the lack of organizational structures, premises, and resources became especially problematic and threatening precisely when the organization seemed to be doing rather well in its attempts to plug the gap left by a disintegrating welfare system. Clothes, food, and toys gathered by a process that the organization's president described as "collective begging" at the doors of church charities, foreign embassies, and international aid organizations had to be sorted, stored, and redistributed to the most suitable of the organization's fifty mothers and their children. These tasks and responsibilities were taken on by the organization's most active members; however, storing goods in their small, often communal apartments was difficult, and telephoning around members to establish who most needed what was time consuming and exposed the women involved to accusations of favoritism. Organizing the collection and delivery of goods was difficult for women who relied entirely on public transport and frequently worked long hours at two or more places of employment.

In September 1995, the founder and president of Tol'ko Mama felt that the organization had a long future ahead of it but added, "I won't demand much of my women because I know their lives are hard." Barely 5 weeks later at a general meeting of the organization, she no longer felt able to be so generous and spoke instead of the overwhelming burden of responsibility she felt for the organization and her regret that unless others took over some tasks she would be forced to disband Tol'ko Mama. The members present promised to contribute more to the running of the organization and insisted that its continued existence was crucial to their own well-being and survival. Several women referred specifically to the vital contact the organization provided to women and children in similar circumstances to their own and the opportunities it afforded to discuss and compare shared experience.

These "emotional" resources were described as equally important to the organization's primary goal of providing material aid and practical support. This shift in focus might have reduced the burden of some of the more logistically complex tasks previously undertaken. Yet the experience of another organization, the Tarusa Association of Women, suggests that a focus on "emotional" support and solidarity might also demand a considerable input of financial and structural resources if the organization was to survive in the long term.

The Tarusa Association of Women was set up on a very different basis than Tol'ko Mama. Though the leader of the latter had deliberately set out to found an organization with the primary goal of offering help and support to women struggling to raise children alone, the woman who had founded Tarusa's only women's organization described its origins as "completely unexpected." She explained that it arose largely out of women's "natural" propensity to find "common ground," her own leadership skills, and her positions as both the editor of a local newspaper and a member of the local Duma. Having founded the Tarusa Association of Women, she quickly found that in the absence of the Soviet system of personal problem solving through appeals to party structures, including via the state-controlled press, it was she, personally, to whom many women looked for a solution to their often extremely difficult problems and circumstances.[3]

During the 12 months before my visit to Tarusa in January 1996, she had dealt with a deeply depressed and potentially suicidal woman undergoing a particularly messy divorce; a case of serious physical abuse and intimidation of another woman's family by a member of the local administration; and a woman who had been to Chechnya to retrieve her wounded son from the army lines and had subsequently been hiding him from the military police. In each instance, she had provided as much practical advice and support as she was able, and had offered a substantial degree of counseling and emotional support.

As difficult and draining as dealing with such cases would have been for any small organization, once again the level of stress and overload experienced by this woman was exacerbated by a lack of resources. With no premises and no separate telephone line, her home and her private number had virtually become a 24-hour crisis center and hotline, leaving her with very little opportunity to retreat and recuperate. Because the organization had no staff and most of its members had initially come to her seeking help, she was also experiencing considerable difficulty in finding anyone with whom to share what was rapidly becoming an unbearable burden of responsibility.

When I left Tarusa in 1996, she was hopeful that some of the longer-standing members would soon take on a leadership role, providing her with the support she felt was vital if she was to continue. When I returned in May 2000, I was saddened, though not especially surprised, to discover that the organization had in fact ceased to function, although it still existed as a legal entity, and that its erstwhile leader was adamant that she could not even consider reviving it unless a source of reliable funding could be secured first.

As she reminisced during an interview in September 2001, she explained that although a lack of funding had not initially been a problem because "everyone worked and everyone just wanted to make something better," she had come to realize that "you can't exploit people's enthusiasm on a long-term basis." She also pointed out that organizations in provincial towns tend by their very nature to take on a multitude of functions and often work in isolation from a broader community of nongovernmental organizations (NGOs). Thus she felt that the only sort of funding that could have saved an organization such as hers would have been some form of reliable, long-term, core funding. She explained that though many of the grants currently available from international funding agencies were generous in the short term, they were based on project activities and did not cover "things that demand continuous expenditure: the rent of premises, a telephone line" over a longer time period.

None of the organizations studied was without funding due to a lack of initiative or a passive mentality. None expected a paternalistic state (or Western funding body) to step in and provide for it with no effort required on its part. On the contrary—mirroring the indefatigable determination and ingenuity of the individual survival strategies pursued by their members—organizations explored numerous avenues in search of reliable sources of funding for their activities. In an attempt to kill two birds with one stone, at least two organizations, Tol'ko Mama and the Club for Women's Initiatives in Tver', embarked on commercial ventures, usually involving the retailing of handmade souvenirs, clothing, and accessories produced by members.

These undertakings, it was hoped, would both provide a regular stream of income for the members involved and produce some surplus that would fund the organization itself. Unfortunately, this strategy proved unsuccessful. Each venture described to me had collapsed or looked doomed to fail, either because the market was already saturated and profit margins were too low or because when such ventures became successful, they generally broke away from the organization altogether.[4]

In addition, women who had taken part in such projects often explained that they had been time consuming and stressful, drawing time and energy away from other organizational aims and activities without providing satisfactory levels of income. Repeated setbacks and often insurmountable obstacles led in many cases to a sense of exhaustion and pessimism, consolidated by some women's perception that both their personal circumstances and their organization's future sustainability were jeopardized and undermined by the indifference and incomprehension of both the Russian state and the international donor agencies that claim to want to support them.

International Aid: A Source of Funding—but Not without Strings Attached

To date, no stable and reliable mechanism for funding the activities of NGOs has been forthcoming from within Russia. Yet the various Western agencies, charitable organizations, and foundations that were established in or relocated to the post-Soviet states in the early 1990s offer a potentially lucrative source of funding. These foundations and aid organizations—usually operating either directly or indirectly on public funds allocated to them by Western government bodies for redistribution to indigenous organizations and charities—have offered numerous rounds of funding to Russian NGOs through project grants awarded after a competitive application procedure. For the organizations that secured such grants, generous funding often facilitated the acquisition of office equipment, including computers, facsimile machines, and photocopiers, as well as paying the rent on premises and staff salaries for a limited period. Clearly, such prospects are attractive to many Russian organizations.

Moreover, the idea that the working conditions made possible, at least temporarily, by securing such a grant are the "norm" for NGOs in Western Europe and the United States is compounded both by the wording of publications announcing new funding opportunities and by the presence in Moscow and Saint Petersburg of well-established Western organizations and foundations. These operations frequently inhabit luxurious premises, equipped with sophisticated technology and employ a relatively large staff on fairly high salaries, at least by Russian standards.

These circumstances do not necessarily reflect the reality of working conditions and organizational infrastructure for many small, local grassroots organizations in the West any more than they do for those in Russia. Nonetheless, the perpetuation of a myth of universally well-funded, professionally staffed, and financially secure organizations in the "advanced West" contributes to a negative sense of hierarchy from West to East and to the notion that the only valid model for civil society activity and structures is that found in the United States and parts of Western Europe. This is particularly disempowering for new groups struggling to justify their existence and facing frequent disappointments in the projects they are able to pursue or the support they are able to offer due to a lack of resources. Many of the women active in women's NGOs in the mid-1990s—being unaware of the more modest reality experienced by many small organizations in the West and believing that winning a grant would be a relatively painless path to achieving a "normal working environment"—were convinced that this was the way forward. It rapidly became clear, however, that international funding comes with strings attached.

The Western governments and institutions making public funds available for redistribution in the post-Soviet states have political as well as social agendas to pursue. This is reflected in the funding programs and grant competitions, which seek to promote and instill values of "democracy," "civil society," and the "free market" in the recipient populations.[5] As a consequence, the power imbalance inherent in almost any donor–recipient relationship is further exacerbated by an assumption, on the part of many funding bodies, that the flow of experience and knowledge is unidirectional, namely from West to East. Where they have been rigidly adhered to, such views have led to problems for both sides.

In the early 1990s, a failure to research properly the specific cultural and social context as well as the political and economic circumstances in which they would be operating led to delays and unforeseen obstacles to the implementation of programs and projects and sometimes hindered communication between Western and Russian partners. In the most extreme cases, Western agencies succeeded above all else in creating a new elite, trained in the language of grant applications and the working methods and priorities of funding bodies, but not necessarily the most able or likely to deliver the project outcomes expected and desired either by those offering funding or by the Russian population.[6]

By the middle to late 1990s, Western agencies had become more adept at negotiating the post-Soviet field, and many employed staff with a close working knowledge of the Russian situation and with well-established links to a number of Russian partners. Nonetheless, where the allocation of funds is at stake it has remained of decisive importance that the applicant identify the crucial buzzwords and use the right language to present her organization or project and its aims and objectives as a good match with the priorities and agendas of the funding body. This has not produced an even playing field upon which all Russian NGOs can compete for funding.

Instead, those with prior exposure to the writings of Western theorists, academics, and activists, not to mention knowledge of the English language, are at a considerable advantage. This has frequently favored larger, more established organizations, often with an academic background or having enjoyed the privileges associated with Communist Party patronage during the Soviet era. In contrast, smaller grassroots organizations, especially those in provincial areas, whose members might have little or no knowledge of English and very limited experience of contact with Western individuals or organizations, have been left at a considerable disadvantage.[7] For women's organizations, an additional set of complicating factors is at play.

Funding Women or Funding Feminism?

Russian women's organizations have not been the main recipients of funding offered by Western funding agencies through their mainstream programs. Instead, a number of Western organizations, foundations, and programs with a specific remit of offering funding to women and women's projects were established and operated in post-Soviet Russia over the course of the 1990s.[8] These women's programs shared the concerns of mainstream programs about the promotion of "democracy," and "citizenship." In addition, they represented a strong commitment to an agenda of equal opportunities and rights for women and tended to subscribe to and seek to promote Western understandings of gender equality and feminism.[9]

On the one hand, the existence of these specific streams of funding for women guaranteed that women's projects and organizations would not be entirely excluded from the funding arena. On the other hand, the lack of alternative sources of funding for groups run by and for women and the focus on "feminist theory and practice" reinforces the exclusion of some of the very small, practically oriented grassroots women's organizations, which reject or remain ambivalent about explicit feminist aims and ideologies.

Funding programs aimed specifically at women have not been immune to the processes of creating new elites or consolidating existing ones. This is not to imply that those organizations and projects that have managed to attract funding have done so without merit. On the contrary, numerous excellent projects and vitally important organizations have received funding, either directly from Western foundations or via collaboration with Western partner organizations and institutions. Yet it is undeniable that many of these groups have been aided along the path to funding by the fact that they are led and represented by women whose higher education and professional status has afforded them access to writings on Western feminist theories and praxis, Western colleagues, and travel abroad, none of which has been readily available to the vast majority of Russia's female population. These privileged opportunities for contact with the West and its concepts and theories have made it easier for them to master the prerequisite language of funding applications—in some cases literally English, in others simply an ability to wield the correct terminology.

The development of aid programs based on unexamined assumptions about the nature of civil society in the funding countries contributes to these divisions. Such programs, which are founded on the premise that "the West knows best," run the risk of placing the highest value on recipients' abilities to mimic convincingly Western language, stances, and structures, rather than on their ability to respond to local priorities and perspectives and to embed their activities and projects within local communities. They may also contribute to a negative construction of Russia and its people as the "other," detracting from rather than consolidating potential points of cooperation and partnership.

Organizations that may be unable to present themselves in such a way as to provide an instant and sophisticated match to these Western expectations may nonetheless have a great deal to contribute to the more broadly stated goals of international aid. The organizations described in this chapter, for example, the majority of which were largely unsuccessful in gaining international funding, were in fact able to empower women at the local level, to encourage active citizenship, and to function as credible and potentially sustainable community-based organizations. It is telling, however, that none of these organizations would have used these terms to describe its activities.

Creating Hierarchies and Mistrust Instead of Networks and Collaboration

Given the fact that many small grassroots women's organizations are struggling to provide considerable levels of practical and emotional support to members without external funding and with little prospect of receiving any, it is perhaps inevitable that the simultaneous appearance of a number of relatively well-funded projects and organizations, many of them run by women from the former intelligentsia, would elicit a certain level of jealousy and resentment.

In a society saturated with rumors of corruption and embezzlement, these jealousies are easily and rapidly translated into accusations of self-interest, nepotism, and deceit. On several occasions during fieldwork in Russia, I spoke with activists in organizations that had not been able to secure Western funding who were convinced that the women running funded organizations—many of whom were, quite rightly, drawing a salary for their work—had been successful because of who they were and who they knew rather than as a result of what they did.

Suspicions of this nature are further exacerbated by some of the practices of funding agencies themselves. Donor organizations have shown a tendency to offer repeat funding to individual women leaders and to certain organizations with which they have established a working relationship and that they view as reliable partners. Once such a relationship is established, naturally, the women concerned are keen to maintain and exploit it and frequently apply for a new grant as soon as the one they are working on is drawing to an end, sometimes working on several projects simultaneously for limited periods.

This practice of repeat funding is different from the provision of long-term, core funding for projects and organizations, which would allow them to become firmly established and achieve a much needed degree of long-term sustainability. The introduction of such forms of funding was very much desired by the overwhelming majority of interviewees. The practice of repeat funding, however, did not necessarily guarantee this sought-after sustainability, for each grant would be allocated for a short-term and distinct project. At the end of each period of funding, a new project (or in some cases, even a different organization) would have to be established to secure further financial support. What remained constant was the relationship between the funding body and a particular individual or group of individuals, and those most able to adapt to the new priorities and "pet projects" of the funding bodies were the most likely to be successful.[10]

Because few alternative sources of funding are available for women, those who have mastered the formulae necessary for extracting funds from specific "women's programs" are likely to present as pro-woman and pro-feminist projects and activities that may in fact have a more general focus and involve a broader base of NGOs. Strategies such as this, though they may be the only option available for the women involved and may appear to them very much as a rational choice, compound the perception that an elite group of women and organizations have managed to become the darlings of Western funding agencies and jealously guard this relationship to the exclusion of others, rather than genuinely seeking to work with and on behalf of Russian women at the grass roots.

Opinions of this nature were expressed with the most vehemence by a group of women who had no direct personal involvement or contact with any women's organizations and whom I interviewed as a "control group" during fieldwork. Their attitudes toward almost any form of women's group or organization were scathing, to say the least. They asserted again and again that the women involved in such activities had no interest in them, their lives, their needs, or the issues they considered important. Instead, they felt, such women were solely concerned with their own private interests:

> Irina: "These issues [length of military service, state provision of kindergartens, pensioners' homes, and cultural institutions] are completely ignored by women's organizations."
>
> Maria: "Yes, because all their attention is directed at improving their own private lives."
>
> Tanya: "That's why we don't believe in them."
>
> Anna: "All they care about is securing their own position."

The criticisms of these women were not based on any close personal or authentic knowledge of the workings of women's organizations in post-Soviet Russia. Yet an assumption that personal gain, rather than concern about key "women's issues," was the driving force behind some groups' activities clearly kept these women at a distance and thereby deprived organizations of support from a more broadly based constituency of women. Among those more closely involved in the work of women's organizations, schisms, hostilities, resentments, and hierarchical structures were also in evidence.

Again, largely as a result of funding agencies' strategies, certain women's organizations and individual leaders effectively become gatekeepers to the Western individuals and organizations that provide access to funding for women's organization activities. Groups that choose to embrace an overtly feminist identity, especially where they function as an umbrella organization or where they have previously received funds for networking and information projects, are viewed by Western funding agencies as a logical point of first contact to other women's groups and organizations. These "partner organizations" collect and disseminate information about up-and-coming funding opportunities and may, in some instances, play an advisory role to the executive committees and boards that allocate grants.

In 1995–96, it was common for representatives of those Western funding bodies offering specific funding programs for women to attend seminars and conferences initiated and run by organizations such as the Moscow Center for Gender Studies and the Independent Women's Forum. There, they made announcements about current or future grant competitions, gathered information on the organizations present, and were available for lobbying and questions from representatives of women's groups. Similarly, at such events, literature providing funding information and advice from other grant-making bodies was available, as were the publications produced by the larger Russian women's organizations, often as a result of Western funding and in collaboration with Western colleagues. More recently, women who played a key role in the founding and consolidation of those Russian women's organizations that have become best known in the West have taken on a coordinating or executive role with some of the agencies delivering women's funding programs.[11]

These activities and strategies have been instrumental in allowing Russian women's umbrella organizations to fulfil one of their primary functions: the dissemination of information about funding opportunities to a wider circle of women's NGOs and the provision of expert advice to funding bodies about the allocation of funds. The power relations inherent here, however, have also had an undeniable effect on the development of interorganizational relations. This method of distributing information via established "partners" has left those groups without close contact to or good working relations with the specific networks and umbrella organizations in question feeling cut out of the loop altogether. Small, often very localized, and highly pragmatic organizations may be either unaware of the existence of some of the larger women's networking organizations or unable to see the relevance of their theoretical and political perspectives to their work and activities. Conversely, overtly feminist organizations with a strong commitment to changing public perceptions of women and improving their legislative and economic status may fail to see the activities of smaller, less strategically focused groups as significant or relevant to their agenda.

This mismatch in perspectives is further reinforced and exacerbated by mutual fears and accusations of self-serving interests from each side toward the other. On the one hand, the leaders and activist members of several of the small, grassroots women's organizations were convinced that they were being deliberately excluded from an "inner circle" of organizations with access to Western funding bodies. Moreover, they felt that these organizations were trying to obstruct any contacts to such agencies or other Western organizations that they might attempt to make independently. Meanwhile, some of the leaders of the bigger umbrella organizations were suspicious of new organizations that sought to become part of their network and wished to be invited to events and included on mailing lists, fearing that they were only interested in gaining access to lucrative Western contacts and might "cream off" hard-won resources without contributing anything substantial to the network as a whole or its broader goals.

Practical issues and structures also have a constraining effect on the work of the larger umbrella and networking organizations, limiting their ability to distribute information more democratically. For example, literature containing information about grant opportunities as well as application forms and procedural guides were readily available in the offices of all of the Moscow-based women's umbrella organizations I visited during fieldwork. The whereabouts of these premises were well known among activists involved in the network of organizations linked to the Independent Women's Forum, to foreign researchers and activists, and to the representatives of funding agencies. They were not, however, publicized more widely, and all were housed within the premises of larger, often unrelated institutions with no external sign to mark their existence and no public access without prior invitation and, hence, the pass necessary to be allowed admission to the premises. Thus, for the uninitiated, they practically did not exist, and even if their location was discovered, they could only be accessed through personal invitation.

This system was not of the making of the women's organizations in question but a hangover from the Soviet tradition of limiting public access to buildings, offices, and organizations. Nonetheless, in the post-Soviet context, it served to exacerbate the sense of those groups and activists on the peripheries of such networks that they were being deliberately excluded and discriminated against.

Similarly, the way in which conferences and seminars were organized caused problems for those organizations with no paid staff and whose members could not afford to take time off from work to attend. A member of one of the organizations involved in my study, which had not had much success in obtaining funding and which she saw as being on the periphery of the more established and, in her opinion, better connected feminist networks, explained the difficulty in becoming more closely involved:

> All these conferences are during the week, on workdays from morning until night, and we all have to work. On the whole, our members don't even work in just one place but in two or three, so before they could go anywhere they'd have to go without a week's pay. . . . I've looked at these

> conference programs and it's always the same—three days in a row. I'd really like to go but I can't afford the time.

She subsequently described these barriers to closer cooperation as having been deliberately set up by women and organizations with no interest in sharing their lucrative contacts and information with "the likes of us." Whether her suspicions of deliberately elitist and exclusionary tactics had any founding in reality or not, the fact that she, and many other activists like her, believed them to be true illustrates how easily funds frequently allocated with a specific remit of fostering movement growth, interorganizational cooperation, and solidarity could unintentionally produce an entirely opposite effect.

For organizations working in small, provincial areas among tightly knit communities, the risk of funding producing jealousy and resentment rather than cooperation and increased activity is multiplied and reaches beyond the membership of organizations themselves to the broader community. For instance, the former leader of the Tarusa Association of Women explained in September 2001 that although receipt of a grant from international funds might have saved her organization in terms of infrastructure and resources, it might just as easily have destroyed it by creating suspicion, jealousy, and resentment, possibly within the organization but even more so from without. The only solution for this, she felt, was to ensure the spread of clear information about grants, their purposes, and conditions to the population through the local press. As she put it,

> You can always justify yourself to the foundation, but it is important that local people don't get the idea that this person is (1) getting rich quick, or (2) working for Western foundations. There mustn't be this feeling that this woman lives among us but I live in poverty, while she lives in luxury.

Certainly it is true that at present—especially in the provinces but also in the larger, cosmopolitan cities of Russia—the population at large has little if any idea of the why and how of international assistance for NGOs' work. It would be in the interest of both those giving and those receiving grant money if this situation were tackled.

The women interviewed put forward a variety of suggestions for how international funds might be used to achieve this increase in knowledge. Some of the most popular ideas were poster campaigns to advertise both the availability of funding programs and the activities undertaken by those organizations in receipt of grants; features in the local and national press and audiovisual media; training programs for journalists working for local and regional publications; and a stream of funding allocated specifically to public awareness campaigns. In each instance, women suggested that such activities could be designed and implemented by existing organizations and grassroots groups.

Conclusion

Russia's grassroots women's organizations have developed in a specific historical, political, and cultural context. Many of them came together in response to the practical and financial pressures experienced by women as a consequence of the post-Soviet reform process. Their aims and activities, therefore, focus primarily on combating these pressures by pooling resources and extending practical and emotional support to members. There is a clear correlation between the prevalence of essentialist discourses of gender in post-Soviet Russian society and many of the gendered effects of post-Soviet reforms.

Yet combating stereotypical attitudes, politicizing issues of language or media representations of women, or fighting for legislative equality and defense of women's rights per se are not necessarily viewed as legitimate primary goals by the members of many of these organizations, nor by large sections of the female population. Indeed, the pursuit of "political" or "strategic" goals is often regarded as legitimate only when it can be seen to have a reasonably direct and immediate positive impact on the lives of members. In this context, it must be understood that the negative connotations of Soviet-style legislative equality and "enforced" emancipation are still very much in the forefront of many women's minds, and as such the imposition of any singular ideological perspective is frequently rejected.

By contrast, engagement in practical projects and activities that can be seen to provide much needed support to women is very much favored. Members often describe an organization's most significant impact as the emotional and moral support it provides and the sense they gain of being part of a collective, being able to make a positive contribution to the lives of others, and no longer having to deal with problems and difficulties alone. In this way, though often they do not articulate it as a "mission statement" or "political strategy," these organizations help to harness and focus women's sense of social responsibility into forms of civic activity and community-based activism that offer both a source of personal empowerment and a form of social safety net to many of the women involved.

Activities of this nature, however, demand a relatively high level of both material and emotional resources. As a consequence, they place a particularly great strain upon members, leaders, and ultimately upon the sustainability of an organization itself. For grassroots women's organizations operating in post-Soviet Russia, this strain has been compounded by a chronic shortage of financial, structural, and membership resources. Although members have contributed a great deal to their organizations through voluntary work and contributions in kind, their personal circumstances significantly restrict the scale and long-term sustainability of such contributions. In these circumstances, many groups have been encouraged by the appearance of Western funding agencies that specifically target women, and they look to the West as a potential source of material support and sustenance.

Clearly, a number of tensions exist between the theory and practice of Western funding for Russian women's organizations. Western bodies provide funding for the development of "civil society" in the hope of producing a stable, "democratic" Russia and with a view to creating sustainable organizations with well-developed ties and cooperative networks. Yet a focus on the promotion of Western standards and values, either real or idealized and mythologized, has meant that the realities of Russian circumstances, culture, and history are ignored at worst or given insufficient attention in the drawing up of funding programs at best.

This situation may lead to problems in the implementation of programs and to contradictions between the donors' expectations and perceptions of what is being done with their money and the reality experienced by organizations on the ground. In recent years, Russian NGOs have become increasingly assertive in their rejection of top-down and patronizing attitudes from Western agencies and in calling for an end to funding approaches that appear to conflate a lack of funding and material resources with a lack of expertise and organizational abilities.[12]

The development of specific programs of funding for women's organizations and projects has helped to prevent the marginalization and exclusion of women from access to financial support. Yet by confining support for women almost solely to a set of programs based on a rather narrow definition of "feminist activities," this approach has in effect excluded many grassroots women's organizations and the broader cross-section of Russia's female population those organizations could reach. The work of these groups does not necessarily fit within a strict feminist ideology, in terms of explicitly advocating equal rights or calling for an end to sexual discrimination. Yet they are directly concerned with improving women's lives and sense of well-being by extending a broader set of options and opportunities to women by pooling material and emotional resources, extending practical support and the experience of female solidarity, rather than via more theoretical, strategic, or legalistic approaches.

It may well be argued that both forms of approach are needed; and it is certain that many of the overtly feminist projects that developed in post-Soviet Russia are engaged in invaluable work, some of which is funded internationally and some of which is also carried out with little if any financial support. Nevertheless, a more flexible approach to funding is needed, and above all a new awareness that expertise and insight emerging from within Russia may be used to adapt Western experience, theories, and practices. Persistent assumptions that "know-how" lies in the West and that it can and should be imported wholesale to the East deprive both sides of what could be a mutually beneficial process of exchange and two-way learning and development.

Notes

1. For examples and analyses of the kinds of survival strategies developed by Russian women see Sue Bridger, Rebecca Kay, and Kathryn Pinnick, *No More Heroines? Russia, Women and the Market* (London: Routledge, 1996); Marta Bruno, "Employment Strategies and the Formation of New Identities in the Service Sector in Moscow," in *Gender, Generation and Identity in Contemporary Russia,* ed. Hilary Pilkington (London: Routledge, 1996); Marta Bruno, "Playing the Co-operation Game," in *Surviving Post-Socialism: Local Strategies and Regional Responses in Eastern Europe,* ed. Sue Bridger and Frances Pine (London: Routledge, 1997); Teela Jyrkinen-Pakkasvirta and Evgenia Poretskina, "Structural Changes and the Position of Women in St. Petersburg," in *Women and Political Change: Perspectives from East-Central Europe,* ed. Sue Bridger (Basingstoke, U.K.: Macmillan, 1999); and Sue Bridger, "Rural Women in Russia: What Does Private Farming Mean?" in *Making the Transition Work for Women in Europe and Central Asia,* ed. Marnia Lazreg (Washington, D.C.: World Bank, 2000).

2. For a full account of this study and its findings, see Rebecca Kay, *Russian Women and their Organizations: Gender, Discrimination, and Grassroots Women's Organizations 1991–96* (Basingstoke, U.K.: Macmillan, 2000).

3. The press played a key role in the system of social checks and balances that existed in the Soviet Union. Citizens who felt that their rights had been infringed or that they had been denied benefits, services, wages, or opportunities due to them by management or local authorities would frequently seek redress by writing to a newspaper or magazine, the editors of which would often name and shame the perpetrators, as well as passing on complaints to the relevant Communist Party authorities and ensuring that

cases were properly settled. See, e.g., James Riordan and Sue Bridger, *Dear Comrade Editor: Readers' Letters to the Soviet Press under Perestroika* (Bloomington: Indiana University Press, 1992), 1–4.

4. See also Bridger, Kay, and Pinnick, *No More Heroines?* 113–16.

5. See, e.g., Katherine Verdery, *What Was Socialism and What Comes Next?* (Princeton, N.J.: Princeton University Press, 1996), 205; Bruno, "Cooperation Game," 172–73.

6. See, e.g., Bridger, Kay, and Pinnick, *No More Heroines?* 198–99; Bruno, "Cooperation Game," 179, 186; and Sarah Henderson, "Importing Civil Society: Foreign Aid and the Women's Movement in Russia," *Democratizatsiya, the Journal of Post-Soviet Democratization* 8, no. 1 (winter 2000): 78–79. See also chapter 13 in this volume by Michele Rivkin-Fish.

7. See chapter 9 in this volume by Andrea Berg for a discussion of the ways in which a lack of information and language barriers have prevented rural women in Uzbekistan from taking an active part in the activities of Uzbek NGOs and have helped to perpetuate preexisting divisions between an urban educated elite and the rural populations their organizations claim to serve.

8. The United States–based Ford Foundation and MacArthur Foundation, as well as the Soros Foundation's Open Society Institute have all set up specific funding programs for women's education and networking projects. The German foundation Frauenanschtiftung has sponsored various women's organizations through its East–West Women's Network, and the Global Fund for Women has offered a series of rounds of project-oriented grants.

9. Henderson, "Importing Civil Society," 65–66.

10. See chapter 14 in this volume by Julie Hemment for a discussion of the problems caused to organizations when funding bodies shift their focus or develop a preference for a new genre of project or organizational activity; in this case the shift is from funding crisis centers to a focus on "trafficking" and international prostitution.

11. A notable example is the Network Women's Program of the Open Society Institute, funded by the Soros Foundation, in which three founder members of the Independent Women's Forum now hold key positions, one as director of the New York office and the other two as program coordinators in the Moscow office. Elena Kochkina, "Resursy dlia zhenskikh organizatsii" [Resources for Women's Organizations], *"We/My" Dialog zhenshchin: Mezhdunarodnyi zhenskii zhurnal* ["We/My" women's dialogue: International women's journal] 5 (1998): 19.

12. "Conference Builds Bridges," *BEAR Trust Newsletter* 32 (February 2001): 2–3.

12

Working at the Local–Global Intersection: The Challenges Facing Women in Armenia's Nongovernmental Organization Sector

Armine Ishkanian

In the anticommunist euphoria of the late 1980s, there was a revival of the grand idée of civil society, which Jean Comaroff and John Comaroff argue was championed with an evangelical zeal by Western scholars and policy-makers on a planetary scale.[1] This link between civil society and non-governmental organizations (NGOs) was a late-twentieth-century phenomenon and one that should be understood in the context of deregulated and increasingly globalized economies.[2] Although this link may be a recent phenomenon, it is nevertheless very significant, and as Janine Wedel points out,

This chapter is based on fieldwork conducted in Armenia between 1993 and 2000. The author thanks the National Research Council, the International Research and Exchange Board, the Academy of Educational Development, and the Department of Anthropology, University of California, San Diego, for their generous support, which allowed her to conduct research in Armenia. She also thanks Julie Hemment, Rebecca Kay, Kathleen Kuehnast, Carol Nechemias, and Michele Rivkin-Fish for their insightful comments, suggestions, and advice in preparing this chapter.

in the postcommunist period donors have seen NGOs as the "connective tissue of democratic political culture."[3] Or, as the NGO Center in Armenia puts it:

> Traditionally, the societal role of NGOs has been peripheral compared with other actors and decision makers. Within the last half of this century, however, the role of NGOs has rapidly increased. This shift logically parallels the emergence of democracy as a universal ideal toward which almost all countries now aspire. Clearly, as democracy becomes a globally held value, it only makes sense that the role of civil society becomes more important.[4]

The NGO Center in Armenia thus links the spread of democracy to the development of civil society and NGOs. However, the argument describing democracy and civil society as "globally held values" is problematic because it overlooks the local manifestations, translations, and adaptations of global models and values (if there are such values). Katherine Verdery contends that since the demise of communism, Western capitalist societies have tended to believe that they have a monopoly on "truth" and can therefore dispense "wisdom" concerning how to build the "proper" forms of democracy and capitalism.[5] Instead, there are multiple understandings, alterations, interpretations, and representations of the "universal" models of democracy and capitalism. Scholars focusing on post-Soviet "transitions" especially confront issues connected to the acceptance or rejection of new models; therefore, research has delved into the complex ways in which the past and present are mediated. Attention has been directed toward the impact of nationalism and national ideologies, and the creation of new identities, social classes, and NGOs.[6] Yet another major aspect of post-Soviet transitions has increasingly gained salience, as scholars accumulate knowledge regarding the "gendered" nature of the post-Soviet transitions.[7]

In Armenia, Soviet and pre-Soviet beliefs about the nature of the family, the state, political leaders, capitalism, and community and social life affect the transition to democracy, a market economy, and the development of civil society. Susan Gal and Gail Kligman argue that the post-socialist transition has vastly expanded the possibilities for political activity and expression and that these expressions are framed in gendered terms.[8] This chapter explores how Armenian women's participation in NGOs has shaped their discourses and actions in the public sphere as they work in the local and global spheres and mediate between thinking—and securing funding—globally and acting locally.[9] I begin by discussing why international donors and Western governments have been interested in developing an NGO sector in Armenia and how this sector has become "feminized." By choosing to work through NGOs, I maintain, women are able to reaffirm the ascribed gender roles and gender-based divisions of labor and avoid the criticisms that they would face if they entered political parties or government but are still able to work in and through the public sector to achieve their personal and community objectives. This analysis takes into account Armenia's historical, cultural, and political context, in particular the impact of imported Western models of civil society and democratization. We will see how NGO actors, who are operating at the nexus of local and global concerns, translate, manipulate, negotiate, and reconcile the imported and global models, discourses, and agendas with traditional and local beliefs about gender roles, relations, and the nature of the family.

This chapter is based on research conducted in Armenia in 1996–97, 1999, and 2000 with the All-Armenian Women's Union, which I use as a case study to demonstrate how NGO members work in and between the global and local levels by adapting their discourses and strategies to work with both local government officials as well as donors. To emphasize the challenges involved in working at the global—local nexus, I discuss local perceptions of and concerns with the issue of domestic violence.

Why NGOs?

Donors were motivated to fund NGOs, because they were perceived as panaceas for the political cynicism, apathy, disaffection, and overcentralization that marked post-Soviet societies. Of course, NGOs also counted as one of the fundamental signs of democratization. In the 1990s, U.S. agencies and other industrial-world donors embraced the idea that the development of civil society was critical to democratization and a "successful transition." This rapidly emerged as a new mantra in both aid and diplomatic circles.[10]

Under 70 years of Communist rule, there had been very little space for civil society or for nongovernmental and non—Communist Party organizations in Armenia. The intense post-Soviet growth in the number and types of NGOs in Armenia has been both a reaction to the past repression of such activities as well as a response to the new funding that has been made available by international agencies and Western governments. Wedel's contention that the aid effort to Central and Eastern Europe, Russia, and Eurasia was not akin to developing-world aid efforts prompted Western donors, in the early 1990s, to reorganize their efforts and management to suit the magnitude of the task.

One of the largest donors of NGOs in the former Soviet Union, the Eurasia Foundation, describes NGO development as "help[ing] build democracy by providing citizens with a formula for collectively voicing their views and lessen[ing] the pain of economic transformation by providing alternative vehicles for the delivery of critical social services."[11] Even the World Bank, which tends to provide more funding to governments than NGOs, described civil society organizations (particularly NGOs) as being important in the transition and development processes taking place in Armenia. In the 2001 World Bank *Armenia Country Assistance Strategy Report,* NGOs are described as "stakeholders in Armenia," as entities with whom the World Bank should consult as it develops its plan of action. The report also calls upon NGOs to "develop a 'social audit' of Government programs and policies."[12]

In the 1990s, Armenian government officials hailed the growth of the NGO sector as "a step in the right direction." They praised NGOs as a sign of acceptance of democracy and civil society, a means to get grants and promote economic development from a grassroots level, and a way to become part of a new global dialogue involving the international NGO sector. As of April 2003, there were nearly 3,500 NGOs registered with the Ministry of Justice in Armenia,[13] and more than two-thirds of these organizations were led by women.[14]

This "feminization" of the NGO sector is due to at least four factors. First, in the early 1990s, the removal of the quota system led to a sharp decline in the number of women in official positions. Although women played a critical role in the independence movement by participating in the demonstrations and work and hunger strikes, by making speeches, and by collecting money for the effort, once independence was achieved, women found themselves excluded from the new government and from political parties.[15] NGOs therefore became a popular, alternative path for women's public participation.

Second, men initially demonstrated little interest in the "nongovernmental" sector, because any man who wishes to be active in political or public life can do so through the government or political parties. Third, men generally regarded the rewards of NGO participation, in terms of grants and microcredit programs, as too small and the bureaucratic details of operating an NGO as too numerous. Men preferred the business sector where they felt they could make more money. Fourth, a preference among donors in supporting women's initiatives and organizations has made NGOs a viable alternative for women. The number of women's organizations particularly grew after the 1995 UN Fourth World Conference on Women in Beijing. The Beijing conference was a watershed event in the development of women's NGOs in Armenia. The women who attended the conference, both as members of the government delegation and as NGO members, returned to Armenia informed and educated about global gender discourses, issues, and concerns; and they proceeded to translate these into the local Armenian context.

The Beijing conference also stimulated greater donor funding and interest in the role of women in development. Donors responded by proclaiming women the more "cost-effective" beneficiaries of development and civil society aid and by apportioning greater funding for gender issues and women's organizations.[16] As Gohar, [17] one of my informants, said,

> You learn what the donors fund and then you talk about that in your grant proposal. They all like gender issues (*genderii hartzer*), so women have a better chance of getting grants as do women's organizations.

"Talking gender" or any of the other "issues of the day," became an important factor in winning grants. Both women's NGOs and women in NGOs in Armenia are adept at employing the appropriate discourses to receive funding from donors. Yet, because they are working in the local context, they are compelled to temper these discourses and use them in conjunction with more "traditional" discourses. These traditional discourses reflect beliefs about gender roles and stereotypes that existed in the pre-Soviet period. These beliefs about gender roles and gender relations within the family and society were reinforced during the Soviet period, as the family became the locus for resistance to Soviet policies. In the next section, I describe the traditional gender ideologies and explain how Armenian women simultaneously use the discourses of tradition and modernity to survive and succeed in the NGO sector.

Gender Discourses and Ideologies: Betwixt and between the Local and the Global

According to Armenian gender stereotypes, a woman, specifically a mother, is considered to be the hearth (*odjakh*), the pillar (*syun*), and the light (*jrak*) of her family. The following excerpt is from the United Nations Development Program (UNDP) *1998 Armenia Human Development Report: The Role of the State.* It provides a glaring example of official political discourse about the family and the role of women within the family in Armenia:

> *Family has been more than just a basic societal unit. In Armenian national mentality, it has traditionally been perceived as being of the highest value in its capacity as an intermediary, situated in between the individual and the state.* In the absence of statehood, the concept of "Nation-as-a-Family," a sui generis "familism," has evolved in Armenian society. *The core and the unifying power of these ideas has traditionally been the Armenian woman, whose role is unique and decisive in the national history and culture.* A history replete with war, invasion, massacre, genocide, and natural disasters shaped the Armenian family into a basic unit for viability and self-preservation.[18] (emphasis added)

The important points in the above paragraph include, first, how the family has become a substitute for the state because Armenia has been stateless for many centuries, and, second, that women play a major role within the family and nation (family writ large). Stephanie Platz suggests that Armenians conceive of traditional kinship as an enduring model that is distinctly and uniquely Armenian, and that kinship is a central part of what it means to be "Armenian."[19]

Another example of the official discourse regarding the role of women and the family in Armenia is from the *National Report on the Condition of Women* prepared by the Armenian National Committee for the Preparation for the World Conference on Women in cooperation with UNDP for the 1995 Fourth UN World Conference on Women in Beijing:

> For centuries, the people of Armenia, a country rarely sovereign, viewed the family as a key value and the primary factor that kept the nation together. Traditionally, the Armenian family has been considered as the main area of a woman's activities. Due to this traditional upbringing, the Armenian woman is more oriented towards her family and children and somewhat less inclined towards an active involvement in politics and social life.[20]

The rhetoric in this second example is almost identical to that in that in the former, except that it takes this argument one step further by adding the comment that "women are less inclined towards an active involvement in politics and social life." The overall intention of the national report is to demonstrate first, that there is no formal, legal discrimination against women in Armenia and second, that women are beginning to play a more active role in public life as the transition period continues.

In the national report, the authors describe NGOs as the ideal intermediary organizations that will "help women overcome traditional beliefs" about participating in public life and politics by "build[ing] up their resources."[21] They maintain, "These organizations [NGOs] have a versatile scope of activities . . . [and] the creation of women's NGO community enables Armenian women to voice the concerns, open a dialogue and jointly seek solutions [with the government]."[22]

The report's authors do not explicitly address how women will overcome traditional beliefs and ideologies, but through my research with various women's NGOs and NGOs led by women, I found that what women did was not directly to attack traditional ideologies in an attempt to overcome them, but rather to reinterpret traditional gender ideologies to meet their needs. For instance, several women in the All-Armenian Women's Union held that just as women in past centuries were charged with the duty of preserving the family and nation and transmitting Armenian cultural beliefs and values to their children, today, their role as both mothers and citizens of the newly independent Republic of Armenia is to promote democratic values, civic responsibility, and self-sufficiency. As Susanna, one of the women activists, noted,

> Since democracy and civil society are inherently social and public activities, we [mothers] can't teach these values in the seclusion of our homes. Instead, we have to work in the communities, at the public level to teach our children the value of civic participation, social responsibility, and other such democratic values.

The women thus saw themselves as playing a critical role in the development of an independent Armenian nation-state, a role that required their presence in the public sector. Because NGOs are operating at the international level as well as the local level, women cannot solely employ these "traditional" discourses about the role of women in the family and society. To successfully operate in and across these levels, women have employed and manipulated the discourses of tradition and modernity simultaneously. By portraying themselves as traditionalists and as antifeminists, the women appease local bureaucrats and politicians who resent the entry of women into the public sphere. For example, in 1994, the All-Armenian Women's Union named its regional chapters "hearths" (*odjakhner*), to symbolize the traditional, familial nature of women's work and to please local bureaucrats and politicians. According to Datevik, the chapter coordinator,

> We decided to call them *odjakhner* instead of chapters (*masnatcyukh*) in order to show that they are doing the work of the family—the larger family.

Women reconcile their use of the contradictory models of modernization or Westernization and of traditionalism by invoking the rhetoric of moral motherhood and insisting that they have entered "public life for the good of the nation." They adhere to the belief that NGOs are the *natural path* for women's activism in the post-Soviet period and that NGOs should be concerned with alleviating social and national problems.[23] Armenian women resist defining their problems as women's problems and instead seek to describe them as national problems or problems of the nation and thus avoid overtly feminist discourses and projects. Ethnonational identity supersedes gender identity, and in this context a women in Armenia is first and foremost an Armenian, then a woman. Therefore, her loyalty must lie with the nationalist aspirations, beliefs, and ideas of the society rather than feminist ideas, aspirations, and beliefs.

The women I spoke with contended that it was wrong to separate women's issues from men's issues. As Datevik told me, "Our goal is not to pursue a divisive feminist agenda, but to work for the good of the entire nation (*ampogtch azgi hamar*)." Armenian female academics (and of course politicians) reinforce this perspective. For instance, in the article "This Is Not about Women's Struggle, but about Society's Common Sense," the chair of the Yerevan State Department of Sociology, Lyudmila Harutyunyan, argues against a feminist approach:

> I don't place the emphasis on the women's movement, since the woman in Armenian society is the pillar of stability and she does not have the right to cause a social implosion that will threaten that stability. Especially since our society is under crisis. Simply, it is important to initiate constructive steps to insure that women play a role in political affairs and governance.[24]

Many women in the NGO sector agree with Harutyunyan's views and consider NGOs organizational forms that allow women to pursue critical social, educational, and health care needs rather than a feminist agenda. This leads them to define themselves and their organizations as "feminine" (*kanatzi*) rather than "feminist." This distinction is crucial, because "feminine" denotes continuity with the past and traditional gender roles and ideologies, whereas "feminist" clearly denotes a break with the past. This rejection of feminism in Armenia is similar to what has occurred in other former Soviet states and in Eastern Europe. At one level, this vilification of feminism stems from 70 years of state opposition to feminism as a bourgeois ideology and counterrevolutionary ideology.[25] At the same time, however, feminism is rejected by women in Armenia who define it as not only anti-male but also as antifamily. Given the high value that is placed on family in Armenia, feminism has not been very popular there, and even women who promote gender equality and criticize the government for not including women in positions of power never define themselves as feminists. Indeed, they often take offense at being referred to as feminists.[26]

As such, these Armenian women's NGOs can be viewed as "practical" because they do not directly challenge traditional gender ideologies.[27] Although the women in the All-Armenian Women's Union, the Helsinki Citizens' Assembly, and the Women's Republican Council, among others with which I conducted research, did not question gender subordination, they used and manipulated their traditional gender roles (i.e., mothers, wives) to enter public life, and they utilized feminist and gender discourses to win grants from donors. Once in the public sector, gender identity became a strategic commodity that was selectively deployed. Depending on the audience, the NGO women were "liberal, progressive women fighting for change" or "caring, nurturing mothers working for the spiritual and cultural renewal of the nation." The next section examines how members of the All-Armenian Women's Union utilize, negotiate, and reconcile the use of competing discourses and ideologies.

The All-Armenian Women's Union: A Case Study

The All-Armenian Women's Union (AAWU) was established in 1994. At that time, an eleven-member coordinating committee led the group, with First Lady Ludmilla Ter-Petrossian acting as honorary president. Given this, the AAWU enjoyed support from government officials and local bureaucrats while Levon Ter-Petrossian and the Armenian National Movement (ANM) were in power. At this time, the AAWU was very much a government-supported NGO, or GONGO,[28] because it operated with the support and assistance of the ANM-led government. Yet, as I will explain below, this situation changed when Ter-Petrossian resigned from office in February 1998. From February 1998 until the time of this writing (February 2002), the AAWU has begun to operate more like a "normal" NGO, in that it struggles for funds, has a small membership, and so on. Before describing the work of AAWU in the postcoup years, I will discuss its operations when it was at the zenith of its power.

Organizational Structure and Projects, 1994–98

The AAWU coordinating committee held weekly meetings to address various issues and make decisions about new projects. The coordinators conducted research, maintained the membership, wrote grants, and the like. In addition to the Central Yerevan headquarters, there were chapters in each of Yerevan's ten municipal districts and roughly thirty provincial chapters in Armenia's regional (*marz*) capitals and larger villages.[29]

Between 1994 and February 1998, the AAWU had more than 5,000 members. The majority of the members were from the old elite (intelligentsia or the Communist Party); these women had transformed themselves into social workers and public servants by acquiring new skills such as grant writing, fund raising, public speaking, computer use, and media relations and advertising. By repackaging their skills and learning the jargon associated with global discourses about women's rights and NGOs, some individuals had forged new roles and reinvented themselves to take advantage of the new opportunities made available to NGOs in the post-Soviet period.

According to the AAWU's leadership, the organization's main objectives included

- increasing the role of women in the society and the state;
- protecting the rights of women and children;
- involving women in the structural processes that take place in society;
- contributing to the improvement of children's education and health services;
- providing for the harmonious development of an individual and the participation of the new generations of children in the society and state in order to have democratic, healthy citizens; and

- reviving and preserving humane traditions that were lost during the totalitarian regime by reaffirming the traditional elements of Armenian life, respect for the culture and the elderly, and increasing community feeling and awareness and responsibility toward the nation.

From 1994 to 1998, the AAWU achieved many of these objectives, including the improvement of children's health and educational services; the provision of social assistance to disabled, poor, and elderly people; the publication of reports and books; and the organization of roundtables and conferences. Its programs received funding from UNDP, UNICEF, the Office of the UN High Commissioner for Refugees (UNHCR), the Norwegian Refugee Council, Médécins Sans Frontières of Belgium, the U.S. Agency for International Development, the U.S. Academy for Educational Development, and other international and foreign organizations. In 1996–97, the AAWU also received political and financial support from the Armenian Ministry of Health, Ministry of Social Security, Ministry of Education, Ministry of Culture, Youth Issues, and Sports, the Ministry of Agriculture, and the Ministry of Internal Affairs.

One of the best received programs the group sponsored was its weekly Untoonelootyoons (Reception) program. These weekly Receptions were organized to help people in need. Every Wednesday afternoon, the AAWU would open its door to the public and invite those in need to come to the office and present their concerns and complaints. These included petitions for assistance with housing, medical, and military conscription problems. The AAWU volunteers would complete the necessary petition forms and submit them to various ministries and agencies.

Because these requests were made by the AAWU and signed by the first lady of Armenia, they received "priority" treatment. If the individuals themselves had made these same requests, it is highly unlikely that they would have been fulfilled so promptly, if at all. I recorded many instances in which requests for aid were successfully fulfilled. For instance, Akel, a 3-year-old boy from a poor family in Avan Arinj, was in dire need of an eye operation, without which he would become blind in a couple of years. His parents, who also had two other small children, were barely making ends meet and did not have the money for Akel's operation. Their request to the AAWU was promptly met, and Akel was given a letter authorizing a free operation to be performed at the Republican Hospital. Akel was successfully operated upon, and his condition was corrected.

In addition to the Untoonelootyoon program, the AAWU was also involved in many community and national level projects. For instance, in 1996 the AAWU was involved in the Healthy Village Project in conjunction with UNDP, UNHCR, and other foreign and international development organizations. After conducting surveys and research to assess the needs of villagers in border villages, where many refugees had settled after fleeing their homes in Azerbaijan, the AAWU organized and implemented various development projects in these villages. In one of the villages, Paravakar, in the northeastern Tavush region, the AAWU found funding from the Norwegian Refugee Council and UNHCR to build a hydroelectric station. Because the village was on the Armenian—Azeri border, there was sporadic shelling of the water wells, and many residents did not have access to artesian and potable water. The hydroelectric station would not only provide artesian and potable water but also generate electricity throughout the village.

At this time, the AAWU was also active in promoting programs and projects to assist children with physical and mental disabilities. For instance, beginning in 1994, the AAWU began actively supported the Kharbert Children's Home and the Oshagan Children's Rehabilitation Center. The Kharbert programs were supported by funds from Médécins Sans Frontières. The Oshagan project, which was supported largely by funds from the Armenian diaspora in France, was unique, in that it also received funds from local Armenian individuals and institutions, including the Holy Seat of the Armenian Church in Saint Echmiadzin, which donated $25,000 to the project, and Yerevan-based sponsors, who donated $115,875. The key coordinators of the AAWU were quite aware of the public relations aspect of its work and kept emphasizing that the AAWU was the ideal intermediary organization, which brought together the people, the government, and international organizations. One member, Monika, explained:

> We are in a unique position to help people since we benefit from state and international support. We can identify local problems through our on the ground chapters and apply our resources to solving those problems.

The organization's 1997 *Annual Report* also acknowledged the central role of international support by noting, "Many programs of the AAWU are in progress owing to the fruitful collaboration with international organizations accredited in the Republic of Armenia."

Discourses

Many members of the Yerevan AAWU chapter spoke about how they became involved in the AAWU to help people, to help their communities, and to help the nation survive the transition process. These women described how they were assisting those in need (e.g., the elderly, disabled, war widows, and orphans), but they were also strong advocates of civil society and democratic reforms. Natalya Martirossian was, and as of May 2003 continues to be, the chief coordinator of the AAWU (she is also the co-coordinator of the Helsinki Citizens' Assembly).[30] She is in her late 40s, married with two children, and a candidate for a doctoral degree in chemical physics. Until the Karabagh Movement disrupted her life, she worked as a researcher for the National Academy of Sciences for nearly 20 years along with her husband, who is also a physical scientist. She was officially the highest ranking member, following the first lady, and often acted as the group's spokesperson when the first lady was absent. Natalya's explanation for why she had become active in public life is illustrative:

> Until the [Karabagh] Movement began I had never really been active in social life. We worked in the Academy and had a relatively normal life. But when the Movement began we became so caught up in the euphoria of that time. I became pregnant in 1988 with my second child and to me it was like a sign of my dedication to the cause of Independence. I was physically expressing my hope for a better future by bringing another child into this world. When our son was born we named him Levon, after Levon Ter-Petrossian [the first president of the newly independent republic]. My son is now [1996] 8 years old and symbolizes my continuing dedication to democracy and an independent nation. I am working, as a mother and as a citizen, to build a democratic society where my children will grow up in.
>
> I first got involved in public life through the Helsinki Citizen's Assembly. Our goal with that group was to serve as civil mediators in the Karabagh Conflict. Only later did I get recruited into the All-Armenian [Women's Union]. Because I had done such a dedicated job for the HCA [Helsinki Citizens' Assembly], they [the committee] asked me to become a part of this organization as well. Since 1988 and the NKR [Karabagh Movement] and the earthquake women had begun becoming more active in public life, politics and so forth. When Independence was achieved, many of the active women were left out of the high-level politics, but we still wanted to be active. It was when we got shut out by the elections that we turned to the NGO sector. We felt that we had an important contribution to make.

For Natalya, there is a close connection between NGO activism and motherhood. Many AAWU women shared the opinion that women joined

NGOs to remain active in public affairs and to assist their families and the nation. One AAWU activist, Susanna, assessed the motivations and barriers facing women as follows:

> Women have great potential and since we cannot express this in the form of government positions we often do so through NGOs. The NGO sector provides women with arenas for participation in public life and community affairs. Through this participation in NGOs, women can gain entry into certain *shrchabadner* [circles, surroundings] that will allow them to realize their goals. Through NGOs, women also are given the opportunity to express their ambitions (political and otherwise). These ambitions are harder to realize in the form of the governmental posts. Traditionalism is truly a problem in Armenia, and people who are stuck on old-fashioned traditions cannot move forward.
>
> Traditionalism is this focus on certain rules about what behavior of women and men should be like. This is changing, but very slowly, and that limits some of our participation. There have been many changes in life since Independence, and people have been forced to change and adapt. But the traditionalism is lingering and holding women back. It's not just the traditionalism or backwardness if you wish to call it that, but that women are also deterred from active participation in public life because of time constraints. Time is a major issue in the life of every Armenian woman; we have to wait for the water, anticipate the electricity shutdowns, and make time for grocery shopping, cooking, cleaning, and taking care of the children. These take up so much time that we are often left with little energy at the end of the day to do anything else. That is why you don't have many women from villages or from working-class families in NGOs. They tend to have husbands who adhere to those traditional ideas that the woman should be at home and waiting on them hand and foot.

Here, issues related to "traditionalism" as well as social class are identified as obstacles to women's political participation. In this context, AAWU women often advanced a rather paradoxical argument: that their public (nontraditional) work was actually the most effective method of promoting and protecting traditions. Their focus on working with children on projects—such as the UNICEF-funded "I Am a 21st Century Citizen"—provides an example of how the traditional role of mothers as nurturers can combine with the goal of producing good democratic citizens.

To promote the UNICEF project, AAWU members traveled around

Armenia and visited schools to talk about democracy and the rights and responsibilities of citizens. They had the children draw and write about their understanding of such concepts as "democracy," "freedom," "oppression," and "citizenship." The goal involved finding out what these terms meant to children and how to better teach them about democratic principles. As Nata stated,

> We have to encourage their dedication to the ideas of freedom and liberty that we have fought for. Children have certain ideas of what democracy is, but often because they hear different things from their parents, friends, or others, they sometimes have a low estimate of it. They sometimes equate democracy with being poor.

AAWU members felt that they were intervening *before* the children succumbed to the overwhelming apathy and disillusion of adulthood.[31]

The Postcoup Period

While the Armenian National Movement was in power from 1991 until February 1998, the AAWU was a force to be reckoned with and imposed its will freely upon local officials and ministry bureaucrats. But following the 1998 coup against President Levon Ter-Petrossian, the membership declined from more than 5,000 to fewer than 20, and the AAWU became, as one member put it, "just another NGO." When I visited Armenia in 1999, the once busy office in Yerevan was deserted and dark, the office walls had begun to crack, the computer was broken, and several of the phones in the multi-room office were disconnected. Subsequently, the AAWU moved to a much smaller office.

Despite the organization's decline, the remaining three AAWU coordinators continued in 2000 to implement the UNICEF "I Am a 21st Century Citizen" project. They were able to do so thanks to continued support from UNICEF. In addition to the UNICEF project, as of 2002 the AAWU continued to support the work of the Oshagan Children's Rehabilitation Center and the Kharbert and Vanadzor Orphanages by working with its United States—based diaspora partner, the Development Services of Armenia nonprofit organization.

Beginning in 2000, the AAWU, together with Development Services of Armenia, found funding and support from the Austrian chapter of the Armenian General Benevolent Union, the United States—based James Tufenkian Foundation, and the U.S. Agency for International Development Social Investment Fund for its work with the orphanages and rehabilitation center.

Beginning in 2002, the AAWU also resumed its educational programs and activities and began organizing master classes and seminars for youths on such topics as human rights, globalization, the Karabagh conflict, and the proposed constitutional reforms in Armenia. In 2003, the AAWU also held a series of training seminars titled "Women's Rights and Their Role in Civil Society" for the sixty-five women participating in the "Raising Women's Empowerment through Professional Training" program, which they cosponsored with the International Accountancy Training Center Educational Fund (IATC), a local Armenian NGO. This project, which was funded by the Swiss Agency for Development and Cooperation, provided unemployed women from Yerevan and the Kotayk, Aragatsgotn, Armavir, and Ararat regions with accounting and financial management skills and civic education trainings aimed at increasing their awareness of their legal and labor rights. Of the sixty-five women who received their certificates in May 2003, forty are already employed in various small, medium-sized, and large enterprises. Following the success of the project, the AAWU and IATC have now received funding from the Institute for International Cooperation of the German Adult Education Association to organize a similar program for women living in the Siunik region of Armenia.[32]

The AAWU has been able to maintain its organization and to continue pursuing its primary objectives. International and diaspora support has been instrumental for this work, and this aid has allowed the AAWU to continue in operation even after having lost local political support.[33] But though international support allows NGOs to implement their programs even after losing local political support, it also carries with it certain problematic aspects, which I will discuss in the next section.

The Problematic Aspects of Working at the Local–Global Intersection

The difficult economic conditions in the post-Soviet period have not allowed for the growth of local foundations that would support NGOs. In Armenia, NGOs must rely on external financial support from foreign agencies or donors from the Armenian diaspora. International support, however, is a double-edged sword. On the one hand, this aid provides NGOs with increased leverage and autonomy at the local level; on the other hand, it exposes them to foreign direction and control.

The dependency of local NGOs on the "uncertain largess of donors," as William Fisher calls it, has direct and indirect effects. He describes these as (1) redirecting the accountability toward funders and away from the group's grassroots constituencies and (2) transforming NGOs into contractors, constituencies into customers, and members into clients.[34] This exposes NGOs to attacks within their own countries, raising questions about whether they truly represent their constituents. This is one of the most difficult challenges facing Armenian women's NGOs, because they walk a fine line between maintaining tradition and promoting more liberal, sometimes feminist agendas. If they sacrifice the local for the global, they are betraying their mission as grassroots organizations. If they ignore the needs and wants of international donors, they risk losing funding that is critical to their survival and success.

The issue of domestic violence, which became a popular funding initiative among donors during the late 1990s, illustrates this quandary.[35] The Armenian authors of the August 1995 "United Nations Review" dedicated to the 1995 Fourth World Conference on Women in Beijing state the following with regard to domestic violence:

> Violence against women, although there are no records kept in Armenia, is a universal phenomenon. Therefore, Armenian women must have experienced some form of violence against them. Reporting of violence is not customary. The definition of violence is not clear. Psychological violence, violence of sexual nature and physical violence are not clearly understood or identified or distinguished.[36]

In 1995 and 1996, domestic violence was still a new topic in Armenia's NGO sector and to some extent a taboo subject. Women's NGOs opposed public discussion of what they deemed a private, family issue. In 1996, members of a transnational feminist NGO called the Young Women and Democracy Program (YWDP)—which had funding from the European Union programs named Poland and Hungary, Aid for the Reconstruction of Economies (PHARE), and Technical Assistance for Commonwealth of Independent States Countries (TACIS)—began work in Armenia to assist in the creation of a coalition of local women's NGOs to address the issue of violence against women alongside other women's empowerment programs.

This group had funding to help local NGOs to begin addressing the problem of domestic violence, but local groups resisted working with the YWDP. They argued that domestic violence was not the most critical issue facing Armenian women and added, "We don't air our dirty laundry in public."[37] Also in 1996, Marineh Khachadour, an American Armenian expatriate, created a study group to examine the problems of battered women. Marineh organized several meetings during the spring and summer of 1996 to discuss the issue of domestic violence in Armenia.

These meetings were attended by American expatriates working in Armenia and by a few local Armenian scholars. At one meeting, which was held at the cafeteria at the American University of Armenia, one of the American participants suggested that women's NGOs should be involved, and in fact take the lead, in addressing the issue of domestic violence in Armenia. In response to this suggestion, an American training coordinator at the Armenian Assembly of America's NGO Center, expressed her concern that many women's NGOs did not want to address this issue and added, "Many of the women's NGOs do not necessarily address women's problems and the issue of domestic violence will not be well received by such groups." Members of various women's NGOs had been invited to attend, but none were present at any of the meetings I attended.

When I asked Anahit, one of these women's NGO members, why she did not attend, she replied, "That is not a problem we wish to discuss in public. If she [Azniv] wants to do so, it is her choice, but she will not receive any support from us." Though Azniv's efforts were well received by the American expatriates and a few low-ranking local women, nearly all of the women's NGOs continued to avoid addressing the issue of domestic violence in 1996–97. This situation began to change in 1998–99, when increased funding was made available by international donors for local NGOs to begin addressing the problems of domestic violence.

As a result of this greater funding, crisis centers and hotlines were created in response to the particular interests of foreign funding agencies. Susanna Vardanyan, president of the Women's Rights Center NGO, has in recent years become the most prominent local advocate of protecting women's rights and addressing the problems of domestic violence; but this was not always so. In 1996, Vardanyan was the leader of the Hayouhi Women's Association NGO, whose mission was to "protect women's rights by extending the role of women in public, social, cultural, and political life."[38] In 1996, Vardanyan did not attend any of the meetings or seminars organized by Azniv, and only in later years did she become involved in addressing the issue of domestic violence. With this shift in focus, she disbanded the Hayouhi Association and formed the Women's Rights Center NGO in 1998. At this point, the mission of her new organization became

> to extend the role of women in public, social, cultural, and political life. To promote democratic reform in Armenia. To protect the rights of women and children in accordance with the RoA [Armenian] Constitution and international treaties. To promote the improvement of women's state confirmed by the main provisions of declaration and activities of Women's 4th International Conference (Beijing 1995).[39]

The first sentence of the new mission statement is identical to the mission statement of the Hayouhi NGO. The remaining sentences reflect how local NGOs often pack their mission statements with a plethora of objectives so as to have the flexibility to apply for a variety of grants and to easily accommodate the shifting discourses, agendas, and funding initiatives of donors. The last sentence in the paragraph confirms my earlier point of how the UN conference in Beijing provided women's NGOs with an introduction to the world of NGOs and a new vocabulary with which they could represent their organizations and activities.

In keeping with this new mission statement, in 2000 the Women's Rights Center published a trilingual (Armenian, English, and Russian) booklet containing the stories of battered women. These stories appear as excerpts from longer interviews, but they are presented without any context or explanation as to how and where the Women's Rights Center members met these women, how and if these women have been helped, and what has happened to them since the interview.

In 2000, Vardanyan also worked with Elizabeth Duban and Delinda Cooper of the Minnesota Advocates for Human Rights, who had traveled to Armenia with the sponsorship of the U.S. State Department to explore how the Armenian government treats domestic violence and whether Armenia was upholding its international legal obligations with respect to women's rights.[40] That same year, the Minnesota Advocates for Human Rights published a report titled "Domestic Violence in Armenia." [41]

In an article in the *Armenian Forum* about the report, Duban and Cooper argue, "In countries moving out of the Soviet past, defensiveness continues to be the more common response to critical questions" and add that they found a lack of willingness on the part of state officials and even some human rights NGOs to address the issue of domestic violence. What they don't recognize or reflect upon, however, is the reason for this defensiveness or reluctance. In Armenia, the domestic violence issue is still considered a "private" issue. Efforts by NGOs such as the Women's Rights Center are not well received, and many women NGO leaders whom I interviewed in 2000 were critical of Vardanyan's efforts. Even if domestic violence is discussed in such public forums as the *UNDP Women's Status Report* and in the *Millennium Generation Gender Studies Report* (2001), as the authors of the UNDP Report point out, "Public opinion is what matters most [and] unfortunately, the opinion prevails that the family is an entirely private sphere and is not open to public intervention."[42]

Although some American feminists working in Armenia recognize that domestic violence formerly was a "private" issue in the United States, they underestimate the historical, cultural, and social differences that determine how issues are addressed and resolved in other contexts.[43] Transferring foreign models or ideologies, even successful ones, is problematic because local conditions affect their translation and implementation. Armenian women's organizations have gone to great lengths to demonstrate that they are working for the good of the family and hence the nation; above all, this means that they do not pursue agendas that could be perceived as threatening the stability of the family and nation. They cannot address the domestic violence issue in the same way as it is done in the United States or elsewhere in the West because they must work in the local context, with its own expectations and limitations. This is not to say that there is no problem of domestic violence in Armenia, *because there is,* but rather to emphasize the necessity of identifying local approaches and solutions.

Scholars of development, including Arturo Escobar, William Fisher, and Jonathan Crush, have contended that to truly make development "work," it is necessary to allow local citizens to define the problems and search for locally based solutions and not to compromise the agency and ability of local groups in determining their own development and political agendas—otherwise, we have failures of well-intentioned development projects.[44] The tendency of donors to shift funding priorities compromises the ability of local NGOs to implement long-term programs because groups are constantly having to shift and adapt their discourses and projects to meet the changing funding priorities of donors instead of the needs of their local communities.

For example, domestic violence is not an issue championed by local groups. It is an issue deemed important by international donors, and local NGOs therefore began to address it to take advantage of available funding. There is a danger, however, that because the issue of domestic violence does not resonate with local NGO actors as much as it does with donors, that when donors' agendas shift, local NGOs will abandon domestic violence in favor of newer funding priorities. This happened in Georgia, for example, where women NGO leaders felt that foreign donor agendas shifted the work of local NGOs away from what local women saw as the needs of their communities.[45] In chapter 14 of this volume, Julie Hemment describes how members of the Russian women's NGO, Zhenskii Svet, were concerned that funders were moving away from supporting the theme of *nasilie* (violence) and toward the new theme *torgovlia liud'mi* (trafficking), and explains their frustration at having "to be like chameleons" to keep up with the changing demands and funding priorities of donors.

Conclusion

As Armenia and many of the other former Soviet states move from poverty toward sustainable development, they enter the "development phase" of the post-Soviet transition, with an attendant rise in the risk that donors will impose their own development agendas.[46] This has already occurred when in the establishment of Armenia's NGO sector, a certain international aid agency suggested that the Armenians follow the "Bangladesh Model." Because the Armenians were dependent on funds from this agency, they duly accepted and attempted to implement this model. Yet they soon discovered that not only did this approach not work in the Armenian context but that it also did not exist in Bangladesh—a fact they discovered after conducting research to find out more about the actual program, rather than in the agency's reports and publications.

As Steve Sampson has pointed out, the problem is not with foreign as opposed to local models but with models in general. Models are created by theorists (or technocrats, as the case may be), and when they are applied to real life situations they must be amenable to adaptation and change. This is not a new discovery or epiphany. Scholars have been writing about the problems of international aid, development, and foreign models for the past 25 years.[47] What is new involves the locations where development and transition are now taking place. The former Soviet states are not developing countries in the traditional sense, because they have highly educated, trained, and literate populations.

If we want to promote democracy, women's rights, sustainable economic development, or any other worthwhile cause in the post-Soviet sphere, it is necessary, as Michele Rivkin-Fish argues in chapter 13 of this volume, to move beyond established, Western bureaucratic forms of engagement and to seek out local initiatives that identify power inequalities, subordination, hierarchy, and institutional forms of repression as well as to democratize our methods of engagement. This entails engaging local actors in dialogue and accepting the idea that there are multiple perspectives on any given topic and multiple ways of addressing any problem.

International aid has been very important to the development of the civil society and NGO sector in Armenia, and it has allowed women to remain active in public life. In the past 10 years, there has been a great deal of progress as NGOs have become more professionalized and established. According to Tania Chichmanian, the NGO program officer at the Armenian Assembly of America,[48]

> While the NGOs aren't financially sustainable, they do have informational, human, and leadership resources, which they have built up over the past 10 years. Many of the NGOs in Armenia are now professionally run and have strategic plans, mission-driven statements, and know where they are going. . . . NGOs are also learning to build social partnerships and to formalize their relationships with the government. This is important since NGOs are trying to define their role in the society.

Even though Armenian NGOs are becoming more professionalized and established, they continue to encounter difficulties working in and between the local and global spheres. Armenian women are dealing with their own society's cultural stereotypes, pressures from donors, and their own personal struggles of surviving in the post-Soviet period and trying to redefine their role in society. As they negotiate the predicament of working locally and getting funded globally, women are contesting, reformulating, and rethinking their role in the development of an independent Armenia. As one of my informants, Susanna, said in an interview in October 2000,

> As we become more professionalized and build our external networks, our situation improves such that local parties cannot destroy us or interfere with us as easily. But, we also have to find ways to combat our culture's gender stereotypes and traditionalism and our own complexes if we want our situation to improve. We can learn from our foreign friends and their experiences. But I don't think we should duplicate the foreign patterns and models wholesale—we have to find what works in our own situation.

In this chapter, I have demonstrated how local NGO actors negotiate, mediate, and reconcile conflicting positions. I have also argued that for transition projects to succeed, it is necessary to engage local NGO actors in dialogue and take into account their concerns, their cultural beliefs and traditions, and their approaches to solving problems. Otherwise, as Marina, an NGO member, said, "You will pretend to be helping us and we will pretend that we are being helped."

Notes

1. John L. Comaroff and Jean Comaroff, *Civil Society and the Political Imagination in Africa: Critical Perspectives* (Chicago: University of Chicago Press, 1999), vii.

2. Chris Hann, "Introduction: Political Society and Civil Anthropology," in *Civil Society: Challenging Western Models,* ed. Chris Hann and Elizabeth Dunn (London: Routledge, 1996), 7.

3. Jane Wedel, quoted in Chris Hann, "Introduction," in *Civil Society,* ed. Hann and Dunn, 1.

4. NGO Center, "Developing Democracy in Armenia," NGO Center, Yerevan, Armenia, 1996 (unpublished), 6.

5. Katherine Verdery, *What Was Socialism and What Comes Next?* (Princeton, N.J.: Princeton University Press, 1996).

6. Daphne Berdahl, Matti Bunzl, and Martha Lampland, eds., *Altering States: Ethnographies of Transition in Eastern Europe and the Former Soviet Union* (Ann Arbor: University of Michigan Press, 2000); Sue Bridger and Frances Pine, *Surviving Post-Socialism: Local Strategies and Regional Responses in Eastern Europe* (London: Routledge. 1998); Mary Buckley, ed., *Post-Soviet Women: From the Baltic to Central Asia* (Cambridge: Cambridge University Press, 1997); Michael Burawoy and Katherine Verdery, *Uncertain Transitions: Ethnographies of Change in the Post-Socialist World* (Lanham, Md.: Rowan & Littlefield, 1999); Gerald W. Creed and Janine R. Wedel, "Second Thoughts from the Second World: Interpreting Aid in Post-Communist Eastern Europe," *Human Organization* 56, no. 3 (1997): 253–64; Nanette Funk, "Feminism East and West," in *Gender Politics and Post-Communism: Reflections from Eastern Europe and the Former Soviet Union,* ed. Nanette Funk and Magda Mueller (London: Routledge, 1993); Susan Gal and Gail Kligman, *The Politics of Gender after Socialism: A Comparative-Historical Essay* (Princeton, N.J.: Princeton University Press, 2000); Steven Sampson, "The Social Life of Projects: Importing Civil Society to Albania," in *Civil Society,* ed. Hann and Dunn; Katherine Verdery, "From Parent-State to Family Patriarchs: Gender and Nation in Contemporary Eastern Europe," *East European Politics and Societies* 8, no. 2 (1994): 227–30; Janine R. Wedel, *Collision and Collusion: The Strange Case of Western Aid to Eastern Europe 1989–98* (New York: Saint Martin's Press, 2001).

7. Gal and Kligman, *Politics of Gender.*

8. Gal and Kligman, *Politics of Gender,* 91.

9. "Thinking globally and acting locally" is one of the most overused phrases in the

NGO sector, and in the past 5 years, it has also entered popular discourse in the United States, where it can now be seen on bumper stickers, advertisements, etc.

10. Marina Ottaway and Thomas Carothers, *Funding Virtue: Civil Society Aid and Democracy Promotion* (Washington, D.C.: Carnegie Endowment for International Peace, 1998), 6.

11. Eurasia Foundation press release, Yerevan, Armenia, 1998, 2.

12. World Bank., *Armenia Country Assistance Strategy Report;* <http://www-wds.worldbank.org/servlet/wdscontentserver/wdsp/ib/2001/05/19/000094946_01050804481521/rendered/index/multi0page.txt> (2001).

13. This is from an interview by the author with Edward Markarian, chief of the State Registry of Social Associations, Ministry of Justice of Armenia, April 16, 2003.

14. Democracy Union, *Women in Armenia* (Yerevan, Armenia: Democracy Union, 1996), 4.

15. In 1985, 121 of 219 members of parliament were women. But it is clear that this was due to an inflated quota system, because once the Soviet system collapsed and a new National Assembly was elected in 1991, the number of female parliamentarians dropped to 8.

16. Mayra Buvinic et al., *Investing in Women: Progress and Prospects for the World Bank (*Washington, D.C.: Overseas Development Council and International Center for Research on Women, 1996), 13.

17. In keeping with anthropological conventions, I have used pseudonyms in the place of the real names of individuals who are not public figures.

18. United Nations Development Program, *1998 Armenia Human Development Report: The Role of the State* (Yerevan, Armenia: UN Press, 1998), 17.

19. Stephanie Platz, "The Shape of National Time: Daily Life, History, and Identity during Armenia's Transition to Independence," in *Altering States,* ed. Berdahl, Bunzl, and Lampland, 118.

20. National Committee in Preparation for the World Conference on Women, *National Report on the Condition of Women* (Yerevan, Armenia: National Committee in Preparation for the World Conference on Women, 1995), 16.

21. National Committee, *National Report,* 16.

22. National Committee, *National Report,* 16.

23. The concept of moral motherhood dates from the late nineteenth century, when women in the United States and Europe argued that they had the right to enter the public sphere because they were promoting "good social housekeeping." Micaela Di Leonardo, *Gender at the Crossroads of Knowledge: Feminist Anthropology in the Postmodern Era* (Berkeley: University of California Press, 1991), 16.

24. Lyudmila Harutyunyan, "Kanants Baykari Masin Che Khoskuh, Ayl Hassaragootyan Vokhcha-khohootyan" [This Is Not about Women's Struggle, but about Society Is Common Sense], *Kanayk Hayots: Nor Dari Shemin* [Women at the Doorstep to the Twenty-First Century Journal] (Yerevan State University), 2000), 21–23. (This journal is released sporadically, i.e., whenever there is funding. Therefore, this issue is not numbered.)

25. Mary Buckley, *Women and Ideology in the Soviet Union* (New York: Harvester Wheatsheaf, 1989).

26. I have explained this resistance in my dissertation, "Hearths and Modernity: The Role of Women in NGOs in Post Soviet Armenia," University of California, San Diego, 2000. In chapter 13 of this volume, Michele Rivkin-Fish also discusses the resistance

and disparagement of feminism by women in Eastern Europe and the former Soviet Union.

27. Maxine Molyneux, "Mobilizations without Emancipation? Women's Interests, State, and Revolution," in *Transition and Development: Problems of Third World Socialism,* ed. Richard Fagen, Carmen Diane Deere, and Jose Luis Coraggio (New York: Monthly Review Press, 1986).

28. Government-supported NGOs are commonly referred to as GONGOs by scholars working on NGOs.

29. After 1998, the Central Yerevan office was the only remaining chapter.

30. Former first lady Ludmilla Ter-Petrossian is now the acting, not honorary, president of the AAWU.

31. A United States—based prodemocracy NGO has also begun working intensively with youths, having come to the conclusion that working with disillusioned adults is not worth the effort.

32. This is based on a personal communication with AAWU staff, May 30, 2003. The Suinik region is the southernmost region of Armenia and is a 5- to 6-hour drive over mountain roads from the capital, Yerevan.

33. For a more detailed discussion about diaspora involvement in development projects, see Armine Ishkanian, "Helping the Homeland: The Impact of Transnational Diasporic Activism on Armenia's Post-Soviet Transition," in *Transnationalism and Diaspora in the Caucasus and Central Asia,* ed. Turaj Atabaki and Sanjyot Mehendale (New York: Routledge, forthcoming).

34. William Fisher, "Doing Good? The Politics and Anti-Politics of NGO Practices," *Annual Reviews in Anthropology* 26 (1995): 454.

35. Lara Olson, "Women and NGOs: Views from Some Conflict Areas in the Caucasus," paper prepared for Women in International Security Workshop, New Bridges to Peace, Washington, D.C., April 27–28, 2001, 9. Also see chapter 14 by Julie Hemment in this volume.

36. United Nations Department of Public Information, "United Nations Review," August 1995, Yerevan.

37. In chapter 14 of this volume, Julie Hemment also documents the resistance and reservations expressed by women activists who did not think that it was the most pressing issue facing Russian women and that they were concerned that so many resources were being put into it.

38. Armenian Assembly of America, *Karabagh and Armenia Factbook.* (Washington, D.C.: Armenian Assembly of America, 1996), 69.

39. See <http://www.ngoc.am/whoiswho/wiw_eng.pdf>.

40. Belinda Cooper and Elizabeth Duban, "Respecting Women: Domestic Violence in Armenia," *Armenian Forum* 2, no. 3 (2001): 77–90.

41. For a more detailed discussion, see Armine Ishkanian, "Importing Civil Society?: The Emergence of Armenia's NGO Sector and the Impact of Western Aid on Its Development," *Armenian Forum: A Journal of Contemporary Affairs* 3, no. 1 (in press).

42. United Nations Development Program, *Women's Status Report* (New York: United Nations Development Program, 1999), 47.

43. Nancy Fraser, "The Uses and Abuses of French Discourse Theories for Feminist Politics," *Boundary 2* (summer 1990): 85. Fraser argues that even in the United States, feminists had an uphill struggle in making domestic violence a public issue. She writes, "Until recently, feminists were in the minority in thinking that domestic violence was a

matter of common concern and thus a legitimate topic of public discourses. The great majority of people considered this issue to be a private matter between what was assumed to be a fairly small number of heterosexual couples."

44. Jonathan Crush, *Power of Development* (New York: Routledge, 1995); Arturo Escobar, "Anthropology and the Development Encounter: The Making and Marketing of Development Anthropology," *American Ethnologist* 18, no. 4 (1991): 658–82; and Fisher, "Doing Good?"

45. Olson, "Women and NGOs," 8.

46. I have intentionally capitalized the concepts of Capitalism, Democracy, etc. to point out how these concepts have become reified by donors.

47. Riall Nolan, "Now That We Know Where the Bodies Are Buried, Who Do We Tell?" Paper presented at the 2001 American Anthropological Association meetings. Michael Cernea, ed., *Putting People First,* 2d ed. (New York: Oxford University Press, 1991). Michael Horowitz, "Development and the Anthropological Encounter: A Reflective Underview," *Development Anthropologist* 16, nos. 1–2 (1998): 44–50.

48. Chichmanian was interviewed by the author on November 30, 2001, in Washington, D.C.

13

Gender and Democracy: Strategies for Engagement and Dialogue on Women's Issues after Socialism in St. Petersburg

Michele Rivkin-Fish

A concern with the lives of women and gender relations has contributed core theoretical insights regarding the political, economic, and cultural unraveling of socialist systems. Although liberal observers initially anticipated that universal benefits would ensue from the creation of markets and representative democracies, evidence from the first decade of post-socialist reforms reveals sharply differentiated sets of outcomes for members of former socialist societies. The turn from planned economies to integration into a capitalist global order has restructured women's and men's relations to the state,

The author's fieldwork in Saint Petersburg, in 1993 and 1994–95 was generously funded by the Andrew W. Mellon Foundation and the Peter B. Lewis Fund of the Center of International Studies at Princeton University. The author thanks the World Health Organization's Healthy Cities Project office in Copenhagen and the delegates who agreed to have her accompany their tour. She also acknowledges the Saint Petersburg Public Health Committee and Saint Petersburg maternal health care providers for their assistance in making this research possible. This chapter benefited immensely from the insights of Elena Gapova, Julie Hemment, and all the members of the Kennan Institute workshop.

society, and family in distinct ways and justified narrow associations between women and the domestic sphere as necessary for societal development.[1] Democratizing transformations are being made in part by means of ideological and institutional practices that, supported by global institutions, exclude women from politics and the labor market.[2]

The need to ensure women's equality as an essential component of democratization has not eluded all global and local participants seeking to shape post-socialist transitions. During the 1990s, projects focusing on women occupied an increasingly prominent place in the global agendas of development agencies and nongovernmental organizations concentrating on the former socialist world. In this chapter, I argue that by addressing women's issues, Western agencies aimed to communicate a specific set of values regarding the ways post-socialist change should be carried out. Such values included the importance for policymakers of addressing the needs of underrepresented groups, vulnerable populations, and women in particular as a disempowered minority. Achieving improvements in the status of women was often equated with the very pursuit of democratic change in former socialist states; unlike many Western economic advisers, these global actors have construed political change as an inherently gendered process.

Yet if the link between establishing gender equality and achieving democracy has been widely theorized,[3] the process of stimulating changes to improve women's status, of intervening on behalf of women's issues *in ways that enact democratic principles,* has been subjected to far less scrutiny. Such an interrogation of strategy in international engagement is necessary for several reasons. Studies of assistance to post-socialist contexts have shown that projects aiming to facilitate democratic change often result in unintended consequences, with resources appropriated for a range of goals that do not necessarily lead to the empowerment of marginalized groups.[4] Projects intended to promote women's voices and women's rights have often been designed without regard to local histories, cultures, and political-economic circumstances, inadvertently contributing to hostile attacks against feminist agendas and opposition to democracy itself.[5] Not of least importance, promoting democracy and women's equality entails making moral kinds of arguments and actions. Pursuing these ends with incompatible, incongruous, or contradictory means may undermine the legitimacy of the claims themselves.

This chapter seeks to advance discussion of the politics of global activism in former socialist states by examining the process of intervening to promote women's status. Put most simply, promoting women's empowerment through global engagements involves the complex deployment of power in local settings. The definition of need, identification of recipients or partners, and concept of assistance that come to shape such engagements may reveal as much, or more, about global activists than about the women targeted for help. In recognizing this, activists may begin to consider the problem of how democratizing change is conceptualized and pursued in post-socialist contexts. This requires exposing assumptions and structures that shape activist interventions but that often remain unexamined in the design and implementation of global projects. We need to concern ourselves with how inequalities between global and local actors are structured, recognized, and managed during engagements for women's issues.

My insights for this analysis derive from my experiences as an anthropological researcher and consultant during a project affiliated with the World Health Organization (WHO) aiming to promote Russian women's health in the mid-1990s. In this capacity, I strove both to analyze the encounter between Russian and foreign experts as a site of cross-cultural dialogue and to affect it. My goal was to interpret for each side the assumptions, experiences, and values of the other, and to suggest new forms of mutually satisfying engagement. This attempt to position myself as a "cultural translator" and thereby help participants avoid the miscommunication and conflict of many global encounters proved untenable, however. Cultural differences by themselves were not the greatest obstacle to mutual understanding and cooperation. Far more detrimental to the collaborative process was how the power of those providing assistance was expressed and deployed.

The issue of power became particularly clear during the process of "needs assessment" that global consultants undertook in Russia, and on which I focus in this chapter. Specifically, I examine the organization of time and space in which encounters took place between international consultants and local experts, and the negotiation of communicative control in their discussions about local "needs." The practices of these consultants were neither unique nor exceptional, but exemplified those typical in development assistance.[6] My critique compares the assumptions and methods that systemically shaped development strategies of engagement with those of the anthropological approach for organizing encounters and negotiating dialogue.

To make sense of these models of engagement, I use the concept of *stance* as an analytic tool for exposing distinct methods of wielding and negotiating power in global encounters.[7] Specifically, I view stance as global actors' self-conception in the collaborative encounter, as expressed in their assumptions regarding their role and potential contribution to the local setting, and in the practical tasks they undertake (and do not undertake) to pursue their goals. It is important to note that the kinds of stance possible for global actors to adopt, and the degree of flexibility, rigidity, and routinization manifest in the choice of stance, are to a large extent effects of the institutional setting in which actors work. Designing projects from within a large bureaucracy, a nongovernmental organization, or a university may involve different sorts of possibilities and constraints, and lead to different kinds of potential contributions.

Nonetheless, individuals also have agency and may be more or less inclined to push the boundaries of their worldview and habits, to experiment with new methods of engagement, or to reproduce institutional frameworks. Consultants affiliated with WHO embraced what I call a "provocateur stance" to urge reforms for women's self-determination in health care. Working as provocateurs, global actors considered themselves as experienced experts with models and skills that could be transferred to the post-socialist context. They viewed their contribution as offering an alternative to existing practices, a new approach or solution to resolving local problems. As a generalized approach, the provocateur stance is expressed in a variety of ways, positioning global actors as experts, consultants, teachers, mentors, evaluators, and the like. It is distinguished by a view of the outsider as having valuable knowledge that is both new to local conditions and relevant for them, having been already worked out (if not always perfectly achieved) in the outsiders' home context.

I contrast the provocateur stance with that assumed in contemporary anthropological research, where the purpose of engagement is to understand difference in worldview and experience. The *anthropological stance* prioritizes principles of cultural relativism and holism in approaching unfamiliar worldviews. This fundamentally sympathetic perspective is distinct from moral relativism, the moral legitimation of any human belief or action. It seeks to place alien ideologies, values, and practices within the context of broader historical experience and cultural systems in order to make sense of them and appreciate their meaningful character to those who espouse them.

The role of the anthropologist in the field is consequently that of novice, student, or initiate. Her primary contribution comes after leaving the field, in her written and oral analyses aiming to convey the humanity of the world she entered to her home audience. Without a doubt, anthropologists struggle with the omnipresent challenge of how to represent cultural practices that they find morally unacceptable, including physical and symbolic violence in local communities. Although there can be no single formula for such interpretive processes, the anthropological imagination makes such moments of discomfort and dissonance themselves the focus of investigation and self-reflexive inquiry.

Consonant with this focus on difference as a source of insight, anthropologists have increasingly exposed and addressed power differentials between researchers and community members as inherent to the ethical character of engagement.[8] Again, there is no single or straightforward way this can be done; the traditional anthropological stance does not involve collaborating with cultural others for anything other than increasing understandings of difference.[9] Applied anthropologists have come closer to seeking a role for outside scholars and activists in helping facilitate the empowerment of local communities where they become involved.[10] They have suggested that engagement in locally defined agendas for change should become a goal of anthropologists, acknowledging that scholarly engagement morally implicates outsiders in the destinies of those whose lives they study, who become, in effect, a source of personal gain. Yet at the same time, recognizing that inequalities inhere in any local community, and that "locally defined agendas for change" are not innocent of power relations, complicates the process of imagining collaboration immeasurably.

As I examine how the WHO affiliates assumed a stance as provocateur, I contrast their strategies of engagement in Russia with the strategies derived from an anthropological stance. The provocateur and anthropological stances enabled distinct kinds of insights about local needs to emerge for outsiders, and led global actors to relate to the process of catalyzing change in different ways. The comparative examination of the provocateur and anthropological stances reveals alternative ways that abstract principles and values about democracy became operationalized in the methods global actors pursued at the most local level of international encounters.

I also attend to the risks, constraints and possibilities of these distinct forms of engagement by analyzing the kinds of responses each elicited from Russian actors.[11] The chapter concludes by suggesting how it may be possible to integrate anthropological modes of engagement with activist approaches to provoking gender equality, to promote the empowerment of marginalized people in post-socialist settings by supporting locally meaningful forms of democratizing action.

Contextualizing Problems

The collapse of the Soviet Union in 1991 marked a notable turning point in the views of public health experts both inside and outside Russia. The socialist health care system, long touted by the regime as a sign of socialism's achievements in welfare and scientific advances, became publicly exposed for its shortcomings and failings. Maternal health indicators were a case in point. In 1992, WHO and the city of Saint Petersburg formally acknowledged that the city's maternal mortality rate approximated 60 per 100,000 live births, 10 times higher than in Western Europe.[12]

If these indicators reflected the poor investments in health of the previous years, local Russian health officials and providers further witnessed the decay of their system as the country's economic crisis surfaced in the health care sector. Although maternity care was still officially free, hospitals were rapidly being closed, crumbling infrastructures were not repaired, and institutions could no longer supply all necessary medications. Inflation soared, but physicians' salaries covered under the equivalent of $100 per month. With 70 percent of Russian physicians being women, remaining in medicine became viewed by these professionals as the "luxury" of those with husbands who could support them, and a devastating new source of female impoverishment for all others. Many physicians increased the number of shifts they worked, others moonlighted in nonmedical spheres, becoming public health educators, salespeople, and taxi drivers. Deep frustration and anxiety pervaded the health care sphere. Moreover, economic and political instability were reflected in the quality of women's health. Rapid increases in both sexually transmitted diseases and other infectious diseases, as well as sharp declines in the birthrate, contributed to physicians' sense that delivering babies in the 1990s involved working in severe crisis conditions.

WHO representatives viewed the collapse of state socialism and poor maternal health indicators in a substantially different way. In investigating maternal morbidity and mortality in the early 1990s, they sought a broader perspective that linked women's poor health to their well-being and autonomy in health care settings. They noted that direct causes of maternal deaths included illegal abortions, cesarean sections, and hemorrhaging; but they argued that a broader set of indirect causes also needed to be addressed, including the "severely dehumanized nature of services," and "older regulations preventing possible change."[13] What WHO referred to in characterizing maternal health care services as "severely dehumanized" was a range of procedures that emphasized institutional dominance over women even when scientific data justifying medical intervention was inconclusive or absent. Hospital concerns surrounding labor and delivery focused on the technological management of women's bodies and appeared to exclude women from participating in their birth experiences as active decision makers. Women were not allowed support companions during labor, and after the birth, mothers and babies were separated as hospitals and medical experts claimed authority over infants.

After viewing these arrangements during tours of local hospitals, WHO consultants targeted the provider–patient relationship and care-giving ideologies in maternity care as necessary components of improving women's physical and social well-being. Their recommendations linked democratization of this former Soviet society to health care reforms that would eliminate Soviet-era regulations supporting medical dominance, thereby "humanizing" childbirth.

WHO's recommendations for Russian health reform had their roots in critical social movements, which emerged in North America and Western Europe in the early to middle 1970s and were oriented to the critical reassessment of systemic inequality in health care. These included the domestic movements for a "new public health," the women's health movement, and the international movement on primary health care.[14] The radical spirit that infused Western Europe and the United States in the 1960s and 1970s led these activists to critique traditional public health policies, characterized by the unquestioned public belief in physician authority and the supreme value of medical technologies over other kinds of investments in well-being. The very superiority of Western biomedicine as a form of healing was increasingly called into question by educated, activist segments of the middle class, who challenged its disassociation of physical, emotional, and spiritual forms of suffering.

In grassroots organizations and academic scholarship, these activists more and more juxtaposed a social model of health to the curative, medical model. The prioritization of community and individual empowerment came to be seen as opposed to the use of technology and reliance on biomedical expertise.[15] One of the most vibrant struggles for change came from advocates for women's health, who steadfastly demanded a reconceptualization of the medical "management" of labor and childbirth, and a renewed understanding of women as healthy, active agents in their birthing processes.[16]

In extending their work to the post-Soviet context, consultants proudly embraced the goal of bringing objectionable ideas to the forefront of established discussions. They described themselves as unabashedly confronting local hospital administrators with the insistence that women's needs for self-determination mattered as a public health issue. Moreover, they conceptualized their advocacy on behalf of women's issues as inherently democratic: In arguing with local Russian health officials, they were giving voice to the needs of those who have been marginalized and silenced—women patients.

In interviews I conducted, consultants spoke of "bringing models" to Russia, and metaphorically of "planting seeds" of the values of democracy and women's rights. But the pragmatic and ethical dimensions of their intervention—how the promotion of women's self-determination could be undertaken in a manner that systematically reflected democratic principles of action—had not been a focus for consideration.

A Framework for Collaboration

The initial encounters between WHO and Saint Petersburg's health care authorities in the early 1990s paved the way for interventions designed to catalyze reforms in local maternity care.[17] In 1994, an independent team of maternal health experts affiliated with WHO secured bilateral funding for a 2-year series of professional training workshops for Russian maternal health providers. Topics to be covered in these lectures included the appropriate use of technology in birth and the importance of focusing on individual empowerment and social well-being for improving women's health. Educational training, as has been noted,[18] serves as a key mode of channeling assistance to the former Soviet world, in part because it enables the distribution of resources in a way that cannot be embezzled or stolen.[19]

The use of educational programming in former socialist contexts replicates the purpose and strategies of development work as conventionally designed for the developing world: It offers solutions to social and economic problems in the form of technical inputs, rather than by promoting changes in political and economic structures of society.[20] Development projects adhere to the principle of governmentality; that is, they view government organs as channels for distributing resources and use them to implement technical inputs, rather than targeting these organs for change as the ultimate source of disempowerment, poverty, and oppression.

In the case of WHO's workshops for health care providers, educational training focused on women's rights and autonomy in childbirth, lending an appearance of political involvement to the intervention. However, as I have discussed elsewhere, when the project design equated the establishment of "women's rights" in birth with Russian providers' attitudes toward women's roles in the birthing process, it failed to address or even acknowledge the institutional structures that gave rise to women's subordination in the state socialist health care systems.[21]

The conceptualization of "women's rights" as an effect of rhetoric and attitudes alone (as opposed to one of structural guarantees and institutional relations) fit the conventional requirements of development interventions: apolitical, technical kinds of input.[22] Yet the severe poverty of health care institutions, the unsustainable level of physicians' salaries, the dire economic pressures women patients faced, and the continued impotence of physicians and patients to affect public policies regarding health despite the emergence of "democratic" forms of government all were ignored.

A Needs Assessment Tour: Organizing Time, Space, and Communicative Control

A "needs assessment" tour is a standard event for development workers, and the consultants studied here received funding for a week-long trip to Saint Petersburg in 1994 for just this purpose. Yet precisely what was to be assessed? The delegation had already been granted more than $200,000 to offer a series of educational workshops to Saint Petersburg health care workers regarding maternal health over a 3-year period. In writing the grant, the consultants had actually articulated a clear vision of what they thought Saint Petersburg "needed" to improve maternal health outcomes, and they had already determined what their task would be in promoting such changes: the provision of training and education for health care providers.

The needs assessment tour, consequently, was to be an opportunity to inquire into the kinds of lecture topics local providers would be interested in learning about from the global experts. It was also intended to expose the state of Russian maternity care to those members of the delegation who had not before been to Russia.

The head of the delegation planned the needs assessment tour, sending international faxes to the translator at the Saint Petersburg Public Health Committee requesting that appointments be set up with chief doctors and key administrators of local maternal health institutions. The organization of time and space during the tour was not just an administrative procedure; it involved a series of decisions that would limit the kinds of interactions global consultants would have and the kinds of knowledge they would find in their encounters. Such decisions included whom to meet, how long the meeting was expected to take, and what its purpose was imagined to be. For example, a typical daily agenda included a meeting at a women's outpatient clinic in the morning, followed by a lunch break, and then an afternoon visit to another clinic or hospital. The evenings were left open, to be reserved for delegates' "free time," including visiting tourist attractions and souvenir shopping.

This rhythm, which mirrored a standard schedule of official institutional practices in the West—rigidly structured meetings between 9 A.M. and 5 P.M., with evenings "off" or reserved for formal events—did not allot specific time for informal exchanges and the development of personal relations with local Russians. The organization of time according to the Western logic of interaction not only limited the kind of knowledge the delegates would find and the kinds of relationships they would develop; as I show below, it also led the delegation unwittingly to reassert their hierarchical status vis-à-vis local Russians.

The incommensurability of this structuring of time in the Russian setting emerged most vividly at the end of one morning's clinic tour, when the chief doctor of the clinic invited the delegation into her office "for a cup of tea." Such rituals are an important way in which Russians offer hospitality; at every encounter the foreign delegation had with local Russians, an invitation to "sit at the table" concluded the official segment of the meeting. By offering a moment of commensality, these rituals also provide the opportunity to shift the tenor of interactions to a less official mode of engagement. Although rituals of "sitting at the table" are a virtual imperative for Russians receiving guests in any capacity,[23] the length of time they consume, the degree of intimacy they involve, and the kind of communication they enable differ from occasion to occasion.

Russians often view the ritual as an opportunity to transcend hierarchical lines of status and cultivate a degree of intimacy with their guests. Supervisors, for example, often refuse to sit at the table with their subordinates. The "play" of these rituals—their indeterminate outcomes—represents what anthropologists see as the improvised, strategic negotiation of relationships in daily practice. Although the form of engagement is ritualized, the work these rituals do in forging ties is not determined in advance, and it holds the possibility that a more enduring sense of trust and obligation may emerge through the reciprocal exchanges begun "at the table."[24]

For the foreign delegates, by contrast, the organization of time and space during the tour was guided by a utilitarian logic: The purpose of the tour was to gain information, and the "receptions" that Russians offered were viewed as a quaint but insignificant procedure in substantive terms. The official component of this particular morning's clinic tour ended close to the time the delegates had scheduled for lunch, and their next appointment was in just over an hour in another part of the city. When the chief doctor invited the delegation to her office "for tea," the leader of the consultants hesitated, and then conferred with her translator: "Will there be a substantial amount of food, so that we can basically eat lunch here, or will it be something merely symbolic?" The translator conveyed the question, and the embarrassed chief doctor admitted that she was not prepared to feed lunch to the eight-person delegation.

The delegation leader then politely declined the offer of tea and explained that they would need to proceed on because they had another appointment in the afternoon. She then asked if the chief doctor knew of any restaurants in the area where they could eat. Taken completely aback, the chief doctor flushed and shook her head—the question was embarrassing, inasmuch as few Russians in the mid-1990s could afford to eat at restaurants, and most had almost no knowledge of where they even existed on the city landscape. The consultants' refusal to partake in the ritual of sitting at the table, and the request for advice about restaurants, emphasized their distance from and disinterest in forging personal relations with their Russian counterparts. The translator shuffled the group onto the bus.

The delegates' view of themselves as provocateurs, as experts equipped with the knowledge of progressive solutions to address Russian women's needs in health care, thus limited the methods they undertook for engaging with Russian public health experts. Their confidence in their own expertise led them to believe that they were competent to judge the local setting, to know what to look for and how to go about finding the relevant information for improving women's health needs. Yet as I suggested above, the provocateur stance precluded the creation of trusting relations gained from informal involvement with Russians, and thus constrained the kinds of insights they would gain. In addition to organizing time according to a logic of Western cultural procedures, the delegation's stance as provocateurs also led them to assert and maintain communicative control over the conversations they had with Russian officials.

In the following excerpt from my fieldnotes, I relate the delegation's tour of an outpatient women's consultation center that provides prenatal care and family planning services in Saint Petersburg. They were escorted around the center by the chief doctor. After viewing the premises, they met with him and his assistant in a conference room of the clinic. In this discussion, the consultants attempted to elicit a list of questions and educational topics that were of interest locally, and which could be addressed in the future lectures they would provide.

Here, the delegates' self-concept as experts and provocateurs led them to restrict the direction of conversation and limit the topics deemed relevant to issues the delegation had determined in advance to be of concern. In response to this strategy of engagement, the chief doctor, a candid and assertive man in his early 60s, spent the meeting struggling to wrest control over the conversation from the consultants. Being anxious to establish that he and his staff were competent professionals, he argued against the consultants' intentions to offer educational materials. To improve maternal health, it was technology and material assistance that Russian health care professionals needed, he insisted. The excerpt from my fieldnotes reads as follows:

> Consultant J: "Is there any topic in particular that you would find interesting and most important?"
>
> Chief doctor: "In terms of this question, we'll be glad to receive any gift."
>
> Consultant R: "We'll be coming back to run lectures over the next 3 years. What major topics would you like to have on prenatal care?"
>
> At this point, the chief doctor turned away from the delegation leader and addressed the Russian translator: "What kind of help? I need a good ultrasound apparatus. Tell them that."
>
> The translator responded first by clarifying the question to the chief doctor: "They're thinking about what kind of literature you'd want." She paused, saw he was refusing to answer in any other way, and turned to the consultants and translated: "I need a good ultrasound."
>
> Consultant D: "You don't have one now?"
>
> Chief doctor: "It's not working well. To diagnose early fetal placental insufficiency, there's only two dots, it's an old model and it doesn't work well. And we can't tell about congenital malformations either. We need a doplar. In terms of literature, I have been given this (shows them *The New Pregnancy Book*). We're now planning to write and publish our own. Do you have this in [your country]? Do all women get such books?"

Consultant R: "Our women get lots of literature."

Chief doctor: "We're trying to make a Russian variant, not to copy this one, but to develop our own."

Consultant R, to the group: "I'll try a different approaches to the question." To the chief doctor: "What are the biggest problems you face?"

Chief doctor: "Economic problems. We can't provide drugs for all women, medications for anemia, microcirculation drugs. We prescribe them, but if the women can't afford them, they don't buy them. With our own money, we bought iron and gave it out to pregnant women, but we've run out of it and there's no money to buy more."

Consultant K: "What would you like to learn more about to help pregnant women?"

Chief doctor: "To know this, we'd have to see how we could do it better, to see how things are in your country."

Consultant K: "Is there any problem you find particularly difficult?"

Chief doctor: "We try to solve all the problems we encounter. We try to do everything we can. The training of doctors here is very good. Everything is done well. The material conditions are bad. Women say, the doctor tells me what to do, but I can't fulfill the recommendations. I don't have the money. For many of these women, it's either food or medicine. So they buy food. We've bought some medications from the TMO and sold them at cost, and it's cheaper than at the pharmacies.[25] When we want a woman to get an ultrasound, here we have only an old machine. To diagnose a problem in time, she needs to go to another women's consultation center, and there it costs money. Even up to 30,000 [rubles]. In terms of our qualifications, they are high. We have good doctors here. I've worked for 25 years in a maternity hospital, other doctors we have here are also from the maternity hospitals. We are all qualified."

At this point, the consultants were getting ready to leave. The chief doctor mentioned that they give women some literature about pregnancy and consultant R asked him if she could get a copy. He had someone bring him examples, and explained that this copy was very old and not up-to-date. "We're planning on publishing some new literature, but as of yet haven't been able to finance it." The delegation leaders, R and K, thanked him for his time, and the chief doctor responded by saying, "Next time you come we can show you our work throughout the complex, and we'll have a bigger table (reception) for you."

The chief doctor then said to consultant R: "I would really like to be able to come and see what you do in your country, to be able to learn about things from seeing them myself."

Consultant R replied politely, as a formality: "Well, perhaps one day you will be able to come and visit us."

The chief doctor responded by breaking her rhetorical attempt to be polite by alluding to the financial impossibility of her suggestion: "No, I don't think I'll ever be able to get there."

Consultant R smiled and said, "Well, then we'll come here to you and tell you about what we do, and that way you'll come to learn about what we do."

In this exchange, the delegates systematically worked to limit the parameters of conversation regarding the needs of health care institutions. They were not satisfied with answers that claimed the need for technology or material resources, which were, in their view, answers that only proved the need for appropriate educational programming and correction. So they consistently sought to redirect the conversation back to possible lecture topics. Moreover, having thoroughly internalized the limitations of what their future intervention could do, they came to believe that information directly related to their intervention was the only knowledge relevant for them to gain.

Thus, when the chief doctor obstinately insisted that technological assistance was of paramount importance, the consultants had no need to confer with each other on how to proceed. They unconsciously harmonized their efforts to elicit a "useful" response by taking turns rephrasing the question in a variety of ways, as if the chief doctor did not understand their question. "Is there any topic in particular that you would find interesting and most important?" "Is there any problem you find particularly difficult?" "What major topics would you like to have on prenatal care?" "What would you like to learn more about to help pregnant women?" Yet, as the exchange the chief doctor had with the translator makes clear, he understood their agenda perfectly, and disagreed with it. At the same time, the chief doctor struggled to gain acknowledgment of his two interrelated concerns: that his clinic's primary needs were economic and not educational, and that he and his staff were knowledgeable, well trained, highly competent professionals.

Had the consultants not been so confident of their own expertise to solve problems in the post-socialist context, they might have searched for insights into local knowledge and strategies for improving women's health beyond appeals for economic assistance. One such moment occurred in this conversation when the chief doctor mentioned the clinic's hopes to develop its own educational literature for pregnant women. Referring to the English language text he had been given by a previous, British group, he stated: "We're trying to make a Russian variant, not to copy this one, but to develop our own." This remark differed significantly from most of his other comments, by breaking from his repeated requests for money and the proud reassertions of his staff's skills. It offered a conceptual entrance into his views on local needs and the creative endeavors he planned to undertake. In response to this comment, the consultants might have opened up a dialogue about the topics deemed relevant for Russian women to know; they could have inquired into the kinds of changes he anticipated would be necessary to write a text suitable for the local context. Yet in their perspective as provocateurs, such a logic of investigation did not occur to them.

Struggles over control of the conversation and the areas of relevance did not take place in every encounter. Many times, Russian experts respectfully received their international guests and dutifully answered their questions without attempting to transform the boundaries of discussion or take control of the dialogue. These exchanges usually unfolded as one-way interviews, with consultants asking questions and local officials offering brief answers and then waiting for the next question. In such cases, Russian health experts did not resist the framework of conversation or its defined topics because they had no expectation that the "foreigners" could ever "understand our life." They held little, if any, hope that they would reap significant benefits from these now ritualized encounters with international delegations, as several doctors in one hospital told me again and again. Indeed, the very significance and purpose of the interaction had become transformed. It was no longer seen as a mutually beneficial encounter for dialogue and understanding, instead, it was a moment for meta-performances about global difference.

Health care administrators and providers engaged in a complex presentation of the collective self during these encounters, viewing the meetings with foreigners as a time for establishing "who we Russians are" and "what we are capable of. "They would offer impeccable hospitality, and, as individuals and as an institution, they would model Russia's "high culture," "civilization," and professional expertise. They felt compelled by these exchanges to assert and perform self-respect and dignity.

This perceived need was evident, for example, at the outpatient clinic described above. When the chief doctor promised that the next time consultants came, "we'll have a bigger table (reception) for you," he indicated that this was a moment not only to petition for help but also to offer hospitality. In trying to manage the fine line between his sense of poverty and his desire to establish his clinic's competence, he also felt the culturally embedded obligation to maintain his self-respect by offering his guests a lavish welcome. That meeting represented profound stakes for the chief doctor's sense of professionalism and identity, and for his hopes to improve women's health through his clinic.

Anthropological Strategies

The traditional anthropological stance, based on the self-concept of novice or student of the local setting, sets flexible boundaries regarding the organization of time and space in the field. The net is cast as widely as possible in determining sites of relevance, persons who may become authoritative interlocutors, and modes of communication. The anthropologist aims to learn about what is considered authoritative knowledge in a local setting, and how such knowledge emerges in the context of specific kinds of relationships. By moving in unofficial circles and accessing people through informal, personal contacts rather than solely through official, bureaucratic channels, the anthropological stance afforded me knowledge about women's health care in Saint Petersburg that was unavailable to consultants.

For example, there were unofficial initiatives under way in Saint Petersburg that paralleled WHO's commitment to viewing health and social well-being as integrally connected. In the course of my research after the consultants left Russia, I met with midwives who worked semi-legally, attending home births in the shadow of the public health care system and holding prenatal consultations in public bath houses. Like WHO, these home birth communities criticized the institutional management of birth and sought a more holistic approach to childbearing and women's health. I came to see how their home births and critiques of technology not only echoed critiques developed abroad but also differed from them, emerging in response to the post-Soviet Russian context. I gained access to such groups by partially releasing control over the organization of time and space in my engagements and following the lead of my Russian interlocutors. Our discussions were interspersed among the rhythms of caring for women, sitting in the bath, enjoying the rituals of sitting at the table.

By developing personal relationships, I also gained insights into the views of health providers in the state hospitals where WHO reforms were taking place. At most of these sites, providers displayed gracious hospitality and took pains to show professional competence to me. But the openness they perceived from the anthropological stance, my disposition as a "student" of their society rather than as an "expert," led them to speak candidly and personally with me. I learned of the dilemmas they faced in their daily work and about the ethical quandaries they faced as members of a reforming Russian society in which the realm of health care no longer followed authoritarian principles. Women's health care providers were more and more being confronted with demands from patients. Some welcomed these patient initiatives, but others perceived such demands to be medically unsound and threatening to their professional authority.

Ethical questions concerning the boundaries of expert authority and patients' self-determination mattered deeply to these health providers, and they often felt frustrated due to their uncertainty about the legal and political implications of their clinical decisions. They would have welcomed the opportunity to discuss such issues with global colleagues if provided a safe atmosphere in which to do so. But meetings with self-conceived provocateurs, who had arrived in Russia with predetermined notions of the kinds of changes the locals needed, largely precluded such conversations.

Attempts to "Apply" Anthropology

At the time of the delegation's needs assessment tour, I was conducting independent fieldwork in Saint Petersburg's maternity hospitals and women's outpatient clinics. I had also agreed to act as a temporary consultant to WHO's European Regional Office, which was encouraging Saint Petersburg's participation in maternal health care reforms through the framework of the global Healthy Cities Project. The responsibilities associated with this consulting work were minimal. I sent periodic reports to the agency describing the process of local reform in women's health care and offering insights into local culture and practices that I considered relevant for enhancing the collaborative process. There was no mechanism in place for incorporating my insights or suggestions into the agency's work; anthropological knowledge was considered interesting "background" material alone.[26]

When the WHO-affiliated delegation came to Saint Petersburg for the needs assessment tour, I expected the consultants to strive to gain as broad an understanding as possible of health needs and social change in Saint Petersburg. I believed my role was to increase their exposure to local experiences and expand their understanding of local developments beyond what they would otherwise learn given their limitations as non-Russian speaking outsiders visiting for a week. The anthropological stance provided few direct insights into concrete steps that could improve women patients' self-determination, but it led me to believe that expanding providers' opportunities to express themselves in safe, confidential, and informal contexts would entail a significant step toward illustrating the value of self-determination and making its realization appear possible to a group that often expressed deep skepticism about such ideals. I thus hoped to facilitate informal interaction and open, frank discussions, and to use my personal relationships with the health care providers to facilitate dialogue and debate—beginning with a sympathetic stance toward their situation.

I offered to set up evening-hour meetings with physicians who were implementing the reforms WHO recommended in the model maternity institutions, so that the consultants could hear about their experiences and critiques. I also invited the consultants to meet with several local health experts whose work seemed to me to be innovative, and whose ideology about health appeared to dovetail with WHO's concerns with social well-being. I urged the consultants to meet with two acquaintances of mine in particular, individuals who were involved with community and professional education regarding infant development and child sexual abuse, respectively. Though both of these topics were far afield from the issue of childbirth, I believed the individuals' work would prove instructive to the delegates, inasmuch as they aspired to address issues that, like women's rights in childbirth, had not been part of Soviet-era public health concerns, were still considered marginal topics for discussion, and emphasized matters of individual social well-being.

Meeting with any of these public health activists, I argued to the consultants, would offer examples of the kinds of local innovations being developed at nongovernmental levels, and of the struggles that pioneering health activists confronted when trying to implement innovative projects. It would expose the consultants to more voices and stories than they could have experienced through official bureaucratic meetings. And perhaps, I thought, it might lead the consultants to enter into new kinds of relationships with Russian health care providers, forms of engagement that seemed to be crucial for building trust in Russian society. Such relations would be based on channels of informal relations—personal acquaintances—and would assume an openness to personal forms of obligation, in contrast to official and bureaucratically formed relations.

The consultants rejected my urgings and invitations to set up meetings with the activists I knew. My suggestions were viewed as a time-consuming digression, an ineffective use of time. “Chatting” with a range of randomly selected people seemed irrational from the point of view of implementing change; such meetings did not relate systematically to a defined set of goals and tasks that could be implemented in a project format. The leader of the delegation explained: “Listen, there are a lot of interesting groups out there doing a lot of good work. We have a mandate, and that means we can’t just run all over the place. We’ve come here with a specific mandate, and that’s what we must fulfill.”

The “mandate” she was referring to was, of course, the funded intervention approved by a foreign bilateral development agency. Outsiders to Russia—the global consultants and their funders—were the ones equipped to determine what was needed locally. Her comment entailed an argument that the delegation’s goal was not to learn about the internal dynamics of Russian society or local strategies of change in health care but to provide information to local health providers about a specific realm of women’s health care. They had come to Saint Petersburg not to learn but to provide expertise on a topic with universal relevance.

In addition, the consultants were sensitive to the fact that encounters would implicate them in new obligations, and they sought to strictly define and control the boundaries of obligation they would accrue toward local communities. Consultant J explained the ethics behind her refusal to meet my acquaintances: “These people you want us to meet [will] want something from us, some kind of help. I’m not sure what we can give them. It’s very problematic to meet people and raise their expectations that you’re going to do something for them, and then you can’t deliver. That’s worse than not meeting with them at all.” Their stance as provocateurs resulted in engagements made from a conceptual and interpersonal distance, and minimized the acquisition of social debt. It also precluded anthropological involvement in the work of provocateurs—making expertise in local experiences, culture, and social change irrelevant.

The anthropological stance was problematic to these consultants because it forced them to recognize the difference between global and local settings—differences in cultural, historical, and political-economic terms. In considering themselves as experts competent to provoke change for women’s empowerment, global activists have tended to minimize questions of how the local context differs from the context of own struggles. In so doing, they have often come to view the Russians as stuck back in time, occupying an earlier stage of history that Westerners have transcended. "They're where we were 25 years ago," the consultants announced again and again while touring Saint Petersburg's hospitals. Some of the procedures surrounding childbirth that Russian providers routinely employed—such as having women go through labor without companions, relying heavily on technologies such as episiotomies, and enforcing scheduled feedings for infants—did resemble the procedures Western hospitals had used and abandoned following pressure from consumers and women's groups in the late 1970s.

However, the consultants failed to explore what kinds of differences existed between the home context of their personal experience and the post-socialist, Russian context—how the experiences of severe economic constraint, the socialist structure of health care, and the breakdown of the socialist system affected providers' relations with women's health care. In neglecting these differences, the consultants also failed to consider the impact of the development framework itself as a context of change, and the role of power and inequality in their own intervention.

Conclusion

An analysis of projects by Western agencies aiming to improve women's status in the former socialist world offers an illuminating entry into the broader processes of conceptualizing, promoting, and enabling democratizing kinds of reforms in this region. This is true despite the fact that gender issues have been ignored by the majority of political and economic initiatives undertaken by American and European advisers, and despite the fact that gender issues account for only a tiny share of the overall funding allocated to former socialist societies by Western sources. The increasing popularity of women's issues among Western organizations working in the former socialist world reveals how democratic change becomes equated with social justice and promises of inclusion.

Moreover, because projects focusing on gender are more likely to embrace critical or radical visions of democratic change and prioritize the creation of equality over other aspects of democracy (e.g., markets), gender-based initiatives are efforts wherein innovative methods of engagement, dialogue, and collaboration might be expected. My goal has been to raise the issue of whether and how the link between gender and democracy is transforming the practice of cross-cultural engagement.

In the "needs assessment" processes described here, both the provocateurs and the anthropologist were constrained by inadequate methods and theories about their engagement in Russia. The stance of provocateur constrained the consultants' encounter with locals in at least two ways. It led the consultants to determine the organization of time and space in which interactions would take place, and to limit discussion to certain narrow topics that could fit into training workshops being planning.[27]

Through these modes of engagement, I have argued, the consultants missed opportunities to hear local perspectives, to understand the complexities of local problems, and to grasp the logic of locally devised solutions. My point is not that experience and expertise developed in Western contexts cannot be valuable for post-socialist actors. Rather, I am arguing that technical expertise on topics such as "public health" alone is not sufficient for devising solutions in a local setting. Knowledge of the local culture, history, and political-economic context, and sensitivity to the power implications of global interactions, are important components of transferring knowledge in democratic ways.

The consultants' self-conception as experts—what I have called their provocateur stance—recreated hierarchical relationships between consultants and local experts that resulted in combative or defensive responses, rather than working toward dialogue and mutual understanding. Russians felt proud or embarrassed, relieved or anxious about reviews of their work by an international agency; but they rarely accepted the agency's recommendations as authoritative. The delegates' dismissal of local concerns made the issues of democracy and women's rights in birth seem untenable, given pressing local economic constraints. Ultimately, the Russians redefined the very purpose of global engagements, from that of participating in collaborative exchanges for beneficial change to those of offering hospitality, showing "high culture," and deriving professional and national self-respect.

The anthropological stance, with its emphasis on holism and cultural relativism, afforded me access to a range of people and projects concerning women's health in Saint Petersburg. But it did not lead to the design of concrete steps for collaborative endeavors. The health care providers I met were eager to share their perspectives and ideas on women's health, but they hoped that their cooperation with me would bring something in return. To only talk about the dire conditions of women's health, of illness, and of national suffering seemed woefully insufficient—and even gratuitous and self-absorbed. My interlocutors had questions about medicine and public health in the West that I could not answer, and they sought assistance in a range of forms that I, in my capacity as an anthropologist, could not provide.

Employing anthropological models of research and engagement in designing projects for gender equality and democracy carries risks. My research, for example, involved the "snowballing" technique of accessing knowledge through acquaintances of acquaintances. This approach, when applied to a development or intervention framework, carries the risks of nepotism and corruption.[28] The moral obligations of exchange that arise with even the most preliminary encounter in local communities are certainly not easy to manage; in some cases, official and personal forms of reciprocity may be called for, and global actors may need to adapt their modes of interaction both to convey respect and to learn about the local context. Although the anthropological stance does not offer simple or straightforward answers for how to organize our engagements in more equitable ways, it does challenge us to address the issue, not to use it as a means of avoiding encounters altogether.

Considering such questions of methodological engagement is crucial for democratizing the interactions between Western researchers and practitioners and the citizens of former socialist states. It is necessary to find women located at a variety of sites, not just those easily available to Western visitors, and to learn multiple *ways of hearing* about their experiences. Westerners must conceptualize collaboration not just as the delivery of professional expertise but first and foremost as the building of relationships based on shared understandings. One step in this direction might be to include viewing the act of dialogue and debate as a democratizing project in and of itself—and even as a required step in developing future collaborative projects. Realizing gender empowerment and democratization all around the globe may first require developing mutual understanding and reciprocity.

Notes

1. Susan Gal, "Gender in the Post-Socialist Transition: The Abortion Debate in Hungary," *East European Politics and Societies* 8, no. 2 (1994): 256–86. Susan Gal and Gail Kligman, eds., *Reproducing Gender: Politics, Publics, and Everyday Life after Socialism* (Princeton, N.J.: Princeton University Press, 2000). Susan Gal and Gail Kligman, *The Politics of Gender after Socialism: A Comparative-Historical Essay* (Princeton, N.J.: Princeton University Press, 2000).

2. Nanette Funk and Magda Mueller, eds., *Gender Politics and Post-Communism: Reflections from Eastern Europe and the Former Soviet Union* (New York: Routledge, 1993); Susan Gal, "Feminism and Civil Society," in *Transitions, Environments, Translations.,* ed. J. Scott, C. Kaplan, and D. Keates (New York: Routledge, 1997). Peggy Watson, "Eastern Europe's Silent Revolution: Gender," *Sociology: Journal of the British*

Sociological Association 27, no. 3 (1993): 471–87. Peggy Watson, "The Rise of Masculinism in Eastern Europe," *New Left Review* 198 (1993): 71–82.

3. Gal and Kligman, *Reproducing Gender.* Also see Peggy Watson, "Civil Society and the Politics of Difference in Eastern Europe," in *Transitions, Environments, Translations: Feminisms in International Politics,* ed. Joan Wallach Scott, Cora Kaplan, and Debra Keates (New York: Routledge, 1997).

4. David Abramson, "A Critical Look at NGOs and Civil Society as Means to an End in Uzbekistan," *Human Organization* 58, no. 3 (1999): 240–50. Marta Bruno, "Playing the Co-operation Game," in *Surviving Post-Socialism: Local Strategies and Regional Responses in Eastern Europe,* ed. Sue Bridger and Frances Pine (London: Routledge, 1997). Julie Dawn Hemment, "Gender, NGOs and the Third Sector in Russia: An Ethnography of Post-Socialist Civil Society," Ph.D. dissertation, Cornell University, Ithaca, N.Y., 2000. Michele Rivkin-Fish, "Health Development Meets the End of State Socialism: Visions of Democratization, Women's Health, and Social Well-Being for Contemporary Russia," *Culture, Medicine, and Psychiatry* 24, no. 1 (2000): 77–100. Janine R. Wedel, *Collision and Collusion: The Strange Case of Western Aid to Eastern Europe 1989–98* (New York: Saint Martin's Press, 1998).

5. Igor Semenovich Kon, *The Sexual Revolution in Russia: From the Age of the Czars to Today* (New York: Free Press, 1995). Rivkin-Fish, "Health Development." Such antipathy is not limited to conservative elements of society. When Western feminist scholars approached late socialist and post-socialist societies with the goals of critiquing women's marginalization and highlighting women's particular experiences, they often found their concerns with gender-based inequality rebuffed by local women. See Nanette Funk, "Introduction: Women and Post-Communism," in *Gender Politics and Post-Communism,* ed. Funk and Mueller; Funk and Mueller, *Gender Politics and Post-Communism.* Beth Holmgren, "Bug Inspectors and Beauty Queens: The Problems of Translating Feminism into Russian," in *Post-Communism and the Body Politic,* ed. Ellen E Berry (New York: New York University Press, 1995). Tatyana Tolstaya, "Notes from Underground: Soviet Women: Walking the Tightrope," *New York Review of Books,* May 31, 1990, 3–6.

6. James Ferguson, *The Anti-Politics Machine: "Development," Depoliticization, and Bureaucratic Power in Lesotho* (Minneapolis: University of Minnesota Press, 1994); Arturo Escobar, *Encountering Development: The Making and Unmaking of the Third World* (Princeton, N.J.: Princeton University Press, 1995); Wedel, *Collision and Collusion.*

7. Robert Emerson et al., *Writing Ethnographic Fieldnotes* (Chicago: University of Chicago Press, 1995).

8. The centrality of questions of global and local power to anthropological studies of culture was inspired by scholars of colonialism, Marxism, and feminism. For some important texts that prompted these developments, see Talal Asad, *Anthropology and The Colonial Encounter* (New York: Humanities Press, 1973); Frances E Mascia-Lees, Patricia Sharpe, and Colleen Ballerino Cohen, "The Postmodernist Turn in Anthropology: Cautions from a Feminist Perspective," *Signs: Journal of Women in Culture & Society* 15, no. 1 (1989): 7–33; and Michael T. Taussig, *Shamanism, Colonialism, and the Wild Man: A Study in Terror and Healing* (Chicago: University of Chicago Press, 1986).

9. It is recognized that an anthropologist who becomes adopted into a community enters relations of exchange, reciprocity, and obligation, but these relations are seen as the individual responsibility of the anthropologist, to be fulfilled in a private manner by

the fieldworker. Obligations to the community of engagement have not been conceptualized as sociopolitical, i.e., as involving the need to participate in or initiate struggles for liberation, freedom, from oppression, etc. Nancy Scheper-Hughes, *Death without Weeping: the Violence of Everyday Life in Brazil* (Berkeley: University of California Press, 1992).

10. Merrill Singer, "Community Centered Praxis: Toward an Alternative Nondominative Applied Anthropology," *Human Organization* 53, no. 4 (1994): 336–44. Merrill Singer and Margaret R. Weeks, "Preventing AIDS in Communities of Color: Anthropology and Social Formation," *Human Organization* 55, no. 4 (1996): 488–92. John Van Willigen, *Applied Anthropology: An Introduction,* rev. ed. (Westport, Conn.: Bergin & Garvey, 1993).

11. I do not mean to suggest here that Russians were always only in the position of responding to, and not initiating or taking charge of, interactions. However, in the context of the day-to-day tours and meetings described here, Westerners were the ones imposing themselves on locals, setting the agenda, arranging meetings, etc.

12. Healthy Cities Project, "St. Petersburg Support Project" (unpublished), World Health Organization, Regional Office for Europe, Copenhagen, 1993.

13. Healthy Cities Project, "St. Petersburg," 4.

14. John Ashton and Howard Seymour, *The New Public Health: The Liverpool Experience* (Philadelphia: Open University Press, 1988). Boston Women's Health Book Collective, *Our Bodies, Ourselves* (New York: Simon & Schuster, 1973). Kenneth W. Newell, "Selective Primary Health Care: The Counter Revolution," *Social Science and Medicine* 26, no. 9 (1988): 903–6. Susan B. Rifkin and Gil Walt, "Why Health Improves: Defining the Issues Concerning 'Comprehensive Primary Health Care' and 'Selective Primary Health Care,'" *Social Science and Medicine* 23, no. 6 (1986): 559–66.

15. Ivan Illich, *Limits to Medicine: Medical Nemesis: The Expropriation of Health* (London: Marion Boyars, 1976).

16. Boston Women's Health Book Collective, *Our Bodies, Ourselves.* Barbara Katz Rothman, *In Labor: Women and Power in the Birthplace* (New York: Norton, 1982). For critical anthropological studies in this vein, see Robbie Davis-Floyd, *Birth as an American Rite of Passage* (Berkeley: University of California Press, 1992); and Emily Martin, *The Woman in the Body: A Cultural Analysis of Reproduction* (Boston: Beacon Press, 1987).

17. Links between Saint Petersburg and the World Health Organization developed in several directions at this time. The city became part of the European Regional branch of the Healthy Cities Project, a network of cities throughout Europe that have made political commitments to WHO's ideas of "health for all" and multisectoral efforts to promote health. Saint Petersburg's participation in the Healthy Cities Project raised its visibility to development organizations interested in promoting democracy and stability in the aftermath of socialism. The project I analyze here built on the contacts established with WHO through the Health Cities Project. It was affiliated with WHO but received funding from an independent, bilateral development organization.

18. Matt Bivens, "Aboard the Gravy Train," *Harper's Magazine,* August 1997, 69–76, cited in Abramson, "Critical Look at NGOs."

19. The reasons for this have to do with issues of Western funders' needs to demonstrate accountability and to remain external to politics, rather than due to objective indicators of local needs. Ferguson, *Anti-Politics Machine.*

20. Ferguson, *Anti-Politics Machine;* Escobar, *Encountering Development.*

21. Rivkin-Fish, "Health Development."

22. Ferguson, *Anti-Politics;* Rivkin-Fish, "Health Development."

23. Dale Pesman, *Russia and Soul: An Exploration* (Ithaca, N.Y.: Cornell University Press, 2000).

24. Pierre Bourdieu, *Outline of a Theory of Practice* (New York: Cambridge University Press, 1977).

25. TMOs, *territorial'nia meditsinskaia organizatsiia,* are an administrative unit within the city's public health system.

26. In important, pioneering study of anthropological contributions to development programs, Judith Justice showed that the mere availability of knowledge about local culture and politics is insufficient for improving development work. I agree with her argument that unless mechanisms are put in place for instrumentalizing anthropological insights and including them in the design of development projects, they are unlikely to affect on the success of interventions. Judith Justice, *Policies, Plans and People: Culture and Health Development in Nepal* (Berkeley: University of California Press, 1986).

27. Even when Russians requested discussion on topics that interested them, e.g., the technical methods by which Western doctors performed cesarean sections, consultants refused to devote workshop time to this issue, which they felt would lend further legitimacy to the technological bias of local health providers.

28. Wedel, *Collision and Collusion.*

14

Strategizing Gender and Development: Action Research and Ethnographic Responsibility in the Russian Provinces

Julie Hemment

In recent years, particularly following the 1998 collapse of the Russian economy, the Western-sponsored project of democratization has come under intense scrutiny. Concepts that have undergirded Western aid—"transition," "democratization," and "civil society"—have been critiqued for their universalism and ethnocentrism. Furthermore, recent scholarly work during this period has emphasized the role of Western and international agents in the failures of the aid effort in Eastern Europe and the former Soviet Union.

These revisionist accounts offer an important corrective to the sanctimonious tone of much self-representation of democratization, and their

This chapter is based on 19 months of ethnographic fieldwork, conducted in Moscow, Tver', and Pskov between 1995 and 2001. The author is grateful to the Cornell University Graduate School, the Einaudi Center for International Studies at Cornell University, and the Cornell University Peace Studies Program for financial support. For their helpful commentaries on this chapter, the author is particularly grateful to Armine Ishkanian, Rebecca Kay, Kathleen Kuehnast, Carol Nechemias, and Michele Rivkin-Fish.

importance is not to be underestimated. However, these critiques may have had some unintended effects. In recent years, liberal triumphalism has been displaced by talk of how Russia is "lost" and is a "failed project."[1] This disturbing narrative switch surely has potential policy implications, and it could pave the way for scaling back support and the eventual withdrawal of aid agencies from Russia altogether, a development that would have serious implications for Russian nongovernmental groups and for the (mostly) women who work for them.

As an anthropologist who has worked with Russian women's groups as both advocate and scholar, I am deeply concerned at this prospect. Although it is crucially important to bring a critical lens to these interventions and processes, we must be mindful of how our critiques are deployed. Whatever the failings of Western aid, Russian women's groups have achieved a great deal with the intellectual and material resources they have received. They make use of the concepts and terms of democratization, which continue to circulate in Russia, appropriating them and giving them local inflection and nuance. I propose that at this crucial juncture, there is an increasingly pressing need for investigations of these local meanings so that we can reassess and reevaluate the status of civil society in Russia. Attention to local meanings and constructions of events can help us to understand where policy has not worked; drawing out the unexpected and unintended outcomes of development initiatives can give us insight into ways to proceed.

In this chapter, I tell the story of Western aid from the perspective of one provincial Russian women's group, presenting insights gained in the course of an action research project I undertook with the group during the period 1997–98. It is a story that I hope will be of benefit to practitioners and scholars alike. Moving beyond the dichotomy of colonization or liberation, I highlight some of the unexpected moments, the creativity, and the dynamism that takes place at the periphery.[2] Over the years, I have followed the group as it entered into its first interactions with Western-identified donor agencies. When I first made contact with the Russian women's group in 1995, it was determinedly independent. That is, group members refused to register the group with the local authorities, were reluctant to formalize their activities into an organization, and kept a skeptical distance from the world of grants and projects.

By 1997, when I returned to the group, I found it at a crossroads, contemplating the changes in the rapidly transforming nongovernmental field. In 1998, I worked with members of the group in an action research project, which resulted in the decision to set up a crisis center in the city. This project has brought women members into contact with a variety of state and nonstate agents, both Western identified and local. As I have followed the group and its shifting identifications, I have become aware that Russian activists make use of the democratization apparatus selectively, drawing tactically on its resources. By so doing, they have been able to use these resources creatively and to root Western models in local concerns.

In exploring this topic, this chapter poses the following ethical and methodological questions: What role should scholars play and how should we position ourselves in relation to local groups and international donors? How can we best deploy the insights that sustained contact with local actors have yielded in a way that does not betray the trust they have placed in us? How can scholars achieve better dialogue with practitioners? Finally, where can we locate and generate new forms of collaboration, beyond seeing civil society as the only desirable outcome? In so doing, the chapter moves toward a theorization of gender and post-socialism that is determinedly global, reflexive (i.e., scrutinizing the contradictions of export models and acknowledging Western researchers' own role as actors in the transition), and practice oriented.

Russian Women's Nongovernmental Organizations and International Aid

Since the late 1980s, when it first became possible to set up independent clubs and associations in Russia, women have been prominent in the emergent nongovernmental sphere.[3] They have been drawn to it for a number of reasons. Implicitly or explicitly, many of the women who work for what are now known as nongovernmental organizations (NGOs) do so as a form of protest against the direction of political and economic reform in Russia. In the late 1990s, their activism, or *obshchestvennaia rabota* (societal work) was often a response to the perceived immorality and disorder of the market. Contra liberal democratic civil society discourses, democratization and the liberalizing economic reforms of the early 1990s marked the demotion of women as a group in Russia and post-socialist countries. Democratization signaled women's loss, not their gain.[4]

For all the very serious flaws and contradictions of officially proclaimed equality, the state socialist system did not relegate women to the private sphere. Although women were clustered in less prestigious professions and underrepresented in decision-making structures, women as a group were represented in the public sphere. Mikhail Gorbachev's *perestroika* reforms brought about crucial shifts in what Katherine Verdery calls the "gender regime of socialism."[5] These were further entrenched by the market-oriented reforms undertaken by Russia's first democratic governments, which resulted in the sharp exclusion of women from key aspects of public life—notably from formal politics and the new business sector. In post-socialist Russia, political power (*vlast'*) is encoded as a masculine domain. This is explicitly and implicitly acknowledged in the pronouncements of politicians and ordinary people alike. In response to this, women have found a niche in the nongovernmental sphere.

Support for women's groups has made up a proportionally small, and yet ideologically significant portion of Western civil society aid. Since they set up in Russia in the early to middle 1990s, major foundations such as Ford, Eurasia, MacArthur, and more recently the Soros Foundation's Open Society Institute have begun to prioritize women's issues as part of their broad mandate to strengthen civil society in Russia. This aid signals some of the interesting gendered realignments of the post-socialist period. Western-identified foundations appeared to be ideal interlocutors for women's groups. Their goals of democratization and civil society development seemed to be in tune with the ideals and aspirations that brought women to this activity. However, the reality has proven to be rather different than the promise. Foundations arrived with a distinct notion of what organizations should look like, and they brought new technologies of organizational development. Their presence has significantly changed the face of women's organizing in Russia. Formerly loose groups and clubs have been encouraged to formalize as "NGOs," to register, and to professionalize.

Concern about these processes has been raised by insiders and outsiders alike, in Southern or developing-country contexts as well as in the post-socialist one.[6] "NGO-ization" has contributed to the formation of new hierarchies and allowed former elites to flourish, as some of the contributors to this volume have documented.[7] What is more, in many cases, it also signals the triumph of Washington- or Geneva-based agendas over local concerns. Certainly this is true of women's organizing in Russia and the post-socialist context; it is a part of the story that researchers including me have felt compelled to tell. However, if we pay close attention to what is happening on the ground, we will see that this is not the whole story. First, NGOs are diverse in status and form and their members are not solely elite. Second, although international aid certainly exerts a powerful influence on group activities, it does not determine them. In the nongovernmental sphere,

Russian women draw on international aid to strategize and make sense of the realignments in their lives and to articulate a way forward. What comes into view if we shift the lens?

Zhenskii Svet: A Story from the Periphery

Zhenskii Svet (Women's Light) is a small, university-based women's group dedicated to women's education and consciousness raising.[8] It was founded in the provincial city Tver' in 1991, long before the arrival of Western foundations, in the first wave of independent organizing in Russia. I first made contact with the group in 1995 when undertaking preliminary research for my dissertation. I was immediately captivated by its founder, Larissa, a professor of sociology, and by her account of the group. She explained to me that the group was explicitly feminist, and explicitly informal. Both facts made it unusual, even anomalous.

Like most provincial groups, Zhenskii Svet existed on the periphery of grants and funding. Unlike most other groups, however, it retained a commitment to its informal, diffuse status. The group was not registered with the local authorities, and it had no bank account, no office space, or telephone. It had managed to achieve a great deal with very little. Over the years, the group had run a number of socially oriented projects for women—such as free health consultations and free computing courses for unemployed women. As Larissa explained to me with a smile, "all we have done, we have done on the basis of enthusiasm."

I chose to base my research with Zhenskii Svet for two reasons. First, galvanized both by the work of development anthropologists,[9] and by debates about feminism between "Eastern" and "Western" women scholars,[10] I sought critical interlocutors in my investigation of the transformations of women's community activism. Zhenskii Svet's anomalous status—its distance from the world of grants and funding and commitment to independence—signaled an interesting perspective on the transformations of the nongovernmental sphere I sought to map. The second reason for choosing the group was that its members were friendly to the methodological concerns I brought to my project.

As I planned my research, I became increasingly preoccupied with the following question: In a context so sensitive to Western intervention, when part of my project was to examine Western intervention itself, how could I go about this in a way that was both sensitive to the people I was working with and also self-aware, in a way that accepted and did not write out my own role and agenda? Anthropology is distinct as a discipline through its commitment to a particular methodology, participant observation. This methodological approach places the researcher in face-to-face contact with the "others" who are the object of study. It necessitates immersion in "daily life" (those banal and taken-for-granted practices that neither local people nor most social scientists deem worthy of commentary). The ideal typical participant observer deliberately opens herself to experience and interactions that are locally determined.

According to the interpretivist tradition (which remains the compass by which most anthropologists navigate), the task is then to make sense of and to represent the "native's point of view." Although there was much about it that appealed to me, the practice of participant observation raised as many questions as it answered. It did little to assist me think through issues of power in the exchange between researcher and researched. Although many anthropologists since the 1980s have raised similar concerns about the politics of ethnographic research and representation,[11] I found few methodological suggestions.[12]

Participatory action research (PAR) methodology suggested itself as a possible answer. PAR is a method for the social investigation of problems that involves the participation of a community group in problem identification and solving. It is designed to be an educational process for both researcher and participants, who analyze the structural causes of problems that they identify through collective discussion and interaction. Finally, it is a way for researchers and the local group to move toward collective action to bring about social change.[13]

In its respect for local knowledge, for the expertise of local people, PAR seemed to represent a way of stepping out of the "Western knower" role that I found so objectionable and that was so widespread in Russia at the time.[14] What is more, it offered a way to explore the tensions of the civil society–building project by engaging these tensions. Larissa and the members of the Zhenskii Svet group were receptive to my project, interested in collaboration, and invited me to join the group when I returned to Russia to conduct my dissertation research. In this way, I located my field site. In 1997–98, I lived and worked in Tver' (teaching at the university and attending meetings of Zhenskii Svet and other NGOs) and made frequent trips to women's groups in Moscow and other provincial cities. After 10 months of participant observation, I initiated a joint research project wherein we discussed the group's trajectory and formulated new projects. It was in this context that the decision to set up a crisis center was made.

Participant observation enabled me to get to know group members and afforded me insight into the meaning the group held for them. The meetings of Zhenskii Svet were public, and though its nucleus was made up of Larissa's acquaintances, new and unaffiliated women showed up quite regularly, having heard of the group through newspaper articles, radio interviews, or the grapevine. The group comprised women of different ages and motivations, though they were almost exclusively of the intelligentsia. First, there were Larissa's students and ex-students, young women mentees, who were drawn by her energy and eager to spend more time with her. Having been newly trained in social work, sociology, psychology, they were all too aware that few employment opportunities awaited them in the provinces and came to the group in search of direction.

The majority of group members were adult women, mostly between the ages of 30 and 55 years. Most were highly educated professionals, teachers, engineers, doctors, and journalists, who either remained clustered in poorly paid or unpaid state employment, or had been squeezed out of their jobs and were seeking new opportunities.[15] Whether married, divorced, or single, whether employed or unemployed, many of the women in the group felt that women suffered disproportionately in the new democratic Russia and that their position had worsened in the past several years. Although it was clear that both men and women were adversely affected by reforms (i.e., had lost their jobs or did not receive their salaries), many of them felt that it was left to women to pick up the pieces. These highly educated women—forced to scrimp, save, and draw on all their Soviet-era reserves of inventiveness and frugality—spoke with alarm of how their own and friends husbands were unable to adapt, and of how they thus found themselves the mainstay of their families' survival and maintenance.

The group offered these women companionship and support as they struggled to find solutions to their daily problems. It also offered a forum for discussion and debate, and as such was very welcome to women struggling to stay intellectually alive through the dull struggle of survival. Beyond this, it offered them a framework to make sense of the changes in their lives. Many of the women I spoke with did not share Larissa's feminist orientation. Although I never heard group members voice any antagonism toward feminism, perhaps out of respect for Larissa, some shied away from it on the grounds that it was "academic," and therefore not relevant, or comprehensible to them.

However, it was clear to me that whatever their interests and orientation, group attendance had caused many of the women to rethink and rearticulate their lives. One of the most striking ways in which Larissa had influenced women's thinking was in communicating the social construction of gender.

In her lectures, Larissa spoke of "social stereotypes" and "myths" of femininity that held women back, and she encouraged the women to explore these themes in their own lives. Several of the women in the group adopted what they called a "gender approach" (*gendernyi podkhod*) in their commentaries on the processes around them. Some members of the group spoke explicitly of the gendered effects of the market and of gender "discrimination." Furthermore, through the rubric of gender, individual women were able to formulate their own projects and plans. The group served as a launching pad for diverse initiatives that were directed toward women—the socially oriented projects I have mentioned. It is illuminating to consider one of these efforts.

Tamara, a doctor and one of the newest and most enthusiastic participants of the group, offered seminars on women's health. She was an assertive, practical woman in her mid-30s who had recently moved to Tver' from Siberia with her husband and young daughter. Theirs was a depressingly familiar post-socialist story. In Siberia, they had lived modestly but well. Then in 1995, shortly after she had completed her medical training, her engineer husband lost his job. They decided to sell their apartment and to move to Tver', his hometown, where economic conditions were less dire. In the first year of their stay in the city, they lost their life savings when the bank crashed and they were forced to move in with his parents. For more than a year, they lived together, tightly packed into a two-room apartment, and Tamara found herself uncomfortably dependent on her in-laws. In the lean post-socialist situation, she had struggled to find a professional niche; this was no mean feat for someone outside local networks of patronage and connection. She worked part time at one of the local hospitals, renting office space with another doctor and drawing a meager salary.

Tamara had learned about the existence of Zhenskii Svet through a newspaper article. She was inspired by the group's activities and its philosophy, and she quickly formed friendships with some of its other members. When I met her, Tamara was looking for a niche, a place to which she could bring her considerable energies and that would give her independence. "I'm not afraid of hard work," she told me, "the main thing is that I am committed to what I do." She dreamed of being able to bring about a unity between what she called her hobby (issues of women's health, the women's movement) and her career, and she longed to build on her seminars to achieve something more substantial.

Strategizing Development

As I explained above, group members had always been resistant to formalization. Larissa in particular was determined that Zhenskii Svet remained an independent *group,* or *club* (not organization). On the basis of their observations of both Moscow-based and local women's groups, the women of Zhenskii Svet were concerned about the influence of international agencies on community groups. They were disconcerted by the market logic that they saw was creeping in and were unsure how to respond to the professionalization they saw beginning to occur.[16] Their perception was that the presence of grants and funding led groups to shift their purpose and fomented a more mercenary attitude among their participants. In our discussions, these women were adamant that nongovernmental or societal work (*obshchestvennaia rabota*) should be more than just another form of business.

By 1997, this had begun to change. Wages were routinely withheld in the city, and women members experienced new economic pressure. Together, we debated the constraints and possibilities of the emergent nongovernmental sphere. Some of the group members felt that it was no longer tenable to operate on a voluntary, informal basis and had begun to consider finding partners to support their activities, both among Western foundations and in the local administration. In the summer of 1998, we decided to formalize this questioning process in an action research project. Four key members of the group joined me in a series of seminars that were designed to assist participants clarify their aims and objectives. As a result of this process, the women devised two new projects—a Center for Gender Studies and Women's History and a women's crisis center. Both involved a high degree of formalization and required resources, and they thus entailed entering into collaborations with local powerbrokers and Western agencies.[17] It is to the crisis center that I will now turn.

International Aid and Crisis Centers

According to the rhetoric of contemporary development discourses, NGOs facilitate the expression of already existing identities and issues, bringing community concerns ("grassroots issues") to the table. Women's issues and identities are presumed to exist and be recognizable. This formulation conceals the ways in which political issues, identities, and needs are created. As Susan Gal puts it, "What can be legitimately political depends neither on people's perceptions of inequality nor on the wherewithal to organize, important though these are. It depends on what identities and activities can count as part of the public in various historical versions of a civil society."[18] The civil society of NGOs that has been stimulated by the presence of international donor agencies in Russia has done much to shape and mold local perceptions of needs.[19] Groups have been encouraged to pursue specific issues because of the resources attached to them.

The Russian crisis center network is perhaps the most striking example of this. It is widely celebrated as one of the most successful cases of collaboration among Russian NGOs. There are now more than thirty women's crisis centers (*krizisnye tsentrii*) in Russia that provide services to victims of sexual and domestic violence. Through telephone hotlines and individual consultations, they provide free and confidential legal and psychological counseling to female victims of sexual or domestic violence. The network has achieved an impressive national profile. With foundation support, crisis centers work with other Russian women's NGOs in a well-orchestrated national campaign, as Janet Johnson documents in chapter 10 of this volume.

However, the ubiquity of the issue in Russia testifies less to local perceptions of needs than to the success of transnational campaigns and the work of international donor agencies. For complex reasons, violence against women is not an issue that local groups were likely to have raised by themselves; indeed, it did not exist as an issue in Russia before the arrival of feminist and NGO activists.[20] The crisis center network in Russia owes its success to the fact that most of the agencies working with women's groups in Russia have devoted funds to the campaigns.

Between 1995 and 1999, I visited a number of crisis centers in Moscow, Saint Petersburg, and the provincial cities Pskov and Sergiev-Posad and became acquainted with other crisis center activists through conferences and seminars. In tracing the genealogy of different projects, I learned that in all cases, the original plan to set up a crisis center had been raised by outsiders. It was either stimulated by travel, when a local activist had traveled to the United States or Western Europe on one of the many trips facilitating the exchange of "know-how," or when visiting foreign scholars, activists, and NGO workers had brought the idea to groups. Further, in almost all cases, these projects were initially met with local incomprehension or resistance.

Indeed, in my research I came across much skepticism about the campaigns expressed in surprising quarters. Privately, women activists, even those involved in the campaigns in some capacity, admitted that they did not think that it was the most pressing issue facing Russian women and that they were concerned that so many resources were being put into it.

Although in this way the campaigns shared the back-to-front qualities of many Western interventions,[21] I had become aware that local groups had been able to use the crisis center model and root it in their own concerns, "translating" it in a way that made sense to them. Clients (men, as well as women) brought different understandings of "crises" with them to the center, mostly problems that were materially based and that affected them not as individuals but as whole families (e.g., concern about military service, poverty, unemployment, and a lack of living space). They did not understand the framing of gendered violence or recognize their own experience in these terms; frequently, they were alienated by it. However, the counselors did not turn these people away but worked with them, providing legal advice and psychological counseling. Occasionally, they suggested novel solutions, encouraging women clients to go into business together.[22]

Through the action research project, I was able to lend my energies to the group as it negotiated the contradictory nongovernmental field. In this context, my status as a Western outsider and my familiarity with donor priorities and grant-making processes became a valuable resource that group members were able to deploy. In the course of my fieldwork, I had amassed a great deal of information about women's crisis centers. I realized that the network offered great possibilities for provincial women's groups, in terms of foundation support and intragroup connections. I shared this information with members of Zhenskii Svet. Some of the women began to see the founding of a crisis center as a way to strengthen and institutionalize some of the more socially oriented programs offered by Zhenskii Svet. They saw it as a potential base from which already existing projects could be run, and as a place where young women could gain work experience. The idea of setting up a crisis center appealed to Tamara because it most closely approximately the "concrete social project" in which she had dreamed of being involved. Furthermore, she was persuaded by the issue. As a doctor, she had noticed that many of her women patients had bruises under their clothes. "It was obvious that some of them had violent spouses, but there was no way to talk to them about it," she said.

In the summer of 1998, with the endorsement of other members of Zhenskii Svet, Tamara and I embarked on a preparatory project to set up a crisis center for women victims of domestic and sexual violence in Tver'. Our aim was to learn more about existing services and to locate sources of financial and material support. We met with members of the local administration and the staff of the local social security services, and we traveled to Moscow and other provincial cities to visit and learn from other crisis centers. It was a whirlwind of activity—and a tremendous amount of fun. As we went, she and I laughed about our strategies to cast her as a *provinsialka* (provincial woman)—"It's like a movie!" she exclaimed.

What is more, it was a successful strategy. The Tver' project coincided with a specific moment of expansion in the network of crisis centers. It was seeking to reregister itself as a national association and was eager to find more collaborators throughout Russia. To this end, its sponsors provided start-up funds for new centers and were glad to make the acquaintance of a provincial woman activist who was well versed in the tenets of the international women's movement.

At the same time, local conditions were ripe in Tver'. Since the mid-1990s, "women's issues" have had political currency in Russia.[23] Throughout the country's regions, officials are now mandated to undertake steps to provide services for women. In this way, "crisis center" had entered the lexicon of government officials and social services personnel and was on the books. We won the support of two key political figures in the city—the mayor (who was preparing for reelection) and the president's representative to the *oblast'* (a woman journalist with an insecure political base who had begun to dabble in the "women's movement" to generate support for herself in the city). They were only too happy to make the acquaintance of a community group willing to undertake such an endeavor.

The Founding of the Tver' Crisis Center and the First International Collaborations

The crisis center was registered as a societal organization in January 1999. It occupies two medium-size rooms in a municipally owned building located downtown, which are provided rent free by the mayor's office. It is tucked away on the third floor, in an inconspicuous location that suits its mission of providing a safe, confidential space for women clients. The first room serves as a reception area and contains a small alcove where drop-in clients receive free legal and psychological consultations. The second houses a desktop computer, printer and small photocopying machine. Its walls are lined with bookcases, which are full of brochures and literature pertaining to the issue of domestic violence and other activities of the Russian women's movement. A small space has been carved out in the corner for the telephone hotline, which now operates between the hours of 8 A.M. and 8 P.M. 5 days a week.

In many ways, the center has succeeded in becoming what the members of Zhenskii Svet wanted it to be. As a model women-run community project, it contributes to Zhenskii Svet's mission of raising the profile of women's issues in the city. It provides a service to local women, acting as a kind of support center to which they can turn in times of need. At the same time, it is a place where women can gain valuable work experience as volunteers. There is a significant dialogue between the two projects of Zhenskii Svet. Many of the crisis center volunteers are students of the Center for Women's History and Gender Studies. Larissa's students and colleagues at the center have also conducted sociological surveys that trace attitudes toward domestic and sexual violence, and a few students have conducted academic work on the topic.

Western aid has been important at both symbolic and practical levels. Funds have enabled the purchase of essential office equipment and supplies and facilitated the installation of a telephone.[24] They also pay modest salaries to staff and have provided occasional financial support to volunteers. Belonging in the network of crisis centers has facilitated access to technology and know-how. Tamara and some of her staff and volunteers have attended Moscow-based training in nondirective listening skills, legal issues, and organizational development. But in the provinces, the symbolic aspect of this Western support is almost as important as the material. Groups can use it as a bargaining chip in negotiations with organs of the local administration. Tamara explained that foundation support has acted as a "shield" against local appropriations.[25] It has also won her the grudging support of those who were very skeptical about the issue.

However, belonging in the civil society of NGOs is an ambiguous experience, as became clear to me during my visits to Tver' since the crisis center was founded.[26] When I last returned in the summer of 2001, I found Tamara preoccupied with new questions. Although she was eloquent about the importance of the work she does, she was alive to its contradictions and eager to discuss the ambivalence of grants and funding.

One day she invited her colleague Natasha, a crisis center colleague from a neighboring city, and me home to discuss these issues. Like many city residents, she and her family live in one room of a communal apartment, sharing bathroom and kitchen facilities with two other families. The room was crowded with the belongings they had brought with them from Siberia and was cluttered with papers. These were crisis center accounts and grant announcements, the paraphernalia of NGO activity. Being the director of an NGO may have given Tamara increased status in the city, but it has not granted her material security. The funds provided by Western donors are modest and of limited duration, and thus do not enable her to focus exclusively on her crisis center work. As previously, she and her colleagues are forced to take on a number of additional jobs to support their families. The chaotic and unstable conditions of her life were strikingly at odds with the professionalism and efficiency required of her as an NGO worker.

In the course of our conversation, it became clear that the two women were dissatisfied and baffled by foundation policies and felt that they were not heard by foundation representatives. Although Natasha and Tamara—both directors of provincial crisis centers—felt that they were doing useful work, they were frustrated that so much time was taken up by bureaucratic activities. What is more, they felt constrained. Grants permit and exclude specific activities, down to the themes of training. Natasha explained that her center had recently been visited by agency evaluators and that it was absolutely clear to her that they were not interested in the content of the center's activities; "they just need pretty numbers, they don't need to hear my thoughts (*razmyshlenie*) about our work."

The two women spoke of their sense of vulnerability. Rather than continuing to provide support for existing centers, Tamara explained that the new policy appeared to be to provide start-up funds for new groups. The very logic of expansion, according to which her project had succeeded, now threatened to leave the group stranded. Further, they were concerned that donors were moving away from supporting the theme of *nasilie* (violence). The new theme, she continued, was *torgovlia liud'mi* (trafficking). Tamara nodded, saying, "We have to be like chameleons to please the foundations. Even if you don't want to take it [trafficking] on, you have to!" Natasha insisted that she was not about to do it, despite the fact that she needs funding. "I don't understand it, it doesn't make sense to me and it's not realistic that societal groups should be required to deal with it!"

Finally, they had begun to feel a sense of futility about the work they had been encouraged to do. They had successfully raised an issue that both felt was real and important, but at the same time, they were aware that it was nested within a host of other concerns. As with the other crisis centers I came across, they found that their clients came to discuss a wide variety of issues. Although they were frequently able to locate (or "uncover") an element of domestic violence in clients' accounts (whether it be verbal or psychological abuse, economic pressure, or actual physical violence carried out by spouses or male relatives), clients most pressingly made reference to material problems that affected both themselves and their families.

Natasha's and Tamara's work with women uncovered issues they felt powerless to address—problems connected with unemployment, unpaid wages, the crisis of living space. "All we can offer is psychological support. It doesn't resolve the main issues," Tamara lamented. "We can't solve the material problems." Natasha agreed, saying, "The global attention to solving women's problems must be the business of the government! Housing, the police, the law— it's too much on our shoulders!"

Conclusions: Reconsidering Russian Women's NGOs and International Aid

Through this examination of one provincial women's group, Zhenskii Svet, I have shown that women's activity in civil society has been both a symptom of and a response to the gendered shifts that have characterized the post-socialist period. Their struggles take place within the broader context of transnational identity politics (the women's movement), the emergence (and subsequent crisis) of "democratization" as a development paradigm, and the influx of international capital in the form of grants and funding.

Through my research, I came to regard the Russian nongovernmental sector as a locus of sense making, life revisioning, and crucial gender realignments. It is a response to the social and economic turbulence of the past decade—both the hope and idealism of the *perestroika* period and the early Boris Yeltsin regime and the disillusionment and impoverishment that have characterized Russia in the late 1990s and more recently. In the case of Zhenskii Svet, "gender" became a rubric through which women members could make sense of their own losses, choices, and options. In their puzzling about the correct role of the nongovernmental sphere, the women posed questions about accountability and responsibility in the post-socialist era. Who should be responsible for child care, for the elderly, the sick, and the needy?

In many ways, Zhenskii Svet and other groups like it functioned as a kind of workshop, a discussion forum in which women could make sense of the privatizations that were taking place—the retrenchment of the state and the related cutbacks in social provisioning that hit women particularly hard. Involvement in *obshchestvennyi organizatsii* (societal organizations) became an endeavor that could enable them to articulate a new role and place for themselves. It was particularly compelling to these highly educated, professional women who worked in education or medicine and who were accustomed to having a particular role or input into society. When assessing its meaning and import, it is important to recognize that although materially impoverished, this activity generated moral capital.

Western aid has played into these shifts in interesting ways. As international agencies arrived and attached material resources to this nongovernmental activity, the meaning of women's involvement in *obshchestvennyi organizatsii* shifted. The presence of grants and funding opened up new opportunities at the same time as it imposed new constraints. In post-socialist Russia (as other developing-country or democratizing contexts), it is impossible to separate out the category of gender from the resources now attached to it. In the new marketplace of NGOs, gender and gender-based organizing have ironically become a specialized system of knowledge and a new basis for professional expertise. Embracing this framing enables groups to undertake new work and new projects, as the Tver' crisis center project illustrates. (Western aid and the domestic violence narrative position Tamara as member of an avant garde; it also guards her from incursions by local actors who may wish to expropriate by taking over the center and displacing her.)

Through my account of the Tver' crisis center project, I have shown the ambivalence of belonging in the civil society of NGOs. Involvement in the nongovernmental sphere can certainly be regarded as a career strategy. To gloss this activity as "elite," however, is to screen out a great deal of complexity. The terms of engagement are rather constrained; groups are encouraged into specific activities and much of their time is taken up maintaining themselves (writing grants, puzzling the policies of funders, securing resources).

Although it certainly provides local kudos, the NGO realm does not provide local security; NGO workers are often highly insecure. Unless they are truly well connected in former Communist Party or state circles, they operate outside state networks of patronage and support and are often materially impoverished. They are not eligible for state benefits such as pensions, and according the logic of the system, they can actually stand to lose professional qualifications.[27]

Far from being a gravy train, NGO work is frequently sustained by the input of spouses, children, and extended family and friends.[28] Partnerships forged with local power brokers are extremely fragile, and they often depend on the symbolic presence of powerful outsiders. Activists are aware of the precariousness of the situation and fearful that foundations will move on, or jettison projects.

As for the content of NGO work, though it is true that international aid has had a powerful impact on activities in the nongovernmental sphere, it does not determine them. Russian women activists draw upon international aid when they can obtain it and Western models as resources, translating them as necessary. In so doing, they are able to root projects in community needs. Through the model of the crisis center, groups provide services for victims of sexual and domestic violence and raise an issue that formerly had no profile in Russia; they also achieve a lot more besides. Clients and volunteers bring their own constructions of problems and crises in ways that both embrace and exceed the domestic violence narrative, and the center provides support accordingly.

What is more, NGOs such as the crisis center serve as model (women-run) community projects. The Tver' crisis center provides a place for young psychology and law students to gain work experience, answering a serious need in the city. Much like Zhenskii Svet, it is a site of contestation and debate about the direction of political and economic reform and the state's role and responsibilities. Unlike Zhenskii Svet, due to its standing in the city, it brings diverse constituencies (municipal authorities, staff of social services, and volunteers) into dialogue.

Epilogue: Forging a Responsible Scholarship

The anthropology of post-socialism has provided important counter discourses to dominant narratives of economic transition. Recent ethnographic accounts have highlighted the complex pathways of post-socialist change and the individual transformations that accompanied the bold macro projects of transition. Some scholars have taken democratization and the project to build a civil society itself as an object, problematizing Western interventions of the period. The emergent critical anthropology of NGOs and civil society has provided a valuable counterbalance to triumphalist accounts by pointing to misallocations, distortions, and the power imbalance inherent in the encounter. But what are our responsibilities in the light of this recognition?

In the past several years, there has been a sharp switch in the zeitgeist. It has become politically correct to critique democratization.[29] I consider this moment to present both practitioners and scholars with specific challenges. Ironically, rather than instigating rigorous critique at home, this narrative switch could lead to the elision of responsibility, and a stance of blaming the victim. It could also potentially have unfortunate policy outcomes, namely, cutting back civil society aid, which would have a disproportionate effect on women. A further challenge is to recognize that scholars do not stand outside; we are implicated in these processes. As scholars of transition, we are peculiar hybrids, recipients of this aid and products of the democratization industry.

In my work, I attempt to theorize the global encounter between local Russian women's groups and international aid in a way that answers these concerns. In my research practice, my strategy has been to challenge the scholar/practitioner divide by bringing action research methodologies to an ethnographic setting. Participatory action research cannot resolve the contradictions of the nongovernmental sphere, but it does engage them. Working with the Zhenskii Svet group as it entered into collaborations with donor agencies meant that I could not avoid confronting these often painful contradictions—inequalities and power disparities between donors and recipients, between local groups and group members, and crucially, between myself and my Russian women friends. It made things visible to me that otherwise might have remained concealed. In so doing, the action research project yielded rich ethnographic results, a truly "thick description" of Russian women's community activism.

In writing this chapter, I have used this ethnographic knowledge to decenter Western aid, examining this activity from a different angle. I have emphasized the strategizing undertaken by women activists before and after the arrival of Western aid and emphasized the continuities in nongovernmental activity. In so doing, I have shown that the civil society of NGOs cannot be described as either a "success" or a "failure." Instead, it is a realm that allows creative processes to take place, and it offers an uncertain, fragile way forward.

Notes

1. For a particularly striking example of this tendency, see Jeffrey Tayler, "Russia Is Finished," *Atlantic Monthly,* May 2001, 35–52.

2. NGOs tend to be regarded in dichotomous terms. That is, depending on the ideological persuasion of the commentator, they are regarded as either liberators, or colonizers. For a discussion of this, see Julie Hemment, "Colonization or Liberation? The Paradox of NGOs in Post-Socialist States," *Anthropology of East Europe Review* 16, no. 1 (1998): 31–39.

3. Independent societal organizations (*obshchestvennyi organizatsii*) were first permitted during the Perestroika era. They mushroomed in the early 1990s in response to the collapse of the Soviet system of social security. See Julia Zelikova, "Women's Participation in Charity," in *Women's Voices in Russia Today,* ed. Anna Rotkirch and Elina Haavio-Mannila (Aldershot, U.K.: Dartmouth, 1996).

4. See, e.g., Susan Bridger, Rebecca Kay, and Kathryn Pinnick, *No More Heroines? Russia, Women and the Market* (London: Routledge, 1996); Susan Gal and Gail Kligman, *The Politics of Gender after Socialism: A Comparative-Historical Essay* (Princeton, N.J.: Princeton University Press, 2000); Hilary Pilkington, "Whose Space Is It Anyway? Youth, Gender. and Civil Society in the Soviet Union," in *Women in the Face of Change,* ed. Shirin Rai, Hilary Pilkington, and Annie Phizacklea (London: Routledge, 1992); Peggy Watson, "Civil Society and the Politics of Difference in Eastern Europe," in *Transitions, Environments, Translations,* ed. Joan Scott, Cara Kaplan, and Debra Keates (New York: Routledge, 1997).

5. Katherine Verdery, *What Was Socialism and What Comes Next?* (Princeton, N.J.: Princeton University Press, 1996), 64.

6. In recent years, a new direction of scholarship that has arisen in response to the rise of NGOs worldwide and shifts within development agendas. See, e.g., Sonia E. Alvarez, Evelina Dagnino, and Arturo Escobar, eds., *Cultures of Politics Politics of Cultures: Re-Visioning Latin American Social Movements* (Boulder, Colo.: Westview Press, 1998); Steven Sampson, "The Social Life of Projects: Importing Civil Society to Albania," in *Civil Society: Challenging Western Models,* ed. Chris Hann and Elizabeth Dunn (London: Routledge, 1996); Janine Wedel, *Collision and Collusion: The Strange Case of Western Aid to Eastern Europe 1989–1998* (New York: Saint Martin's Press, 1998).

7. See chapters 9, 11, and 12 of this volume. Also see James Richter, "Citizens or Professionals? Evaluating Western Assistance to Russian Women's Organizations" (unpublished), Carnegie Corporation, New York, 1999; Valerie Sperling, *Organizing Women in Contemporary Russia: Engendering Transition* (Cambridge: Cambridge University Press, 2000).

8. Following anthropological conventions, in this section I have used pseudonyms to protect the identity of members of the group.

9. Recent poststructuralist anthropological work has taken "development" as an object. These authors examine development as a historically and culturally specific project that is more to do with the exercise of power over the developing world than solving objective problems. See, e.g., Arturo Escobar, *Encountering Development: The Making and Unmaking of the Third World* (Princeton, N.J.: Princeton University Press, 1995); James Ferguson, *The Anti-Politics Machine: "Development," Depoliticization and Bureaucratic Power in Lesotho* (Cambridge: Cambridge University Press, 1990).

10. Here I refer to the sometimes acrimonious debates between Eastern European and U.S. or Western Europe–based women scholars over the meaning and significance of "feminism." See, e.g., Nanette Funk and Magda Mueller, eds., *Gender Politics and Post-Communism: Refl ections from Eastern Europe and the Former Soviet Union* (London: Routledge, 1993).

11. See, e.g., critiques raised by Lila Abu-Lughod, "Writing against Culture," in *Recapturing Anthropology: Working in the Present,* ed. Richard G. Fox (Sante Fe, N.M.: American School of Research Press, 1991); James Clifford and George Marcus, *Writing Culture: The Poetics and Politics of Ethnography* (Berkeley: University of California Press, 1986); Gananath Obeyesekere, *The Apotheosis of Captain Cook: European Mythmaking in the Pacific* (Princeton, N.J.: Princeton University Press, 1992); Gayatri Chakravorty Spivak, "Can the Subaltern Speak?" in *Marxism and the Interpretation of Culture,* ed. Cary Nelson and Lawrence Grossberg (Urbana: University of Illinois Press, 1988).

12. In chapter 13 of this volume, Michele Rivkin-Fish also discusses these issues in her comparison of "stance."

13. PAR did not originate in anthropology. It sprang from sociopolitical critiques of oppression, and it is rooted in Marxist theory and the adult critical literacy work of Paolo Freire. See, e.g., Paolo Freire, *The Pedagogy of the Oppressed,* trans. M. B. Ramos (New York: Herder & Herder, 1970). It was revitalized (and subjected to critique) by feminist scholarship in the 1980s. For feminist post-structural reworkings of action research, see Michele Fine, *Disruptive Voices: The Possibilities of Feminist Research* (Ann Arbor: University of Michigan Press, 1992); J. K. Gibson-Graham, "'Stuffed If I Know!': Reflections on Post-Modern Feminist Social Research," *Gender, Place and Culture* 1, no. 2 (1994): 205–24; Patti Lather, *Getting Smart: Feminist Research and Pedagogy with/in the Postmodern* (New York: Routledge, 1991).

14. At the time my research took place, Russia was full of Western European and U.S. "experts"—consultants and advisers who in many cases had little knowledge of Russian culture and society and who seemed to presume Russia to be a blank slate. I came to refer to this stance as the "Western knower" role. In chapter 13 of this volume, Rivkin-Fish expresses this well in her description of the "provocateur stance."

15. Wages were routinely withheld during the period I lived in the city.

16. Here I do not mean to suggest that this ambivalence can be attributed simply to resistance to foreign aid, or to "capitalism." The group's commitment to independence was an important way of distinguishing itself from official (state-sanctioned) organizations of the Soviet era. Suspicion expressed toward "business" can be regarded as symptomatic of the gendered redrawings of the post-Soviet period, whereby the market is encoded as masculine (and dishonest).

17. The Center for Gender Studies and Women's History was founded in 1999 by Larissa as a program of the Department of Sociology and Political Science at Tver' State University. It has received funding from the Ford Foundation.

18. In this section, I am drawing on interesting new body of scholarship that has emerged out of a dialogue between women scholars of East and West and which has been attentive to the historical and cultural specificity of feminism and the differences in gender configuration in the East bloc. See, e.g., Susan Gal, "Feminism and Civil Society," in *Transitions, Environments, Translations,* ed. Scott, Kaplan, and Keates.

19. In chapter 13 of this volume, Rivkin-Fish makes similar points about the politics of global activism by tracing interactions between global consultants and Russian health officials.

20. This is not to say that domestic violence does not occur, or that individual Russian women are not concerned about it. Rather, I mean that it is not widely recognized as an issue that is specifically gendered, or that can be isolated from other factors—such as

poverty and alcoholism. Hence, without the encouragement of Western funding and Western outsiders, the issue would not have been conducive to mobilization.

21. By this I mean that agendas are often not set locally, but rather in Washington or Geneva.

22. I explain resistance to the campaigns, the work of these centers, and this process of translation in more detail elsewhere; Julie Hemment, "Gendered Violence in Crisis: Russian NGOs Help Themselves to Liberal Feminist Discourses," *Anthropology of East Europe Review,* 17, no. 1 (spring 1999): 35–38; and Hemment, "Global Civil Society and the Local Costs of Belonging: Defining 'Violence' against Women in Russia," *Signs* 29, no. 3 (forthcoming, spring 2004).

23. This is in part as a result of international pressure. Russia's integration into the international community has forced it to take international declarations such as the Convention for the Elimination of all forms of Discrimination Against Women seriously.

24. Since the center was founded, it has received modest grants from the American Bar Association, the Open Society Institute and the International Research and Exchange Board.

25. Municipal support, though welcome, also involves some risk, as Tamara discovered. On several occasions, she had heard rumors that other local women who were close to the mayor wanted to take over the center and displace her. Her relationship with donor agencies protected her from this, because agency representatives commonly prefer to work with those they know and trust (and those they have trained).

26. Since completing dissertation research, I have made three return trips to Tver'. As a member of the Board of Directors and friend of the project, I continue to work with Tamara and the crisis center as much as I can.

27. Professional qualifications automatically increase with service within state structures. In addition, state employers will sponsor employees to take higher education courses and additional exams. Workers in the nongovernmental sphere doing similar work are denied such support.

28. An interesting point to note, is that a high proportion of women activists (particularly the younger generation) had supportive husbands—Larissa proudly celebrated the fact that her Gender Studies Center comprised four married couples (where the husbands would provide computing and technical support as well as provide material support through their own income).

29. At a recent panel on corruption at Colgate University, Janine Wedel and Louise Shelley, two prominent critics of some of the processes in question, commented on the sudden popularity of their message. During the early to middle 1990s, no one had wanted to hear about democratization's failures; however, after the 1998 economic crisis in Russia, they have found themselves much in demand.

Contributors

David Abramson is an American Association for the Advancement of Science fellow in the Office of International Religious Freedom at the State Department and a research associate at the Institute for European, Russian, and Eurasian Studies at George Washington University. Abramson has published in *Human Organization, Political and Legal Anthropology Review,* and in *Census and Identity: The Politics of Race, Ethnicity, and Language in National Censuses,* edited by David Kertzer and Dominique Arel. He is currently conducting fieldwork on the anthropology of foreign policy and is also collaborating on a research project on contemporary shrine pilgrimages in Uzbekistan.

Andrea Berg, a research fellow at the Institute of Peace Research and Security Policy at the University of Hamburg, Germany, has conducted field research in Uzbekistan. Berg was a consultant in Kyrgyzstan and Tajikistan in the past several years, focusing particularly on problems of democratization, gender issues, and community development.

Susan A. Crate is a postdoctoral fellow at the Havighurst Center for Russian and Post–Soviet Studies at Miami University in Ohio. Crate's published work and ongoing research and teaching interests include cultural ecology, ecological anthropology, human geography, sustainable development, post-socialism, circumpolar peoples, Russia, Siberia, and the Sakha Republic.

Elena Gapova is the director of the Centre for Gender Studies at European Humanities University in Minsk, Belarus. She is the author of articles on gender, nationalism, and postcommunism and the co-editor (with Almira Ousmanova) of *Antologiya gendernoi teorii* (Anthology of gender theory) and *Gendernye istorii Vostochnoi Evropy* (Gendered histories from Eastern Europe), and co-editor (with Sibelan Forrester and Magdalena Zaborowska) of *Over the Wall/After the Fall: Postcommunist Cultures under the East-West Gaze* (forthcoming). Gapova's current research project is focused on information techlogies, gender, and high-tech migration from the former Soviet Union.

Katherine E. Graney is an assistant professor of government at Skidmore College. Her research interests include federalism, ethnicity, Islam, and gender in the Russian Federation, with a particular focus on these issues in Tatarstan and Bashkortostan, where she has done extensive fieldwork. Graney's publications have appeared in journals such as *Europe-Asia Studies* and *Problems of Post-Communism.*

Julie Hemment is an assistant professor in the Department of Anthropology at the University of Massachusetts, Amherst. Hemment's research interests include gender and postsocialism, NGOs and global civil society, feminist anthropology, and Participatory Action Research Methodology. She is the author of "Global Civil Society and the Local Costs of Belonging: Defining Violence against Women in Russia" in *Signs* and is working on a book entitled *Gendered Interventions: Women's Activism and Action Research in Postsocialist Russia.*

Armine Ishkanian is a postdoctoral research fellow at the Institute of Slavic, East European, and Eurasian Studies at the University of California, Berkeley. Ishkanian's research interests in Armenia include NGOs, gender, development, and the cultural and social implications of the post–Soviet transition. She has published articles on the role of NGOs in Armenia, the impact of western aid in their development, and the effect of the post–Soviet transition on Armenian women.

Janet Elise Johnson is an assistant professor of political science at Brooklyn College and former postdoctoral fellow in women's studies and political science at the Havighurst Center for Russian and Post–Soviet Studies at Miami University in Ohio. Johnson's current research interests include gender and postcommunism, civil society, global feminisms, and violence against women. Recent publications include "Privatizing Pain: The Problem of Woman Battery in Russia" in the *National Women's Studies Association Journal.*

Rebecca Kay is lecturer in Russian culture, politics, and society at the Department of Central and East European Studies at the University of Glasgow, Scotland. She is author of *Russian Women and Their Organizations: Gender, Discrimination, and Grassroots Women's Organizations, 1991–96.* Kay's current research interests include the impact of post–Soviet social, cultural, and economic change on Russian men.

Kathleen Kuehnast is a research associate in the Institute of Russian, European, and Eurasian Studies at George Washington University. Her research interests concern gender-related problems in Central Asia, including the impact of poverty on women. She is the recipient of numerous academic awards, including most recently, a Mellon Foreign Area Fellowship at the Library of Congress and a Title VIII Research Scholarship at the Kennan Institute for Advanced Russian Studies at the Woodrow Wilson International Center for Scholars. In addition to her academic interests, Kuehnast has a decade of experience in development anthropology, including conducting poverty studies for international assistance organizations. Kuehnast has published widely in both academic and development journals and books.

Carol Nechemias is an associate professor of public policy at Penn State University, Harrisburg, where she serves as coordinator of the Public Policy program and as a member of the Steering Committee for the Women's Studies program. Her areas of specialization include Russian domestic politics and women in politics. She has published articles on women in U.S. politics in *Western Political Quarterly* and *Legislative Studies Quarterly.* Her work on Russian living standards has appeared in *Slavic Review, Soviet*

Studies, Urban Studies, Studies in Comparative Communism, and *Social Science Quarterly.* Her essays on women's status in post–Soviet Russia have appeared in such journals as *Women and Politics* and *Demokratizatsiya* and as book chapters focusing on such issues as women's access to legislative seats in the Soviet Union/Russia, the development of a women's movement in Russia, women's political participation, and women's health issues. Nechemias is co-editor with Norma Noonan of *The Encyclopedia of Russian Women's Movements.*

Ludmila Popkova is associate professor of history and director of the Gender Studies Center at Samara State University, Russia. Popkova's current research focuses on women's political participation and the women's movement in post–Soviet Russia , gender policy in Russia and Western countries in the twentieth century, and the history of feminism. She is the author of many publications, including chapters in the first Russian textbooks on gender studies. She also works as an expert for women's NGOs, foundations, and regional administrations.

Nancy E. Popson is deputy director of the Kennan Institute of the Woodrow Wilson International Center for Scholars. She has been at the Kennan Institute since 1996, where she has coordinated the institute's program on Ukraine and worked on projects related to regional and rural development in Russia and the evaluation of Western assistance programs to the newly independent states (NIS). Her research interests include women and politics in the NIS, nation-building in Ukraine, questions of ethnicity in Ukraine (in particular in Kyiv), and assistance programs to the NIS. Her publications include *The Ukrainian History Textbook: Introducing Children to the Ukrainian Nation; Fragmented Space in the Russian Federation* (co-editor with Blair Ruble and Jodi Koehn); *Ukraine and Its Western Neighbors* (co-editor with James Clem); and "Kyiv's Nontraditional Immigrants," *Post-Soviet Geography and Economics* 41, no. 5 (2000): 365–78 (co-author with Blair Ruble).

Michele Rivkin-Fish is assistant professor of anthropology at the University of Kentucky. Rivkin-Fish's research examines how Russian women's health care, health strategies, and reproductive politics reflect broader processes of postsocialist change and neoliberalism. Some of her articles have appeared in *American Anthropologist, Social Science and Medicine,* *and Culture, Medicine and Psychiatry,* and she is currently completing an ethnography on global and local efforts to improve Russian women's health.

Blair A. Ruble is director of the Kennan Institute of the Woodrow Wilson International Center for Scholars in Washington, D.C., where he also serves as co-coordinator for Comparative Urban Studies. He has edited eight volumes, including two reference works and six collections of articles, and is the author of four monographic studies. His book-length works include a trilogy examining the fate of Russian provincial cities during the twentieth century: *Leningrad: Shaping a Soviet City*; *Money Sings! The Changing Politics of Urban Space in Post-Soviet Yaroslavl*; and *Second Metropolis: Pragmatic Pluralism in Gilded Age Chicago, Silver Age Moscow, and Meiji Osaka.*

Nayereh Tohidi is an associate professor of women's studies at California State University, Northridge. Tohidi has taught at the University of Iowa, the University of Minnesota, the University of Southern California, Harvard University, and the University of California, Los Angeles, and has been a consultant for the United Nations on gender and development in the Middle East and post-Soviet Eurasia. She is the recipient of postdoctorial fellowships at Harvard, Stanford University, and the Woodrow Wilson International Center for Scholars, and a Fulbright lectureship and research award at the Academy of Sciences of the Soviet Republic of Azerbaijan. Tohidi's latest publication is *Globalization, Gender, and Religion: The Politics of Women's Rights in Catholic and Muslim Contexts* (contributor and co-editor with Jane Bayes).

Cynthia Werner is an assistant professor in the Department of Anthropology at Texas A&M University. Werner has traveled extensively to Kazakhstan conducting research on a variety of topics, including gift exchange and household networking, the practice of bride kidnapping, and the development of international tourism. Her current project examines risk perceptions related to nuclear testing in northern Kazakhstan. She is also writing an ethnography based on her research in rural Kazakhstan.

Tatiana Zhurzhenko is an associate professor at V. Karazin Kharkiv National University in Ukraine. Her research interests focus on transformation processes in post-Soviet Ukraine: feminisms and nationalisms;

gender aspects of transition to market economy; nation-building and citizenship; border construction and regional identities; and language politics. She is a Lise Meitner Fellow at the University of Vienna, Austria, Institute for East European History. Recent publications include *Social Reproduction and Gender Politics in Ukraine* (in Russian); and "(Anti)national Feminisms, Post-Soviet Gender Studies: Women's Voices of Transition and Nation Building in Ukraine," in *Oesterreichische Osthefte* (in English).

Index

Note: Page numbers followed by *n* or *t* refer to notes or tables.